PARIS FASHION AND WORLD WAR TWO

Global Diffusion and Nazi Control

CAPTIONS FOR COVER AND ENDPAPER IMAGES:

COVER IMAGE:
Adapted from 'Göta Trägårdh's fashion drawing: *Hats in Red* - copies of Paris couture millinery designed and made by Stockholm milliners, **Bonniers månadstidning**, November, 7.1942.' (See Chapter 4: *'Much News from the Fashion Frontier:' Swedish Neutrality and Diffusion of Paris Fashion during World War II.*)

END PAPERS:
Five colour print design, 'Friendship,' by Marie Gudme Leth, on twill woven cellulose fibre fabric, 1943, Designmuseum, Denmark, no. 198_1999; photo by Pernille Kemp. (See Chapter 8: *Fashion in Denmark in the 'Five Dark Years.'*)

PARIS FASHION AND WORLD WAR TWO

Global Diffusion and Nazi Control

Edited by
Lou Taylor
Marie McLoughlin

BLOOMSBURY VISUAL ARTS
LONDON • NEW YORK • OXFORD • NEW DELHI • SYDNEY

BLOOMSBURY VISUAL ARTS
Bloomsbury Publishing Plc
50 Bedford Square, London, WC1B 3DP, UK
1385 Broadway, New York, NY 10018, USA

Bloomsbury Publishing Ireland, 29 Earlsfort Terrace, Dublin 2, D02 AY28, Ireland

BLOOMSBURY, BLOOMSBURY VISUAL ARTS and the Diana logo are trademarks of Bloomsbury Publishing Plc

First published in Great Britain 2020

Selection, editorial matter and individual chapters © Lou Taylor and Marie McLoughlin, 2020
Individual chapters © Their Authors, 2020

Lou Taylor and Marie McLoughlin have asserted their right under the Copyright, Designs and Patents Act, 1988, to be identified as Editors of this work.

For legal purposes the Acknowledgements on p. 7 constitute an extension of this copyright page.

Cover design by Dani Leigh
Cover image: Adapted from 'Göta Trägårdh's fashion drawing: *Hats in Red* - copies of Paris couture millinery designed and made by Stockholm milliners, *Bonniers månadstidning*, November, 7.1942.'

All rights reserved. No part of this publication may be: i) reproduced or transmitted in any form, electronic or mechanical, including photocopying, recording or by means of any information storage or retrieval system without prior permission in writing from the publishers; or ii) used or reproduced in any way for the training, development or operation of artificial intelligence (AI) technologies, including generative AI technologies. The rights holders expressly reserve this publication from the text and data mining exception as per Article 4(3) of the Digital Single Market Directive (EU) 2019/790.

Bloomsbury Publishing Plc does not have any control over, or responsibility for, any third-party websites referred to or in this book. All internet addresses given in this book were correct at the time of going to press. The author and publisher regret any inconvenience caused if addresses have changed or sites have ceased to exist, but can accept no responsibility for any such changes

Every effort has been made to trace copyright holders and to obtain their permission for the use of copyright material. If any have been inadvertently overlooked, the publishers will be pleased to make the necessary arrangement at the first opportunity.

A catalogue record for this book is available from the British Library.

A catalog record for this book is available from the Library of Congress.

ISBN:	HB:	978-1-350-00027-8
	PB:	978-1-350-00026-1
	ePDF:	978-1-350-00028-5
	eBook:	978-1-350-00029-2

Typeset by Lachina Creative, Inc.

To find out more about our authors and books visit www.bloomsbury.com and sign up for our newsletters

Dedication

To our families – past, present and future.

Table of Contents

Acknowledgements 7
Notes on Contributors 9

Introduction 13
Marie McLoughlin and Lou Taylor

Chapter 1
From Berlin to Paris 25
Lou Taylor

Chapter 2
The Lyon *haute nouveauté* fashion textile industry during World War Two: design making, exhibition and international diffusion 53
Lou Taylor

Chapter 3
Shortages in Paris 1940–1945: frivolous accessories become essential needs 77
Dominique Veillon

Chapter 4
'Much news from the fashion frontier': Swedish neutrality and diffusion of Paris fashion during World War Two 97
Ulrika Kyaga

Chapter 5
From Paris haute couture to New York: maintaining the French domination of fashion across the Atlantic, 1939–1946, through women's magazines 115
Sophie Kurkdjian

Chapter 6
New York and Paris fashions during World War Two: a competitive love affair 139
Sandra Stansbery Buckland

Chapter 7
Lisbon as a centre of couture fashion in World War Two and its Paris and international connections 161
Alexandra Gameiro and Lou Taylor

Chapter 8
Fashion in Denmark in the 'Five Dark Years' 183
Kirsten Toftegaard

Chapter 9
The diffusion, reception and use of Paris style information in Brazil and its couture salons: 1939–1946 203
Cláudia de Oliviera

Chapter 10
Annexed, neutral and occupied: the worlds of couture in Austria, Switzerland and Belgium and their relationships with Paris couture, 1939–1946 225
Lou Taylor

Chapter 11
1944: London plans to become the 'meridian' of world fashion 247
Marie McLoughlin

Chapter 12
Paris fashion: an international product for an international clientele 271
Marie McLoughlin, with postscript from Nancy Yeide

Chapter 13
The liberation of Paris and the state of the haute couture industry: late August 1944–1946 303
Lou Taylor with Marie McLoughlin

Chapter 14
The end of the war in Europe to 1947: rejuvenating the international business of haute couture 319
Lou Taylor with Marie McLoughlin

Conclusion 333
Lou Taylor and Marie McLoughlin

A Letter from Nuremberg, 1946 338
Lou Taylor

List of Illustrations 341
Index 349

Acknowledgements

The images in this book tell our story just as much as our text and we are consequently deeply grateful to everyone who has helped us find them and track down copyright owners. We were awarded grants toward related costs from the Centre for Internationalising Design History, the Dissemination Fund and the Dress History Research Fund – all at the University of Brighton, as well receiving as awards from the Pasold Research Fund and the Design History Society. We are grateful to them all. At the University of Brighton, we have received financial support related to developing the research for this book over many years from Dr. Paddy Maguire, Head of the School of Humanities. Other staff who have given us constant support include Nicola Cooke and George Sykes for expert technical advice, Lolita Stein Johnson, Mel Searle and Jerry Loft for help with our accounts. We received exceptional help over research and tracking images from Giulia Bonali for Chapter 9 on Lisbon, which could not have been produced without her help and advice. Nele Bernheim, Asia Gallien, Sophie Kurkdjian, Marie Laure Gutton, Beezy Marsh, Alexandra Palmer, E-J. Scott and Ben Wubbs have also enabled a successful conclusion to many of our picture hunts. Josephine Gladstone and Cristina Volpi carefully checked some of our chapters. We thank them, every one.

The following journals and their staff generously awarded us free use of images from their 1939–1945 editions: *Marie Claire* (Pauline Husband-Clement); *Annabelle* (Zurich – Denise Alt); *L'Illustré* (Lausanne – Valerie Pellet). Jane Hattrick, Janet Hammond and Carolyn Last have allowed us to use items from their family archives and collections whilst Li Thies-Lagergren granted us permission to use the drawing by Göta Trägårdh, her grandmother, on our cover. The following libraries have kindly also given us generous permissions to use their images: *Bibliothèque municipale de Lyon* (Philippe Rassaert); *Hemeroteca Municipal de Lisboa* (João Oliveira); *Biblioteca Nacional, Rio de Janeiro* (Clara R. Chianello Ramos); *Kungliga Biblioteket* (Amanda Almroth). We thank them all.

We have also received very real kindnesses from the following archives and their staff: Archives Cartier (Paris-Anne Lamarque and Violette Petit); Cartier Archives, London (Jenny Rourke); Christian Dior (Perrine Scherrer); Kerry Taylor Auctions; Sebastian Wormell at the Harrods Company Archive; *Narodowe Archiwum Cyfrowe*, Warsaw; the BundesArchiv; *Magasin du Nord* Archives, Copenhagen; Lambeth Archives, Lambeth Borough Council, London (Susan Shanks); Peter Ascher of the Ascher Archive and Nadine Meisner for notes on Kangol. Thank you.

Museum curators and staff in their photographic departments have been endlessly patient and helpful over sorting images and permits for us, many helping us far beyond the norms of duty: *Collection départementale des Musées de l'Ain/Fonds des Soieries Bonnet* (Nathalie Foron-Dauphin); *Musée des Tissus*, Lyon (Audrey Mathieu); *Musée des Métiers de la Chaussure* (Sandy Antelme); Musée d'Histoire Militaire de Lyon (Col. André Mudler); *Schweizerisches Nationalmuseum*, Zurich (Joya Indermühle); *Musée Suisse de la Mode* and the *Archive Piguet*, Yverdon-les-Bains (Anna Corda); *Wien Museum*, Vienna (Regina Karner); Munich Museum (Isabella Belting); *Gemeenteuseum*, the Hague (Madelief Hohé); *Mode Museum*, Hasselt (Karolien De Clippel); *Traje Museum*, Lisbon (Clara Vaz Pinto); the Fashion Institute of Technology, New York (Valerie Steele and her team); the Jewish Museum, Milwaukee (Patti Sherman-Cisler); Ohio State University, College of Education/Human Ecology Historic Costume & Textiles Collection (Gayle Streger); Bexhill-on-Sea Museum (Julian Porter); the University of Brighton Dress History Teaching Collection.

With special thanks to Bloomsbury Press: Frances Arnold, Editorial Director; her Editorial Assistants, Pari Thompson and Yvonne Thouroude, and Lauren Crisp, Visual Arts Production Editor.

Notes on Contributors

Alexandra Gameiro

Alexandra Weber Gameiro was born in Lisbon. Alexandra holds a Master of Art, Heritage and Theory of Conservation for her dissertation 'Fashion and the Dressmakers in Portugal during the Estado Novo – the changes of the post-war (1945–1974)' and is currently working at Cabral Moncada Auctioneers in Lisbon.

Sophie Kurkdjian

Sophie Kurkdjian, PhD in History, University Paris I, is Associate Researcher and seminar organiser of the Dress History Group of the Institut d'Histoire du Temps Présent (IHTP-CNRS) and Associate Researcher at the Centre d'Histoire Sociale/Université Paris I Sorbonne. She was co-curator of the exhibition 'Mode & Femmes, 14-18', Bibliothèque Forney, Paris, 2017. Her research interests include the history of fashion press, of fashion publishers and journalists, of fashion during World War One and World War Two and the intellectual property applied to fashion press (copy and counterfeit of fashion magazines, nineteenth and twentieth centuries).

Ulrika Kyaga

Ulrika Kyaga holds a doctorate in fashion studies. She defended her thesis at the Centre for Fashion Studies at Stockholm University and holds a masters degree in fashion studies and a Master of Science in Business and Economics from Karlstad University. Ulrika has worked in the PR and communication sector for a number of years, specialising in fashion, and is in great demand as a guest lecturer and expert on issues related to Swedish fashion. She also works as an editor and curator for fashion-related exhibition project.

Marie McLoughlin

Marie McLoughlin is senior lecturer at the University of Brighton, UK. Her PhD, on the founding of the English art school fashion degree, focused on Muriel Pemberton and St. Martin's School of Art. After studying fashion at St. Martins, Marie worked as a fashion designer, later taking her MA at Winchester School of Art focusing on the British Utility fashion scheme. Publications include contributions to *Picture This: Artist as Illustrator*, ed. Sylvia Backemeyer (2005); twenty-six entries on twentieth century fashion designers in the *Bloomsbury Encyclopaedia of Design* (2015); and the text for artist Howard Tangye's book *Howard Tangye: Within* (2013).

Cláudia de Oliveira

Cláudia de Oliveira holds a PhD in Social History from the Federal University of Rio de Janeiro (UFRJ), Brazil, and the University of Bristol, UK (2004). She has been Professor of Brazilian Culture at the School of Fine Arts, Federal University of Rio de Janeiro since 2010, where she also lectures in postgraduate visual arts. Her research focus lies in the fields of fashion, body anthropology, gender and history of women in Brazil. She has written and organized several books on these themes, published in Brazil.

Sandra Stansbery Buckland

Sandra Stansbery Buckland, PhD, is professor in the fashion merchandising program at the University of Akron, US. She earned her doctorate at the Ohio State University. Her research includes the World War Two American fashion industry, the promotion of American designers and the media campaigns aimed at American women maintaining the homefront. Her publications include 'Fashion as a Tool of World War II: A Case Study Supporting the SI Theory', *Clothing and Textiles Research Journal 18*, no. 3 (2000); '"We Publish Fashions Because They Are News': *The New York Times* 1940–1945", *Dress* 25 (1998); and "Promoting American Designers 1940–1945: Building Our Own House", in *Twentieth-Century American Fashion* (2005).

Kirsten Toftegaard

Kirsten Toftegaard, who is a curator at Designmuseum Danmark, is the keeper of the museum's Dress/Fashion and Textile Collection. She has arranged several exhibitions at Designmuseum Danmark, including 'Walk on the Wild Side – Margit Brandt Fashion Design 1965–1980' in 2010; 'Rokoko-mania' in 2012; 'British Post-War Textiles' in 2013; the permanent exhibition 'Fashion & Fabric' in 2014; 'Marie Gudme Leth – Pioneer of Print' in 2016; and 'I Am Black Velvet—Erik Mortensen Haute Couture' in 2017–2018. In 2015, she curated an exhibition on 'Modern Danish Tapestry' at the State Hermitage Museum in Saint Petersburg. Her research field has, in recent years, focused on twentieth-century Danish fashion and textiles. From 2005 onwards, Kirsten has been a member of the Conseil du CIETA (Centre Internationale d'Études des Textiles Anciens), representing Denmark.

Lou Taylor

Lou Taylor is Professor Emerita in Dress History at the University of Brighton, UK. She has worked as a dress history curator and university lecturer in Brighton since the mid 1970s. She is author of *Mourning Dress, a Costume and Social History* (1983,

2012), *The Study of Dress History* (2002) and *Establishing Dress History* (2004); co-author with Eleonor Thompson and Amy de la Haye of *Family of Fashion, the Messels – six generations of dress* (2005); and with Jenny Lister and Cassie Davies-Strodder of *London Society and Fashion: the wardrobe of Heather Firbank, 1905–1925* (2015).

Dominique Veillon

Dominique Veillon is Director of Research at Institut d'Histoire du Temps Présent, CNRS, Paris. She is a researcher, writer and post-graduate supervisor on the Resistance from 1940–1945, and everyday life and fashion in France under the German Occupation. Her recent books include *La Mode Sous L'Occupation, Débrouillardise et coquetterie dans la France en guerre (1939–1945), Payot* (1990 with French reprints, including 2014 and English edition 2002); *Nous les enfants* (2003) and *Résistance: histoires de famille* (2009), both with Dominique Missika; *Jean Moulin, Artist, Préfet, Résistant, 1899–1943* (2013) with Christine Levisse-Touzé; *Pour Vous Mesdames – La Mode en Temps de Guerre* (2014); *Centre d'Histoire de la Résistance et de la Déportation de Lyon* (2014) and *Yves Saint Laurent: The Scandal Collection, 1971* (2015) with Olivier Saillard; *Les jours sans, 1939–1949, Alimentation et pénurie en temps de guerre* (2017).

Nancy Yeide

Nancy H. Yeide, MA, was head of the Department of Curatorial Records at the National Gallery of Art, Washington, from 1990 until her retirement in 2017. Her primary interest is in the history of collecting, particularly during the nineteenth and twentieth centuries, a topic on which she has published regularly in such journals as *Apollo, Archives of American Art Journal, Burlington Magazine* and *Museum News*. Since 1997 she has conducted World War Two–era provenance research on the National Gallery of Art's collection, and has spoken and written widely on the subject. In 2001 she co-authored the *American Association of Museums' Guide to Provenance Research*. Her research on the art collection of Reichsmarschall Hermann Goering resulted in her *catalogue raisonné* of his personal, looted collection, *Beyond the Dreams of Avarice, the Hermann Goering Collection* (2009) and an appearance in the documentary film *The Rape of Europa*, discussing Goering's collection.

Introduction

Marie McLoughlin and Lou Taylor

Premise

This book examines the world of Paris haute couture in World War Two and the international activities of Paris couturiers – their businesses, designs and their clients – throughout the dark years of 1940–1944. Dress history has it that World War Two wrought a dramatic change to these circumstances and that almost no fashion news or exports came out of Paris once German forces occupied the city from summer 1940 until August 1944. This book challenges this view.

Following respectfully as we are in the footsteps of Dominique Veillon and Fabienne Falluel, this social/dress history and material culture study connects wartime Paris haute couture to the world of international couture for the first time, examining links to its Paris clients, friends and competitors throughout the war. We have highlighted as examples the continuing links with Berlin, Zurich, London, New York, Stockholm, Copenhagen, Lisbon, Brussels and Rio de Janeiro. A closely related second theme that runs all through this text is an examination of the energetic war time national appropriation of couture fashion in many of these countries.

In the midst of the slaughter and the vast traumatic upheavals of this period, a text with its focus on couture clothes might seem positively shocking, even perverse, and our commitment to examining fashion history in the midst of all of this needs an explanation. Daniel Roche was clear that assessing historical clothing 'is another way of penetrating the heart of social history' (Roche 1994: 5). He emphasises that dress history can usefully and validly expose the differences in the social life of all classes. 'Clothing', he writes, 'is a good indication of the material culture of a society for it introduces us immediately to consumers' patterns and enables us to consider the social hierarchy of appearances' (1987: 160). Beatrix Le Wita shared this interest in the hierarchy of appearances and also carefully justified her ethnographical research into the study of the fashions selected by young upper-class women in a wealthy district of Paris in the 1990s. She found that her focus on dress offered a precise approach for her analysis of how these rich young women used the carefully selected details of their clothes to create 'distinction [which] enables [man] to mark out a sphere for himself in which he will live with himself and his fellows' (1994: 57).

FIGURE INTRO.0
Summer hat, straw with silk flowers and veiling, by Agnès, Paris, *Modes et Travaux*, June 1943, Dress History Teaching Collection, University of Brighton.

Also enmeshed in our story is the issue of fashion as a vast international business involving the professional colleagues of the Paris haute couture salons all over the world: the fashion press, illustrators, fashion textiles manufacturers, ready-to-wear fashion companies and their designers at all market levels, buyers, retailers and so on. Many of these in France, as elsewhere, were Jewish and their fates are also deeply entwined in the stories in our book.

It was a complete understanding of all these issues that inspired Fabienne Falluel, dress curator at the Musée de la Mode de la Ville de Paris, Palais Galliera, to spend years quietly collecting couture accessories worn in Paris through the Occupation, an activity that many would have considered taboo because of the shadows still hanging over the exaggerated couture fashions designed and worn in Occupied Paris. The results were finally shown in a profoundly moving exhibition at the Mémorial du Marechal Leclerc de Hauteclocque et de la Liberation de Paris, Musée Jean Moulin, in Paris in 2009, curated by Christine Levisse-Touzé and Dominique Veillon. Here the luxury fashions and accessories of 1940–1944 were set in the contexts of the terrible events taking place in occupied Paris. Catherine Join-Diéterle, then director of the Musée Galliera, wrote in her introduction to the exhibition's accompanying book by Fabienne Falluel and Marie-Laure Gutton, that

> some may be astonished that this exhibition of objects... intelligently collected over a period of thirty years by Fabienne Falluel ... should be shown at all. Worn throughout the Occupation, these accessories conjure up fashions of the period, but they also offer far more than that. They exude history. Put together and placed in front of us, they make us relive, disturbingly, those difficult and tragic years where lightness of spirit was rare. The collection in the Galliera Museum contains many other artefacts just as equally charged with the weight of history from revolutions and from the [Paris 1871] Commune. These accessories from the last war however were mostly worn by women we have met and who still carry memories and sometimes stigmas from these terrible years – memories filled with emotion. For all those who did not live through the Occupation, this research enables us to measure the consequences on the daily life of Parisiennes.
>
> (Falluel and Gutton 2009: 4–5)

The seminal research by Dominique Veillon, director of research, Institut d'Histoire du Temps Présent, CNRS, Paris, published in her book, *La Mode sous l'Occupation* of 1990, was weighted with the same concerns. She questioned whether the study of fashion was 'anything more than a frivolous activity which impacted basically only on the wardrobes of the ruling classes'. Whilst agreeing with Roche, she confirmed her view however that fashion carries 'quite other significances because its roots lie in the practices of society'. She emphasised that these issues, when set in the traumatic period of the Occupation, needed to 'be posed and contemplated'. Her approach is a perfect example of Roche's close 'penetration' of the correlation that exists, between, as Veillon confirms, the 'phenomenon of fashion and specific social happenings . . . [and] is a way of understanding how a society re-acts to the pressure of events on its ways of being and dressing.' 'Were these years a parenthesis, a turning or a rupture?' Veillon asks (1990: 7–9). Our book respectfully embraces and builds on the material culture and social history research approaches of Roche, Veillon and Falluel. It is our view that these dark years were not a 'rupture', nor even an isolation, but were a continuous, albeit traumatic, turning of the wheel of the long-established international business and style development of Paris haute couture fashion. Another fresh contribution we offer here is to set this world into its wider international wartime business setting, showing for the first time that Paris style was not confined within the borders of France alone but was diffused right across Europe and to Sweden, the USA and Brazil.

Since well before the nineteenth century, Paris couture salons had dressed international royalty, the new plutocratic rich, great actresses and the upper classes across Europe, North America, Scandinavia and Russia. Grumbach writes that in 1911, the most elite salons separated themselves from the existing large trade organisation of tailors, dressmakers at all levels of manufacture which had been established in 1868. In separating themselves, they created the *Chambre Syndicale de la Couture Parisienne* (Grumbach 1993: 24). Its elite members, and only them, made individual Paris-based haute couture bespoke clothes for their customers, made to the very highest levels of craft dressmaking and tailoring standards using only the most luxurious fabrics, furs, artisan craft-made embroideries, trimmings and accessories. Grumbach writes that the Chambre thus separated itself from more ordinary levels of French couture manufacture through its stress on luxury, fashion 'savoir faire' and by celebrating design creativity (Grumbach 1993: 26). E-J. Scott has shown that the commercial astuteness of the great salons also led them to produce several quality ranges of garments, from those at the most luxurious haute couture level made with almost no consideration of cost, to far more bread-and-butter garments made for the still rich but somewhat less wealthy consumers (Scott 2014). Membership in the Chambre was strictly controlled with adherents having to be sponsored by two committee members (Grumbach 1993: 25). By the 1930s an annual calendar of haute couture presentations was formalised, with each salon obliged to show one hundred garments made to haute couture standards of skill and luxury (Grumbach 1993: 26). By 1939 the Paris haute couture and Lyon silk trades had thus been designing, making and exporting these luxury couture garments globally for generations and the taste and design influences of leading Paris haute couturiers had long dominated the style of the international fashion industries and that of their professional and private clientele.

This book, the work of dress historians from across the world, examines the diffusion of information about seasonal haute couture style out of Occupied Paris throughout the war. It will show that the businesses of Paris haute couture went to extraordinary lengths, with some success and with the help of committed fashion professionals and clients around the world, to keep up every overseas contact they could under the most extreme of difficulties in Occupied, neutral, Axis and Allied countries. The Paris salons were driven by the not unreasonable fear that New York or London might find the opportunity to snatch the lucrative and status-giving commercial leadership of fashion away from France. London and New York, independently aware of the economic opportunities, watched, waited and did indeed discuss possible plans to take over this trade themselves. This book examines these activities.

This book argues too that it is important to establish these facts because they help explain the successful re-establishment of the luxury international business of Paris haute couture and its status of global fashion supremacy after the Liberation of Paris. Even though this took two to three years and did not go unchallenged in the post-war period, this was possible because of the firmly held allegiances of so many of their international professional contacts and private clients all through the war years. Decisions taken in July 1940 by the *Chambre Syndical de la Couture Parisienne* in Paris and the *Chambre Syndicale des Fabricants* in Lyon, across the demarcation line in Vichyist France, to keep their companies and international contacts running by whatever means they could, were of key significance. Whether they were based in or out of France, the international businesses and export networks of Paris haute couture, though damaged, were not ruptured by the Occupation.

The development of our research

These chapters are the result of ten years of targeted research co-operation by dress historians from the University of Brighton's School of Humanities, members of the Histoire de la Mode Research Group of the Institute d'Histoire du Temps Présent, CNRS, Paris and of commissioned research from colleagues around the world, to whom we are deeply grateful. Sharing a material culture, social, dress and business history approach to the fashion history of World War Two, the chapters in this book, which cover the 1939–1947 period, focus on analysing surviving garments, textiles, accessories, the international fashion press of the period and government and business archives and memoirs. As the chapters have come together, similarities and differences from country to country have become apparent, as have many unexpected direct links from one country to the other. We were unaware of many of these when we set out on this project. This collective research highlights the fact that news about seasonal Paris haute couture styles did indeed spread around the world, often by surprising and circuitous routes, as our chapters will show.

FIGURE INTRO.1
French fashion magazines, 1942–1943 (University of Brighton, Dress History Teaching Collection).

The impetus for this research

In 1990 Dominique Veillon's research exploded the commercially useful myth persistent for more than sixty years that the Paris couture salons closed down between 1940–1944 and were therefore untainted by any accusations of poor behaviour during the war years. Her text was reprinted by Payot in 2001 and then published in English by Berg in 2002. Veillon has since also been involved in two major French exhibitions on French Occupation fashion. Firstly came the exhibition 'Accessoires de Mode sous l'Occupation, Paris 1940–44' with its related book by Fabienne Falluel and Marie-Laure Gutton, discussed here already. The second exhibition was titled 'Pour Vous Mesdames, la mode en temps de guerre', and was held at the Musée de la Resistance et de la Deportation in Lyon, from November 2013 to April 2014, also with a published catalogue of the same name. Both exhibitions included surviving garments, fashion textiles, hats and accessories designed by Paris haute couturiers and milliners, including some discussed in Chapter 1.

Other major exhibitions testify to the growing international interest in the material culture and social contexts of women's fashions in World War Two. To give a few examples: the Imperial War Museum, London, included fashion for the first time in their 1995 'London at War' exhibition. In 2015 their successful exhibition 'Fashion on the Ration: 1940s Street Style' dealt entirely and intelligently with the British austerity style of women's clothes and included many examples of British wartime fashions, uniforms, accessories and textiles for women. Interestingly in the USA, the Museum of Fine Art in Boston also dealt with British wartime fashion textiles in its 'Beauty as Duty: Textiles and the Home Front in WWII Britain' exhibition held in 2011. In 2015, Isabelle Belting's landmark exhibition (and related book) at the Munich Stadtmuseum, *'Gretchen mag's mondän!"Damenmode der 1930er-Jahre'*, with its 150 garments, dealt largely with wartime design work of the German School of Fashion in Munich (see Chapter 1, Figure 1.2B and Chapter 10).

Our understanding of the reality of these wartime events has therefore moved on a long way from the dress histories of the 1980s. Following the publication of Veillon's book, most dress history books now acknowledge that the businesses of Paris haute couture kept running all through World War Two. However there has been little analysis of the continuous development of Paris couture style and accessories

Veillon in Chapter 2, here, notes that 1943 saw the full flourishing of the extravagant full skirted, broad shouldered, high hatted, platform soled, Occupation style which lasted until well after the Liberation of Paris in August 1944. The diffusion of this style outside wartime Paris has never been debated.

The structure of our book

In order to understand why and how this industry kept going and to expose the extremes of compromise and accommodation that were forced on the Paris haute couture salons and on the Lyon silk companies by the Germans from 1940–1944, the economic, cultural and racist policies imposed by Nazi Germany on their conquered French territory are discussed here in Chapter 1, including attitudes to fashion in Nazi Germany itself. This chapter also describes the shift in membership of the highest social circles of '*Tout Paris*' in Occupied Paris, where the haute couture salons worked under the most difficult of circumstances to dress this changed clientele.

Dominique Veillon, in Chapter 2, details the extraordinary levels of craftsmanship, creativity and subtly subversive design found in Paris couture accessories made under the extremes of Occupation shortages. In Chapter 3, Lou Taylor assesses the fate of the Lyon silk industry, which provided luxury fabrics to the Parisian couturiers. Ulrika Kyaga's Chapter 4 details the continuing links between the worlds of couture in neutral Sweden and Paris, with an account of

FIGURE INTRO.2
Paquin, green chiffon evening dress with gold sequins for winter 1939 (Kerry Taylor Auction House, Lot 60, June 2010).

FIGURE INTRO.3
Cover of *Modes et Travaux*, June–July 1944 (University of Brighton, Dress History Teaching Collection).

the related wartime work of Stockholm's couture salons. In Chapter 5, Sophie Kurkdjian discusses Lucien Vogel and Michel de Brunhoff, leading pre-war figures in the publication of French *Vogue*, detailing their courageous struggles to keep international awareness of the continuing work of the Paris couturiers alive.

In Chapter 6, Sandra Stansbery Buckland gives a fresh account of the stressed relationship between the American fashion press and industry, Occupied Paris fashions and the Vichy regime after America joined the war on 1 December 1941. Alexandra Gameiro and Lou Taylor, in Chapter 7, reveal the importance of Lisbon in neutral Portugal as an information hub and as a city selling both original Paris and Lisbon couture throughout the war. The stresses and shortages in the fashion

FIGURE INTRO.4
Summer straw hat with silk flowers and veiling by Agnès, Paris, *Modes et Travaux*, June 1943 no 528, University of Brighton, Dress History Teaching Collection.

world of occupied Denmark are the focus of Kirsten Toftgaard's Chapter 8. Here information on Paris style was thin on the ground and unwelcome efforts were made by the German occupiers to replace this with German and Austrian fashion style. Chapter 9, by Cláudia de Oliveira, is set in Brazil, which went to war on the Allied side in 1942. She focuses on the development of Brazil's own couture world and on the extraordinary lengths to which both the British and French governments and couturiers went to keep alive their rival lucrative couture markets in Rio de Janeiro and São Paolo. Lou Taylor's Chapter 10 examines developments in the couture trades of annexed Austria, neutral Switzerland and Occupied Belgium in the context of Nazi German economic and anti-Semitic policies. Marie McLoughlin, in Chapter 11, reviews British hopes to be the centre of world fashion following the liberation of Europe and the failure of government departments to capitalise on the expertise newly available from European emigrés into the textile industry and Paris couturiers working in London as part of the Incorporated Society of London Designers. In Chapter 12, Marie McLoughlin opens up a new debate examining Paris couture as a fundamentally international industry rather than a uniquely French trade, through her assessment of the varied wartime careers of designers including Molyneux, Piguet, Creed, Balenciaga, Schiaparelli and Mainbocher, none of whom were French, and all of whom had successful haute couture houses before the war. Finally, Chapters 13 and 14 set down the shocked reaction to the extravagance of Paris Occupation style reported in the British and American press after the Liberation of Paris in August 1944 and the efforts made in the French and international fashion industry to overcome them and to re-establish Paris as queen of fashion. Our conclusion then summarizes our collective findings.

Conclusion

Fascist German economic and cultural policies spread their tentacles around the world during World War Two with profound impacts on dress and textile industries across Europe. The war triggered a movement of highly talented professionals in the fashion and textiles world, most of them Jewish, away from Germany, Austria, Czechoslovakia, Poland and France to Britain, South America and later to Australia (Sydney Jewish Museum, 2012) where they made major creative and business contributions throughout and after the war.

This book, whilst addressing the differing national fashion developments across Europe and in the USA, also shows that the crisis of World War Two triggered competitive international wartime propaganda campaigns conducted through the medium of fashion. These were targeted not only at keeping national exports alive but, in the cases of London and New York, also at the possibility of wresting the lucrative crown of couture away from the city of Paris. Well aware of the threatening competition after the Liberation of Paris in August 1944, the city's haute couture industry immediately set in place efforts to re-establish its prewar position of global fashion domination, as Pouillard (2013) has detailed. Its most successful form of self-promotion, discussed in several chapters in this book, was the displaying of the *Théâtre de la Mode* in capital cities around the world in 1945–1946, where Paris couture clients and the international press were eagerly waiting for news. This set of sophisticated little stage sets, with its quarter-size wire dolls dressed by the top couturiers in seasonal styles for spring 1945 opened to great acclaim in Paris in March 1945. Thereafter in order to quickly reach the widest audience, it may well be that either more than one version of the Thèatre was made and/or that the original Paris version was split into groups that were sent separately around the world. Thus whilst one set of scenes was displayed, for example, in London in September 1945, another set was on view in Rio de Janeiro in the same month, as is further detailed in Chapter 9 and in our Conclusion. In January 1946, Copenhagen received just three of the sets, albeit to huge acclaim (see Chapter 8). This book therefore details the national and international activities of the Paris haute couture salons during the fearful years of the Occupation of Paris and at its end.

This text thus examines war time couture trades across Europe with a focus on the diffusion of Paris haute couture style to these countries. It assesses the consequences of the enforcement of Nazi economic, cultural and racist policies on couture industries in Germany itself, in Nazi-annexed Austria and in German-

FIGURE INTRO.5
Jeanne Lanvin, Paris, evening dress in beaded, ivory rayon satin, 1944 (Kerry Taylor Auction House, Lot 94, 23 June 2015, with thanks).

occupied Denmark and Belgium and on the European Jewish community involved in the couture industry. The routes of diffusion of Paris style to the neutral countries of Portugal, Sweden and Switzerland are probed and finally this text examines the reactions to all of this in the fashion worlds of Allied countries: Britain, America and Brazil. All of these issues form the heart of the discussions in this book.

References

Belting, I. (2015). *Gretchen mag's mondän!" Damenmode der 1930er-Jahre*, Munich: Hirmer Verlag.

Doré-Rivé, I. (ed.). (2013). *Pour Vous Mesdames, La mode en temps de guerre*, Lyon: Libel.

Grumbach, D. (1993). *Histoires de la Mode*, Paris: Seuil.

Huff, A.B. and Sharf, F.A. (2012). *Beauty as Duty Textiles on the Homefront in WWII Britain*, Boston: Museum of Fine Arts.

Falluel, F. and Gutton, M-L. (2009). *Accessoires de Mode sous L'Occupation, Paris 1940–44*, Paris: Paris-Musées.

Le Wita, B. (1994). *French Bourgeois Culture*, Cambridge: Cambridge University Press.

Pouillard, V. (2013). 'Keeping designs and brands authentic: the resurgence of the post-war French fashion business under the challenge of US mass production', *European Review of History*, vol. 20, no. 5: 815–835, DOI: 10.1080/13507486.2013.833720.

Roche, D. (1994). *The Culture of Clothing: Dress and Fashion in the Ancien Regime*, Cambridge: Cambridge University Press.

Scott, E.J. (2014). 'The Pennington-Mellor collection of House of Worth haute couture 1885–1920: The overlooked case of the consumption of less expensive haute couture', MA History of Design and Material Culture Dissertation, University of Brighton.

Sydney Jewish Museum. (2012). *Dressing Sydney, the Jewish Fashion Story*, Sydney: Sydney Jewish Museum.

Veillon, D. (1990). *La Mode Sous l'Occupation*, Paris: Payot.

Chapter 1
From Berlin to Paris
*Lou Taylor**

Nazi Germany

Building on their certainty of the supremacy of the German Master Race, the goal of Hitler and his Third Reich was to create an empire that would last a thousand years, incorporating the whole of Europe and beyond. Kershaw writes that 'The barbarism and destructiveness which were inherent in the vain attempt to realize [the goal of racial purification and racial empire] were infinite in extent, just as the expansionism and extension of aggression to other peoples were boundless' (Kershaw 1999: 240).

In every annexed and occupied country these policies were set in place by Hitler's military leaders, troops, civilian administrators and their collaborators, all sharing a ruthless sense of national and personal entitlement to own everything in their path. Based on his personal wartime experiences, Airey Neave wrote in 1978 that 'No reconstruction can convey the true extent of their infamy' (Neave 1978:25). In last two years of the war, Neave had been the chief organiser of MI9, a secret organisation master-minding underground escape lines in occupied North-West Europe. For this, Neave received the Distinguished Service Order (DSO). He was also awarded the French Croix de Guerre for his work with the French Resistance. In 1945 he was employed by the British War Crimes Executive at the Nuremberg War Crimes Tribunal. His first job was to serve indictment warrants personally on the twenty-two surviving Nazi leaders jailed in Nuremberg and charged with war crimes and crimes against humanity. These included Goering, Frank, Hess, Ley, Speer and Sauckel.[1] After witnessing the Tribunal, he wrote:

> these trials 'revealed in plain language, the character of the Nazis's' system. Without evidence, the world might never have known the full truth of the Jewish extermination plan and the slave labour programme of Albert

FIGURE 1.0
1941-42, German Reich, Nazi Occupied, neutral, and Allied territories across Europe. (Map adapted from Wikimedia Commons, licence CC-BY-SA-3.0).

---

*All translation from French by the author.

Speer. It demonstrated what kind of people perpetuated these colossal racial abominations. They were not supermen. They were 'ordinary people' ... invested by Hitler with unbridled power. ... As their power increased they learned to wield it without restraint. Manipulation, perversion and corruption of the law, allied to absolute rule unchecked by legal or democratic sanction, turned many of them into beasts.

(Neave 1978: 25–27)

Elwyn-Jones, on the British prosecuting team, stated plainly that at the 1946–1949 American-run trials of leading Nazi industrialists, including some who oversaw spoliation of industries in Occupied France, their 'criminality' too became clear. To give examples, Emil Puhl, vice president of the Reichsbank, was charged and jailed for receiving and disposing of gold from occupied territories and from concentration camp loot (Elwyn-Jones 1983: 128).[2] Hans Kerl, who oversaw textile industries across Germany and in France and other conquered European territories, was charged with 'spoliation in occupied territories' and sentenced to fifteen years in jail (see Chapter 2, p. 60 and Figure 2.3). As also became clear at these trials, Nazi anti-Semitic legislation was applied energetically in both annexed regions and occupied territories. Jews were deported to concentration camps from all of these – except in Denmark, which was the only country to actively resist the deportation of its Jewish community. Secretly warned that round-ups were to start, 7,200 Danish Jews were helped to leave, mostly by small ships to neutral Sweden.[3]

Nazi high society

Nazi military, diplomatic and industrial leaders and their wives, weighted with self-aggrandizement and with this same ruthless sense of entitlement, lived lives of extreme luxury built on the spoils of war wealth, from the gold teeth of those murdered at Auschwitz, from bribes, from the looting of Jewish banks, businesses and property and from public and private art and museum collections, whilst their wives wore couture, competing with each other over leadership in German fashion.

By 1933 Reichsmarschall Herman Goering was Hitler's second in command, a leading member of the Nazi Party, head of the Luftwaffe, founder of the Gestapo and a 'fervent anti-semite'. He was named at Nuremberg 'as the instigator of the concentration camps' (Neave 1978: 92, 243). By 1933, having already amassed a fortune, Goering built himself a huge, luxury country residence, Carinhall, northeast of Berlin. As Nancy Yeide proves, here he stored and exhibited much of his huge looted art collection, which included 1,570 old master paintings pillaged from all over annexed and occupied Europe and also from various German collections (Yeide 2009: 28–213). Edsell writes that 'he was denied nothing' (Edsell R., quoted in Yeide 2009: 3). Yeide further shows that Goering visited Paris twenty-five times in 1941–1942, selecting freely from looted paintings stored at Nazi art repository at the Jeu de Paume and attending auctions at the Hotel Drouot to buy paintings (Yeide 2009: 13).[4] With such frequent travel to Paris, it is no surprise that find that Goering's second wife, the retired actress Emmy Sonnemann, wore couture clothes made in Paris as well as Berlin (Figure 1.1A).

Goering, with his wife Emmy, finally surrendered to the American 36th Infantry Division on 9 May 1945 (Yeide 2009: 17), still in direct possession of six Memling paintings. When Goering, who kept emeralds in his pockets (Edsell R., quoted in Yeide 2009: 3) and who had a 'passion for jewellery,' arrived under US guard at Nuremberg jail with his 'finger nails varnished red,' he brought with him 'sixteen monogrammed suitcases, a red hat box and a valet' (Neave 1978: 68).

FIGURE 1.1A
Emmy and Herman Goering with Magda and Joseph Goebbels, Reich Minister for Propaganda, attending a press ball in Berlin, 3 February 1935 (Getty 541086559).

FIGURE 1.1B
Hans Frank, Governor General of Occupied Poland's General Government, with his wife, Brigitte, and Goebbels at a soirée in Krakow on 1 September 1940, marking the first anniversary of the outbreak of war (with thanks to the National Digital Photographic Archive, Warsaw, no: SM02-3385. Photograph by Paul Brander).

Chapter 1: From Berlin to Paris 27

Hans Frank, Governor General of the Occupied Polish Territories from October 1939–1944, lived in luxury in one of the greatest historical palaces of Europe, Wawel Castle in Cracow, just seventy kilometres from the concentration camp at Auschwitz. When his private villa in Bavaria was searched in 1945, American forces found Leonardo de Vinci's painting *Lady with an Ermine* dated to 1490 and Rembrandt's *Landscape With the Good Samaritan*, both stolen from the world famous Czartoryski Gallery in Cracow and both finally returned to the city.[5] Frank's wife, Brigitte, an ex-secretary, became the First Lady in the General Government. Not so young or slim, nevertheless photographs show that she wore fashionable bias-cut satin evening dresses, furs and jewels. She liked to be called 'the Queen of Poland'.[6]

With his fashionable wife, Maria, and living grandly too in another vast castle, was Arthur Karl Greiser, the Reich Governor of the Poznan Region of Eastern Poland. This huge fortress was being rebuilt as Hitler's home in his Eastern Territories (Michal 2004: 25).[7] Wearing couture clothes was thus just one of the many benefits of the war for the wives of these men. Some continued to procure their couture clothes in Paris as well as Berlin all through the war.

FIGURE 1.1C
Arthur and Maria Greiser at the Hunters Ball, 5 November 1937. (Copyright Bundesarchiv 183-C15532.)

Luxury goods and couture fashion in Nazi Germany

High-ranking leaders and their wives therefore lived lives of great luxury, attending many occasions when wearing fashionable evening dress was required – at concerts, balls, the opera, for soirées and receptions at the best restaurants in Berlin, with elegant day wear worn at Nazi public occasions and official functions.

Anneliese Ribbentrop was a leading Nazi fashion celebrity. Probably whilst her husband was German Ambassador to London, in 1936–1938,[8] one of their daughters was placed in a private finishing school in Bexhill, the Augusta-Victoria

FIGURE 1.2A
Anneliese Ribbentrop, Inge Ley and Mme. Alfieri, the wife of Dino Alfieri, the Italian Ambassador and leading Italian Fascist, at a reception on 22 May 1939 (Getty 545920705).

FIGURE 1.2B
College blazer badge for the Augusta-Victoria College, Bexhill-on-Sea, Sussex, attended by one of Ribbentrop's daughters, in about 1937 (Bexhill Museum, no. BEXHM: 2018.41.1, with thanks to Julian Porter, curator).

College, which featured the swastika and the flags of Germany and Britain on the school blazer badge.

The German couture industry provided the elegant clothes required by women from this circle, whose photographs were published widely in the German press for the general public to admire and copy and whose images were seen in filmed news reports.

Significantly for the story in this book, both Irene Guenther and Isabelle Belting state that Paris remained the arbiter of German fashion throughout the war years. In her meticulous and moving 2004 study of the high fashion world of Nazi Germany, Guenther makes this perfectly clear (Guenther 2004: 170–72). Belting also detailed this in her 2015 exhibition Gretchen mag's mondän!Damenmode der 1930er-Jahre, at Munich's Stadtmuseum, and in a related book. Hence, Germany as a whole, and Berlin in particular, continued to source fashion style from Paris as well as Berlin. Guenther notes that leading German couturiers included Hilda Romatzki, who was Jewish and who was named 'the German Maggy Rouf' (Guenther 2004: 191). Her salon also received Magda, the elegant wife of Joseph Goebbels, the new Reich Minister for Public Enlightenment and Propaganda (Guenther 2004: 133). Romatzki attended couture shows in Paris right up to the autumn of 1939 (Guenther 2004: 203–4). Guenther references other famous couture salons, many of them

FIGURE 1.2C
Left: Summer evening dress in purple silk crepe georgette and gelatin sequins, salon of Stanowksi, Dussledorf, 1936–1938 (No. T-A79/252). Right: White evening dress in rayon tulle, 1938, worn by the actress Gundel Thormann (No. T-80/654). Both garments from the Münchner Stadtmuseum, with thanks to Isabella Belting.

also Jewish. These included Annemarie Heise, Paul Kuhnen, a Jewish couture salon 'where all the most stylish women in Berlin society went to be dressed" (Guenther 2004: 133), as well as Richard Goetz, the Schulze-Bibernell salon, Hermann Gerson, Harald Mahrenholzp, Clara Schultz and Max Becker amongst others (Guenther 2004: 133, 137, 180, 189, 173).

In 1933, the German National Fashion Institute (the Deutsches Modeamt, later Deutsches Mode-Institut (DMI), the Central Fashion Organisation) was founded. Guenther devotes an entire chapter to the DMI, describing it as the only organisation 'with full [Nazi] governmental support at ministerial rank" (Guenther

2004: 167). It fell under the protection of Goebbels. Guenther explains that its task was 'to unite all existing artistic and economic forces in the nation for the creation of independent and tasteful German fashion products' so that these 'can successfully enter into competition with the designs of Paris haute couture" (Guenther 2004: 170–71). This was to be achieved through the organisation of fashion design training, the holding of fashion shows at home and abroad and the promotion of German fashion goods of all kinds both at home and for export (Guenther 2004: 167–201). Guenther shows that by November 1938, the powerful Robert Ley was the head of the German Labour Front (Deutsche Arbeitsfront or DAF), the Nazi labour organisation which had replaced the democratic national trade union organisation (Guenther 2004: 185). Ley was also accordingly Head of DAF's Textile, Clothing and Handiwork Group.[9] Guenther adds that some of Ley's DMI offices were run by 'avid Nazis" (Guenther 2004: 186). Ley's blonde, fashionable wife, Inge, was a leading Nazi socialite and famous for her couture clothes.[10] Shirer noted that Max Amman, who was close to Hitler, was president of the Reich Press Chamber and wealthy czar of the Nazi publishing house, the Eher Verlag[11] (Shirer 1939: 461).

There was no law imposing an official 'Reich Fashion'. However, as Belting and Guenther both state, despite the fact that high fashion in Germany followed Paris/Berlin lines all through the war, the traditional dirndl costume, the *trachtenstil*, was promoted as ideal dress representing German womanhood and patriotism. Guenther writes in detail about the cultural meanings attached to the '*Trachtenkleidunge*' style in Nazi Germany (2004: 109–119), noting that it was viewed in Nazi eyes as 'the most suitable example of racially and culturally pure clothing" (2014: 110). Dirndls had been worn in rural communities across Southern Germany, Alsace, Switzerland,

FIGURE 1.3
Robert and Inge Ley in a motorcade, 6 June 1930, with Max Amman (photograph by Hugo Jaeger, Timepix/The LIFE Picture Collection/Getty Images, 50714939, 1939).

FIGURE 1.4A AND B Fashionable linen suit and dirndl, both from *Der Goldene Schnitt*, Hamburg, 1938 (with thanks to the Dress History Teaching Collection, University of Brighton).

Austria and Alpine Italy for many, many years before that, as seen, for example, in F. Meyer's *Collections de Costumes Suisse Originaux*, published in Zurich in 1837. The dirndl was a style worn popularly across urban Germany and Austria in the 1930s, as witnessed in the dressmaker patterns offered alongside fashionable Paris fashion copy styles. Additionally, 'Tyrolean' dark green loden suits trimmed with heavy passementerie and worn with feather-trimmed felt hats were equally popular, a style embraced by fashion internationally by the late 1930s (Guenther 2004: 117).

It needs to be clarified here that the wearing of a full dirndl costume before 1940 did not automatically signal support for Hitler and the Nazi party. A photograph taken by Dr. A. F. Haffner, researcher at the Technical Institute, Karlsruhe, in the summer of 1937, shows his cousin, Frau Mia Renner, showing off her newly adopted baby to her neighbours' children on a summer's day. Dr. Haffner's daughter, Janet Hammond, writes that these clothes were 'probably home-made' and that Frau Renner was 'far from being a Nazi sympathiser'. Her schoolteacher husband, Wilhelm, had in fact 'been disciplined for refusing to teach Nazi songs at his school'.[12]

Whatever styles were favoured, the German fashion industry was obliged to function in the context of both Nazi anti-Semitic legislation and Nazi National Socialist policies for women. From 1933, the industry was increasingly aryanised. Guenther comments that by 1936 most Jewish fashion salons had been aryanised,

FIGURE 1.5
Frau Mia Renner and children in dirndl styled dresses, Karlsruhe, summer, 1937. (Photographer Dr. A.E. Haffner, with thanks to Janet Hammond.)

liquidated and 'had vanished from view" (2004: 151–54, 165, 189). Once the war started, popular German magazines 'aggressively promoted nationalism in fashion' replacing photographs of 'enemy fashions' (English and French) with Italian, Austrian and German designs (Guenther 2004: 204). From 1941 until it closed down in April 1943, a new high-fashion German fashion magazine, *Die Mode*, was used as 'external cultural propaganda for the Third Reich, through distribution all over Scandinavia, Spain, Italy and elsewhere?' (Guenther 2004: 213–14). Guenther contrasts the elegance seen in this publication most meaningfully with the realities of the extreme struggle undergone by most German women to get hold of any clothing at all by 1944.

For the First Ladies of Fashion in Germany, their husbands' travels to Paris offered useful opportunities to obtain Paris couture clothes. Guenther notes importantly for this investigation that Nazi officials, visiting or on duty in Paris, frequented the better fashion salons for purchases for their German wives or French mistresses (2004: 212). *The New York Times* of Friday, 1 September 1944, at the moment of the Liberation of Paris, reported that Goering ordered four gowns for his wife, Emmy, from the couture salon of Paquin just two weeks before the liberation of the city. Baroness von Stohrer, the wife of a leading German diplomat involved in Spanish politics and with German attempts to kidnap the Duke and Duchess of Windsor in 1940, selected many clothes from collections of the House of Schiaparelli, purchasing them on her not infrequent travels through Paris from Berlin and Madrid. She stayed at the Ritz Hotel, also the headquarters of the Luftwaffe, where Chanel lived through the Occupation with her Nazi lover Baron von Dincklage. Kerry Taylor notes that surviving invoices addressed to Baroness von Stohrer at the Ritz reveal that she purchased practical garments such as a waterproof coat and a house coat in 1942 from Schiaparelli, her favourite couture salon, as well as day and evening gowns. The Baroness had a preference for fashionable turbans.[13] Veillon confirms such sales, noting that from July 1942, all private clients of Paris salons were obliged to obtain a personal '*Carte-d'acheteur couture-création*'. Whilst the French clients buying these varied in number from 2,000 to around 1,300, German numbers remained at 200 from 1942 through 1 April 1944. German permit cards were ordered directly by the German Military High Command for France (the *Militärbefehlshaber in Frankreich*) based at the Hotel Majestic (Veillon 1990: 164–65).

There was therefore no dictatorship of fashion by Nazi Germany. Guenther writes of the hypocrisy latent in Nazi attitudes to Paris couture (2004: 212). Adlington details the Upper Tailoring Studio, in Auschwitz, where Jewish seamstresses and French women imprisoned for their anti-Nazi Resistance work were put to work by 1942 creating Paris-inspired outfits for the wives of the camp's elite Nazi SS Officers (2018: 96–99). Belting too confirms the deep gap between the aggressive and hypocritical hostility towards Paris couture within Nazi theory and amongst Nazi women's organisations and the reality of the sartorial practices of the wives of powerful Nazi leaders (Belting 2015: 255). As Guenther clarifes significantly for this study, the Nazi occupying forces in Paris could have shut down the entire Paris couture world had they wished to do so. She writes that many historians of the Third Reich believe that 'when the Nazi government was truly intent upon accomplishing a certain goal, there was little that evaded its terror or its grasp" (Guenther 2004: 210–11). Instead, they opted to turn Paris couture into a trade subjugated to their will and functioning only with their permission.

France and its couture trade in 1940

The desperate and humiliated situation that conquered France was in must be made clear. After the defeat of France on 22 June 1940, whilst General de Gaulle flew at once to London to set up a French Government in Exile with its own force (Forces Françaises Libre or FFL), the aged Maréchal Pétain became Head of State (Azema and Wieviorka 2000: 309). Despite this national title, Pétain and his cabinet were in control only in the Zone Libre, with its capital at Vichy in south-central France across the German militarised Demarcation Line, until November 1942, when this region was also invaded by German forces.

The rest of France, in the Occupied Zone and Military Zones, fell under direct German control. Azema and Wieviorka write that 'The French state's policy of collaboration irrevocably compromised it in the eyes of the Allies' (2000: 309). Halls, in one sentence, confirms Nazi intentions for the future of France. The 'master race' planned from the start 'to preside over the destinies of a France dismembered ... whose function would be to provide food, luxuries and pleasure for their conquerors" (Halls 1981: 2).

FIGURE 1.6
Map of divided France, June 1940 (Map adapted from Wikimedia Commons, licence CC-BY-SA-3.0).

Thus it was that in the defeated country, both the couture trade in Occupied France and the luxury silk trades in Vichy, France, permitted by their vanquishers to continue functioning, were caught in the rapacious and inescapable embrace of the Nazi authorities. Occupied regions were obliged to pay huge levies for the cost of their own occupation and to tolerate the looting of any of their raw materials and goods that the Nazis desired (Durand 1989: 65). A system of tightly controlled repression was set in place immediately. By the end of the war, 240,000 French and 75,000 Resistants died (*Tricolore* 1945: 54) as well as 25 per cent of the Jewish population of France. This included 10,000 Jewish children who were sent to the camps (Bertin 1993: 152–55, quoting Klarsfeld S., 1983; Fayard 1983: 191).

All aspects of life were controlled – law, business, diplomacy, manufacture, medicine, imports and exports, the police, postal and telephone services, transport, travel, rations, the press (see Chapter 5), all publishing and culture, including the art world of galleries, theatre, film, museums and exhibitions. As a mark of ownership, street direction signs were erected in German in Paris and a huge V sign for victory and banner, also in German, was stretched across the great neoclassical front of the Chambre des Deputés in Paris, which read 'Germany Triumphs On All Fronts'. Celia Bertin was haunted later by memories of 'the atmosphere of fear, intolerance and madness that ruled then" (Bertin 1993: 242).

FIGURE 1.7
Chambre des Deputés in Paris, 1941, with German V for victory sign and banner: "Germany Triumphs On All Fronts" (Getty 3313255).

Nazi control over French culture

Cone writes that 'one of the first acts of the German Occupiers after the June Armistice was to set up a branch of Goebbels' Propaganda Ministry, the *Propaganda Abteilung*, part of the German army... to keep the French press and art worlds under surveillance' (1992: 9). She adds, importantly, that Goebbels 'had the ambition of transforming the arts into a modern instrument of political stewardship" (Cone 1992: 9, 66). French 'Romantic Realist" art that reflected German National Socialist art and its love of 'return to the soil' imagery (Cone 1992: 34) was heavily promoted whilst art defined by Hitler as 'Judeo-Marxist-Decadent' was banned and destroyed. 'Decadent' art included Cubism and Modernism (Cone 1992: Chapters 2 and 7). Jewish artists were forbidden to exhibit their work and Jewish galleries were aryanised (Cone 1992: 12–13). As noted above, looted art collections were stored at the Musée de Jeu de Paume in Paris before shipment to Germany (Cone 1992: 72–73). A series of major exhibitions were held in Paris to promote Goebbels' concept of 'art as an instrument of political stewardship'. A massive retrospective of the work of Hitler's favourite sculptor, Arno Breker, was held at the Orangerie in the summer of 1942, for example (Cone 1992: 157). Artisan crafts were heavily promoted in exhibitions in both the Free and Occupied zones (see Chapter 2).

As well as arts and crafts shows, joint propaganda Franco-German trade exhibitions were held on a regular basis to demonstrate to the French public the commercial benefits of German economic reorganisation and the take-over of much of French industry. At the 'Exposition de la France Européene' in June 1941 at the Petit Palais, Paris, German and French synthetic fabrics were shown together, as is further discussed in Chapter 2. Every effort, dependent of course on German permission, was also made by French designers and manufacturers of luxury dress and textiles to hold couture fashion shows abroad. This is a story that runs its way all through the chapters in this book.

Otto Abetz and 'cultural cooperation'

From August 1940, Otto Abetz, the German 'Ambassador' to France, and his French wife, Suzanne de Brouckère (once secretary to the leading French collaborationist journalist, Jean Luchaire, a close friend of Abetz), lived in the grandest of style in the Hotel Beauharnais, Rue de Lille. This Napoleonic palace, hidden behind tall walls and high wooden gates, was, and is still, furnished with its original early nineteenth-century Empire decoration, chosen by Empress Joséphine. Amongst the many grand reception rooms is, for example, the Four Seasons saloon, with midnight blue walls and five great crystal chandeliers, regarded still as one of the greatest examples of surviving decorative arts of this period.[14] Here receptions, dinners and parties with the best of foods and wines were held for the new *Tout Paris* social circles. These were a mix of high-ranking German military staff, diplomats, French collaborationist politicians, businessmen, leading journalists and their wives, writers, artists, actors, film stars and some couturiers and their clients.

Barbara Lambauer writes that Abetz strongly supported the ideals of Joseph Goebbels' Propaganda-Abteilung and its Propaganda-Staffel (the propaganda organisation and controller of the French Press and publishing) during the Occupation, believing that Goebbels' ideas could be implemented through establishing 'cultural collaboration' between the occupiers and the occupied. Abetz also strongly supported Hitler's ideas of racial purification. Lambauer notes too that the persecution of French Jews from the summer of 1940 was triggered in large part by the actions of Abetz. In the process, he pillaged the Paris apartments of the Rothschild family to find decorative art to further enhance the decoration of his Embassy (2007: 157–59).[15] Lambauer explains, importantly, that the policy of establishing Franco-German 'cultural collaboration' was based on the premise that a continuation of French intellectual life, re-aligned on a Nazi axis, played into German determination to create the illusion that a 'normal life' was continuing in Paris.[16] It is in this context that the continuation of the work of Paris couture through the Occupation needs to be set, as a highly successful example of 'cultural collaboration', despite the wishes of most of the couturiers.[17]

The Paris couture trade after Occupation: June 1940

As outlined in this book, the German authorities reorganised the French fashion and textile industries, including the couture salons, under close Nazi control, to serve Nazi business and cultural interests, not French ones. In reaction, leading Paris couturiers, led by Lucien Lelong, determined that, at whatever the cost and despite fearful shortages, their industry must survive (see Chapter 4). Nearly all the leading members of the *Chambre Syndicale de la Couture Parisienne* in Paris continued to create bi-annual designs season after season without pause. Thanks to research by Veillon and Grumbach, these facts and the ever-more flamboyant and exaggerated Paris occupation styles from 1943–1945 are now known. The salons had, however, to come to terms with the fact that the continuation of their businesses was permitted only on German terms and on the understanding that the conquering Nazis were now in charge and could close their trade down at any moment should they wish to do so. This policy was still in place in 1943 when the journal *International Textiles* (published in London and other centres, but not in Paris; see chapter 12) noted in June that 'news which filters out of France to-day [sic] brings the story of creative talent carrying on, of fashions retaining a high standard of artistic merit despite the poor quality materials in which they are executed'. The report concluded that whilst Germans do not like to see the women of France 'proudly flaunting their elegance', they have 'no desire to see the French fashion industry and the *Haute Couture* crushed" (International Textiles 1943: 25).

Deeply concerned about keeping their international businesses alive, the couturiers were also determined to retain their highly specialised staff, trained by generations of craftsmen and women, and to prevent them from being sent to

Germany on forced labour. The couturiers in Paris kept 12,000 in work,[18] 97 per cent of their force, saving many from what turned out to be very real traumas of forced labour in Germany.[19] The *Chambre Syndicale de la Couture Parisienne* and its president, Lelong, successfully argued against the German proposal that their trade should move to Germany (Veillon 1990: 152–54), but nevertheless the salons were forced to adapt to the demands of the Nazi authorities and so Paris couture continued, and indeed, as Veillon clarifies, prices escalated and business even improved (Veillon 1990: 205).

Nazi anti-Semitic legislation

Many Jewish specialists worked in the Paris couture trade, from textile designers to tailors, models, couturiers, milliners, jewellers, furriers, shoemakers and business people at every level of design, manufacture and retailing. Bertin (1993: 146–59) and Veillon (see Chapter 2) detail how all became subjected to Nazi anti-Semitic legislation, forbidden to own their businesses, which were forcibly aryanised, and thousands were put on transportation trucks to the death camps. The Jewish couturier Jacques Heim, for example, under the protection of an influential Spanish customer, escaped transportation, but his business was aryanised 'voluntarily'. Veillon writes that his war experiences have never been fully recognized (1990: 180). Far grimmer fates were those of Odette 'Fanny' Berger, the young Jewish milliner cited by Veillon in Chapter 2 and Elisabeth, the estranged, non-Jewish wife of Philippe, Baron de Rothschild. Having refused publicly to sit next to Otto Abetz's wife at a Schiaparelli show, Elisabeth was deported (Veillon 1990: 210) and died at Ravensbrück in March 1945, seven months after the Liberation of Paris and one month before the end of the war.

The reactions of the couturiers

Leading couturiers in Paris reacted each in their own way to the inescapable circumstances of the Occupation, as is detailed in several chapters in this book. Not all favoured the extremes of the Occupation style, and not all mixed with the occupiers socially, though many did. Jacques Fath's salon flourished. He frequented soirées at the German Embassy at the Hotel Beauharnais with his beautiful model wife, Genevieve. His staff numbers grew along with his business success, from 76 employees in 1942 to 240 by 1944 (Guillaume 1993: 29). Veillon discusses Maggy Rouff and Marcel Rochas, who were both closely involved with designing fashions made from German-French synthetics for public Franco-German propaganda exhibitions (1990: 124, 128). Odette Fabius, a Resistant, remembered that Rochas refused to publicly acknowledge his Jewish clients once they were forced to wear yellow stars. He would cross the Paris streets to avoid them (Veillon 1990: 179). *Falbalas*, a film by Jacques Becker, starring Micheline Presle and Raymond Rouleau and set in a fictional Paris haute couture salon, featured designs by Rochas and survives as witness to his extravagant late Occupation-style designs, with hats by

FIGURE 1.8A
Evening dress in cream-coloured lawn with red, white and blue floral embroidery and lace ruffles, 1939–1940, Chanel, Paris. (Museum of the City of New York, no. 45.111.3A and B. Gift of Mrs. Harrison Williams, 1945. © The Metropolitan Museum of Art Photograph Studio.)

FIGURE 1.8B
General Schellenberg, head of the SS Intelligence Service in Berlin, September 1943. (Copyright Bundesarchiv 101III-Alber-178-04A. Photographer Kurt Alber.)[21]

Gabrielle.[20] The continuing businesses of the salons of Molyneux and Piguet are discussed in Chapter 12.

Coco Chanel, a long term anti-Semite, became a 'horizontal collaborator' during the Occupation. She designed her last collections in 1939, including her ravishing, patriotic, 1939 tri-colour evening dress beautifully embroidered with the field flowers of France (see Chapter 2.)

Chanel closed her salon in 1939, once war was declared. Her collaborationist activities are now widely known, fully documented by Hal Vaughan in his 2011 book *Sleeping with the Enemy: Coco Chanel – Nazi Agent*, based on surviving Berlin and Paris police archives. To summarise, Chanel lived in the Ritz Hotel in Paris through the war and after, with Baron Hans Günther von Dincklage, who was working directly for the German Abwehr, the German Foreign Intelligence Service. Amongst other documented activity, Chanel undertook a failed mission (code name Modellhut) to Madrid in 1943 for General Walter Schellenberg, head of the SS Intelligence Service in Berlin, visiting him in Berlin to receive her instructions. Vaughan details Chanel's Abwehr agent number as 7124 (Vaughan 2011: 161–72).

Wartime couture clientele

Ideal couture clients, wherever they came from in the world, understood the effort needed to obtain couture clothes – the need to attend fittings for each garment and to know the precise correct etiquette for wearing which costly garment for what occasion, whether public or private. They also knew the importance of wearing matching fashionable, seasonal accessories – hats, gloves, shoes, bags, jewellery and so on (see Chapter 3). They knew that all of these were badges of identity and public signals of membership of the highest international social, political and business circles and of wealthy artistic and creative worlds. They and their couturiers understood their need to keep slim and to spend time on all aspects of creating a soignée appearance, from a perfect hairstyle and makeup to perfectly matching accessories, whether worn in town, country, beach, travelling or at cocktails or balls, and all of these up-to-date and in constant style flux. In occupied Paris, the Polish writer Andrzej Bobowski, who kept a journal all through the Occupation, noted that above all, in the 1939–1941 period, classic black suits became almost a uniform for day wear in such circles (Trojanowski, 2015: 127).

Some wealthy, regular, pre-war couture clients, particularly those with sympathies for the Occupation and Vichy regimes, simply continued their usual patronage of Paris haute couture. As we know now from the research of Professor Yves Pourcher,[22] one such was Josée Laval, the only child of Pierre Laval, Prime Minister of France from 1931–1932 and 1935–1936, to whom she was devoted. In 1934, she had ordered her clothes from Lelong, Chanel and Caroline Reboux. She married Comte René de Chambrun, a Franco-American aristocrat, international lawyer and businessman, in 1935 (Pourcher 2015: 46, 61). Josée, Countess de Chambrun, spent her Occupation life entrenched in the most powerful levels of collaborationist *Tout Paris* political and social circles. From 12 April 1942 to 19 August 1944, Pierre Laval became head of the Vichy Government and Pourcher writes that he was 'master architect of the policy of collaboration with Germany' and that he 'placed the [French] government and police at the occupier's disposal, handing over Jews, opponents and forced labourers' (Pourcher 2012: 110–11).

And so, for example, the Countess met Goering, in the winter of 1942, on one of his visits to Paris. He promised her a painting from his [looted] art collection (Pourcher 2015: 115). Pourcher writes after reading her diaries: 'I . . . saw what mattered to her: titles, châteaux, signs of affection, recognition, or rejection, horse races" (2012: 116). Moving constantly between Paris, Vichy, Biarritz, Deauville and her father's castle at Châteldon in the Puy du Dôme, the Countess evidently felt the need to keep her couture wardrobe up to date throughout the war years and her diaries give a detailed account of her purchases. On 11 December 1940, for example, she bought a black dress and a chestnut-coloured coat from Lanvin and was vastly pleased by the designs at Marcelle Chaumont (Pourcher 2012: 97). She sat at the bedside of her father, who had been the target of an unsuccessful assassination attempt on 25 August 1941, wearing a Lanvin dress in spotted lavender blue (Pourcher 2015: 111). In June 1942, whilst Laval was occupied signing the Service du Travail Obligatoire legislation with Gauleiter Sauckel, Josée ordered another blue dress from Lelong (2015: 124). Balenciaga's darker-coloured designs pleased her later that year (2015: 128), though by 5 January 1943 she preferred a red Balenciaga dress and two days later purchased another lavender blue dress at Schiaparelli (2015: 134). In September 1943, by which time her father had become head of the infamous *Milice*, she declared that designs at the House of Lelong, where both Dior and Balmain were working (Balmain 1964: 14, 18) 'lacked imagination'. She turned instead to Marcel Rochas, Lanvin, Schiaparelli and Maggy Rouff (2015: 151) and by Easter 1944 she returned to Schiaparelli, buying a green hat (2015: 153).

As the Allied, Free French and Resistant forces fought their way to Paris in July and August of 1944, Josée was still attending her regular lunches at Maxim's, having tea at the Institute Allemande and making visits to the Auteuil races, as if her *Tout Paris* collaborationist luxury life would never end (Eder 2006: 95, quoting Pourcher Y., *Pierre Laval, vu par sa fille*, 2002). Laval was tried in France and executed by firing squad on 15 October 1945 for collaboration (Poucher 2012: 111). The Countess de Chambrun died in 1992 and her husband in 2002. Pourcher noted in 2012 that 'Hubert de Givenchy had asked for her Balenciaga gowns for the museum dedicated to that fashion designer. The remaining gowns were finally given to the Galliera museum' (Pourcher 2012: 122).

The salons were deprived through the Occupation of most of their international clientele, though Veillon writes that wealthy South American and Spanish women were still 'assiduous' clients and many very elegant (Veillon 1990: 212). Else Rijkens, a Dutch concert singer, and Aimée de Hereen, a wealthy Brazilian socialite, were just two examples of elegant international clients who were unable to directly order Paris couture clothes from summer 1940 but recommenced as soon as they could, after autumn 1945 as soon as the Liberation was over (see Chapter 14). New arriviste, haute collaboration customers soon made their way to the salons, the wives and mistresses of the new rich *Tout Paris* circles. Veillon and Bertin have written at length about these women (Veillon 1990: 187–217; Bertin[23] 1993: 99–130). They were a bizarre mix of the wealthy wives and mistresses of some leading Nazis officers and diplomats, including Emmy Goering, Inga Ley and Baroness Stohrer, as already noted, alongside Suzanne de Brouckère, who favoured Schiaparelli and Francoise and Corinne, the wife and daughter of the leading collaborationist journalist Jean Luchaire. They were joined by a class of often beautiful, intelligent, dissolute women, who Eder calls 'Les comtesses de la Gestapo'.[24] Eder describes them as stylish women with 'fabulous jewels and toilettes by the great couturiers . . . wearing a veneer of decorum . . . the stars of the world of the demi-mondaine" (Eder 2006: 12). Some were French, others foreign and all were determined to amuse themselves. One source of their fortunes was through German 'purchasing agencies' set up to buy and loot French goods. The most infamous one was the large-scale Bureau Otto, run by the SD Sicherheitsdienst des Reichsführers, the Intelligence Agency of the SS and the Nazi Party, which worked through French collaborationist intermediaries (Eder 2006: 11). Michel Szkonikoff, the biggest provider of goods of all kinds to the

Germans, became vastly wealthy in the 1941–1944 period (Eder 2006: 24, footnote 2). His German wife, Elfrieda, owned twenty-four couture fur coats (Veillon 1990: 208). These elegant 'horizontal collaborators' dined at the Tour d'Argent and at Maxim's with high-ranking Nazi officers and attended receptions at Abtez's Hotel Beauharnais. One grand soirée celebrated the opening of the mammoth Arno Breker exhibition (Cone 1992: 163). Jean Luchaire held his own reception to mark the publication of the hundredth edition of his collaborationist newspaper *Nouveaux Temps* in February 1941. Veillon writes that 'ambassadors of haute couture [who attended] included Lanvin, Dormoy, Paquin, Agnès, Rochas, Dèsses and Fath. Corinne Luchaire wore a glamorous, full skirted, evening dress by Rochas" (Veillon 1990: 191). Paquin's Spanish designer, Castillo, told Bettina Ballard, a leading American fashion journalist, that during the war 'he had made dresses for the very smart weekend parties at the millionaire Charles de Bestegui's Chateau Groussay, to the west of Paris, where all the women were asked to dress fashionably, regardless of war" (Ballard 1960: 197).

Corinne Luchaire (Bertin 1990: 104–112) was a blonde, young and exceptionally pretty film star. Bertin writes that at the age of twenty, Corinne 'began to share her life with profiteers of the regime of injustice and oppression" (1990: 111). She wore ravishing dresses from Marcel Rochas with white fox fur stoles (1990: 106). After interviewing her, Bertin, who had served with the Resistance, wrote of women who had behaved in the same manner as Corinne Luchaire, that:

> no-one never asked where the money came from and [they chose to forget] that the country was ruined, that most people were suffering because they were poor, starving, humiliated and scandalized by what was happening. Corinne and those like her pretended that they did not know that some of the population was persecuted, deported, put to death by their Nazi and French friends.
>
> (1990: 112)

Corinne's husband, Guy de Voisins de Laverniere, worked with the Bureau Otto (Bertin 1990: 126).[25] By the time of the Liberation of Paris, most of these women had fled to Germany, Portugal, Brazil, Argentina and elsewhere. They were so infamous and so compromised that they dared not stay in Paris. Most ended up with their goods confiscated and abandoned by everyone they knew, as did Corinne Luchaire.

BOF women

Next came the BOF women (Boeuf, Oeufs et Fromages), who had made fortunes on the food black market and who in prewar days could never have afforded couture. With their working-class, red knees, they were mocked at the Lelong salon, by his designers, Dior and Balmain (Balmain 1964: 72–77). Bettina Ballard, a leading US journalist but working then with the US Red Cross in Europe, visited Balenciaga's salon in Paris in December 1944. She knew him well. She remembered the shock of witnessing

> a group of noisy, fat, fancy-hatted women with hard vulgar voices – the kind of voices that I remembered hearing in the early morning at *Les Halles* market screaming at the customers and at each other ... looking at models *en solde* ... One of the women was counting thousand-franc notes from her purse, paying cash for a dress that she was carrying away with her in a white and blue Balenciaga box.
>
> (Ballard 1960: 196)

Later Balenciaga told her privately and apologetically that he tried to discourage them. 'They would buy anything, models much too small for them, and pay at any price, always paying cash out of bulging pursers. "*Elles sont tellement cursi*" – his Basque word for vulgar and unattractive" (Ballard 1960: 196).[26] Nevertheless, he needed and accepted their custom.

Resistants in the world of French couture

These wealthy corrupt women did not 'represent' French women during the Occupation. They were a small dissolute minority, albeit of financial importance to the survival of Paris haute couture. Most women in France, as explained in Chapter 2, struggled through the years of the Occupation to find food, clothing and warmth for their families in the cold, cold winters of the war. Millions and millions of French women just survived somehow. Most women kept their distance from the Occupiers as best they could, including for example Micheline Presle, noted above as the star of Becker's film *Falbalas*. Unlike Corinne Luchaire, however, she did not circulate in the wealthy, corrupt Occupation *Tout Paris* circles. She wrote in 1998 in her autobiography, *L'arrière-memoire* that she 'detested the Germans. I did my best not to see them. It wasn't an act of heroism; it wasn't an active resistance. It was an attitude.'[27]

Thousands of other women all over France, of all classes and ages, committed themselves even more directly to actively working with the French Resistance in full understanding of the terrible dangers of doing this. A good few of these courageous and selfless women were involved with the couture industry, either as workers or still as faithful clients. Odette Fabius worked for the Resistance Information Service. She was impeccably elegant in her couture clothes and could therefore usefully spy on *Tout Paris* collaborationist circles. Veillon writes that Fabius was often arrested, once in a Lanvin suit. She survived deportation to Ravensbrück (Veillon 1990: 210; Bertin 1993: 215). Josephine Baker, a couture client, worked secretly for the Resistance before joining the Free French Army in North Africa. In pre-war days she had favoured the salon of Vionnet (Jules-Rosette 2007: 144).[28] Veillon and Levisse-Touzé write that Antoine Sasse, a charming, sophisticated and elegant life-long couture customer, was, by 1940, a member of the Resistance and lover of the Resistance leader Jean Moulin. By May 1943 he was secretly organizing the United National Council of Resistance on behalf of de Gaulle in London. In her diary, Sasse noted down her war-time fittings at Jean Lanvin, Maggy Rouff and at the milliner Rose Descat. A simple, beige wool jacket she bought at Lanvin in 1943 survives,[29] as does her couture buyer's card. Sasse was Jewish and risked arrest at any time. Sasse worked closely with Moulin until he was betrayed, captured and tortured to death by SS Obersturmführer Klaus Barbie in Lyon in June 1943. She continued to work for the Resistance Military Information Service even when forced to flee to Geneva. Genéral de Gaulle awarded her the Resistance Medal with Rosette on 22 September 1945 (Veillon and Levisse-Touzé 2016: 12–25).

Chapter 3 details the committed anti-Nazi, pro-de Gaulle stance and activities of the luxury jewellery company Cartier in Paris, London and New York. Marie Louise Carven, who opened her Paris couture salon in 1942, aged twenty-one, held very opposite views to those of Chanel. In 1943, during a Jewish round-up, she arranged to hide the wife and children of her Jewish tailor, Henry Moise Bricianer. He was sheltered in her workshop throughout the remainder of the Occupation. She found safe places elsewhere for his family, who also survived. The Yad Vashem World Holocaust Remembrance Center in Jerusalem declared her to be 'Righteous Among the Nations' at a ceremony in Paris in August 2000.[30]

Violette Szabo was the most unexpected of all Resistant couture clientele. Half French, with a British father, she grew up in Stockwell, in South London, in a modest home. In 1943, aged twenty-two and already war-widowed with a little daughter, she trained as a Special Operations Executive, Courier (F. Section). Small, dark and pretty, she was parachuted into France just across the Channel into the dangerous Zone Militaire on 6 April 1944, carrying equipment to give to a Rouen resistance group. She found this group had been betrayed and was broken and after undertaking important work on her own initiative, she went to Paris, astonishingly visiting the couture salon of Edward Molyneux as a private customer on 24 April using a false identity (see Molyneux in Chapters 11 and 12). It was, however, no haphazard chance of fate that took her there. Szabo knew that the chief executive of the SOE, Wing Commander Forest Yeo-Thomas, had been the business manager of Molyneux's Paris salon before the Occupation. In the presence of 'several German officer customers and well-dressed sophisticated German women', Szabo ordered four Molyneux couture oufits. Szabo's daughter Tania kept the bill in her archives, so we know that Szabo ordered a heavy black silk crepe de chine evening dress, an 'écossais day dress – a crimson and deep-blue plaid dress trimmed at the neck and cuffs in midnight blue velvet', a navy blue and white floral silk dress with 'small dark blue flowers on a white background with short puffed sleeves and piping at the

FIGURE 1.9
Carven, Paris, summer suit with hunting print, 1945 (Kerry Taylor Auction House, LOT 73, 23 June 2013, with thanks).

FIGURE 1.10
Violette Szabo in floral print dress, probably 1942–1944, from a Lambeth newspaper published in 1946 (by kind permission of London Borough of Lambeth, Archives Department, lambethlandmark.com).

neck' and finally a yellow 'golf' jumper. The tartan trimmed dress had to be altered and thus after meeting sadly with the writer and French Resistance leader, Andre Malraux, to tell him that his brother had been killed at Rouen, she returned to the Molyneux salon three days later to collect her purchases, paying in counterfeit cash. The bill was huge: 37,475 francs. On 30 August she and her suitcase of Molyneux clothes were picked up by an RAF Lysander plane bound for London (Szabo 2015: Ch. 20). On her next mission in June 1944, Szabo was arrested and finally executed by Nazi officers at Ravensbrück prison in January 1945, alongside her tortured SOE colleagues, Denise Block and Lilian Rolfe (Perrin 2017). Szabo was awarded the George Cross and the French Croix de Guerre posthumously. Her Molyneux clothes survived in her wardrobe in London. They may exist today, but searches have proved sadly fruitless. Through the trauma of the Occupation, continuing to wear couture clothes was not always the mark of collaborating women.

References

Adlington, L. (July 2018). 'Sewing for the Nazis, the Dressmakers of Auschwitz', *BBC History Magazine*, Collection Edition.
Azéma, J.P. and Wieviorka, O. (2000). *Vichy*, 1940–44, Paris: Perrin.
Balmain, P. (1964). *My Years and Seasons*, London: Cassell.
Bertin, C. (1993). *Femmes sous l'Occupation*, Paris: Stock.
Belting, I. (2015) *Gretchen mag's mondän! Damenmode der 1930er-Jahre*, Munich: Hirmer Verlag.
Cone, M. (1992), *Artists Under Vichy, a case of Prejudice and Persecution*, Princeton: Princeton University Press.
Durand, Y. (1989). *La France dans le Deuxieme Guerre Mondiale: 1939–45*, Paris: Armand Colin.
Eder, C. (2006). *Les Comtesses de la Gestapo*, Paris: Grasset.
Elwyn Jones, F. (1983). *In My Time*, London: Weidenfeld and Nicolson.

Guenther, I. (2004). *Nazi Chic, Fashioning Women in the Third Reich*, London: Berg.
Guillaume, V. (1993). *Jacques Fath*, Paris: Paris Musées,
Grumbach, D. (1993). *Histoires de la Mode*, Paris: Seuil.
Halls, W.D. (1981). *The Youth of Vichy France*, Oxford: Clarendon Press.
International Textiles. Seaweed and Cactus Tweeds—and Balenciaga's 'lovely evening dresses'. Issue 1 (Jan.) 1943.
Jules-Rosette, B.P. (2007). *Josephine Baker in art and in life: the icon and the image*, Urbana: Univ. of Illinois Press
Kershaw, I. (1999). *Hitler: 1889–1936: Hubris*, London: Penguin Press.
Levisse-Touzé, C. and Veillon. D. (2016). *Antoinette Sasse, Rebelle, Résistante et Mécene (1897–1986)*, Paris: Paris Musees.
Neave, A. (1978). *Nuremberg, a Personal Record of the Trials of the Major Nazi War Criminals in 1945–6*. London: Hodder and Stoughton.
Perrin, N. (2017). SOE Agent Profiles: Violette Szabo. Accessed 3 August 2017, from nigelperrin.com/violetteszabo.htm.
Pourcher, Y. (2012). 'Laval Museum', *Historical Reflections*, vol. 38, Issue Spring, pp. 105–125.
Pourcher, Y. (2015). *Moi, Josée Laval*, Paris: Le cherche midi.
Pouillard, V. (2013). 'Keeping designs and brands authentic: the resurgence of the post-war French fashion business under the challenge of US mass production', *European Review of History*, accessed 24 Oct 2013 from http://www.tandfonline.com/loi/cerh20.
Shirer, W.L. (1941). *Berlin Diary, the Journal of a Foreign Correspondent*, London: Hamish Hamilton.
Szabo, T. (2015). *Beautiful, Young and Brave, Missions of Special Operations Executive, Violette Szabo*, e-pub ISBN 978 0 7509 6472 2 (first published 2007, Stroud, the History Press).
Taylor, L. (1992). 'Paris Couture 1940–1944', in Ash J. and Wilson E., *Chic Thrills, a Fashion Reader*, London: Pandora.
Tricolore. (1945). London: Carlton Gardens, Jan. 1945.
Trojanowski, K. (2015). 'La mode francaise sous l'Occupation allemande dans le journal; d'Andrzej Bobkowski 1940–44', *Critacao and Critica* no. 15, pp. 126–133, www.revistas.usp.br/criacaoecritica/article/view/102295.
Vaughan, H. (2011). *Sleeping with the Enemy. Coco Chanel – Nazi Agent*, London: Chatto and Windus.
Veillon, D. (1990). *La Mode Sous l'Occupation*, Paris: Payot.
Yeide, N. (2009) *Beyond the Dreams of Avarice, the Hermann Goering Collection*, New York: Laurel.

Endnotes

1. Airey Neave – barrister and politician – was the first British officer to successfully escape from the Colditz German prisoner-of-war camp. In last two years of the war he was the chief organiser of M.I.9, a secret organisation master-minding underground escape lines in occupied North-West Europe, which brought back to Britain over 4,000 Allied servicemen. See Neave, A. (1969) *Saturday at M.I.9*, London: Hodder and Stoughton. He was murdered by the IRA in 1978.
2. Lord Elwyn Jones (1909–1989) was Lou Taylor's father and author of books warning of the threat of Fascism: F. Elwyn Jones (1937), *Hitler's Drive to the East*, London: E.P. Dutton; *Battle for Peace* (1938), London: Victor Gollancz; *The Defence of Democracy* (1938), London: E.P. Dutton. Elwyn Jones's name was listed ('no. J 44 Writer') in the 'Black Book', the Nazi special-wanted arrest list drawn up in 1940–1941 by the office

of SS General Walter Schellenberg at the *Sicherheitsdienst des Reichsführers-SS* (the Security Service of the SS). After the 'successful Nazi invasion of Britain', the 2,820 men and women listed were then to be immediately arrested and investigated by the Reich Security Service. *Hitler's Black Book*, Forces War Records, accessed 3 October 2018 from https://www.forces-war-records.co.uk/hitlers-black-book. (See also Figure 1.8B.)

3. Rescue in Denmark, United States Holocaust Memorial Museum, Washington DC. Accessed 20 August 2017 from https://www.ushmm.org/outreach/en/article.php?ModuleId=10007740.

4. Yeide clarifies that by 1948, 90 per cent of Goering's art collection had been recovered through the work of the Monuments, Fine Art and Archives (MFAA) organisation of the Western Allied Armies: the Monuments Men (Yeide, 2009: 17, referencing Letter 2 March 1948 from the US Political Advisor for Germany to the American Legation in Bern, NARA/RG84/Entry 3223 Safe Haven Files, Box 31).

5. Keyte, M. (2017). '13 Stunning Art Works Stolen by Nazis', *Culture Trip*. Accessed 8 August 2017 from https://theculturetrip.com/europe/articles/13-stunning-artworks-stolen-by-the-nazis/.

6. *Krakow Post*. (2015, Feb 15). 'Looking Back 70 Years: Wawel Under Occupation'. Accessed 8 August 2017 from http://www.krakowpost.com/8702/2015/02/looking-back-70-years-wawel-under-occupation. Neave wrote that Frank idolised Hitler. Arrested by the Americans in 1945, he was tried at Nuremberg, convicted of war crimes and crimes against humanity and hung in the Nuremberg prison on 15 October 1946 (Neave 1978: 108–115).

7. Greiser was primarily responsible for the murder of tens of thousands of Poles and 98 per cent of Jews – more than 380,000 – from his region of control. He was arrested by Polish forces in 1945, tried and publicly executed in Poznan in July 1946. (Unger, M., 2004, *Reassessment of the Image of Mordechai Chaim Rumbowski*, Jerusalem: Yad Vashem, 25 and footnotes 44 and 45). See also Epstein, C., 2012, *Model Nazi, Arthur Greiser, and the Occupation of Western Poland*, Oxford: Oxford University Press.

8. Von Ribbentrop was hanged at Nuremberg on 19 October 1946 after being found guilty of crimes against humanity and other charges (Neave 1978: 317).

9. Robert Ley, leading Nazi politician and 'drunkard', was indicted at the Nuremberg War Crimes Tribunal for conspiracy, war crimes and crimes against humanity. He committed suicide in the cells of the Nuremberg prison on 25 October 1945 rather than face trial. (Neave 1978: 64, 131–32).

10. Inge Ley committed suicide at her home in 1942.

11. Max Amman was sentenced to ten years hard labour in 1948. Released from prison in 1953, he died in poverty in Munich. Jewish Virtual Library, Max Amann (1891–1957), https://www.jewishvirtuallibrary.org/max-amann.

12. Caption on photograph and email correspondence between Janet Hammond and Lou Taylor, July 2017, with kind permission of Janet Hammond, daughter of Dr. Haffner.

13. Kerry Taylor auction sale. Bill from Schiaparelli, Lot 81, 9 December 2014.

14. Bordeau, M. (2014). 'Hotel Beauharnais. Journées du patrimoine: Sous les dorures de l'Hôtel de Beauharnais, l'incroyable résidence de l'Ambassadeur d'Allemagne', *Huffington Post*. Accessed 8 August 2017 from www.huffingtonpost.fr/…/journees-du-patrimoine-2014-hotel-de-beauharnais.

15. Lambauer B. (2007). 'Francophile contre vents et marées? Otto Abetz et les Français, 1930–1958', *Bulletin du Centre de recherche français à Jérusalem*. Accessed 3 August 2017 from http://bcrfj.revues.org/40, 153–60.

16　Lambauer B. (2003, Dec.). 'Otto Abetz, le Manipulateur', *La Revue des Anciens Eleves de l'Ecole Nationale d'Administration, Numero Hors-Series*, 'Politique et Litterature. Accessed 12 August 2017 from http://www.karimbitar.org/politique_litterature.

17　See also Lambauer, B. (2001). *Otto Abetz et les Francais*, Paris: Fayard. In July 1949 a French court sentenced Abetz to twenty years of imprisonment for crimes against humanity. He was released on 17 April 1954 and died in Germany in 1958 in a mysterious car accident.

18　Alison Settle Archives, December 1944, University of Brighton, AS.B. 44.7.

19　Veillon, D. (1987). 'La Mode et les Restrictions: 1940-1944', *Actes du 112e Congrès National des Sociétés Savantes, Lyon Vol. 1 Textile: Production et Mode*, Paris: CTHS.

20　*Falbalas* was shot in Paris from January 1944 at the Pathé studios and on street locations. Filming took place at night due to daytime electricity outages and stopped altogether during the Battle for the Liberation of Paris, when the filmmakers recorded documentary evidence of the fighting. Falbalas was finally shown on 20 June 1945 (Vignaux, V., 2000, *Jacques Becker: L'exercise de la Liberté*, Paris: Céfal, p. 65).

21　SS General Walter Schellenberg, who testified to the Allies against other Nazi leaders after the war, was tried at Nuremberg for war crimes and sentenced on 4 November 1949 at the Ministries Trial to six years imprisonment (AVALON Project, Yale University, http://avalon.law.yale.edu/imt/01-04-46.asp). Released from prison after two years on the grounds of serious ill-health, he moved to Switzerland. Here he renewed contact with Coco Chanel, who paid his medical expenses and supported his wife and children financially. Schellenberg died in Turin in 1952. Vaughan, H. (2012, large print). *Sleeping with the Enemy: Coco Chanel's Secret War*. Rearsby: W.F. Howes. See also Chapter 2, Figure 3, Hans Kerl, Chief of the Textile Department of the Reich Economic Ministry, who was arraigned and sentenced at the same trial.

22　Pourcher, Y. (2012). *Historical Reflections*, vol. 38, Issue Spring, pp. 105–125. In 1995, three years after the death of his wife in 1992, René Chambrun granted Yves Pourcher, Professor of Political Science at the University of Toulouse-Le Mirail Research Group LISST-CAS, free access to her personal diaries. These diaries formed the basis firstly of Pourcher's 2002 book, *Pierre Laval vu par sa fille, D'après ses carnets intimes* (Paris: Le cherche midi) and then a novel written through the eyes of Josée Chambrun's diary, *Moi, Josée Laval* (Paris: Le cherche midi, 2015). With thanks to Josephine Gladstone to the reference to Pourcher's work.

23　Celia Bertin was a French writer, journalist, biographer, winner of the 1953 Prix Renaudot and French Resistance fighter. Author of the first serious study of the haute couturier Charles Worth, she died in 2014. Accessed 28 July 2018 from https://www.lemonde.fr/disparitions/article/2014/11/28/celia-bertin-1920-2014-resistante-romanciere-journaliste-et-biographe_4531322_3382.html.

24　Eder, C. (2006). *Les Comtesses de la Gestapo*, Paris: Grasset.

25　Corinne Luchaire and her father were arrested by the Americans having fled to the Nazi Sigmaringen enclave in Germany. Jean Luchaire was shot by the French for gross collaboration (Bertin 1993: 111, 105).

26　Ballard, B. (1960). *In My Fashion*, London: Secker and Warburg.

27　IMDB. (2018). Micheline Presle Biography. Accessed 14 September 2018 from https://www.imdb.com/name/nm0696163/bio.

28 In 1957, Baker was awarded the French Legion of Honour and the Croix de Guerre with Palm Leaf. Chardonnet, P. and Firmin, F. (2014). 'Josephine Baker', Société d'Histoire du Vésinet, accessed April 2014 from http://histoire-vesinet.org/jbaker-resistante.htm.
29 Jacket by Jeanne Lanvin, 1943, no.1989-117-43. Galliera, Musée de la Mode de la Ville de Paris.
30 Yad Vashem, The World Holocaust Remembrance Centre. 'Marie-Louise Carven, France'. Accessed 6 April 2019 from http://www.yadvashem.org/righteous/stories/carven.

Chapter 2
The Lyon *haute nouveauté* fashion textile industry during World War Two: design making, exhibition and international diffusion

*Lou Taylor**

> *A tragic year has passed in the most troubled of circumstances that we have ever known. . . . Will [next year] bring any alleviation to the bloody conflicts?*
>
> (*Bulletin de Soies et des Soieries et du Tissus de Lyon*, 16–31 December 1942)

Introduction

This text, building on the seminal work of Dominique Veillon's *La Mode sous L'Occupation* of 1990, focuses on the fashion textiles industry of Lyon during World War Two. It assesses its design, manufacturing, exhibition and import/export activities undertaken in Lyon during that time. The city's merchants, manufacturers, spinners, dyers, designers, weavers and printers were renowned worldwide for their exclusive, specialised and creative contemporary silk designs produced seasonally for the great fashion salons of Paris. For less exclusive customers, they also manufactured on a large scale plain, brocaded and printed fashion silks, albeit still costly, and from the late 1920s, innovative rayons. Leading Lyon companies were known worldwide, some indeed since the eighteenth century and many more from the late nineteenth century. The city was dependent on this trade, which employed many thousands of

FIGURE 2.0
Jacket and pleated skirt in red, white and blue, Lanvin, *Modes et Travaux*, May 1943, no. 527, with thanks to Dress History Collection, University of Brighton.

---

*All translation from French by the author.

workers from generation to generation. The key focus of this chapter rests on the 1940–1944 seasonal sample books belonging to Coudurier-Fructus-Descher, one of Lyon's most prestigious fashion textile manufacturing companies and now in the collection of the Musée des Tissus, Lyon (Coudurier-Fructus-Descher sample books 1898–1968 nos: 38985-39879).

Context

By the eighteenth century, Lyon, historically a Catholic town, situated on the confluence of the great Rhone and Soane rivers in South Central France, was already a great city with an imposing feature, the Place Bellecour. It had by then blossomed into Europe's premier luxury silk manufacturing centre, supplying the royal courts of Europe from Versailles to St. Petersburg and from Stockholm to London with the finest dress and furnishing fabrics. This sophisticated international trade relied on raw silk coming from and through Italy, the Levant, China and Japan. In the early 1860s Lyon silk traders were amongst the first Europeans to conduct business once Japan had opened up to Euro-American trade (Medzini 1971: 52). In parallel, Paris couture salons blossomed from the 1860s, dressing European royalty and aristocracy, American dollar princesses, great actresses and wealthy, fashionable women from all over the world. The Paris couturiers and Lyon *fabricants* together developed unique seasonal fabric designs, including modern, technically complex, jacquard silk fabrics. Grumbach explains further that from 'the time of Worth' (late nineteenth century) until the 1960s, it was this symbiosis that created the unique international export market for French luxury fashion textiles (Grumbach 1993: 67). As *Soie Informations*, the journal of Centre de la Soie in Paris, explained (May–June 1939: 3), a key proportion of Lyon business also came from sales to international couture salons and the great department stores around the world, who purchased fabrics for their legal copies of couture garments and provided the city of Lyon with a high proportion of its business. By the 1930s all the great Paris couturier businesses had therefore long been tightly twinned commercially and creatively, if not geographically, with the silk manufacturers of Lyon.

The city was thus the centre of a truly global luxury industry dependent on large numbers of highly skilled workers – spinners, dyers, weavers, printers, designers, merchants, silk dealers and so on. *Soie Informations* trumpeted (May–June 1939: 3) that Lyon silk fabrics had just been made up into dresses by Mainbocher for the Duchess of Windsor, by Molyneux for the Queen of Iran and by Chanel for the Egyptian court. By then, the famous silk manufacturing company, Bianchini Férier, had branches retailing their *haute nouveauté*, highest quality, seasonal, fashion silks in Paris, Brussels, Geneva, London, New York, Montreal and Buenos Aires. Coudurier-Fructus-Descher sold through Paris, London, Brussels, Milan, Vienna, New York and Montreal, whilst Chatillon-Mouly-Roussel sold out of Paris, Nice,

Brussels, Stockholm, Warsaw, Cairo and Alexandria (*Soieries Lyonnaises de 1800 à nos jours*, 1943). In 1942, with travel and trade seriously curtailed, Henry Morel, the President of the Lyon Chamber of Commerce, described the Lyon silk merchant as 'a citizen of the world', wistfully remembering the excitement of his first trade travels as a young man in 'the sunny Midi . . . in China, Japan and the USA. It is a trade . . . with its windows open to the world' (Morel BSS 1942: 3349).

Lyon at the start of World War Two

In the panic of the 'Exode' – the Exodus – of early June 1940, as German troops neared Paris, millions fled the city including the government itself. The couturiers Schiaparelli, Lelong, Balenciaga, Heim, Patou and Molyneux, having also fled – to Bordeaux – collectively agreed on 12 July 1940 to keep their businesses open no matter the circumstances. Molyneux left at the last minute for London (see Chapter 11) having helpfully agreed, as Edna Woolman Chase noted, to divide his Biarritz salon into three, sharing it with Schiaparelli and Lelong and determined to sell clothes to the USA (Woolman Chase, 1954: 286). Paris was occupied two days later by German forces on 14 June 1940 and defeated France was divided into German Occupied France and Pétain's collaborationist 'Zone Libre' with its headquarters in the city of Vichy. This established the eighty-four-year-old Maréchal Pétain, a French World War One war hero, as Head of State of Vichy France with sovereignty over the whole of France, at least in theory.

FIGURE 2.1
Checking papers at a French police station at the Demarcation Line between the Vichyist Zone Libre and the Nazi-Occupied zone, at Moulin, Auvergne, 1940. (Roger Viollet. Getty 92424721).

German forces took control of Lyon on 19 June 1940 (Amoretti, 1964: 16). In the second half of 1940, under orders from Goering, large quantities of luxury silk yardage and head squares were being pillaged freely out of Lyon (Veillon 1990: 183) as swastikas were raised over all public buildings. After the Armistice was signed by Hitler on 25 June 1940, German troops withdrew into Occupied France and the city was controlled by French Vichyist forces. Once the Allies landed in North Africa, two years later, the Germans invaded the Free Zone again and were back occupying the city by November 1942 (Amoretti 1964: 21–25).

From mid-July 1940 to November 1942, the Demarcation Line tore the Lyon fashion textiles trade apart from its sister couture business in Paris. All movement after that was Nazi and Vichy controlled. The city's fashion textiles manufacturers, organised through their Syndicat des Fabricants des Soieries et de Tissus de Lyon, allied themselves, as did millions of others, to the Pétainiste/Vichy regime's ideological axis, in the hope that this stance would protect them from the worst of Nazi rapaciousness, but by the end of 1940, as import/export markets were closed off one by one, the textile industry of Lyon had already reached crisis point. Under these new circumstances, this luxury trade struggled desperately to function at all in defeated, humiliated and divided France. A veritable cult built up around the aged Pétain, Halls calling it only just 'this side of idolatry' (Halls 1995: 13).

The three tenets of Pétain's *Revolution Nationale*, *Travail*, *Famille* and *Patrie*, were at first seductive to a terrified population wanting, as Bertin explains, 'a protective reassuring paternal image' (Bertin 1993: 42). Halls links Vichy culture 'to a return to an almost medieval vision of France' (1995: 210) with its revival of rural, vernacular artisanal architecture and crafts. Constant visual references were made to Pétain's 'return to the soil' nationalism, with its glorification of the French artisan, folklore traditions with a celebration of the French countryside and its wild field flowers, as well as use of French colonial imagery. Through all of this, it must be remembered that Lyon also became 'the Capital of the Resistance' and the centre of the Free French press all through the war (Amoretti 1964: 69–70).

Heavily dependent on the Paris couture market as the Lyon silk trade was, the fact that the Paris seasonal shows continued without break all through the war came as a relief, despite the contact difficulties. Lelong, president of the *Chambre Syndicale de la Couture Parisienne*, struggling with the German authorities and needing to make links to the new Vichy/Nazi cultural landscape, found a way to pragmatically ally Paris couture directly to the Vichy regime. In an interview with Georges Costebelle in early March 1942, Lucien Lelong declared that there was a close symbiosis between the hand craft worlds of Pétain's much promoted French rural artisan craft skills and the artisan work of sewing, tailoring and embroidering in the haute couture salons of Paris. Thus haute couture was sometimes shown at Vichy and German propaganda craft and decorative arts exhibitions, albeit incongruously, alongside French rural crafts (Costebelle 1942: 14–15).

FIGURE 2.2
Pétain propaganda poster featuring wild field flowers, 1940. (Alamy CW8ME9.)

Organisation of the French textile industries under Nazi control

As Veillon confirms, all French textile manufacturing (including wool and cotton in the northern zones, not discussed here) was forced to function under the direction of Hans Kehrl, Chief of the Textile Department of the Reich Economic Ministry and 'Führer' of French textiles (1990: 124). By August 1940, the German authorities, having looted and requisitioned vast amounts of French wool, cotton, linen and silk yardage (Veillon 1990: 125) banned imports of raw materials from Australia, the USA and the Far East. France was left desperately short of fabrics for basic clothing (1990: 133). In 1940, a strict control of all French textile manufacture was imposed by the Nazi authorities through a set of committees, one for each fabric type and each with an experienced French industrialist director. They were answerable to M. Hartman, the German Head of the Textiles Service of the German Administration of the Occupied Territories (1990: 124) through his *Comité General D'Organisation de l'Industry Textile*. Luxury silk manufacture, organised within its own *Groupement Haute Nouveauté*, fell under the control of the *Branche de la Soie*, whose first director was the successful Vichyist silk manufacturer Jean Barioz (1990: 183). The director of the *Branche Fibres Artificielles* was another manufacturer, Edmond Bizot (1990:

130). Both the Vichy and Nazi authorities set about systematically eliminating Jews from ownership of fashion, accessory and textile companies, many of which were forcibly aryanised from October 1940 (Green 1997: 97).

On 16 August 1940, Nazi plans for the future of French textile manufacture tightened under the 'Plan Kehrl' presented at a meeting between Kehrl, Hartman and Jean Bichelonne, a leading Vichy technocrat soon to be appointed Head of the Bureau Central de Repartition des Produits Industriels. All the French textile committee directors were instructed to attend. Veillon explains that the Kehrl Plan declared that all stocks of textiles available in France on Armistice Day were now to be placed at the disposal of Germany, especially wool, and that some French textile factories were to be kept running on condition that large amounts of their products went to Germany (1990: 127). The French authorities, through Bichelonne, were made to understand that France had also to turn both its textile manufacture and clothing production towards the manufacture and use of synthetics. To enable all of this, France was to receive German cellulose pulp and fibres ('rayonne' filament as well as 'fibranne', short staple lengths to be spun into yarn). As Veillon stresses, the amount proposed was disproportionately small when compared to the quantities of finished woven textile yardage that France was forced to send to Germany (1990: 126). In 1942 the German authorities established a controlled account of 100 million Reichsmarks 'for the purchase of [textile goods for export] not classed as indispensable to the internal French market' (Archives Nationale, Paris, F12/10547, Letter to the Directeur de la Soie Lyon, 30 April 1943)– clearly referencing luxury fabrics, which under wartime conditions were extremely hard to produce. The French were warned to accept these plans or face further requisitions and lack of German support for developments in French synthetic textile manufacture (1990: 125). The manufacture and export of French synthetic fabric thus became dependent on uncertain German raw material supplies, whilst both silk and rayon yardage required complex German import/export permits to even survive.

Lyon silk and synthetic textile design and manufacture under Nazi control: 1940–1944

The Syndicat des Fabricants determined that the trade would survive somehow – under the protection, they believed, of Maréchal Pétain. Thereafter, for the duration of the war they exhibited their products literally under his name and image. They vowed to keep seasonal trade practices and workers in place even in their desperate situation, but by January 1942, the *Bulletin de Soies* reported that silk trade was 'functioning at only one fifth of normal operations . . . the war worsens: hopes of a return to work are paralyzed. Silk companies content themselves with minimum orders which they scrape together wherever they can' (BSS 1–15 Jan 1942: 3353).

By spring 1942, the *Bulletin* noted that 'The Milan market is shut. The New York market has almost ceased to exist. The Chinese market is under Japanese control and the Japanese keep everything for interior consumption' (BSS 1–15 April 1942: 3359). By July, it detailed that companies, allowed by then to operate for only forty hours a week, could not even find a way to use the allotted time because the shortages of raw materials were so chronic (BSS 16–31 July 1942: 3366). The *Bulletin* nonetheless urged those in the trade 'not to get discouraged,' adding that the silk industry's usual seasonal *carte de nuances* – its colour forecast shade card – for spring 1942 was published, 'demonstrating determination not to stop the search for *nouveauté* designs' (BSS 1–15 January 1942: 3353). By August, noting the profound lack of dyes and coal, M. Brochier, as president of the Syndicat des Fabricants de Soireries, mourned that collaboration between Paris and Lyon 'is made more difficult by the distressing separation between the two zones; and the impossibility of even making telephone calls across the line' (BSS 1–16 August 1942: 3385). By December, Brochier repeated that the silk industry found itself 'in the midst of a shipwrecked economy' (BSS 16–31 Dec 1942: 3376.) By January, 1943, the reduction of the electricity supply obliged the town's industries to shut down in sequence: dye works on Monday, textiles on Tuesday, printing on Wednesday.[1]

Three months later, the president of the Lyon Syndicat des Marchands de Soies, Albert Cotte, reported that their trade was both internationally isolated and virtually at a standstill (BSS May 1943: 3382). By May 1943, Brochier reported that the Syndicat was struggling to help destitute families of textile workers who had been killed, were missing, imprisoned or who, when unemployed, has been sent on forced labour to Germany (BSS 18 May 1943: 3387). By September, 269 firms in Lyon were running soup kitchens serving their staff daily.[2] The trade, having hoped for protection from Pétain, had found none.

Replacement textiles

Manufacturers soon had no choice but to use synthetic replacement raw materials. Pre-war Lyon had already successfully developed some innovative pure synthetics destined for haute couture use, such as Coudurier-Fructus-Descher's new stretch velvet synthetic elastic, Cinamomo, which Ana de Pombo used in her 1939 designs for Paquin (Sirop 1989: 28). Veillon has identified the fundamental role played by replacement textiles in wartime France (1990: 123–149). Lucien François, looking back over the previous four years in 1944, remembered that textile manufacturers had to 'get over their repugnance' and use replacement textiles far more generally – 'yarns which until then they had only used to add specific high lights to luxurious fabrics'. *l'Art et la Mode* supportively declared that 'they did so in exemplary professional ways': softening *fibranne* with angora, mixing brittle rayon with silk to give it a natural feel, making unrecognizable fabrics with a high class touch' (1944, no. 2700, 12–13).

The Nazi Occupiers thus made self-interested efforts to established and build up replacement textile manufacture across France based on German cellulose and viscose rayon paste and fibres imported under the direction of Kehrl (Veillon 1990: 133). Martin, an American who worked for the Economic Warfare Section of the Department of Justice and Chief of the Decartelization Branch of the US Military Government in 1946, noted that Kehrl, an SS Brigade Leader, had been the leading pre-war German artificial textile industrialist through the Phrix combine and as organiser of 'the Kunstseide Ring', a group of twelve German cellulose fibre and by-product companies established in 1935. This group had been developing new processes and by 1940 were far in advance of French developments (1950: 131). There was therefore much self-interest in Kehrl's four-year textile plan for Europe and France.[3]

Despite the fact that Lyon manufacturers had successfully lobbied to receive a fairer share of the distribution of German synthetic fibres across France (Veillon 1990: 128), by March 1942, the *Bulletin* declared that 'We have to take each day as it comes and be content with a small amount of business, which we can only do thanks to research into new fabrics' (BSS 16–31 March 1942: 3358). Veillon notes that, trying urgently to counteract the wariness of French consumers who had experienced shrinkage and other problems when using replacement fabrics, press reports were soon extolling their virtues (1990: 132–133).

FIGURE 2.3
Hans Kehrl, in his uniform as the Head of the Planning Office, Ministry of Armaments and War Production, Germany, 1942. (Bundesarchive, 183-1998–0525–500/CC-BY-SA 3.0. Bundesarchiv 101III-Alber-178-04A. Photographer: Kurt Alber.)

The highest levels of Lyon chemical, technical and design skills were rapidly applied to try to develop viable replacement fashion fabrics made from locally available wild broom, reeds, pine needles and bean fronds (Veillon 1990: 144). The *Bulletin des Soies* reported the use of recycled jute sacks, goat and camel hair and rayon stockings, noting new developments in rare petro-chemical-based nylon (BSS 1–15 Oct 1942: 3371). An article, 'Allo, New York, Paris Vous Parle', was published in *l'Art et la Mode* before America joined the war with the Allies and whilst US clients were still free to get to Europe (January/February, 1940: no 2649.29). In this text, Juliette Lancret appealed to US fashion buyers both in the USA and also those who had struggled to Paris to attend the fashion shows in February 1940 via Genoa (Snow 1962: 136) to buy these new French textiles. Featuring images of the latest fabrics, Lancret declared that despite the 'thousand daily difficulties', French manufacturers had created designs of pre-war quality, concluding that 'Paris has not lost its courage, its creative spirit nor its taste envied by the world'.

Every type of fabric was produced in synthetic form by French manufacturers, from imitation wool cloth to delicate crepes and nylon made from rare petrochemicals. Each new fabric, as *l'Art et la Mode* detailed in 1943 (no: 2682.20) was given its own alluring name: *crepe geobal*, *sergesciai* (woven from rayon and silk), *l'organzagaze* ('adorable in silk and rayon') and *Famisole* (a synthetic crepe georgette). Risking their elite professional reputations, manufacturers were forced also to produce everyday fabrics to keep their companies alive and their staff in work. Public concern continued to be expressed over shrinkage related to the new fabrics – even in a heavy rainstorm (Green 1997: 9). By 1943, this industry however was also in serious danger of collapse (BSS 18 May 1943: 3387). In an effort to keep up morale, *l'Art et la Mode* advised its readers in 1944 not 'to search too hard to find out about the raw materials from which the most recent fashion textiles collections were made', reassuring them that these were nonetheless 'supple, resistant, comfortable, and seductive to touch' (no 2694, Feb 1944: 12–13).

Designing Lyon fabrics

Haute nouveauté seasonal fashion fabrics had been designed in Lyon and Paris in hundreds of freelance studios or in-house company studios since the mid-eighteenth century (Miller 1988). By the 1940s silk designers belonged to a professional protective, promotional society, Les Artists Dessinateur des Textile Haute Nouveautés, working closely with the leading fashion *createurs fabricants* in Lyon. Not a few of the designers were Jewish. By May 1941, the German Chamber of Commerce, invoking Nazi anti-Semitic aryanisation legislation, complained that: 'This trade seems to be still conducted by some Jewish studios despite our prohibition.' Letters were sent to Daniel Gorin, Administrator of the Couture Group 1, demanding the names of Jewish designers in Paris. Gorin noted that the Nazis were demanding, 'to use their term . . . the "purifying" of the trade' and that they would only permit sales of textile designs on paper to Germany on condition that 'Jewish houses are closed'. The bogus charge was that these designers were undermining design quality through poor wholesale work. The German authorities demanded a list of 'maisons israélites de Dessins pour Textile'. After strenuous efforts made by Gorin to avoid this request, a list of thirteen Jewish names was finally forwarded. The fate of these designers is not known.[4]

As was the tradition, most textile designers' names were publicly unknown. Usefully, however, the catalogue of the Paris exhibition at the Musée des Arts Décoratifs, 11 March to 18 April 1943, *Soieries Lyonnaises de 1800 à nos jours, Tissus pour la Robe, la Mode, l'Ameublement* named leading studios and their designers. These included Suzanne Janin, one of the best known, who designed for Ducharne and the House of Combier et Cie. The studios of Vourlat Pienoz sold designs to Merieux et Cie, whilst Margirier and Bergarol supplied Maison Algoud, Girousée et Dumas designed for Montessuy, de Villetroy for Alliance Textiles Rayon and Robert Charles for H. Chavanis. Rosillon explained later that, during these years, *createurs fabricants* commissioned new designs that were only produced in small yardages simply in order to keep their design teams intact and to fulfil the annual legal requirements that kept their unique professional status intact (Rosillon 1945: 174). They also created yardage for exhibition purposes, though undertaken without hope of commercial profit. These contemporary designs were widely exhibited in non-sale exhibitions to prove that their industry was still functioning, as is discussed below.

Vichyist designs

Fashion fabric designs printed or woven in Lyon in the years 1940–1944 contained the usual basic flowers, spots and stripes but these quickly and deliberately became suffused with clear Vichyist imagery. Manufacturers, having aligned themselves publicly with the Vichy regime, also did so through their designs, using pretty folklorish prints and weaves drawn from the same neo-Fascist *Retour à la Terre* imagery that was attached to Vichy posters. In the process a new fashion textile style was launched. This lauded the three tenets of Pétain's *Revolution Nationale, Travail, Famille* and *Patrie*, with its glorification of French folklore traditions and artisans. Pétain's portrait in his Maréchal's uniform was seen everywhere on posters, often with figures of French peasantry, rural scenes and wild field flowers (Figure 2.2). It was printed patriotically on coloured silk and rayon head scarves produced by the famous *haute nouveauté* fashion textile company of Colcombet.

At the autumn 1941 International Lyon Textile Fair, the stand of the Syndicat des Fabricant de Soieries featured a vast 3.25 m x 1.75 paper mis-en-carte (squared paper weaving plan) for a 'magnificent' black-and-white jacquard tribute portrait of Pétain – a 'true chef-oeuvre of the Lyon artisan' – a patriotic gesture organised by M. Fructus, Head of the Syndicat des Fabricants de Soie and Director of Coudurier-Fructus-Descher (Sorbet 1941: 306).

FIGURE 2.4
Montage of fifteen Coudurier-Fructus-Descher silk and rayon designs (Musée des Tissus, Lyon, 1941–1942 with one of 1942, no 21397 from Collection Départementale des Musées de l'Ain/ Fonds des Soieries Bonnet, with thanks).

MT 39848.6.6

CDF 1942 . vol. 82. no. 25521

CDF 1941, vol. 101, no. 53978

MT 39847.8verso.43137

MT 39848.19.2.47154

MT 39847.6.1

MT 39847.14 verso

MT 39847.7 verso.43126

MT 39843.7recto.43125

CDF 1943. Vol.111.46072

CDF 1942, Vol.113, no.25544

Soieries Bonnet.1942, no 21397 from Collection Départementale des Musées de l'Ain/Fonds des Soieries Bonnet.

CDF 1942, vol. 97. 37

MT 39843.10recto.43144

MT 39848.9.8. 47121

MT 39843.5verso.43109

FIGURE 2.5
Photograph of the giant paper mise-en-carte jacquard weaving plan of 1941 for the silk portrait of Pétain published in *l'Illustration* (5 July 1941:306; with thanks to Lou Taylor Collection).[5] Small silk copies (45 cm x 35 cm) were sold to raise funds for the Secour Nationale. One example remains in the *Musée des Tissus* today.[6]

The 1940–1944 samples books of Coudurier-Fructus-Descher confirm that creative play with the *tricolore* of the French flag was a major characteristic of wartime fashion textile design, just as it was in couture garments and accessories. One design of 1941 is a skillful, abstract, warp-printed weave with a red, white and blue moiré effect. This reflects the widespread use of red, white and blue in fashionable couture ensembles.

FIGURE 2.6A
Abstract, warp-printed and woven sample, with a red, white and blue moiré effect, 1941. (Coudurier-Fructus-Descher, vol. 111. no 53978. Musée des Tissus, Lyon with thanks.)[7]

FIGURE 2.6B
Jacket and pleated skirt in red, white and blue, Lanvin, *Modes et Travaux*, May, 1943, no. 527 with thanks to the Dress History Collection, University of Brighton.

FIGURE 2.7
Lelong, 1943, summer dress with pleated tartan skirt, *Modes et Travaux*, July 1943. (No. 52 with thanks to the Dress History Collection, University of Brighton.)

Veillon clarifies that the use of these colours could be 'read' as either as a patriotic gesture or as a subversive Free French statement or as support for the Vichy regime or as support for the Allies (1990:219). The Nazi-occupied city of Paris was referenced too, as witnessed in a 1943 city map design by Robert Bonfils for a scarf,[8] and as on a pretty daisy print by Bianchini Ferier with the word 'Paris' printed across the white petals (*l'Art et la Mode* 1940 no. 2649: 29) and also as a post-Liberation 1945 print with the words '*J'Aime Paris*' in red, white and blue by Chatillon-Mouly-Roussel (Rossillon 1945: 102). Tartan, long fashionable in France, and in the war a coded symbol of solidarity with Britain, was popularly worn, as shown in the pleated tartan skirt of a white summer dress designed by Lelong in July 1944.

Reflecting the public allegiance of the Lyon industry to Pétain, many fashion fabric designs also reflected *Retour à la Terre* themes. Nostalgia for a romanticized medieval or nineteenth-century past with coaches and horses and crinolined women with parasols were popular, as were scenes of bucolic country life and nursery rhymes (see Figure 2.4). One repeat print on white toile, for example, showed a scene of a farmer's wife milking a cow surrounded by donkeys, rabbits, ducks and field flowers.[9] Another print with the words of the popular song '*Tous vas trés bien, Madame La Marquise*' featured images of sleeping horses and peasants.[10] Robert Charles designed two small repeat nursery rhyme prints on white voile: the first, '*Meunier, tu Dort! Ton Moulin vas Trop Vite*', in red with sleeping millers and a windmill[11] and the second, in tricolour, with pretty little sheep: '*Il pleut, il pleut, bergere*'.[12] In 1942, Coudurier-Fructus-Descher produced a reversible jacquard design of tiny gamboling goats, geese and rabbits (see Figure 2.8A).[13] Even food shortages found their way ironically into textile prints as *l'Art et la Mode* (2694 1944: 8) noted: 'Today's preoccupations about food have been spiritually interpreted by Chatillon Mouly Roussel – through coquilles St. Jacques shells . . . and ducks ready to be roasted.' Rosillon also noted patterns of swedes – a hated French wartime staple food (1945: 175).

Used by Raoul Dufy in 1914–1916 silk print designs, field flowers were ever more popular in wartime France in the 1939–1944 period (see Chanel evening dress, Figure 1.8A), inspired perhaps by their ubiquitous presence on Pétain/Vichy posters (see Figure 2.2). Tricolore games were played with these floral designs too, through designs using together oxe-eye daisies, (white), poppies (red) and cornflowers (blue). In 1940, Coudurier-Fructus-Descher printed a charming but significant small repeat daisy design with their yellow centres recoloured in red white and blue, for example (see Figure 2.8B).[14]

FIGURE 2.8A
Sheep, rabbits and geese, reversible weave, Coudurier-Fructus-Descher, 194 (CDF 1942, Vol. 113, no. 25544). (Musée des Tissus, with thanks.)

FIGURE 2.8B
Daisies with red, white and blue centres, Coudurier-Fructus-Descher 1940, MT 39847.7 verso.43126. (Musée de Tissus, with thanks.)

Bianchini Ferier's New York branch even filed a US Federal Trademark Registration for a design called 'Marguerite' in 1942.[15] Images of ears of wheat, loaded as they had now become, with Fascist and Vichyist resonances of the sanctity and fecundity of the German and French soil, were often found on Occupation-period textiles, such as two Coudurier-Fructus-Descher examples. The first, from mid-winter 1942, a de-lustered rayon marocain, highlighted ears of wheat and butterflies woven in gold on plain red, blue and dull yellow grounds.[16] The second, a pretty repeat *erstaz* print of 1944, showed wheat with red poppies and blue cornflowers[17] (Figure 2.4). Palais Galliera owns a chic shocking-pink, ribbed taffeta jacket by the House of Schiaparelli of 1942, with large ears of wheat in gold embroidery falling from the shoulders onto the crown of the sleeves.[18] The typically small size of the repeat print and woven patterns ensured no wastage of fabric occurred during the pattern cutting process. Often wittily executed by sophisticated designers, these patterns survive today as reminders of France's complex cultural, political and economic responses to Occupation.

The exhibition of couture and *haute nouveauté* textiles

Couturiers and fashion textile manufacturers regularly showed their seasonal designs at public exhibitions throughout the war, but now in the context of wartime scenarios, especially Vichyist artisan craft exhibitions and propagandist, collaborationist Franco-German trade shows. At one, the 'Exposition de la France Européene' at the Petit Palais, Paris in June and July 1941, as Veillon highlights, German synthetic fabrics by Deutche Zellwolle-und Kuntseide-Ring (Kehrl's own organisation) were shown alongside fabrics by France Rayonne, with a display of couture creations made from these fabrics by Lelong, Piguet, Hermes, Blatt and O'Rosen (Veillon 1990: 134).

Lyon manufacturers still also continued to show their seasonal collections at the bi-annual trade fairs (*Foires de Lyon*) all through the war, making every effort to invite overseas buyers. At the fair of 27 September to 5 October 1941, in homage, the huge 'magnificent' jacquard silk portrait of Maréchal Pétain (Figure 2.5) hung over the display of the Syndicat des Fabricant de Soieries.[19] March 1942 witnessed the major Zone Libre fashion event of the entire war – the 8–10 March visit of 'Paris friends from Haute Couture who have courageously overcome all the difficulties . . . [to demonstrate] the vitality of the couture trade and its close links to silks made in Lyon'. This was for publicity purposes only – nothing was for direct sale. With German permission, on the initiative of Lelong and with models and trunks travelling in a special train from Paris to Lyon, eighteen leading couture salons showed their latest collections to 'several thousand professionals' from the trade, alongside Lyon textile displays and a great theatrical event at the Theatre Celestine, organised by Serge Lifar (BSS 1–15 March 1942: 3357).

The 1942 Palais de Tokyo Salon des Artistes Décorateurs textile section was later shown in Lyon and finally invited to Zurich (see Chapter 10 and Figure 10.5). In March 1943, forty examples of contemporary fashion and furnishing textiles were shown, as already noted, in the *Soieries Lyonnaises de 18 à nos jours* and survive today in the museum's collection.[20]

FIGURE 2.9
Paris haute couture fashion show in Lyon, March 1942. (Getty 558642441, photo by Keystone-France/Gamma-Rapho.)

Exhibitions abroad and import/export

As discussed below, from 1940 the industry's access to its lifeblood export markets was minimal. Opportunities to export were few and slow to arrange. Every opportunity was taken to invite overseas buyers and exhibitors to Lyon, such as to the Lyon Fair of September 1942, when participants came from Romania, Spain and Switzerland (BSS 1–15 Oct 1942: 3371). Veronique Pouillard writes that buyers from the Hirsch Department store in Brussels were just about able to travel on buying trips to Lyon, but with great difficulty (see Chapter 10). Exhibitions and fashion shows were tolerated by the Occupier as long as nothing was directly sold. All sales had to be agreed by the Chef de la Section Textile de l'Office de Repartition (the Head of the Nazi Office of Textiles Distribution in Paris). Thus, on 30 May 1942, Maison Diggonnet was granted permission to export *tissue de luxe* (in this case, lamé) to Germany.

On 26 June 1942, Schultz and Stockman of Hamburg proposed to buy a thousand made-up, hemmed, natural silk mouselline squares, printed in two or three colours and of eighty square centimetres. Six months later, on 2 December 1942, the sale was still not concluded. The German Textiles and Leather Distributor noted that if 'the House of Live Michel et Cie, 21, Rue Desirée, Lyon, wish to supply the Hamburg firm, they require an export licence from us.' Coudurier-Fructus-Descher sought an export licence to sell 'lamé and velvet fabrics' to Germany, finding they required four key documents: firstly the agreement of the Head of the German Distribution Office in Paris, secondly the intermediary actions of the Etablissement Zeman-Courband, 8, Rue de Montyon, Paris, a German merchant export company, and thirdly, official assurance that this sale fell within the ten million Reichsmark fund. Finally the Distribution Office wrote to the Branche de Soie, Lyon, on 27 July 1943: 'We inform you that this House may, without difficulty from the German authorities sell these fabrics' (Archives of the Federation des Soieries, Lyon, NA, Paris: F/12/10547).

Efforts to keep up the high levels of pre-war business with Italy were a complete failure. In January 1942, the *Bulletin des Soies* noted that 'it had been hoped that discussions with Italy would lead to the delivery of some quantities of silk to satisfy the most pressing demands for fabric but these were dashed. Not only did the silk not arrive but the amounts available there were skeletal' (BSS 1–15 January 1942: 3376). Schemes to sell to Sweden and Finland also came to nothing by early August 1942. Hungary, as an Axis country allied to Hitler, was in theory open for business. A letter to the Comité d'Organisation de l'Industrie de Textile, Branche Soie, from Paris, 26 July 1943, confirmed that permission had been given to establish a financial accord with Hungary on April 1943 but little evidence seems to exist that much trade resulted (Archives of the Federation des Soieries, Lyon, NA, Paris: F/12/10547).

Spain

One unique success for French couturiers and textile manufacturers was their joint participation in the Barcelona International Fair, which opened on 8 September 1942. This took place before the Nazi takeover of Vichy, France in November 1942. The Lyon industry bulletin *Informations* (26 September 1942) reported that the French haute couture and *nouveauté* textiles organisations, with their stress on artisan manufacture 'as a symbol of prestige', again featured the giant portrait of Pétain (Figure 2.5) as the centre point of the stand. This was 'surrounded by a sumptuous décor, which showed clearly that a new weaving style, including many replacement fabrics, has been developed reflecting the new circumstances.' On 1 November 1942, *Metiers de France* noted the displays from Germany, Italy, Switzerland and Romania at the fair. Legal fabric sales from France to Spain were possible, although rarely. Whether from the Zone Libre or Occupied France, all requests went through the German authorities in Paris. A permit was granted on 2 October 1943 allowing Louis Noth, a textile merchant of 11, Rue de la Fayette, Paris, a 'laissez passer' to travel to Spain (as he had recently done to Switzerland) to arrange the export of luxury fabrics made by Maison Diggonet, within the remit of the statutory ten million fund (Archives of the Federation des Soieries, Lyon, AN, Paris, F/12/10547).

Switzerland

As to Switzerland, Paris couturiers had long used Swiss silk fashion fabrics, especially fashionable machine embroideries from St. Gall, whilst Switzerland had long imported both French fashions and Lyon silks. In late 1942, organised before the Nazis took over the Zone Libre, Zurich's Palais de Congrès received the textile section of the Paris 1942 Palais de Tokyo textile exhibition (see Chapter 10). The lengths of silks were once again shown beneath the same Pétain *mise-en-carte* portrait (BSS Nov 1942: 3388). The show, as in Paris, was arranged in sections to illustrate each of the key tenets of Pétain's ideology.

In reality, legal, direct fabric exports from France to Switzerland were difficult, especially once the Free Zone was occupied by German authorities again. A letter from the Textile Distributor in Paris to the Director of the Branche de la Soie, Lyon, of 30 April 1943 noted that

> it is extremely difficult at the moment to get passports for Switzerland. The Representative of the Weaving Branch, to whom the question was personally put by M. Bichelonne, received very discouraging advice, although he will put in hand procedures for licences with the authorities in St. Gall. Please send the names and ages of those wishing to go to Switzerland.
>
> (Archives of the Federation des Soieries, Lyon, AN, Paris. F/12/10547)

And so, as minimal lengths of luxury Lyon dress fabrics were produced, exhibited and a tiny few exported, the traumas within Lyon's *haute nouveauté* fashion textiles trade grew worse year by year, whether under direct Vichy or Nazi rule.

The end of the war

The Nazi elite retained their proprietorial attitude to Paris haute couture and Lyon fabrics right up until the last minute. In early August 1944, Emma Sonnemann, the actress wife of Goering, shopped at Lanvin's salon. The *New York Times* of Friday, 1 September 1944 commented that 'anticipating that the shops of Paris would not always be at her disposal, the wife of Field Marshal Herr Goering visited the fashionable establishment here just two weeks ago before the city was liberated and had four dresses made.' As the war turned against them, German reprisals against Resistance fighters and their supporters became more and more savage. Paris was liberated on 25 August 1944 and Lyon on 3 September 1944.

The war continued for eight more traumatic months as battles continued across Eastern France with Allied forces fighting through the fearful winter of 1944–1945 in the Ardennes and along the Mediterranean and Atlantic coasts before the unconditional surrender of the German High Command on 7 May 1945. After that, across ruined France, serious shortages of everything from food, coal, electricity and textiles still continued.

FIGURE 2.10
The Liberation of Lyon, 3 September 1944. French parachutists of the Forces Françaises Libres and Allied troops meet up with French Forces of the Interior soldiers of the French Resistance at Lyon Town Hall. (Bibliothèque Municipale de Lyon no.P0706 001 00004, photo by Pik, with thanks.)

The initial shocked reaction of Allied press reporters and fashion professionals to the extravagance of the Occupation fashion styles they found in Paris is detailed in Chapters 13 and 14 of this book. Most accepted the French 'High Hat Resistance' argument – that the Paris couturiers, milliners and clients had indomitably resisted the Nazis through extravagant fashions. Rosillon, Sécretaire Générale de L'Office Professionnel, Art et Creation, writing in 1945 after the Liberation of both Paris and Lyon, declared that luxury fabric manufacturers, too, had in just the same way, mocked the Occupier through their designs. 'Laughing at their misfortunes in their incorrigible way, French men found... yet another means of mocking the German Occupation' (Rosillon 1945 : 175). As Veillon astutely comments, making 'readings' of design choices was complex and thus, in a time of acute shortages, wearing Vichyist styles in fabrics and clothes, such as making a peasant-style skirt from two printed head squares, 'did not automatically imply support for *Retour à la Terre*, but rather that these items were ration free' (1990: 235).

FIGURE 2.11A
Floral print summer dress, *Modes et Travaux*, July 1943, no. 529. (With thanks to the Dress History Collection, University of Brighton.)

Exaggerating the reality of the tiny number of Resistance fashion textile designs, (which did indeed exist), Rosillon, in the post-war French and British press, gave these much publicity. He published an image, for example, of a tiny print design by Colcombet, probably never printed. This played on the double meaning of the word '*canard*' (duck/lie), showing ducks alternating with images of the collaborationist newspaper *Gazette du Soir* (Rosillon 1945: 175–76).[21] Here the defiance was clear. Rosillon, however, made no mention, of the many, many hundreds of specific Pétainist *Retour à la Terre* textiles designed in Lyon between 1940–1944 and flaunted in the name of France at exhibitions in Lyon, Paris and Zurich in 1942, as discussed in this chapter.

FIGURE 2.11B
Design for Resistance fabric print '*canard*' by Colcombet, Lyon, 1940–1944, The Studio, December 1945, vol. CXXX, no. 633, 175–176. (With thanks to St. Peters House Library, University of Brighton.)

Trapped as they were in the dark years of the 'moral misery' of defeated and divided France (Bertin 1993: 133), it remains the case that the wartime public actions of the Lyon fashion textiles *Groupement Haute Nouveauté* demonstrated continuous public support for Pétain and the Vichy regime, whatever the private opinions of the members of the organisation and its workers may have been. This support was epitomised by the decision to hang the large portait of Pétain over exhibition displays in Lyon, Paris, Zurich and Barcelona. It is further confirmed by the specific and deliberate choice of '*Retour à la Terre*' fabric designs for all these exhibitions, however technically skillful, witty and sophisticated they were. Significantly, these fabrics were not, thereafter, exhibited in France for over fifty years.[22]

Celia Bertin remembered above all 'the atmosphere of fear, intolerance and madness that ruled' through the Occupation (1993: 242), whilst Mouré concluded that the Vichy regime was 'the bastard child of the defeat, to be disowned by the Liberation' (2007: 122). Pétain, having been relocated by the Nazis to the French government-in-exile Sigmaringen enclave in Germany in September 1944, was finally arrested on the Swiss border on April 26, 1945, returning to France (Ousby 1999: 312).[23] Azéma and Wieviorka write that as a national unifying act, General de Gaulle, leader of the 1944–1946 post-war Provisional Government, 'forged a myth of a France which was unanimously resistant' and that consequently 'the memory of Vichy faded to a curious amnesia' (2000: 294). The memory of these Vichyist fabrics faded away too. Brought out into the light today, the sight of these innocent-looking, charming and often infantilised fashion prints and weaves, made under the most traumatic of circumstances, raises the ghosts of profound and still often unresolved areas of conflict, tragedy, courage, bravery and, inevitably, compromise.

References

Archives Nationales, Paris: AN.
Amoretti, H. (1964). *Lyon Capitale 1940–44*, Paris: Broché.
Azéma, J.P. and Wievorka, O. (2000). *Vichy, 1940–44*, Paris: Perrin.
Bertin, C. (1993). *Femmes sous l'Occupation*, Paris: Stock.
Bulletin des Soies et des Soieries et de Tissus de Lyon: BSSAU: Please complete this reference information.
Costebelle G. (1942). 'De L'Artisanat a la Couture', *Métiers de France*, 1 March: 14–15.
Green, N.L. (1997). *Ready-to-Wear and Ready-to-Work: A Century of Industry and Immigrants in Paris and New York*, Durham, USA: Duke University Press.
Grumbach, D. (1993). *Histoires de la Mode*, Paris: Seuil.
Halls, W.D. (1995). *Politics, Society and Christianity in Vichy France*, London: Bloomsbury Academic.
Medzini, M. (1971). *French Policy in Japan in the Closing Years of the Tokugawa Regime*, Cambridge, USA: Harvard University Press.
Martin, J.S. (1950). *All Honorable Men*, Boston: Little Brown.
Miller, L.E. (2014). *Selling Silks – A Merchant's Sample Book 1764*, London: V and A Publishing.
Miller, L.E (1988). *Designers in the Lyon Silk Industry, 1712–1787*, PhD, Brighton Polytechnic.
Morel, H. (1942). 'Causerie sur Lyon et le Commerce Internationale de la Soie', *Bulletin des Soies et de Soiereries* 1–15 April, no. 3349.
Mouré, K. (2007). 'Economic Choice in Dark Times: The Vichy Economy', French Society, Culture and Politics 25, no. 1: 108–130. http://www2.univ-paris8.fr/histoire/wp-content/uploads/2007/03/frenchpoliticscultureandsociety-2007.pdf.
Ousby, I. (1999). *Occupation. The Ordeal of France,1940–44*, London: Pimlico.
Rosillon, C. (1945 Jan.). 'Tissus', French *Vogue*, Special Liberation No. Jan: 102–111.
Rosillon, C. (1945). Dress Materials, *The Studio*, Vol CXXX, Dec. no 633: 175–176.
Rousiers, P. (1928). *Les Grandes Industries Modernes*, Vol. 111 Les Industries Textiles, Paris: Armand Colin.
Soieries Lyonnaises de 1800 à nos jours, 18 March to 9 April 1943, Paris: exhibition catalogue, Musée des Art Decoratifs, Paris. (Photocopy Musée des Tissus Library, Lyon.)
Sorbets, J. (1941). 'Portrait en Soie du Marechal', *l' Illustration*, 5 July, no. 5130: 306.
Snow, C. and White Aswell, M.L. (1962). *The World of Carmel Snow*. New York: McGraw-Hill.
Veillon D. (1990). *La Mode sous l'Occupation,* Paris: Payot.
Woolman Chase, E. (1954). *Always in Vogue*, London: Victor Gollancz.

Endnotes

1. *Archive du Chambre de Commerce et d'Industrie de Lyon, Proces Verbaux*, 14 January 1943, *Sous-Série 1 ETP.* Archives du Département du Rhône et de la Métropole de Lyon, with thanks.
2. Ibid., 30 September.
3. Kehrl was sentenced to fifteen years imprisonment at Trial 11, the Ministries Case, of the Nuremberg War Crimes Tribunal in 1948. By the end of the war, having moved on to become General Referent for the German Iron and Steel Industries, he became Head of the Central Planning Office, Ministry of Armaments and War Production. Himmler appointed him as an SS Brigade Fuhrer in 1943. He was released in 1951. (See B.R. Kroner, R.D. Muller and H. Umbreit (2003: 362–365), 'Organisation and Mobilization in the German Sphere of Power – Part 11,War Wartime Administration, Economy and Manpower Resources 1942-44', in *Germany and the Second War War*, vol. V/II, London: Clarendon Press, and Phillips Nuremberg Trial Collection, Alexandra Campbell King Law Library, University of Georgia, http://libguides.law.uga.edu/c.php?g=177170&p=1164760, accessed 14 April 2017.
4. *Archives Nationales*, Paris, F.12.10297. LRP/ym/BO781. Letter to the German Chamber of Commerce, Paris 6, Rue de Presbourg, of 19 May 1941, from M. Libert, Member of the Official Consultative Commission of Group 1, Section A. Sous Direction Vetement, stamped with Comité d'Organisation du Vêtement, Rue Taitbout. *'Nous joignons cette liste affin que vous puissiez la communiquer, si vous jugez nécessaire'.* Received 17 May 1941. Attached was this list of names and addresses: LISTE DES MAISONS ISRAELITES – ARTISTES DESSINATEURS: (Fred Levy) 8, Rue St. Marc, Paris; ATELIER PAX (M. Spreirezen) 47, Ave de l'Opera, Paris; STUDIO ROSAL, 4, Rue de la Paix, Paris; E.P. SEBES, Rue St. Marc, Paris; ATELIER du HELDER (M. Gottesmann, 7, Rue Sribe, Paris; BRODSKI, 10, rue st. Marc, Paris; JOS BRONSTEIN, 97, Rue des Petits Champs, Paris; FELDMANN et Cie, 11 bis, Blvd. Haussmann, Pari; ATELIER DES CAPUCINES (M. Aelion) 9, Blvd. des Capucines, Paris; M.A. FLASHNER, 48, rue des Abbesses, Paris; M.A. FRAENKEL, 9, Rue Verniquet, Paris; HAJOS (M. Semann) 7, Rue des Italiens, Paris; ETABLISSMENT LANG, 8, Rue de Monthyon, Paris.
5. This Pétainist journal became increasingly pro-Nazi. By 1943 it had become a foremost collaborationist journal edited by Lesdain and was shut down at the Liberation. (Perrin, J-P., *Jacques de Lesdain, Redacteur Politique A L'Illustration, Itineraire d'un Collaborateur* (3ème partie: 1940–1944)); http://histpresseillustree.blog.lemonde.fr/tag/jacques-de-lesdain/.
6. No: 44300. Musée des Tissus, Lyon.
7. C.D.F. 1941, vol. 111, 53978. Musée des Tissus, Lyon.
8. 1943 no. 36140. Musée des Arts Décoratifs, Paris.
9. Chatillon-Mouly-Roussel, 1943, no. 35176, Musée des Arts Décoratifs, Paris.
10. 42864 c-44 Musée des Tissus, Lyon.
11. Soieries H. Chavanis, 1943, no. 35149, Musée des Arts Décoratifs, Paris.
12. Soieries H. Chavanis, 1943, no. 35144, Musée des Arts Décoratifs, Paris.
13. CDF, 1942, vol 82, no. 25544, Musée des Tissus, Lyon.
14. MT 39847.7 verso 43126, Musée des Tissus, Lyon.
15. Serial number 71455583, filed on Thursday, 17 September 1942; http://www.trademarkia.com/.

16 CDF, 1942, vol 82, no 25521, Musée des Tissus, Lyon.
17 MT 39847.6.1, Musée des Tissus, Lyon.
18 August 1942 griffe, no. 84.1/35. Musée de la Mode de la Ville de Paris.
19 *Textiles*; Bulletin du Comité General d'Organisation de l'Industrie Textile Bibiloteque Nationale, Sept. 27 1941.
20 Musée des Arts Decoratifs: nos. 35143-35176.
21 Hilaire Colcombet, the son of the famous Colcombet fashion textiles company director, was in the Free French Army, training in Surrey in 1943. In July 1944 as Captain of the 1st company of the 3rd SAS regiment, he and his company were parachuted into the Saone et Loire region and organised sabotage and ambushes. *Memoire et Espoirs de la Resistance*, http://www.memoresist.org/resistant/hilaire-colcombet/.
22 See exhibitions '*Accessoires et objets, témoignages de vies de femmes à Paris, 1940-1944*', Mémorial du Maréchal Leclerc de Hauteclocque et de la Libération de Paris, Musée Jean Moulin, Paris, 20 May to 15 Nov 2009 and *Pour Vous Mesdames – La Mode en Temps de Guerre*, Centre d'Histoire de la Résistance et de la Déportation de Lyon 28 Nov to 13 April 2014.
23 Pétain was tried over July and August 1945 by a French court for treason. Sentenced to death, De Gaulle commuted this to life imprisonment after the Court's recommendation for mercy. Pétain died in 1951.

Chapter 3
Shortages in Paris 1940–1945: frivolous accessories become essential needs

*Dominique Veillon**

From 1939 to 1945 Paris fashion underwent a series of unimaginable upheavals bought about by the war. Set against the national catastrophe, modifications to clothing practice would seem to be just one of many others – were it not for the fact that they combined economic, social as well as aesthetic forces. The fundamental setting was one of basic shortage, deprivation and, more than ever, that ways of dressing reflected above all the desperate actuality of daily circumstances. Clothing issues became totally enmeshed in the daily lives of millions of women as they were obliged to feed and clothe themselves using all available resources, whilst at the same time refusing to abandon their commitment to style. This was now inevitably driven by resourcefulness, such as the use of pheasant feathers available from the French countryside in millinery rather than exotic feathers from abroad.

French wartime fashion thus offers an ideal target through which to observe the sartorial adaptation skills of a population coping with a seismic shock for which they were completely unprepared. The word 'worn out' disappeared from the French vocabulary, for example, as, in order to renew and refresh their outfits, women were forced to turn to whatever was still available to them – and this was the skillful use of fashion accessories. Times were far removed from the luxuries of the 1930s.

Economic and political contexts

Within a few months of the defeat of the French Army, the signing of the Armistice with Germany and soon after the Nazi Occupation of Paris in June 1940, France was rapidly denied its basic overseas imports and colonial resources, such as the raw cotton and silk needed to support its textiles industry. France was at once divided

FIGURE 3.0
Turban in beige jersey with brown bow, c. 1943 (Kerry Taylor Auction House, Lot 307, 12 February 2013, with thanks).

---
*Translation from French by Lou Taylor.

FIGURE 3.1
Hat and muff by Agnès, *Marie Claire*, January 20th, 1943 (copyright SIC/Marie Claire France, 269, with kind permission).

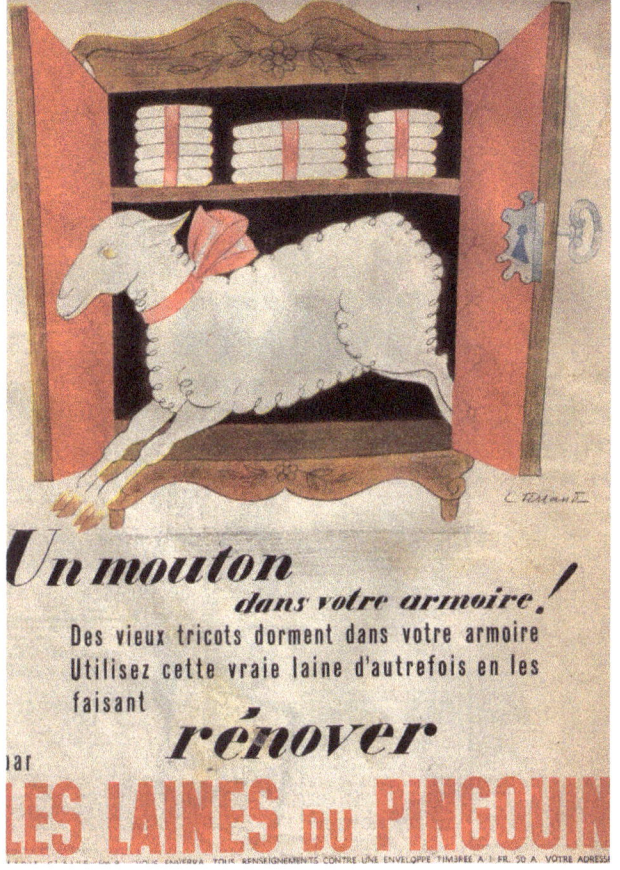

FIGURE 3.2
'A Sheep in your Cupboard', advertisement for Pingouin Wools, urging the re-knitting of old jerseys. *Marie Claire*, back page, 20 January 1943 (copyright SIC/Marie Claire France, 269, with kind permission).

into four tightly controlled administrative regions by the victorious German authorities: Occupied France, with its centre in Paris, secondly the so-called Free Zone (the 'Zone Libre'), governed directly by the defeated Maréchal of France, Pétain, from its capital at Vichy in Central and Southern France, then the coastal Zone Militaire Littoral (the Atlantic Wall in Brittany and the Atlantic coastline) and finally the German Military Administration Zone of Belgium and North France. Great swathes of Eastern France were forcibly absorbed into greater Germany, including the Strasbourg region (see Figure 1.6).

All of this led at once to supply problems between zones. Paris no longer received fabric supplies coming the North, from the Pas de Calais and from the Vosges region in Eastern France (Veillon 2014: 80). The population, industries and businesses in these militarily walled-off regions were at once trapped, controlled and isolated from the Occupied zone. The *Journal de la Chaussure Française* noted on 2 November 1940, that 65 per cent of French shoe factories, for example, were based in the Northern Occupied Zone with only 30 per cent in the Free Zone, and that Northern shoe manufacturers had become unable to honour contracts made with their Free Zone customers. Added to this were a series of other insurmountable problems – shortage of skilled labour caused by the fact that so many workers were prisoners of war in Germany, by the enforced exodus of Jewish artisans active in the accessory sector and already excluded from all commercial activity by Nazi Aryanisation laws, and by the profound shortages set in place as a result of German requisition orders. These became unbearably demanding. After 18 October 1940, as the first step towards Aryanisation, Jewish businesses were placed under the 'guardianship' of non-Jewish, French provisional administrators. More than 80 per cent of companies labeled as Jewish and thus subject to Aryanisation were small, typical Parisian businesses – two-thirds of them working in textiles and leather (Margairaz 1999: 9–10). Pierre Audiat noted that leather, textiles, ready-to-wear and hat-making were almost entirely in the hands of 'non Aryans' (1946: 67). One young Jewish milliner was Odette Fanny Bernstein, trading under the name of Fanny Berger with very real success through her a fashionable boutique in Avenue de Wagram, Paris. Nazi legislation forced her to close her business by late April 1941. A few of her hats survive, but she did not. She was murdered at Auschwitz-Birkenhau in July 1943. She was thirty years old.[1] Three hats we know of, each with her boutique label stitched carefully inside, remain as witness to her millinery talent.

Under the Armistice agreement, the Nazi regime had the right to demand delivery of French stocks of leather and cotton to Germany. Thus, to give one example, after the obligatory signing of a contract with Dr. Grumberg, Director of the Office of the German Leather Industry in Berlin (Veillon 2014: 91), France was obliged to deliver six million pairs of shoes to the Reich in November 1940 (Veillon 2014: 85).[2] Due to the carefully arranged advantageous exchange controls, the Occupiers were able freely to pillage disposable goods from department stores and specialist boutiques – from stockings to leather shoes. The consequences on France were dramatic. A decline in textile production was soon recorded, leading to the development of ersatz products such as artificial textiles – fibranne and rayon – as discussed in Chapter 2, much used for the manufacture of stockings.

Because of the imposition of strict controls on both the production of textile yardage and the sale of textile and leather products, new regulations soon dominated the daily lives of the population, who were forced to submit to a system of ration books and coupons. In February 1940, before the German Occupation, French consumers were already learning how the new rationing system was applied to all clothing items, creating a situation seen as an intolerable intrusion into private life – one resented by many as an intrusion into personal privacy. From spring 1941, after the Occupation, legislation controlling shoes, and from July 1941, legislation controlling textiles, became even more complex and harsh.

Obtaining a new dress became an unreal possibility for ordinary women and consequently new was made from old, though those who had the financial means continued to dress as before, through couture houses. Even so, and rapidly

FIGURE 3.3
(top) Two hats by Fanny Berger, in white and pink felt, 1940–1941 (Musée de la mode de la Ville de Paris Palais Galliera, GAL.1959. 43.3 and 4, © Topfoto and Roger-Viollet) and (bottom) a hat in fine black straw with feather trimming, 1940–1941 (Caroline Last Collection with thanks).

Chapter 3: Shortages in Paris 1940–1945: frivolous accessories become essential needs

for everyone else, the only way to renew an outfit was through the addition of new accessories – which thus became essentials. The world of fashion soon placed a rare focus on these and from then onwards, belts, bags, gloves and above all, hats, were the only means through which to transform the same simple day dress, for example, into a formal mid afternoon outfit. *Ganterie, Revue technique de la Ganterie française* reported in May 1942 that 'Wardrobes are barely renewed and many women have been wearing the same tailored suit for two or three years! It is through accessorising their toilettes that they can most easily add that certain sense of refinement.'

Accessories and their multiple wartime functions

The elegant new silhouette was accompanied by accessories which, as indicated above, were transferred from one outfit or another. To underline the increasing complexities of everyday life, from 1941 some women wore a specific medieval French symbol, '*la croix et la bannière*'. This was a cross and a banne (a symbol of difficult and complicated times) pinned on the lapels of their constantly worn tailored suits, demonstrating both humour and pluck in the service of chic. The May–June 1943 edition of the journal *Ganterie* posed the question: 'Are you invited for dinner, to play bridge, to a theatre premier ? You no longer ask yourself: which dress shall I wear? But what hat? Because everyone knows that you are still wearing your black suit and that only your hat will indicate the type of event you are attending' (*Ganterie*, May 1942).

Artisan makers became highly inventive in response to the exacting fashion demands of their wealthy clientele. The journal *Les Nouveaux Temps*, on the 7 May 1941, reported that, for example, once the width of leather belts for women was restricted to a maximum of four centimetres, leather makers, forced to observe this strict regulation, created a fashion for narrow belts, which caught on because it flattered the slim waists of their clients, who by then had become ultra slim, if not indeed thin. Short of leather, all kinds of materials were substituted. As reported in *Images de France* in October 1941, some ingeniously created designs laughed ironically at the times, such as a black suede belt decorated in gold letters with the word 'swede' – a vegetable hated in France because it was a clear symbol of shortage – or another, made by the famous luxury accessory company Henry à la Pensée, which was encrusted with patriotic designs evoking the countryside with the words '*retour à la terre*' – 'back to the soil' – Pétain's key Vichyist propaganda slogan. The prize for the most eccentric design went to an artist who designed a buckle fastening showing a tiny kitchen cooking pot containing ninety grammes of meat – the weekly ration, as *L'Oeuvre* reported on 15 April 1941. Six months earlier, in November 1940, Marcel Lasseux had written an article titled '*La haute Mode de Paris*', published in *Images de France*, which noted that the famous house of Hermès, in Rue du Faubourg Saint Honoré, had replaced leather with metal on belts and offered a fine, twisted metal chain to be worn with a dress or a sweater. Schiaparelli recalled that she had used 'dog leads for suit fastenings and to hold dresses in place' (1954: 134–135).

More commonly, the wartime French, middle-class fashion image was typified by the use of accessories patched together from every possible source. Women searched for advice in the feminine press, which acted as a news service, and journals were immensely popular. *Le Petit Echo de la Mode* had 253,000 subscribers in 1942 with a print run of 630,000[3] (Veillon 2014: 112). *Marie Claire* bulged with advice for overcoming shortages. Old-fashioned techniques were revitalised for making buttons, belts, bags and fashion jewellery. To replace belts, less well-off consumers used furniture webbing, selvedge edges of furnishing fabrics, colored ribbons, *paper maché* or woven straw plaited into twine. Resourcefulness and inventiveness played an integral role in women's behaviour, driven by ingenuity – as seen in a design for a belt buckle made from an electricity isolator, published in *Mode du Jour* on 9 October 1941. Nothing, however, equalled the courage of a young Parisienne, Jo Cardin, pupil at the Sévigné College. Once the Jewish population of the Occupied Zone were forced to wear yellow stars by a Nazi decree of 29 May 1942, she made herself a cardboard belt on which the word *Victory* could be read – with each letter made from tiny linked yellow stars made from scraps of leather she had managed to find. She was arrested and jailed for making this gesture (Veillon 2014: 98).[4]

Handbags

Regulations were just as strict for handbags. From 1941, the manufacture of leather handbags was forbidden, though this failed to prevent the making of practical handbags of immense size, using unregulated materials such as felt, *passementerie*, calf skin, snake and python skin. Amongst commonly used products, wallets (once leather was no longer available) were made of cloth and became essential for any citizen out and about in search of provisions. The most popular bag design was a vast hold-all of waxed linen fastening with a cord. It was ironically nicknamed 'Restrictions', and it could even look elegant if made from a heavy fabric, such as those designed by the House of Worth (Veillon 2014: 99). Large double designs, like saddle bags, as well as housing shopping, contained a series of small compartments that enabled women who were invited out to tea to discreetly take with them some sugar and bread ration tickets.

Other ideas came spontaneously to ingenious women living as they were in a world of scrounging, substitution and recycling. In her wartime Paris diary, the writer Colette remembered that her mother's Kashmir shawl ended up as 'a hand bag with faux blonde shell handles' (Colette 1944: 105). Once cycling became the common means of transport, as well as wearing their ubiquitous tartan skirts, young girls wore back-strap bags so they could carry large amounts of goods. Micheline Eude-Altman, then aged eighteen, remembered with emotion her hold-all with

FIGURE 3.4 Handbag by Duvelleroy made from a Kashmir Shawl of the 1850–1870 period, Paris, 1943. (Palais Galliera, Musée de la mode de la Ville de Paris GAL.1998.83.1, 1942. © Topfoto and Roger-Viollet.)

its false bottom in which she carried clandestine leaflets and documents for the Resistance group *Franc-Tireur*.[5]

In the great haute couture salons, the use of lizard and crocodile skin fed the expectations of clients who could still afford an expensive handbag. These were deeply fashionable. Thanks to their sophisticated skills, companies such as Hermès continued production even if they had to bend the regulations. Geneviève and Gérard Picot comment that 'A new hand bag especially if in good condition, became a valuable commodity for barter and exchange on the black market. A Hermès bag was worth the same exchange value as fifty kilos of sugar and a lorry tyre' (1993: 118). In February 1941, the couturier Lucien Lelong, daring to mock reality, included a wooden handbag shaped like a log in his collection (Veillon 2014: 100). Later, in 1942–1943, tapestry bags became fashionable, either used as a trimming to complete designs made from rare raw materials such as embossed calf skin, or on their own. The journal *Toute La Vie* on 1 October 1942, advised its readers to recycle old tapestry bags from the back of their cupboards or to stitch new ones themselves using *petit point*, mounting them on simple gold fastenings. Geneviève and Gérard Picot note that in 1944, the company Fernande Desgranges (a company run by two women) presented a handbag named 'Cartridge' (*Cartouche*) made of leather and parachute silk (1993: 121).

Gloves

Gloves, vital accessories for any outfit, became more necessary than ever in the winter. They were the epitome of elegance at the salons of Maggy Rouff, or at the House of Worth when made up in peccary (Mexican pigskin) or ocelot, albeit that their prime function was simply to keep hands warm. For winter 1940, Hermès offered pairs of double-layered gloves – the first layer in white angora with cuffs turned back over the second pair, made of lambskin. Fur, which was not rationed, was used in all kinds of ways, though there were clear differentiations in its use across the social classes, with fox and coney for some and astrakhan and mink for others. Rabbit fur was much in vogue amongst milliners, whilst faux furs were proposed for sports gloves and morning shopping expeditions. Embroidered Eskimo gloves were sold along with mittens, which women could keep wearing in their poorly heated apartments. They met with much success, as did mittens lined with sheep skin. Another much valued design was the woolen 'metro glove' with an extra pocket designed to hold transport tickets. In the summer, amongst young women, the fashion for wearing gloves declined and they went bare handed, whilst fashionable women wore gloves of lace or crochet, and, soon enough, also of rayon and other artificial fibres.

Stockings

Supplies of silk stockings were quickly affected by the restrictions and their near disappearance posed real problems, because the very notion of going out in public without stockings had never even entered the minds of French women. Famous couturiers, such as Nina Ricci, proposed instead a design of gaiters coloured to match shoes, boots or gloves. Henri à La Pensée made them out of dark brown angora.

FIGURE 3.5
Winter shoes with wedge heels of cork covered in brown leather and with knitted brown gaiters attached, c. 1943–1944. (Fonds Chauvin, with kind permission of the Musée des Métiers de la Chaussure, Saint-André-de-la-Marche. Photo copyright Olivier Rahard.)

In 1941 the last silk stockings disappeared or were priced out of reach and it became difficult even to get hold of cotton ones. Some beauty institutes invented a new dye system for legs, imitating stockings. The illusion was even more convincing if a fine stocking seam line was drawn on along the back of the calf. This idea was started at the Elizabeth Arden studio in Paris and was then democratised through *Filpas*, a leg dye whose use became a symbol of the knowledgeable woman. The journal *Le Nouveaux Temps* declared on 26 June 1941 that Elizabeth Arden 'invites us to shade our legs, without worrying about ladders, without hitting our budgets, whilst maintaining the propriety of our outfits and our elegance, as simply as possible.' The company sold this leg dye at thirty-three francs a bottle (plus two francs for the container). The cheaper *Filpas* sold at twenty-five francs. Advertisements in the same edition of *Le Nouveau Temps* marketed the product with the words 'Silk on your legs but without the silk.' Young women either used iodine or went bare legged. In the winter, many women unravelled old jerseys and knitted themselves stockings of wool. Stockings were much sought after on the black market. An inquiry made by the Commissariat Général about Jews living in Troyes, noted in January 1943 that on the legal market, a pair of cotton or rayon stockings cost between twenty-five to thirty-nine, whilst rare silk ones sold at sixty-five to eighty-five francs. On the black market, basic rayon stockings sold at two hundred and fifty francs and silk ones at three hundred (Veillon 2014: 105).

Jewellery

As to jewellery, master craftsmen drew inspiration from the times, some of it humorous, some, again, ironic or patriotic. In spring 1941, they created brooches that reflected Pétain's Vichyist propaganda slogan of '*retour à la terre*' – 'return to the soil' – offering other designs of elegant peasant women holding watering cans made of emeralds. Designs of bicycles with wheels of sapphire, as well as designs of boxes of sugar referenced the shortages whilst more prosaically, brooches of gilded metal shaped like rakes, shovels and a watering can were also available. A few less well-known artisans displayed their new work, including Max Boinet at his establishment near *la Madeleine*. He created a brooch design shaped in gilt metal, of a fashionable hat with flowers and violets to be worn with a tailored suit. Reine Bailly launched the fashion for portable sugar containers – a little, decorated pocket box with the words 'A thatched cottage, a heart and some sugar' (Veillon 2014: 106).

Earrings were in fashion, such as the long pendant ones worn by Arletty, whilst there was a popular vogue for cheap metal designs with animals, figures or geometric shapes. Gold chains were made into necklaces and bracelets were embellished with fashionable amulets. Crosses of Lorraine (the symbol of General de Gaulle and Free France) were widely worn in 1941, laying their wearers open to the risk of reprisals (Veillon 2014: 106). One inexpensive brooch became a symbol of the defeated country and of the French prisoners of war held far from home. It was designed in the shape of a map of France with a heart, on which could be read 'All for Him and for Her'.

Throughout the war the world-famous jewellery company Cartier resolutely supported General de Gaulle. Cartier archivists in Paris and London today believe that once de Gaulle had settled in London in 1940 to established the Free French Forces, George Charity, one of their London designers, may well have created little brass and enamel badges for the Free French Forces, including a Forces Navales Françaises Libres officer's badge. This, like the others, featured the Cross of Lorraine and was worn on the breast of their uniforms. The badges have issue numbers stamped on the back, which may indicate a registered design and patent date of early 1941.[6] Jenny Rourke, Cartier Archivist in London, confirms that their London archives contain

> a few sketches for Cross of Lorraine charms and brooches. . . . Mr. George Charity, [a] designer with Cartier, was asked to produce a number of designs which could be used as the Insignia of all the Free French Forces. He did this and eventually General de Gaulle chose the Cross of Lorraine with Insignia, which became the emblem that was worn with their uniforms.[7]

FIGURE 3.6
Forces Navales Françaises Libres Officer's badge in enamel and brass, probably designed by George Charity in the Cartier Studio, London and made in London, c. 1941–1943 (with thanks to Jane Hattrick).

In Paris, in 1942, the company produced a luxury fashion brooch, '*Oiseau en Cage*', featuring a bird made of multi-coloured precious stones trapped in a golden cage, a symbol of Occupied, trapped France.[8] At the moment of Liberation, the company created '*Oiseau Libre*' with the freed diamond and lapis-lazuli bird perched outside its little gold cage as a symbol of liberated France.[9] Only the tiniest, wealthiest minority could have afforded to buy either of these designs (Veillon 2014: 251). At the other end of the jewellery market, popular cheap charms in blue, white and red were to be found everywhere.

FIGURE 3.7
Left: 'Freed Bird' brooch, Paris, 1944, in gold, diamonds and lapis-lazuli (photo by Vincent Wulveryck, Archives Cartier, Paris, © Cartier Collection, Paris, with thanks to Anne Lamarque and Violette Petit).

FIGURE 3.7
Right: Design in gouache on paper for 'Captive Bird' brooch, Cartier, Paris, 1942 (Archives Cartier, Paris, © Cartier Collection, with many thanks).

Head Scarves

Head scarves were widely worn as fashion accessories during the Occupation period, often featuring printed designs inspired by Pétain's Vichyist *Révolution Nationale* imagery. They brightened up austere styles and could also be twisted into pretty head coverings. By the summer of 1941 many textile manufacturers were choosing such patriotic and Vichyist rural, '*retour à la terre*' design themes. Some, including ones designed by the famous Lyon silk company of Colcombet, reproduced images of, and visual references to, Maréchal Pétain, with, for example, his portrait as the great soldier hero of Word War One set against a back ground of his oak leaf symbol. Another design featured the coats of arms and names of the many great cities of France that supported Pétain and which he had ceremoniously visited. Others featured the 'Great and the Good of France': Joan of Arc, Bayard (a mystical heroic horse from twelfth-century French legends) and portraits of Henri IV and Louis XIV (Veillon 2014: 249). During the period of the Liberation of France, a far more modest accessory was widely used: a patriotic handkerchief featuring designs of the French tricolour flag with a portrait of General de Gaulle, the leader of the Free French Forces.

Shoes and hats and creative imagination

From the spring of 1941, shoe manufacturers were asked to produce designs for non-rationed shoes, that used neither leather or skin and avoided use of all rationed materials. To mitigate the lack of leather, wooden soles were widely used. According to the *Journal de La Chaussure* of 5 November 1940, the shoemaker Perugia developed a flexible wooden sole – though this design failed because it 'clogged up with sand and mud'. The first to successfully launch the wooden sole, this journal noted, was the Heyraud company with the gypsy sandal in lacquered wood with built-in anti-noise, anti-shock and anti-slip characteristics (Veillon 2014: 88). One French manufacturing group secured the use of a German patent for the *Zierold* sole, known under its French name of *Smelflex*. This was a laminated, articulated and very supple wooden sole (Veillon 2014: 87). Whilst such shoes were the common lot of most women, a few chic bootmakers launched the fashion for soles made of cork. Others, such as Perugia, as reported in *l'Oeuvre, Images de France* on 30 March 1941, developed a mix of artificial and vegetable materials for shoe soles that looked like leather but got rid of the exhausting and unpleasant clog-like clatter of wooden soles. Ingenious artisans found ways to improve the look of wooden soles by covering them in suede and lizard skin.

Every kind of material was used for the uppers: artificial leather or '*Synderme*', moleskin, woven felt, waxed cotton, raffia, straw and rattan. If it was summertime, consumers made do with sandals and espadrilles. In winter, the fashion was for short, little fur-trimmed boots, felt ankle boots or fur-trimmed clogs. *Pour Elle*, on 19 November 1941, noted that the company Gresy offered 'ankle boots with soles and heels of varnished wood and uppers entirely covered in real astrakhan'. In October 1942, at an artisanal fair at the Port of Versailles, Paris, as reported by the *Journal de la Chaussure Française*, 24 October 1942, interchangeable soles that fastened on with zips were on offer. Sandy Antelme notes that at the New Shoe exhibition in 1942, designs displayed by twenty-five shoe makers were 'true fashion phenomena. Stands overflowed with sandals whose soles were sculptured or pierced . . . with shoes decorated with coloured slashings . . . and with geometric or floral motifs' (Antelme 2006: 28). In the same mindset, human hair, too, had to be utilised. A law of 27 March 1942 ordered that waste hair must be collected at hairdressing establishments.

FIGURE 3.8
'Pagode' shoes with rigid wooden soles and red leather uppers recycled from stitched-together belts or handbag handles, made by the 'Imperial' brand at Aixe-sur-Vienne (with kind permission of the Neuville collection, Musée des Métiers de la Chaussure, Saint-André-de-la-Marche; photo copyright: Olivier Rahard).

When cleaned and mixed with artificial fibres, the resulting fabric could be used in the manufacture of slippers, gloves and handbags (Veillon 2014: 155). At the other end of the price range, during the period of the Liberation, the shoemaker Di Mauro created an elegant, heeled, bespoke tri-colour shoe, featuring the French and Allied flags, in red, white and blue but unaffordable for most women (Veillon 2014: 96).

Hats

One of the few freedoms allowed to women lay in the design of their head wear. As the last sartorial space left where women could indulge their imagination, hats became unexpectedly central to wardrobes – their use symbolising an escape from everyday problems. Hats underwent spectacular developments as milliners made them from non-rationed materials. Tulle, veils, feathers and flowers became the basis of the most extraordinary designs. This burst of creativity had started well. Felt was king: in brown, red, black, bottle green, it was shaped into conical or pointed skull caps and bound with ribbon or mousseline. The journalist Violette Leduc, writing in *Pour Elle* on 4 September 1940, advised her readers to use an autumn scarf of cotton, surah silk or flannel, either in one plain colour or spotted or striped and which could be worn in many styles: as a bandeau, a head scarf or, most popular of all, as a turban.

Sometimes additional trimmings were added, such as the large brown bow on this high, draped beige turban. For cycling, Reine Bailly created a fashion for 'a blue faux-suede turban, nicknamed 'windscreen', because it kept hair in place and ensured that a woman still looked well dressed.' For reasons of practicality, Simone de Beauvoir adopted and adapted this style of turban (Veillon 2014: 126).[10] Felt hats and berets were much appreciated by all women.

The freezing winter of 1940–1941 saw a wider use of hoods. All styles, at all prices, could be found from the most modest designs in tartan or camel hair in Little Red Riding Hood style, through to formal wool cloth hoods bordered with fur, available at Hermès. The most practical of all was a design that could be knitted at home, in two colours of knitting wool, black for the outside and another plain colour inside. The most fashionable were hoods by Patou in bright wool cashmere: 'almond green, coral or pimiento red, sapphire blue and the colour of champagne.' (Veillon 1990: 115).

The explosion of dress regulations restricted the content of women's wardrobes. Seeking some kind of redress, this situation pushed them into the arms of their milliners and made them susceptible to the range of original creations offered to them. From the summer of 1941 through to 1944, millinery design took opposite directions. Small at the start, flowers, ribbons and fruit were piled high on boaters and straw hats. This was '"*retour à la terre*" in its most gracious form', declared Violette Leduc, writing in *Tout et Tout*, 19 April 1941.

Then designs degraded as Gérard d'Houville lamented, and soon 'hats defied all common sense' (1943: 46). Colette shared the same opinion: 'it is not to be believed how a woman's common sense deserts her when she visits her milliner.

FIGURE 3.9A
Two models wearing scarves made into fashionable turbans, Paris, 1944. (Getty 2696639. Photo by Fred Ramage.)

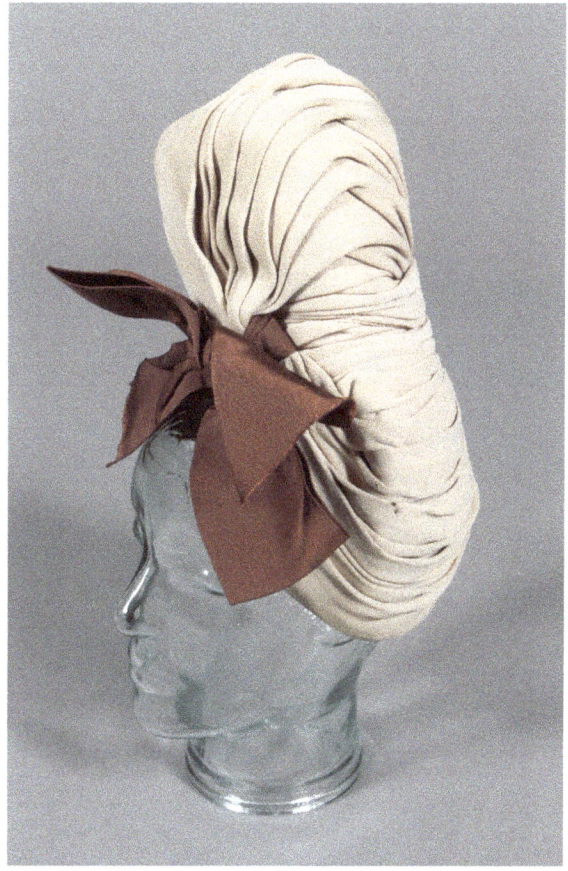

FIGURE 3.9B
Turban in beige jersey with brown bow, c. 1943 (Kerry Taylor Auction House, Lot 307, 12 February 2013, with thanks).

Setting out full of caution . . . a women of taste returns home with a ball of violets worn over her nose' (1944: 89). Everyone was amazed at the aggressive new fashion for long feathers, nicknamed 'knives', worn placed vertically on small hats, as *Les Nouveaux Temps* reported on 12 June 1941 (see Figure 3.10B).

By November 1942, types of available millinery fabrics became limited. Lacking felt, silk and exotic straws, some designers showed no hesitation at all in turning to unusual materials. They set out to prove that haute couture was far from dead and that they were more than capable of creative invention, no matter how problematic their situation was. Thus Madame Agnès created ravishing models in cotton wool and skeins of raw wool, whilst a most original design made from wood shavings became an immense success. The collaborationist journal *La Gerbe* noted on 9 October 1941 that Rose Valois had presented a highly successful collection of hats. 'Some, made of blotting paper, were half veiled with Chantilly lace, whilst others were made from folded and puckered newspaper.' The famous millinery house of Albouy also put its energies into making large hats out of newsprint paper. If some of these designs signalled the unassailable attachment of chic Parisiennes to their hats, the vast size and eccentricity of hats from 1942 became so marked that some saw in these designs a kind of irreverent sniping at the enemy.

Elsa Schiaparelli had no hesitation later in stating that the complicated, hideous, heavy and unseductive hair styles and hats 'proved that a convulsed and

FIGURE 3.10A
Straw boater piled with wide coloured ribbons, cover, *Marie Claire*, 12 April 1940 (copyright SIC/Marie Claire France, 163, with kind permission).

FIGURE 3.10B
Felt hat with 'knife' feather, shown at the haute couture fashion show in Lyon 8–10 March 1942 (Getty 558642453).

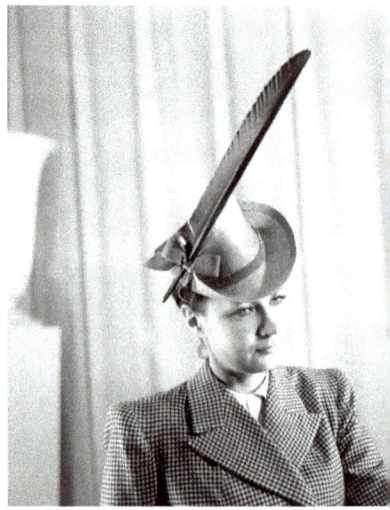

FIGURE 3.11A
High red felt hat with black-and-white striped silk trimming, 1943–1944 (Musée de la Mode de la Ville de Paris, Palais Galliera, no GAL. 1959. 43.3 and 4, © Topfoto and Roger-Viollet).

FIGURE 3.11B
High green felt hat with feather trimmings by Gabrielle, dress by Jacques Heim, *Modes et Travaux*, December 1943 (with thanks to the University of Brighton Dress History Teaching Collection).

crushed Paris had decided to defend its true personality by establishing a battle front deliberately bordering on ridicule' (Schiaparelli 1954: 150). In 1944, the Germans, faced with the ever-growing size of hats, determined to bring an end to this profligate use of materials. The Liberation of Paris ended these discussions.

FIGURE 3.12
Red, white and blue prototype, wedge-heeled shoe, designed to celebrate the Liberation of France, Manoukian, Paris (Musée Carnavalet, 1944 OM 4248. © Topfoto and Roger-Viollet).

Conclusion

For the majority of women in France during the period of 1940–1945, fashion used the unusable. Germaine Beaumont, writing in *Album de Mode de Figaro* of 1944, commented that 'fashion used subterfuge – cheating on the regulations, plaiting paper, carving wood . . . Fashion did this with elegance, arrogance and with extravagance. Women wore hats blown up like balloons and heels and soles which clattered on the ground as if applauding these indulgences' (Levisse-Touze and Veillon 2014: 49).

The Occupation thus saw the birth of a new style in Paris, a style forced to make constant adjustments depending on whatever could be found. These finds were transformed into fashionable accessories, confirming that in this period when everything was lacking, French fashion, true to itself as ever, flowed with creativity.

References

Audiat, P. (1946), *Paris pendant la Guerre*, Paris: Hachette.
Antelme, S. (2016), *Se Chausser sous l'Occupation*, Paris: Libel.
Colette. (1944, reprint 2004), *Paris de Ma Fenêtre*, Paris: Fayard.
de Beauvoir, S. (1960 reprint 1985), *La Force de l'Age*, Paris: Gallimard.
d'Houville, G. (1943), *La Parisienne et la Mode*, Paris: Arts, Lettres, PUF.
Ganterie. (1942), *Revue Technique de la Ganterie Française*, May.
Images de France (1940 Nov; 1941 Oct).
Journal de la Chaussure Française. (1940 2 Nov; 1942 25 Oct and 5 Nov).
Kurkdjian, S., L. Vogel and M. de Brunhoff. (2013), 'Parcours crioses de deux editeurs de 3 press illustrée au XX siecle', Phd thesis, University of Paris 1 Panthéon Sorbonne.
La Gerbe. (1941 9 Oct).
Lasseux, M. (1940 Nov.), 'La haute mode de Paris', *Images de France*.
Le Nouveaux Temps (1941 12 and 26 June).
Levisse-Touze, C. and D. Veillon. (2014), 'La Condition de la Mode en Guerre', in *Pour Vous Mesdames! La Mode in temps de guerre*, Lyon: Centre d'Histoire de la Resistance et de la Déportation.

L'Oeuvre, Images de France. (1941 15 April).

Margairaz, M. (1999), Preface to Verheyde, P., *Les Mauvais Comptes de Vichy, L'Organisation des entreprises juives*, Paris: Perrin.

Mode du Jour. (1941 9 Oct).

Picot, G. and G. (1993), *Le Sac a Main*, Paris: du May.

Pour Elle, (1940 4 Sept and 1941 9 Nov).

Raulet, S. (1985), quoted in Bony A. (1985) *Les années 40*, Paris: du Regard.

Schiaparelli E. (1954), *Shocking, Souvenirs d'Elsa Schiaparelli*, Paris: Denoel.

Tout et Tout, (1941 19 April).

Toute La Vie, (1942 1 Oct).

Veillon, D. (1990, 2014 edition), *La Mode sous l'Occupation*, Paris: Payot and Rivages.

Veillon. D. (2009), '1940-44: Le Front de La Mode', *L'Histoire*, no.3456, September 78-82.

Endnotes

1. Unable to continue her business under Nazi/Vichy Aryanisation legislation of 1941, Odette Fanny Bernstein was caught and arrested on 19 September 1942 trying to cross the demarcation line into Vichy France. Moved from one camp to another in France, by 1943 she was in the Drancy internment camp outside Paris and on 18 July 1943 was transported to Auschwitz-Birkenau in Poland. She was gassed soon after her arrival. See Falluel F. and Gutton, M-L., *Elégance et Systeme D*, Paris: Paris Musées, 2012: 62. See also the documentary film by her niece, Catherine Bernstein (2005) *Assassinat d'Une Modiste*, 2006. IO Productions/Arte.

2. For further details see Archives Nationales, Paris, AJ 4179, AJ 41 171.

3. For further details on the history of Occupation journals see Kurkdjian, S., *Lucien Vogel et Michel de Brunhoff, parcours crioses de deux editeurs de3 press illustrée au XX sie*cle, Phd thesis, University of Paris 1 Panthéon Sorbonne, 2013.

4. The belt was confiscated: oral testimony given by Jo Cardin-Massy in 1987 and Archives de la Prefecture de Police, quartier de la Sorbonne, Télégramme 34, carton PJ 33. Veillon D., *La Mode sous l'Occupation*, Paris: Payot. 1990: 93.

5. Oral testimony collected by D. Veillon in 1974 from Micheline Eude-Altman who worked in Lyon for the resistance group *Franc-Tireur*.

6. Boseley, S. *Regimental Badges, a division of Coldstream Military Antiques.* https://www.regimentalbadges.com; accessed 12 September 2017.

7. Jenny Rourke, Archivist, Cartier, London, in e-mail to the author, 5 December 2016 and with quote from testimony recorded by Joseph Allgood, Managing Director of Cartier, London during World War Two. We thank her for this information.

8. The display of this jewel was drawn to the attention of the Nazi Abwehr, the counter espionage and military intelligence service. Jeanne Toussaint, Cartier director, was summoned to 'answer for the intolerable provocation' caused by this design – such a 'self evident symbol of the Occupation'. She answered that she simply 'loved birds'. Raulet, S. in Bony, A. (1991: 55), *Les Années 40*, Paris: Du Regard.

9. Maison Cartier, London, in immediate support of de Gaulle when he arrived in London in 1940 to establish the Free French Forces, placed their offices and the firm's Bentley (and chauffeur) at de Gaulle's disposal. Eleven of Cartier's Paris staff were imprisoned by the Nazis, including designers Lachassagne and Remy (Nadelhoffer, H. (2007: 313) Cartier, London: Thames and Hudson.

10. For further details see de Beauvoir, S. (1960 reprint 1985: 577) *La Force de l'Age*, Paris: Gallimard.

Chapter 4
'Much news from the fashion frontier': Swedish neutrality and diffusion of Paris fashion during World War Two

*Ulrika Kyaga**

> *Future scholars will certainly struggle when writing the history of fashion in the years 1940 to 1944, since during these times of confusion it is not possible to define what actually is in fashion.*
>
> Rydeberg (October 1944)

Introduction

The turbulent years during the events of the World War Two were times of insecurity and thus challenging for the world of fashion. Within the dress history world 'until recently, a common perception among historians is that Paris was completely isolated and consequently that no fashion information was spread outside of Occupied France' (Kyaga 2017: 111). Yet as this book will clarify, this was not the case in Sweden. The Swedish situation was different, not least due to its standpoint of neutrality. Another clear distinction was that the latest fashion news from the Occupied city of Paris was published on a regular basis in the elite periodical *Bonniers månadstidning* (Kyaga 2017: 111–112). This meant that readers could follow the Parisian fashion ideal, though they were also made aware of the couturiers' exposed situation when struggling with Nazi regulations. This situation

FIGURE 4.0
Göta Trägårdh fashion drawing *'Hattar i rött'* (Hats in Red), *Bonniers månadstidning*, November 1942 (with many thanks to Li Thies-Largergren).

---

*Translation from Swedish by the author.

has been overlooked by historians and not written into the history of Paris as a centre for fashion in the years 1940–1944. Taking the journal *Bonniers månadstidning* as a starting point, this study examines what type of fashion news was produced and circulated through Swedish fashion journalism. In so doing, this chapter contributes new knowledge through the lens of a neutral country.

The Swedish policy of neutrality

According to historian Alf W. Johansson, the policy of neutrality is a significant characteristic in the Swedish self-image (1997: 183) and Sweden's neutral standpoint during World War Two is much debated (Linder 2002; Boëthius 1999). Scholarly writing on this policy gives various interpretations of the Swedish role during the war. The main discussion concerns the question as to whether Sweden was actually neutral due to their concessions to Nazi Germany during their invasion of Sweden's Nordic neighbours. According to Christine Agius, 'neutrality means different things to different countries . . . For some, it is a means to an end, for others, it is a way of staying out of war', and I believe the latter describes the Swedish situation (2006: 50).

In his text *Att bo granne med ondskan: Sveriges förhållande till nazismen, Nazityskland och Förintelsen* ('Living next door to evil: the Swedish relationship with Nazism, Nazi Germany and the Holocaust'), Klas Åmark highlights several questions that deal with this matter, such as 'Was it really right to look primarily to one's own interests, for the preservation of peace and to keep up continuous trade with Nazi Germany?' (2011: 17). He also asks 'did the media extensively reported in detail so that the catastrophe was understandable or was it passed over in silence?' (ibid.). These questions are, according to Åmark, more relevant rather than questioning whether Sweden was neutral or not, in order to understand the consequences of Swedish political standpoints on developments of the war (2011: 29). As Åmark notes, at issue were both economic relations with Nazi Germany, which became important, and also the situation of press relationships, since news distribution was linked to the politics of foreign policy (2011: 69–70).

Historian Jan Linder argues that it is a 'myth' that the Swedish government willingly co-operated with the Germans. Linder suggests, rather, that accepting press censorship and sending Swedish journalists on Nazi-arranged study tours to Germany was a delicate decision for the Social Democratic Prime Minister, Per-Albin Hansson (2002: 66). As Åmark observes, having a good relationship with Sweden was important for the Nazis; the original plans were never to invade Sweden but rather to control its cultural institutions and individual artists, because high culture was of propaganda interest for Hitler (2011: 30).

The Social Democratic Party and its foreign minister Richard Sandler had established the policy of neutrality in the 1930s (2011: 74). It was not until April 1940, after the Nazi invasion of Norway, when this standpoint was questioned in Sweden. Swedish friendliness to Germany is primarily associated with the granting of permission for the transportation of German military material through Sweden to Norway, the *Permittenttrafiken* ('Permittent Traffic') (Linder 2002: 60–61), signed on 8 July 1940. This became the symbol of the Swedish betrayal of its neighbouring countries and a mark of the strength of its resolution for true neutrality. This agreement allowed German military transports through Sweden to northern parts of Norway (Linder 2002: 63). To keep good relationships with all countries was, however, according to Åmark, both a strategy of the Prime Minister and also of the Swedish press. With the Swedish media describing the war situation as a great-power war, Sweden was able to see itself as outside and neutral and thus could continue its relationships with the United States and England, while also trading with Nazi Germany (Åmark 2011: 182).

That business connections with Sweden were important for the Nazis can be illustrated by wartime plans for fashion export activities. Historian Dominique Veillon describes how, since

> almost all the Berlin *couture* houses were closed, it would be difficult to make it known to these businesses that the Parisian *couturiers* remained open, unless the latter agreed to accept a change of direction. It was high time they made a useful contribution to the European economy – for example by expanding their exporting activities to countries such as Sweden, Spain, Italy and Portugal.
>
> (2002: 97, quoting 'Discussions at the Majestic between Jacques Deligny and Dr. Schilling', Archives Nationales, F12 10503 and p. 151, Appendix 2)

The Nazis also 'required French fashion, merged with Viennese and Berlin *couture*, to participate in the promotional exhibition in Stockholm planned for July 1944' (Veillon 2002: 97), an event that never took place. Nevertheless, this quotation reflects how fashion was seen by the Germans as an important trade link when Paris was under occupation and that haute couture became a significant link between Sweden and Germany.

Paris fashion industry under occupation

The German invasion of the French capital on 14 June 1940 was an event that challenged Paris hegemony and its position as an international centre for fashion production. The Nazis, however, acknowledged the importance of Parisian haute couture and, whilst imposing complex controlling regulations, a majority of the fashion houses consequently remained open during the war. One main purpose for permitting this situation was that the Germans wanted to acquire invaluable knowledge of French fashion production, to be used in the development of their domestic German fashion industry. Indeed, the initial plan was to move the entire Parisian couture production to Berlin or Vienna, but the president of the *Chambre Syndicale de la Couture Parisienne*, Lucien Lelong, managed to prevent this through intensive negotiations with the Nazi leaders (Veillon: 85–86). Historian Diana de Marly summarizes, 'It was better to deal with the devil then to kill off the industry altogether' (1980: 197). In Sweden, *Bonniers månadstidning* warmly sympathised with Lucien Lelong and his determination to preserve Parisian couture traditions, which can be observed in its February 1941 issue:

> Why do they work? For many reasons. To prevent unemployment within their industry and defend Paris's position as the capital of Fashion, to avoid getting interrupted – but also for the work itself. They simply cannot resist.
>
> (Marque, February 1941: 20)

In spite of Lelong's negotiations, the French industry was subjected to a number of regulations and limitations, and as Veillon notes, the number of pieces in the collections, as well as the choice of material, was controlled. The purpose of this control was two-fold. Firstly, the Nazis wanted to control the French fashion industry. Secondly, by introducing rationing in France, the Nazis could also help resolve the urgent need for textile goods in Germany (Veillon 2002: viii).

The war situation resulted in a change of customers for the salons and instead of the usual returning international buyers and private international clients, a new group were seen in the dressing rooms at the Paris salons. Veillon describes these as the 'nouveau riche', also nicknamed the *Beurre-Oeufs-Fromages* ('Butter-Eggs-Cheese') women, abbreviated as BOF, because they were trading food on the black market (2002: 121). Their new economic wealth gave access to the elegant world of fashion, but still they differed from the social elite, in terms of taste. This was a phenomenon that was also commented on in *Bonniers månadstidning* where a so-called BOF woman was described in terms of 'a pig adorned with a diamond necklace' or as a newly rich butcher's wife who, irrespective of wealth, can never manage to reach the cultural level of the Parisian countess and her inherent 'spiritual and physical nobility' (*Jean de France*, November 1942: 6, 10).

However, in order to understand the extent of this ongoing fashion production, it is relevant to review the number of couture houses that actually were open during the occupation. Lou Taylor refers to the words of the British journalist Alison Settle, who reported that 'over 100 *couture/création* houses were open in Paris' (1995: 34). According to Alexandra Palmer, this figure implies that 97 per cent of the couture employees remained at work in the industry (2009: 17). My findings in *Bonniers månadstidning* show that it was especially the eleven most famous and leading couture houses that were mentioned in the Swedish fashion periodicals during the war period. These were Schiaparelli, Lelong, Patou, Molyneux, Alix, Heim, Piguet, Paquin, Fath, Lanvin and Maggy Rouff. A number of these couturiers arranged for their salons to remain open even after they had left the country. Schiaparelli left for America, and Molyneux returned to his London salon and became one of the designers responsible for the 'Utility Dress Design Committee' in the UK. Because of his Jewish heritage, Jacques Heim was forced to leave Paris, but continued his business from his country villa outside Paris, under Nazi surveillance, but under the protection of a wealthy and influential Spanish clientele (Taylor 1992: 131).

Censored fashion information

In spite of Swedish neutrality, the freedom of the Swedish press was threatened during the war (Linder 2002: 156–166). Linder summarises how the Swedish Coalition Government tried to avoid conflict with Hitler, who considered any 'free press as a red rag'. This resulted in an inescapable situation where German press censorship had to be accepted and Swedish journalists 'withheld their thoughts and avoided making a fuss!' (2002: 157). In 1940, the Swedish *Statens Informationsstyrelse* (SIS; the Government Information Board) was established. Its main duty was to check up on the Swedish press and thus, as Linder notes, the news agency *Tidningarnas Telegrambyrå* was forbidden to make any comment on German actions that were laced with Swedish 'sarcasm, ironical and insulting attacks'. According to Linder, this resulted in a situation where the SIS became considered a 'secret authority rather than an information authority' (2002: 158). A minority of Swedish newspapers were subsidised directly by German funding, but still they did exist (2002: 163). There were also newspapers that which, even if they did not receive any financial support, were accused of being pro-German; one example was *Stockholms-Tidningen* (2002: 164), a local newspaper that also offered a regular coverage on fashion.

In France, however, fashion journalism was affected by tough German censorship and journals, which refused to work under German inspection, had to cease their businesses. According to Taylor this was the case for *Vogue* and *Femina*, among others. Still, many journals such as *Marie Claire* and *Mode du Jour* accepted these new conditions and continued to publish (1992: 129). That fashion information from Paris was not seen in any other part of the world has become the common history of fashion in the years 1940–1945. My findings therefore fill in a gap of knowledge. Swedish circumstances were exceptional because the latest fashion news from Paris was published on a regular basis. As this chapter will show, the major Swedish fashion journals focused on the latest Paris collections but also included articles on the Paris couture industry and its struggle with Nazi regulations. The fashion correspondent Marque wrote in *Bonniers månadstidning*'s February 1942 issue that everything was almost the same as before except for the new guests on the front rows of the fashion shows – 'the German officers' – who were 'smiling, polite, amused and of course treated kindly' (Marque, February 1941: 18).

My findings show that fashion news from France was present in almost every issue of *Bonniers månadstidning* in the permanent column 'Fashion Letter from Paris'.

Correspondents reporting on Parisian fashion were based in Paris through the war, writing under pseudonyms such as 'Jean de France' or 'Madame in Paris'. Despite the large number of reports covering the latest fashion shows, information sent from Paris was censored. Even five months before the Nazi occupation of Paris, in its January 1940 issue, *Bonniers månadstidning* chose to publish an image of the official stamp of the French government's wartime censors printed on the magazine's Paris fashion reports, in order to inform their readers about this important alteration in wartime publishing (Kyaga 2017: 112–113).

> This is the French censorship's official stamp, which appears on every page of the manuscript to this article as well as on the back of the photographs. Not a single word, no drawings, no photographs seem to leave France in these days without being reviewed by the military censor. This explains why we sometimes have to wait up to fourteen days on our French correspondence
>
> (Marque 1940: 15).

FIGURE 4.1
French censorship stamp in 'Från modefronten mycket nytt', *Bonniers månadstidning*, January 1940 (with thanks to the National Library Stockholm).

Three years later, in 1943, and under Nazi rather than French censorship regulations, press censorship in Occupied France became even stricter, and according to Veillon all publications of Paris couture fashion photographs were prohibited in February 1943 (2002: 119, 96). This could explain why the number of hand-drawn fashion illustrations increased in the Swedish fashion journals, but despite this prohibition, fashion photographs did still appear in the Swedish press, such as the one from March 1944 (*Bonniers månadstidning* 1944: 48). This high presence of French couture fashion indicates that the Nazi occupiers tolerated the diffusion of fashion information. That original information from Paris was published in the Swedish media is further confirmed by published drawings of 1942 by the leading fashion illustrator Pierre Pages (Jean de France 1942: 21).

A Swedish fashion correspondent, Ingeborg Markström, who visited Occupied Paris in 1941, revealed some of the reporting problems to her readers, explaining that photographs as well as entire articles disappeared after being posted to Stockholm. All information had to be sent to Stockholm via the German Ministry of Propaganda in Berlin. Some letters were lost and did not even arrive in Sweden. Furthermore, she confirmed that the Nazis removed all texts containing Jewish as well as English family names in a situation described by Markström as 'bizarre', since fashion was, at the same time, considered seriously by the Germans (1941: 20).

FIGURE 4.2
A typical French fashion image by the Parisian photographer Laure Albin Guillot. Couturier unknown. *Bonniers månadstidning*, March 1944 (with thanks to the National Library Stockholm).

FIGURE 4.3
Fashion drawings by the French illustrator Pierre Pagès. Report by Jean de France titled 'Modebrev från Paris', *Bonniers månadstidning*, September 1942 (with thanks to the National Library Stockholm).

The presence of Paris fashion in Swedish fashion periodicals was seen by the publications as a rare and precious coup. As Kyaga (2017: 113–114) notes, *Bonniers månadstidning* was aware of this and thus highlighted these Paris contacts in their promotion of the journal: 'A fresh fashion letter directly from Paris. In spite of censorship, restrictions and all kinds of difficulties, we have the benefit of providing our female readers with latest news from Paris in the January issue of *Bonniers Månadstidning*' (*Dagens Nyheter* 1942: 10). This quotation indicates that the Nazis tolerated the sending of fashion material to Sweden, probably because of the Swedish neutrality policy. This is confirmed by the fashion correspondent Markströom, who confirmed that the Germans approved her right to cover the latest fashion news, although the information – text and photographs – still had to be transferred through the censorship process after it had been delivered to 'the German information bureau [in Paris], from where they, via the Propaganda Department in Berlin would transfer it to Stockholm' (1941: 20).

Parisian war fashion

Fashion history writing on the first half of the 1940s has traditionally focused on the isolation of Paris during the Occupation and consequently, the simple and narrow British silhouette with military influences has become what the design historian John A. Walker would call a 'canon' of the fashion image of this period (Walker 1989: 62). This image is perfectly illustrated by the legendary fashion photograph 'Fashion Is Indestructible' by Cecil Beaton of 1941, showing an elegant model in a London tailored suit viewing the rubble that once was the famous Middle Temple Inn of Court (Seeling 2001: 195). Yet, as a contrast to Beaton's picture, the fashion style that developed in Paris during the 1942–1944 period can be described simply as extravagant, with full skirts, narrow waists and enormous hats. This fashion is well described by historian Jacqueline Demornex: 'As the threat of war loomed ever larger, couture sought refuge in a nostalgic elegance. Huge gigot sleeves, full skirts and Second Empire crinolines all made a come-back' (2008: 81). Veillon interprets the 'frivolous' fashion as a 'revolt against the occupier' and the courage of not giving up (2002: vii). Swedish fashion journals paid tribute to the Parisian woman and her excessive style, as fashion editor of *Bonniers månadstidning* Célie Brunius wrote in January 1944:

> One may have different views on this provocative clothing. But it helps the city to look happier. It helps the petite French women to endure in a life, which for most of them are very hard. It makes them look livelier, healthier and younger.
>
> (1944: 21)

Practical yet stylish war collections

At the war's outbreak, a number of leading Paris couturiers were called up for military service, but only for a brief period of time, since they almost immediately received official leave permits and could return to work as designers. For this reason the collections released in the autumn were named '*Les Collections des Permissionnaires*'. They contained both a practical and a more elegant line (Taylor 1992: 127–128). Some designs were evidently functional as fashion adapted to the current war situation and the need for practical clothing in bomb shelters, for example. The journalist Marque wrote a report in *Bonniers månadstidning* in January 1940 on Christmas shopping in Paris a month earlier in December of 1939. She noted that shop windows were packed with military-inspired products such as:

> elegant gas masks boxes, jewellery in colours of the tricolour, articles of clothing in Scottish and the fashion colours '*bleu Royal Air Force*', '*vert canon*', '*rouge legion*', '*bleu Maginot*', '*Camouflage*', '*gris Avion*' etc. Of course all [of these] originate from the *demi-saison* collections, also named as the war collections.
>
> (Marque 1940: 15)

According to Taylor, the functional lines were designed for the domestic market, while the evening collections were still aimed at the export market (1992: 128). It is significant that pictures of these war-oriented garments were published in Swedish journals because, in spite of Swedish neutrality, there was a constant threat here too of German invasion and consequently bomb shelters were built in Sweden. One of the most characteristic images of the practical bomb shelter fashions was the 'air-raid shelter suit' from Piguet (*Bonniers månadstidning* 1940: 38).

FIGURE 4.4
Piguet design in *Bonniers månadstidning*, January 1940 (with thanks to the National Library Stockholm).

This situation also inspired Swedish fashion studios to create war-oriented products, for example 'the evacuation dress – warm, strict and of course in grey', which was reported as the major showpiece at Leja's fashion show in January 1940 (Rydeberg 1940: 17). According to Veillon, it was not only the war but also the cold weather in autumn of 1940 and winter 1941 that contributed to this warm and functional fashion image (2002: 32–33). Another contributing factor to this style was the change in methods of transport because of the lack of petrol. In Paris, the Metro became an interesting meeting place, which also inspired fashion designers. On the platforms, people from all social levels were represented, from 'lower middle-class women, secretaries and dress-makers assistants' to 'society ladies'. Veillon argues that the Metro had an enormous influence on, and almost 'dictated', the new fashion image, especially the skirt length, since shorter skirts (for evening wear) were required in order to manage to catch the last Metro departure '23.00 train' (2002: 31).

During the Occupation, another transport characteristic of the Parisian cityscape was the bicycle, again due to the rationing of petrol for cars (ibid.: 28).

The bicycle also had a great impact on the fashion image and garments specially adapted for cycling – primarily culottes – were featured in the main collections. In Paris, separate fashion shows were held for these 'bicycle suits' and the journalist signing herself Sabine in *Bonniers månadstidning* wrote about one particular show at the Pavillon d'Armenonville in Bois de Boulogne (Sabine July–August 1942: 27).

Changes in Parisian fashion style

The British fashion historian Ernestine Carter wrote in 1977 that 'fashion everywhere was frozen' and did not change until the introduction of the 'The New Look' in 1947 (Carter 1977: 230). This quotation, however, does not reflect the situation within Paris as clarified here already, let alone the situation in Sweden. When analysing *Bonniers månadstidning* in the years 1939–1945, it becomes evident that this argument is incorrect, because already by 1942 a new line, with smaller waists and fuller skirts, had already been established by the couturiers in Paris.

A number of fashion historians confirm my observations that the fashion image in the mid-1940s was moving towards a more feminine expression (Taylor 1992; Veillon 2002; Steele 1998). According to the journalist writing under the pseudonym Jean de France in *Bonniers månadstidning*, the wasp-like waist was the most-talked-about style in 1942 (Jean de France October 1942: 24–25). The new line was described as the 'amphora line', which proclaimed the use of a corset (*Sabine* May 1942: 40). A year later, in 1943, further changes were seen, with the main focus placed on the larger new sleeves, noticeable in headlines such as 'A new sleeve line is visible within Paris fashion' (*Bonniers månadstidning* 1943: 18–19).

FIGURE 4.5
Paris haute couture fashion spread, 1943, including designs by Lanvin, Jacques Fath, M. Dormoy, Bruyère, Maggy Rouff and Hermès. In 'Paris just nu', *Bonniers månadstidning*, July–August 1943 (with thanks to the National Library Stockholm).

The fashion silhouette by then could be described in terms of these wide and full sleeves, a wide but softer shoulder line and full skirts with emphasis on tiny waists, with the 'wasp' still in fashion. Other details dominated the fashion image, too, such as draping and pleated skirts and large hats. In 1944 the 'new' large sleeves were still popular and evolved to become even more voluminous. Swedish fashion journals continued to publish and favour this 'modern sleeve line' as well as the wasp waists and jersey turbans (Rydeberg April 1944: 34–35). Probably the most extreme changes in fashion (which after the Liberation caused strong reactions outside France) were women's hats, which were extremely exaggerated in design.

Following Paris Occupation couture style development in Sweden

It was rare to have access to these monthly fashion reports charting the changes in Paris couture style, but Swedish women could still, nevertheless, follow their favourite Parisian designers. Thus, the Swedish situation played a key but as yet unrecognised role in supporting and maintaining the international existence of the French fashion industry. A significant example of the implementation of the extravagant Occupation fashion style in Stockholm is found in the April 1944 issue

FIGURE 4.6
Göta Trägårdh's illustrations of Paris couture garments sold in Stockholm, *Bonniers månadstidning*, April 1944 (with thanks to the National Library Stockholm).

of *Bonniers månadstidning*, with text written by Marga Rydeberg and illustrated with Göta Trägårdh's fashion drawings, some four months before the Liberation of Paris. These, significantly for this study, show examples of 'original' Paris couture model garments that were being bought and sold by leading Swedish fashion studios, including a 'Schiaparelli at Märthaskolan', 'a Paquin model at Edman & Andersson' and 'a Balenciaga at MEA' (Rydeberg April 1944: 35).

Ethnologist Viola Germain confirmed in 1988 that indeed original French models arrived in Sweden from the start and during the war, entering the country via Spain and Italy (Germain 1988: 169–170). In October 1940, only four months after the Occupation of Paris, *Bonniers månadstidning* had informed its readers that two original model garments from the salons of Lanvin and Alix had managed to reach the Swedish market, after an even more roundabout journey from America – which had not then joined the war with the Allies (I. af S. 1940: 3). In 1941, *Bonniers månadstidning* added more details about Sweden's continuing access to international fashion as stemming from the availability of 'a mix of original models from Paris, Vienna, Switzerland and Prague' (Marque April 1941: 17). A more easily available means of accessing Paris couture seasonal couture style was through exported paper patterns.

The journalist writing in *Bonniers månadstidning* in October 1943 noted that original Paris couture design models (in the form of paper patterns) were available for Swedish buyers albeit that these were extremely expensive (at around 4,000–5,000 francs) (Elisabeth 1943: 33). According to Marga Rydeberg too, still in 1944 before the Liberation of Paris, some Swedish fashion studios had access to the latest 'original drawings' and 'French toiles'. One other alternative for Swedish designers, as well as private and home dressmakers, was to create their own models based on original press sketches or illustrations they found in American and French fashion magazines, as well as in Swedish journals such as *Bonniers månadstidning*. Another Göta Trägårdh drawing proves that in 1942, Swedish milliners were also directly inspired by Parisian extravagant hat fashion styles, such as the red model by Edman & Anderson. The 'crumpled up' design in the middle of this fashion drawing was an original design by Gerda Janson & Co (see Figure 4.7).

This text has therefore confirmed that both Paris Occupation-style fashion images and even a few actual Paris couture garments were available for sale, especially to wealthy Swedish fashion consumers, throughout the war years. The Swedish also designed and made copies of Paris hats by 1942. Finally, this article shows that Swedish-made couture versions of Paris designs were created by Swedish couture studios for sale in their own salons, such as at Leja's fashion show in January 1940, discussed above. Swedish designers were able to do this because of the stream of fashion reports coming over from Paris. Veillon confirms these copying process and stresses that whilst most foreign buyers failed to come to fashion shows, a new kind of writer appeared, aiming to glean information or steal ideas (Veillon 2002: 34).

FIGURE 4.7
Göta Trägårdh fashion drawing, 'Hattar i rött', (Hats in Red) *Bonniers månadstidning*, November 1942 (with many thanks to Li Thies-Largergren).

Other literary sources too confirm that Sweden, despite the Paris Occupation, was allowed to trade with the French fashion houses, or as Walford puts it: 'Spain, Sweden and Switzerland, all neutral countries, continued to purchase French couture for the duration' (Walford 2008: 145). According to Veillon, by April 1943, the Occupying Nazi authorities proposed that the Parisian couture industry should be allowed to continue some of its foreign trade to Sweden, as well as to Spain, Italy and Portugal (all either Axis or neutral countries). This was permissible, as confirmed by Dr. Schilling (representing the German Occupying Administration), at his meeting with Jacques Deligny (Director of the Comité d'Organization de Habillement et du Travail des Etoffes) because by then the Paris salons were under Nazi control. Thus, as a consequence of the closure of Berlin couture studios, they were no longer in competition with Berlin salons.

As Veillon notes:

> The Germans therefore considered forming a 'continental consortium' in Berlin, a trading concern that would take over items of *haute couture* produced in France for resale overseas. An overall plan was to be drawn up for the Paris ateliers to be integrated into the scheme with a cloth quota fixed annually.
>
> (Veillon 2002: 96–97)

Paris was liberated before this scheme could be put into operation. In responding to Nazi demands, Lucien Lelong's intent, throughout the war, had been to build on this situation, which allowed Parisian couturiers to continue their business, even if in a limited manner.

Despite all this activity, the number of French original models exported to Sweden had clearly decreased and was replaced by other models from abroad, including from a few leading fashion houses in Switzerland, such as Gaby Jouval (*Bonniers månadstidning*, February 1944: 16) (see Chapter 10, Figures 10.8 and 10.10B). This situation was illustrated in the September 1940 issue of this journal, which noted 'This Autumn a Swedish fashion cocktail – with a little Italian and Swiss lace, and maybe – you should never give up hope! – even French' (Pia H. af S. 1940: 16). What I interpret from these fashion journals is that throughout the period of the German Occupation of Paris, there are clear indications that some original Paris model garments, as well as fashion plates and paper patterns, were present in Sweden, though considerably fewer than before the war.

Conclusion

The aim of this chapter has been to investigate the circulation of Paris couture fashion news in the Swedish press during the events of World War Two. Previous histories have placed a great deal of emphasis on the lack of fashion news from Paris as a consequence of the German occupation from 1940–1944. However, as my findings have shown, Swedish readers could follow the impact of the war situation on Paris haute couture in the French capital, month by month in their fashion press. In spite of strict Nazi press censorship regulations, they were able to follow the changes in Paris style and the development of the exaggerated Occupation fashions. Thus, in the Swedish case, the German censors seem to have tolerated the regular diffusion of this information to Stockholm, whilst from time to time interfering with its free circulation.

This chapter thus recognises the extensive circulation of seasonal information on the Parisian Occupation fashion style that was available in Swedish periodicals on a regular basis throughout the period of the Nazi Occupation of Paris. It has also bought into the light the arrival in Stockholm of some original Paris couture garments and even more couture paper patterns, even if by very circuitous routes from Vienna, Prague, Switzerland and America. These enabled the close copying of seasonal Paris couture style by Swedish couture salons, dressmakers and milliners through the war years.

The findings of this Swedish case bring new perspectives to the issue of the diffusion of the new couture style of Occupied Paris, from the viewpoint of a politically neutral country. They also raise issues about the international trade of Parisian haute couture during World War Two. What becomes clear from my analysis is that these findings redraw the fashion historical map of World War Two by including the story of a small country: Sweden.

References

Fashion Periodical Articles

(1940) 'Paris: just nu', *Bonniers månadstidning*, January.
(1943) 'Paris just nu', *Bonniers månadstidning*, July–August.
(1944) 'Typiskt franskt mode av idag', *Bonniers månadstidning*, March.
(1944) 'Berthen i olika varianter', *Bonniers månadstidning*, February.
Advertisement (1942) *Dagens Nyheter*, January 14.
Célie Brunius (1944) 'Paris skapar av intet', *Bonniers månadstidning*, January.
Elisabeth (1943) 'Modellerna skapas: en titt bakom kulisserna i några av våra större modehus', *Bonniers månadstidning*, October.
I. af S. (1940) 'Höstlöv och höstkläder: lockande för vår håg', *Bonniers månadstidning*, October.
Markström, I. (1941) 'En modekåsör försöker förstå', *Bonniers månadstidning*, April.
Jean de France (1942) 'Modebrev från Paris', *Bonniers månadstidning*, September.
Jean de France (1942) 'Höstmodet 1942', *Bonniers månadstidning*, October.
Jean de France (1942) 'Rik men ändå fattig', Bonniers månadstidning, November.
Rydeberg, M. (1940) 'Förenkling: är just nu det stora slagordet, som vi alla villigt lyssnar till' *Bonniers månadstidning*, January.
Rydeberg, M. (1944) 'Vi ser på kläder. . . i Stockholm', *Bonniers månadstidning*, October.
Rydeberg, M. (1944) 'Moderond i Stockholm', *Bonniers månadstidning*, April.
Marque (1940) 'Från modefronten mycket nytt', *Bonniers månadstidning*, January.
Marque (1941) 'Likt och olikt från Paris: och många modenyheter', *Bonniers månadstidning*, February.
Marque (1941) 'Nya svenska grepp på vårmodet', *Bonniers månadstidning*, April.
Pia H. af S. (1940) 'Höstmodet – hur blir det: kanske svenskt, kanske italienskt', *Bonniers månadstidning*, September.
Sabine (1942) 'Amforalinjen omhuldas alltjämt i Paris', *Bonniers månadstidning*, May.
Sabine (1942) 'Franska cykeldräkter', *Bonniers månadstidning*, July–August.

Books and Journals

Agius, C. (2006). *The Social Construction of Swedish Neutrality: Challenges to Swedish Identity and Sovereignty*. Manchester: Manchester University Press.
Boëthius, Maria-Pia. (1999 [1991]). *Heder och samvete*. Stockholm: Ordfront.

Carter, Ernestine. (1977). *The Changing World of Fashion: 1900 to the present.* London: Weidenfeld and Nicolson.

De Marly, Diana. (1980). *The History of Haute Couture: 1850-1950.* New York: Holmes & Meier.

Demornex, Jacqueline. (2008). *Lucien Lelong.* London and New York: Thames & Hudson.

Germain, Viola. (1988). Märthaskolan. *Kläder* (ed. Ingrid Bergman) Nordiska museet: Fataburen.

Johansson, Alf W. (1997). Neutrality and Modernity: The Second World War and Sweden's National Identity. *War Experience, Self Image and National Identity: the Second World War as Myth and History* (ed.) Stig Ekman and Nils Edling. Hedemora: Gidlund.

Kyaga, Ulrika. (2017). "Swedish Fashion 1930–1960: Rethinking the Swedish Textile and Clothing Industry". PhD diss., Stockholm University, Centre for Fashion Studies.

Laver, James. (2002). *Costume and Fashion: A Concise History.* 4. ed. London: Thames and Hudson.

Linder, Jan. (2002). *Andra världskriget och Sverige: Historia och mytbildning.* Luleå: Svenskt Militärhistoriskt Bibliotek.

Palmer, Alexandra (2001). *Couture & commerce: the transatlantic fashion trade in the 1950s.* Vancouver: UBC Press, in association with the Royal Ontario Museum. (2009). *Dior: A New Look, A New Enterprise (1947-1957).* London: V&A Publishing.

Seeling, Charlotte. (2001) *Mode: designernas århundrade: 1900-1999* (trans. Andrea Resch) Köln: Könemann.

Steele Valerie. (1998). *Paris Fashion: A Cultural History.* New York: Oxford University Press.

Taylor, Lou. (1995). The Work and Function of the Paris Couture Industry During the German Occupation of 1940-44. *Dress* Vol. 22. (1992) Paris Couture 1940-1944. *Chic Thrills: A Fashion Reader* (ed. Juliet Ash and Elizabeth Wilson) London: Pandora Press.

Veillon, Dominique. (2002). *Fashion under the Occupation* (transl. Miriam Kochan) Oxford and New York: Berg.

Walford, Jonathan. (2008). *Forties Fashion: From Siren Suits to the New Look.* London: Thames & Hudson.

Walker, John A. (1989). *Design History and the History of Design.* London: Pluto Press.

Wilson, Elizabeth & Taylor, Lou. (1991). *Through the looking glass: a history of dress from 1860 to the present day.* New York: Parkwest.

Åmark, Klas. (2011). *Att bo granne med ondskan: Sveriges förhållande till nazismen, Nazityskland och Förintelsen.* Stockholm: Bonnier.

PIGUET
et paillettes d'or.

Chapter 5
From Paris haute couture to New York: maintaining the French domination of fashion across the Atlantic, 1939–1946, through women's magazines

Sophie Kurkdjian

FIGURE 5.0
'Velasquez', Piguet evening dress, *l'Album de la Mode du Figaro*, 1943 (from De Holden Stone, 'French Fashion Survives the Nazis', *Art and Industry*, July 1945, vol. 39, no. 229: 3, London, with thanks to St. Peter's House Library, University of Brighton).

Introduction

Far from being neglected during the Occupation, the French fashion press became a defensive propaganda tool for the Parisian haute couture threatened by the war. A study of *French Vogue* (June 1920) and *Jardin des Modes* (October 1920), published by Lucien Vogel and Michel de Brunhoff, the two major fashion publishers before the war, who were brothers-in-law and who introduced an aesthetic revolution to the fashion press with the creation of *La Gazette du Bon Ton* in 1912, reveal the traumas the fashion press faced during this period (Kurkdjian, 2014).

The intent of this chapter is to show that it assumed an economic and highly symbolic dimension, which put it at the heart of tensions between the German Occupants and the occupied French. During the interwar period, *French Vogue*, read by the wealthy class, and *Jardin des Modes*, read by the social elite and the middle class, were two of the most important fashion magazines in France, showcases of the Parisian couturiers and fashion artists.

At the beginning of 1939, the American publisher Condé Nast, who ran the magazines (Seebohm 1982: 317, 390; 'Gloss Leader' 2016: 104) expected and relied on Vogel and Brunhoff to continue their publications with the same success as before. The Phoney War (*drôle de guerre*) period, which extended from the declaration of the war on 3 September 1939 to the invasion of Belgium and the Netherlands on 10 May 1940, showed that they did so. To prevent the Germans from seizing their magazines, Brunhoff, editor of *French Vogue*, ended their publication, before creating *l'Album de la Mode du Figaro* dedicated to the Parisian Couturiers. Vogel helped

FIGURE 5.1
German censorship of the French Press May 1944. (Getty 46390343.)

FIGURE 5.2
Michel de Brunhoff and the staff of French Vogue before the war, in 1937. (Getty 110260487.)

him until June 1940, when he left France. An enemy of Germany because of his anti-fascism, he fled to New York, where he worked for Condé Nast Publications, promoting the Parisian couture.

Saving *French Vogue* and *Jardin des Modes* in the Phoney War period

When the war started, Michel de Brunhoff set in order the business of US-owned French *Vogue* and *Jardin des Modes*, before leaving for Normandy (CNA.B2 F22). As for Lucien Vogel, due to his early anti-fascist and left-wing political beliefs – he was close to the Communists during the Spanish War in 1936 – he anticipated it would not be safe for him to remain in France (CNA.B11 F15). In the middle of September 1939, Brunhoff and Vogel had to make difficult decisions for themselves, their families and for their magazines. Most French people thought that the war would be long and Paul Reynaud, the Minister of Finance of the Front National asked everyone to resume their normal activities. Brunhoff met Lucien Lelong, the President of the *Chambre Syndicale de la Couture Parisienne*, to discuss measures to protect the couture. Lelong, as Brunhoff explained, 'is strongly determined to do all what he can, so that the couture resumes its activity immediately' (CNA.B2 F22). However fashion magazines, such as *Femina* and *Modes et Travaux*, announced at this time their intention to close – though in fact finally they did not (AN. F41 1429) – and their decision encouraged Nast to also temporarily suspend *French Vogue* and *Jardin des Modes*. Brunhoff confessed to Nast his distress:

> I do not need to tell you how shattered I am to see this office which has lost its collaborators and employees who were so deeply tied to your company and to you personally; and an office which did, I believe, do such a great job these ten last years.
>
> (CNA.B2 F22)

After a two-month interruption, as the Phoney War continued, Brunhoff and Vogel resumed contact with Nast on 21 November 1939, explaining that, despite the fact that material and psychological conditions changed daily, they wanted to resume publication of *French Vogue* and *Jardin* in the next few months. Considering them as colleagues and friends, Nast wrote to Brunhoff and Vogel to express his full confidence in their judgment (CNA.B11 F15), but at the same time, he confessed that it would be probably wiser to stop their publication permanently, especially as a bad decision could put in danger the future of all the Condé Nast publications. To persuade him to the contrary, Brunhoff and Vogel presented three reasons to prove that the fashion industry was about to re-establish business (CNA.B11 F15).

First, they had been told that Daniel Gorin, the Secretary of the *Chambre Syndicale de la Couture Parisienne*, had distributed circulars asking workers in the couture trade to report where they were in France in order to be able to recall them quickly when the couture houses re-opened. Secondly, Brunhoff and Vogel were informed that Gorin and leading couturiers had expressed their intention to gather in November 1939 in Biarritz to resume their activities, including Mme Lanvin, Jean Patou, Germaine Lecomte, Marcelle Dormoy and Madeleine de Rauch – Schiaparelli, Balenciaga, Molyneux and Alix had already even expressed by this time their intention to present a mid-season collection, 'made up with materials left from the last openings'. In reality, the *Chambre Syndicale* never sent the official order to join Biarritz, the couturiers decided to stay in Paris (Veillon 2015.32) and the collection of winter 1939–1940 was presented in Paris in November. According to Vogel and Brunhoff, these indications, despite the confusion, clearly highlighted that the couture, and the fashion press, would soon be able to resume their activities (CNA.B11 F15). Nast was convinced by their argument especially as, he admitted, another interruption would be fatal to the magazines and to his business in Europe (CNA.B11 F15). However, until the spring of 1940, although their resumption was decided by common agreement, the magazines appeared irregularly.

The issues of September and October 1939 of *Jardin* were not published. It resumed however from November 1939 to June 1940, appearing regularly in a new format better adapted to the times, presenting more daily fashion advice and more patterns for dressmakers. As for *French Vogue*, finally it ceased production in October 1939 and resumed only in March and April 1940. At the end of 1939, Vogel and Brunhoff were still trying to find a solution for the Nast magazines. Despite his personal difficulties, Vogel explained that he was acting 'just like a ship's captain of 20 years [who] strives to find, with his owner, calm waters again' (CNA.B11 F15).

At this time, while French *Vogue* was confronted with major difficulties, American *Vogue* continued to be published twice a month. As the situation became worse, the latter published more articles sent by European journalists on the situation in France and in the UK. As for *British Vogue*, after being temporarily suspended in October and November 1939, it decided to publish one issue per month instead of two. Deeply marked by World War One, when the magazine was created, the British magazine quickly grasped the impact of a new war on its publication. Aiming to repeat the attitude of resistance, courage and dignity it adopted during 1914–1918, *British Vogue*, as early as 1939, called upon women to help and support their menfolk (Packer 1989: 108). The three editions of *Vogue* thus faced three very different situations: *French Vogue*, following the Nazi Occupation of Paris in 1940, became a major economic and ideological battleground between the Occupants and the Occupied, while *British Vogue* continued to publish throughout the London Blitz despite paper shortages and a bomb-damaged office. At the other side of the Atlantic, the situation was different: before America entered the war in December 1941, and even during the following years, the American edition was in a way protected from the reality of the war.

By the beginning of 1940, little had changed in France and Brunhoff and Vogel still worried about the Parisian couture. As in 1914,[1] they wanted to guarantee the continuation of the French industry. Their main anxiety was over the American attitude regarding Paris. On 1 December 1939, a French *Vogue* editorial stated "Our office has never been closed . . . It was good, it was useful, that everyone knows, among our friends in America, that even in the anxiety of the first days of September, that the Parisian Couture still existed, and would not die." Foreign competition was a cause for concern for the Paris couture: early in 1940 the idea of developing a fashion industry that was independent from Paris design influence appeared in America.[2] To combat this threat, Vogel and Brunhoff knew that they had to ensure that American *Vogue* continued its promotion of the Parisian Couture as the magazine had always done. That is why Brunhoff indicated very early to Nast that despite the interruption of publication of French *Vogue*, he would soon provide the editorial board of American *Vogue* with news about fashion and life in Paris, such as its shuttered shops and women without hats, carrying their gas mask boxes. This sending of news to the American edition was a sign that French *Vogue* was still alive.

The break of the Exodus

Everything accelerated on 10 May 1940, as German forces moved into France after the Battle of Sedan, and magazines entered a 'stand-by' phase (TKP.B1F30). The Vogel family moved to *La Valade*, near Bordeaux, where the French crisis government of the Council and President Paul Reynaud also took refuge (TKP.B2 F3). Once Paris was occupied by the Nazis from 14 June 1940, Brunhoff decided with the American manager of French *Vogue*, Thomas Kernan, to close down the magazine entirely. Significantly, its offices and studio were immediately occupied by the Germans. For *Jardin*, the June issue was already underway and appeared on the 15th. After the Belgian capitulation and the evacuation of the British Army from Dunkirk, Brunhoff joined Vogel in Bordeaux on 16 June, the day Paul Reynaud resigned to be replaced by Marechal Pétain as Prime Minister of France, and then Head of the Vichy regime established on 10 July (CNA.B2 F22). Two days later, whilst General de Gaulle, who had flown to London, spoke to France by BBC radio, Lucien and his wife, Cosette Vogel, left Bordeaux to escape the Germans.

Vogel had been told that his name was on a list of people considered as 'greatly in danger' (TKP.B1F30). Before the war, Vogel, who was sympathetic to various Communist causes, not only published fashion magazines but also *Vu*, created in 1928, dedicated to photojournalism, where Vogel had expressed his interest in the USSR, his anti-fascism and his support for the Spanish Republicans in 1936.

During the interwar period, he continually used the magazine, and the others he supervised (the two leftist journals *Le Petit Journal* and *Marianne* in 1937, and *Messidor*, a trade-union newspaper, in 1938), as political platforms. The French

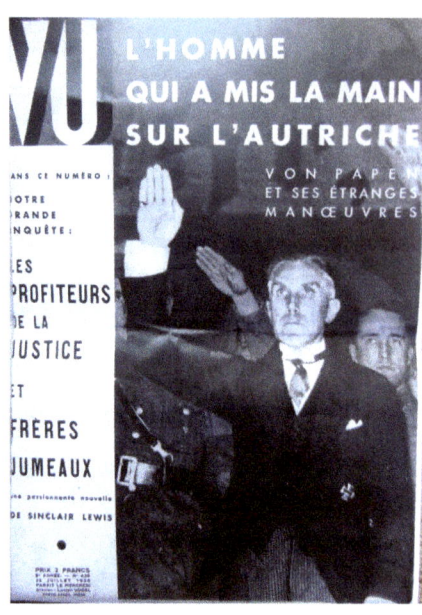

FIGURE 5.3
(left) Cover of *Vu*, no. 436, 22 July 1936 (with thanks to the Dress History Teaching Collection, University of Brighton). (above) Vogel's name on cover as Director of *Vu*, no. 436, 22 July 1936 (with thanks to the Dress History Teaching Collection, University of Brighton).

Intelligence Service from 1930–1939 suspected that Vogel was working as a Soviet undercover agent with the aim of infiltrating the French press through publishing magazines articles that favoured the Communist party and its interventions in French politics, and for example, in the Spanish Civil War in 1936. The Intelligence Service files offer no proof that Vogel ever was a Soviet agent, though they clarify that he did receive money from the Soviet Union for his publication *Vu* and had Communist friends and work relations. His pro-Communist and Soviet Union articles for this magazine played a key role in his exile to New York in 1940, because the Occupying Nazis considered Vogel an influential and dangerous enemy.

Had he stayed in France, his life would have been threatened (AMAE série Z Europe, URSS 948).[3] The political involvement of his daughter, Marie-Claude (a member of the Communist Party,[4] who married the leading Communist politician and journalist Paul Vaillant-Couturier in 1937), also strengthened suspicions against Lucien Vogel. In June 1940, Vogel and his wife therefore decided to leave France and join Condé Nast Publications in America. The Vogels reached Portugal around 23 June 1940, arriving in New York on 12 September 1940. As a consequence of this move, Lucien Vogel lost his French citizenship. A decree of the 23 July 1940 removed French citizenship from those to whom it had been granted up to 1927, and to all people who resisted the German Occupation and to those who left France in May and June 1940,[5] as Vogel had done. From this period onwards, Brunhoff and Vogel's futures differ, though both pursued the same basic objective: to save the future of French *Vogue* and of *Jardin*, and defend France and Parisian fashion.

FIGURE 5.4 Photo of Lucien Vogel and his daughter, 1931. (Getty 541041423.)

The war represented for both of them a period of physical, moral and professional trauma: Vogel was forced to leave France without his three children[6] and a country where he had a prominent position in the press, society and fashion worlds. On the 29 June 1940, Vogel confessed to Yoxall 'everything that happened since these last weeks is like a nightmare' (TKP.B1F30). During the war, he suffered from this exile, from the distance from his family, friends and colleagues, fearing never being able to regain his citizenship after the war. As for Michel de Brunhoff, he stayed in Paris, but, as will be explained, refused to obey Nazi regulations. Wartime was thus a period of deep personal, moral and material traumas, especially when, at the end of the war in June 1944, his son, Pascal de Brunhoff, aged 21, a Resistant, was shot by the Nazis. Both de Brunhoff and Vogel thus sacrificed their way of life, their careers and their families to struggle against the Nazis.

During the war, despite the geographical distance, Vogel, Brunhoff, Nast and Edna Woolman Chase (overall international Vogue editor based in New York) and Harry Yoxall, who had been colleagues and friends since the twenties, kept up communications, demonstrating their strong commitment to Condé Nast Publications and to the united family formed by these three editorial boards. On 15 June 1940, Brunhoff and Vogel sent a message to the American board detailing the defeat and the Exodus, and how they felt about what they were witnessing – the end of an era. On the 15 October 1940, American *Vogue* asked 'There are 3 *Vogues*: an American one, a French one and a British one, but what about French *Vogue*? Several of our readers have raised this question. . . . Are there still three *Vogues*?' ('What About French *Vogue*?' 1940). Thereafter, Iva Patcévitch of American *Vogue* and Yoxall regularly exchanged letters about the situation of French *Vogue*, but also others too about the personal situations of Brunhoff and of Vogel (Yoxall 1966: 269).

French Vogue and Jardin des Modes under Nazi censorship regulations

Immediately after invading France, the Germans seized the French press, whose control became both an economic and a deeply ideological issue (Eveno 2009: 23). Until 1942, the French press was subjected to two different sets of censorship depending on whether publication was in the Occupied Zone under the direct authority of the Nazi military command in France (except for the regions North and Pas-de-Calais attached to the military command in Belgium), or in the Free Zone in the south, with its capital at Vichy (Bellanger 1972–1976: 10). In the Occupied Zone, the German authorities took total control of the press. With this control as part of their general economic exploitation of the zone, the Germans determined to manipulate the popular spirit as well as the French press companies from which they hoped to earn significant income.

At the end of May 1940, two weeks after the Occupation of Paris, the Germans announced a decree suspending publication of all journals, decreeing that all printed material had to be submitted to the Nazi imposed censorship system run by the *Propaganda-Abteilung*, Berlin, created on 18 July 1940 and directed by Joseph Goebbels. In Paris, all submissions passed through its Paris Kommandantur, Major (later Lt. Colonel) Heinz Schmidtke. This decree was strongly enforced through extreme levels of Nazi propaganda placed throughout the world of press, books and radio, determining which journals could or could not be published, whilst overseeing the control of vital paper stocks and their distribution (Dunan 1951: 19–32).

Because no clear directive was given in May 1940 by the French government to the Parisian journals, there was no united action. The dilemma for the owners and journalists was whether to publish again or close down for good (Martin 2005: 254, 103). Amongst the fashion press, as in the daily press, some journalists thought of withdrawing to Lyon, the economic capital of the Free Zone from 1940–1942, especially those in Bordeaux, where the French government had taken refuge on 14 June. Each editorial board reacted in its own way. After the Armistice on 22 June 1940, two choices can be observed (Constantini 1963: 320, 61). Some journals shut down conclusively; amongst these quite a few disappeared even before the debacle, such as *Votre Bonheur* and *Femina*, while others were published irregularly from September 1939 to June 1940, before finally closing permanently, including *Journal de France*, French *Vogue* and *Jardin des Modes*. At the same time, other journals reappeared in Paris after only a short interruption, submitting themselves to the German censorship regulations, such as *Modes et Travaux* and *l'Art et la Mode*. Others withdrew to the South to be published again in Lyon, such as *Marie-Claire* (Auclair 1978: 429) and *La Femme Chic*.

The German invasion called into question the decision taken by Vogel and Brunhoff at the end of 1939. The publication of the French *Vogue* and *Jardin des Modes* was now no longer a financial matter, but depended directly upon German controls. In the Occupied Zone, in order to use existing French journals as propaganda tools, the German authorities organized a system of authorization prior to publication (Eveno 2009: 26) which, from July 1940, Brunhoff and Vogel were obliged to obtain. To prepare their submission and to get a precise insight of the couture's situation after the Occupation, Kernan, who was American and publisher of French *Vogue*, went to Paris on 21 July 1940.[7] By 26 July 1940, back in Bordeaux, where the leading couturiers had regrouped, he had become convinced that *Jardin* should resume publication because during his stay in Paris, he noticed that the magazine's offices were still 'safe and sound', that Brunhoff's secretary had already opened the *Jardin des Modes* paper patterns' shop to avoid its confiscation by the Germans[8] and that French women came daily to the *Jardin*'s offices to beg for their magazine.[9] Kernan's opinion about French *Vogue* however, was not the same. He reported that 'French *Vogue* will do nothing, unless the couture does mid-season collections for the German buyers.'[10]

Agreeing with these views, Brunhoff decided to develop a future for *Jardin*, bearing in mind that, given the economic situation, women would look for practical ideas to make their own dresses. *Jardin*, where 'each line, each page would be a help for the readers',[11] could therefore become a source of information and support for them. This insistence on the practical dimension of fashion reflected closely the real world of French fashion during the Occupation, a time of improvisation where the rationing 'System D' was the main recourse of women (Veillon 2014: 107). Since January 1940, French people had suffered shortages of bread, sugar, milk and more, and were obliged to use rationing tickets to obtain food from September 1940. Further ration cards were established to deal with clothing and fabric shortages, marking the beginning of the French rationing system (Veillon 2014: 108). None of this met the reality of women's needs, so they tried to circumvent shortages by developing their inventiveness. Thanks to advice from the magazines they recycled old dresses, used their husband's clothes and so on.

At the beginning of August 1940, Brunhoff returned to Paris from Bordeaux and to the raided offices of French *Vogue*, where the doors and safe had been forced open by the Germans, who also requisitioned the studio. Parts of *Jardin*'s offices had also been sequestered.[12] Summoned by the Propaganda-Staffel, Brunhoff and Kernan were informed that French *Vogue* and *Jardin* were among the magazines the Germans wanted to see published again but that their publication would be within a German controlled press group. The Propaganda-Abteilung had established a buy-back policy through its business man, Dr. Gerhard Hibbelen (Dioudonnat 1981: 309), who bought most of the stocks of French publishing houses, including those of fifty magazines (Dunan 1951: 19–32). At first, Brunhoff played for time, giving evasive answers to the Germans (De Holden Stone 1945: 8), realising that he must provide for his employees needs and prevent the Germans from seizing the magazines in order to promote German fashion to the detriment of the French fashion industry.

The political and economic dimension of fashion

During the Occupation, fashion became a key economic and cultural battleground. Economic, because the Germans intended to maintain their stranglehold on French production, and cultural, because French hegemony in the world of couture was being challenged. Alongside growing American fashion competition, France had also to fight direct German interference. In July 1940, the Occupying authorities, for example, seized documents at the *Chambre Syndicale de la Couture Parisienne* dealing with the creation and export of French models. Lucien Lelong, who became the intermediary between the Germans and the Parisian couture, was the first to be informed of German intentions that 'Parisian haute couture will be integrated in a German structure whose head offices will be in Berlin and Vienna' (AN.C5 Z6) and that 'the French couture salons will make available their workforce and their fashion designers to Vienna or Berlin' (Veillon 2014: 162). It is in this context of the planned transference of the French couture to Berlin – something that Lelong categorically opposed and that the Germans finally abandoned – that the Germans took over French fashion magazines. In seizing them, they wanted to assert the supremacy of German fashion on the international stage.

Another action set in place by the Occupants was to create their own imitations of French magazines. *Pour Elle*, published on 14 August 1940, looked like *Marie-Claire*, while *Notre Coeur*, created on 13 September 1940, followed the format of *Confidences*, created by Paul Winckler in 1938, who, some months before, had refused to transfer 60 per cent of his capital-stock to the Germans.[13] Stakes were therefore huge for Brunhoff and Kernan (Kernan 1944: 319, 31) who quickly understood that, beyond the issue of the transfer of capital stocks, they were also being obliged to demonstrate to the Nazi authorities that neither journalists nor Nast's financial capital and professional relationships were of Jewish origin (Chase 1954: 381, 323). Without accepting German requirements, Brunhoff submitted the authorization application for both magazines on 21 August 1940.[14] Each application took the form of a documentary file containing the name of the owner, date of creation, size of print run, description of functioning principles and also details about Brunhoff, whose life and career are detailed from his birth.

On 21 October 1940, the German response was that no authorization would be forthcoming for either magazine[15] and that *Jardin* and French *Vogue* would no longer have a place in France. Thereafter, it only remained for Brunhoff to liquidate the assets, attend to liabilities, sell the remaining paper to obtain some cash and to remove the business ledgers. In December, Brunhoff and Kernan were approached by several French intermediaries such as Eugène Schueller,[16] director of *Votre Beauté* and owner since 1909 of the cosmetic company *L'Oréal*, who proposed to help them to obtain the authorization to republish the magazines, explaining that they had not contacted the correct person and advising them that, provided they collaborated, 'everything could be resolved'.[17] Whist declining these proposals, Brunhoff realized that money could solve problems.[18] After placing French *Vogue* under the *Tribunal du Commerce*'s protection to prevent its seizing by the Germans,[19] Brunhoff sought to find a way to work without being accountable to the Germans.[20] In 1941, he therefore started two activities linked to fashion: the development of the existing pattern department of *Jardin* and the creation of a new elite fashion album to replace French *Vogue*.

Working without having to say 'please' to the Germans

Before the war, *Jardin* had directly sold fashion textiles and patterns to its readers for home dressmaking and, in 1940, it still had stocks of wool and silk. A first German decree on 9 July 1940 required that all textile stocks be declared; another on 6 August 1940 imposed the same rule on stocks of 'all textiles, leather and animals skin' (Veillon 2014: 133). The Kehrl Plan (see Chapter 2) further controlled French access to their own textiles, especially wool. All of this jeopardized Brunhoff's plans for *Jardin* to sell fabric alongside dress patterns for home dressmaking. He managed, despite this however, to complete this project. Firstly, he presented a falsified inventory to the Occupation authorities, and, as early as March 1941, started to build up an unofficial stock of textiles. Then, in February 1942, he bought on the black market his first stock of paper for the *Jardin* fashion patterns and in this way managed to generate additional turnover. Despite the difficulties of finding enough paper, the sale of patterns was successful since, at the Liberation, *Jardin* in its 1945–1946 edition declared 'as you know, the *Jardin des Modes* patterns were sold without interruption during these long years, when [the magazine] . . . could not be published. Their everlasting success proved to us the affection of our faithful readers' (*Jardin des Modes*, June 1945).

In spite of this successful activity, daily life remained difficult. In April 1941, Cosette Vogel was warned by her daughter that Michel de Brunhoff, who had already lost eleven kilograms, was in 'a terrible morale state of mind, unable to take decisions'[21] and by September 1941, Brunhoff himself admitted that he was suffering from his Parisian solitude and his idleness.[22] So, when the *Chambre Syndicale* asked Brunhoff to publish a new fashion magazine as a supplement to the daily *Le Figaro*, he accepted. In 1942, he thus became the editor in chief of *l'Album de la Mode du Figaro*,[23] whose aim was to promote elite French fashion abroad. As his niece wrote in September 1942, 'Michel is doing better, even morally. He regained his vivacity thanks to the work he does for *Le Figaro*: a fashion catalog that he prints in Monte-Carlo. He is happy, he works with some of his more loyal colleagues: Solange d'Ayen, Monique de Sereville.'[24]

Looking for a neutral location free from Nazi censorship for the magazine, *Le Figaro* chose neutral Monte-Carlo and the *Editions Publicitaires* of Monaco. The magazine easily received publication authorization in Monte Carlo and even an endowment of paper and thus could publish its first issue in December 1942. Sold at seventy-five francs, the issue presented an illustration by Benito on the cover and articles such as '*Aux âmes sensibles*' (for sensitive souls), '*Le poids des choses légères*' (the weight of slight things) and others of a lighter tone such as '*Des robes du soir*' (evening dresses) and '*Un portfolio couture*' (a couture portfolio). In contrast to other fashion magazines suffering from paper restrictions, *l'Album* represented an exception, achieved 'practically single-handedly by Michel de Brunhoff' (De Holden Stone 1945: 7). The luxury magazine was, however, not circulated in the Occupied Zone (or illegally) and, from the current state of documentation, it is also hard to say how much it circulated in the Southern Zone. In order to publish the first issue, Brunhoff was helped by former colleagues, including Germaine Beaumont as fashion director, famous and well-established fashion illustrators Pierre Mourgue, Bernard Blossac and Pierre Pagès and the well-known writers and journalists Paul Valéry and Georges Duhamel. The second issue was published during the summer of 1943, whilst the other issues, no longer published by Brunhoff but by Louis Ferrand, were produced in October 1943, May 1944 and January 1945.

Through the development of this professionally produced and elegant magazine, Brunhoff gained a reputation as an ardent defender of Parisian couture. An artistic director of English *Vogue*, De Holden Stone even compared the role played by Brunhoff with that of Lelong in his struggle to protect haute couture against the German authorities. According to De Holden Stone, both men played similar roles, playing 'a subtle game of give and take' (1945: 10) with the Nazis. Brunhoff built up this reputation because of the risks he undertook in printing the magazine. Indeed, he went so far as to collect the texts and drawings from Paris, himself crossing the Demarcation Line between the Occupied and Free Zones to reach Monte Carlo, where the issue was typeset and printed. Lelong was aware of the importance of publishing such a magazine since it was he who sponsored Brunhoff in his application to the Nazi authorities to obtain both an identity card and an *ausweiss*, to enable his travel. These round trips of Brunhoff were closely supervised by the Nazis who remarked on the 17 December 1942 'De Brunhoff came to the non-occupied zone to take care of the publication of a fashion album published by the EDP in Monaco . . . Lucien Lelong was the intermediary between the German authorities and Michel de Brunhoff.'[25]

In 1945, Brunhoff explained

> after the horrible choice of defeat . . . there was no honourable way of publishing a magazine under the Germans; there was no honourable way without compromise and collaboration . . . Finally I found a way of publishing Fashion Albums without having to say *please* to the Germans. It was very complicated: it jumped borders and involved quite a lot of risk – but it was exciting.
>
> (De Holden Stone 1945:8)

While the publication of such a magazine, featuring Paris fashion, was considered by Brunhoff as an act of resistance, the British press did not share this opinion. The popular, left-wing *Picture Post* on 1 May 1943 described, for example, the fashions shown in *l'Album de la Mode du Figaro* as 'clothes for the 2,000 wealthy collaborators . . . what the smart collaborators wear' and as 'fashion for traitors', giving in particular the example of a Robert Piguet dress, influenced by Velasquez.

FIGURE 5.5
'Velasquez' Piguet evening dress, *l'Album de la Mode du Figaro*, 1943 (from De Holden Stone, 'French Fashion Survives the Nazis', *Art and Industry*, July 1945, vol .39, no. 229.3, London, with thanks to St. Peter's House Library, University of Brighton).

The judgement was harsh. British journalists were not aware of Brunhoff's intentions, nor the personal risks he was taking. Writing in 1945 after the Liberation, De Holden Stone remembered that

> A short time ago, a fashion magazine came into this office... It was packed with beautiful drawings of magnificent clothes. It showed a wealth and luxury which is the last thing one associates with Paris in war. We wanted to find out more about these fashions. Perhaps the whole magazine was propaganda?
>
> (1945: 10)

This accusation was, as this text has shown, unjustified, because *l'Album* had been published by Michel de Brunhoff outside Nazi press control and especially because de Brunhoff had expressed his clear refusal to collaborate with the Nazis. This story, however, showed that there was both widespread suspicion abroad surrounding Paris couture and related fashion journals and that there were no direct contacts through which to explain the true reality of publication until after the Liberation of Paris. While Brunhoff worked in the fashion press, Vogel started to do the same in the USA, where the objective was the same: defending Parisian couture.

Defending Parisian fashion in New York against accusations of collaboration

During his exile in New York, Lucien Vogel was forced to reinvent his life since he had no job and no responsibilities anymore. Over four years, his daily life became completely different from his previous life in Paris, where he was a famous publisher, left-wing activist and friend of leading journalists, artists, photographers, couturiers and politicians – a man of national standing – whose activities were numerous and diverse. In New York, his main objective was to earn money to live with his family. His wife, Cosette Vogel, was also obliged to work, first by publishing fashion design albums and secondly, by working for Simplicity Patterns, where she was in charge of the creation of patterns books.

For his part, Vogel used his presence on American soil between September 1940 and November 1944 to defend and promote Parisian couture and through his energetic efforts especially to make Americans understand that French couture was not synonymous with the enemy, nor with the collaborating Vichy regime of so-called Free France and that supporting French fashion was not synonymous with supporting the collaboration policy of Pétain. For Vogel, this point was essential: he believed that the future of Paris as a fashion centre depended on this clarification and reality proved he was right to be worried. When some information about the couture reached the world outside France, it indeed sometimes provoked scandal as already shown here with the case of reaction of *Picture Post* in London in May 1943.

Remaining connected to the fashion field during his exile, Vogel had several occasions to evaluate the American opinion about French couture. For example, he attended a lecture by Elsa Schiaparelli, who was in New York during the war from 23 June 1940 and who gave talks to convince her American friends and the US public of the legitimacy of the Parisian couture's pragmatic choice to stay open. Living in the USA and actively promoting and selling her work, as an Italian from an Axis regime, she could, however, be categorized as an enemy alien.

After attending one of her lectures (Schiaparelli 1954: 256; 'Paris Still Centre of Fashion' 1940), Vogel wrote to Brunhoff that Schiaparelli had upset many American people by being provocative when, in answering a question from an American journalist 'do you think that our designs can develop themselves and create an American fashion?' she replied 'How can you believe that we can develop

FIGURE 5.6
Evening jacket, House of Schiaparelli, Paris, *Modes et Travaux*, December 1941 (with thanks to the Dress History Teaching Collection, University of Brighton).

what doesn't exist; by adding 0 to 0, it always makes 0.'[26] For Vogel, whilst such a speech could have had a positive impact for French couture in the USA, the fact that Schiaparelli herself was perceived in the USA as representing the Vichy regime meant that her comments were not well-received. Words were no longer powerful enough to 'save' the reputation of the French couture against the Americans. Vogel explained:

> If we really want to have an impact on American opinion, at a time similar to the position of the French couture in 1914 when America thought it could replace Paris couture, we have to deal with the fact that all promotion for it now in the USA, is seen as a form of approval of collaboration.[27]

For Vogel, Paris couture needed far more convincing spokespersons – couturiers and journalists – if it was to establish a clear separation between the worlds of couture and the politics of Vichy France in American popular opinion.

Vogel pursued this policy during spring 1941, after being informed about a serious crisis between American *Vogue* and French *Vogue*. On 20 January 1941, eleven months before the USA joined in the war, Solange d'Ayen, the pre-war fashion director of French *Vogue*, who planned to go to New York in order to help publish Parisian models in American *Vogue*, was told that Edna Chase, editor-in-chief of *Vogue*, did not want to include images of French models in American *Vogue* any more. D'Ayen cancelled her trip but wrote to Vogel that they must not yield to pressure to exclude Parisian couture from the American press.[28] This message did not fall on deaf ears and Vogel decided to promote Paris fashion in American *Vogue* from spring 1941 on. He asked his family in France to send him by postal service information – texts and illustrations from the French press about the new fashions, 'details on what is going on in France . . . and if it is a good article, we can try to place it the American press.'[29] His daughter wrote to him to find out if 'articles on the practicalities of [French] life' would be of interest, such as 'how are people living without money and without fabric' or 'How do they replace silk stockings' [. . .] or social gossip about Kostio de War who 'is in Cannes: would photographs and articles about her be interesting.'[30]

Simultaneously, he confessed that it was 'impossible to publish an article which highlighted the names of French couturiers at this moment here.'[31] This was because American magazines were instead promoting American designers because Paris couturiers could not provide new collections of garments for sale to the USA from the end of July 1940, once Paris was occupied. The German Occupiers, intending to move the haute couture from Paris to Berlin, controlled all exports (see Chapter 2). Because Parisian couturiers were associated with the enemy Vichy regime, presenting their collections in the USA would also appear to offer approval of the puppet government of Pétain. This opinion was not just Vogel's impression, but was a political opinion shared by Condé Nast Publications. Vogel thus requested that this documentation, described as 'fashion information for *Vogue* and sketches', was to be sent to his personal home in New York and not to the Condé Nast Publications headquarters where it could have been deliberately put aside by the American editorial board.[32]

In March 1941, Vogel also sent an explanatory report to Edna Chase entitled 'Attitude of American Couturiers and Manufacturers', explaining, 'The attitude taken during this war, as in 1914 by the American couturiers and manufacturers toward Parisian couture interests me greatly, as you know. I understand perfectly that *Vogue* is again in a critical position. This attitude also disturbs me.' Using bullet points, Vogel indicated firstly, that in the seven months of war since the German invasion of France the 'creative spirit of the Parisian Couturiers' had not been destroyed; secondly, that the few months of confusion from July 1940 to February 1941 could not have been sufficient 'to allow the American dressmakers and manufacturers to create a New York fashion, entirely uninfluenced by the creations of Parisian designers'. At the same time, his pragmatism made Vogel understand that, despite the logic of this approach, *Vogue* would find it difficult not 'to submit to pressure brought by the Seventh Avenue advertisers' by denying prominence to 'all the attempts made by American dressmakers and manufacturers to create new fashions'.

Vogel made several suggestions to Nast over what measures *Vogue* should take to resolve this problem. According to Vogel it was impossible for *Vogue* not to inform its readers of what Parisian couturiers were doing under the Occupation and how harsh the living conditions were there. *Vogue*, needed to 'show the models created by the Paris designers for women whose apartments are unheated this winter'. In reproducing French models in *Vogue* and in emphasizing that they had been sketched in Paris, *Vogue* would 'prove the resistance of the French couturiers to German domination and their refusal to be transferred to Berlin even though the manufacturing conditions were more advantageous'.[33]

From fashion to political activities

At the same time, Vogel took advantage of his presence in the USA to continue his reflection on the international world of fashion press. Aiming to use the Condé Nast publications as an experimental laboratory, he proposed to Nast that he should become his technical and editorial adviser.[34] Vogel's work consisted firstly in the revision of *Glamour*, as co-publisher of the magazine with Walter Mass and Elizabeth Penrose,[35] as early as 27 May 1941 (Sumner 2010: 242, 93).[36]

Secondly, Vogel's work consisted in the study of new photographic possibilities for the fashion press,[37] writing reports on 'Colour Photography', on 'Artists and Photographers' and 'The Photographers of the Studio'.[38] However, Vogel ceased to write his *Vogue* reports when Condé Nast died in September 1942. Nast's death marked the end of an era for Condé Nast Publications and constituted a break in

FIGURE 5.7
Cover of *Glamour* USA, Christmas 1943. (Getty 531289852.)

collaboration between the New York editorial board and the French one, started in 1920. Iva Patcévitch became the new president of Condé Nast Publications.

After the loss of Nast as his patron, Vogel turned to active political involvement through the France Forever Association. This American association, founded on the 26 September 1940, united everyone who refused to accept the German domination in France and who wanted to fight for the Allied victory.[39] It promoted the actions and policies of General de Gaulle, leader of the Free French Forces, based in London. As ex-editor of *Vu* and member of the executive committee of the Association, Vogel was in particular in charge of the association's magazine, *Free World*, which he helped to create. Responsible for the French version[40] as soon as October 1941, Vogel wrote articles but also took care of the technical aspects of the magazine's layout.

Vogel's involvement can be explained by two issues: not only had he lost the friendship and 'protection' of Condé Nast and thus at the same time, the work Nast offered him, but Vogel also wanted to actively take part in the French Resistance movement. His daughter Marie-Claude Vaillant-Couturier had been arrested on 9 February 1942. Incarcerated in the Prison de la Santé on 23 March, then at the Fort de Romainville on 24 August 1942, she was deported to Auschwitz on 24 January 1943,[41] before being moved to Ravensbrück on 2 August 1944. Vogel's deep involvement in this journal was for him one way to actively resist Nazi fascism. His daughter survived and came back in Paris in November 1944, where she found her father. The period of exile marked both for Vogel and Brunhoff a period of suffering, separated as they were from their families and their traumatised country.

Conclusion

During the war, Vogel and Brunhoff were both fully committed to protecting and promoting French haute couture, as they both had done since the beginning of their careers. Their magazines, as did fashion itself, became political and cultural spaces trapped within the economic and cultural struggles against the Nazis. This text has shown that the hegemony of French couture was challenged not only by the Occupying Germans, but also by the Americans and British. Unlike World War One, this threat however continued after 1945 when the growing self-confidence of the American fashion industry was confirmed, as was clear in the pages of magazines such as *Glamour*.

Unlike the period of World War One, the political dimension of World War Two and of the Nazi Occupation of France placed intense pressure on Vogel and Brunhoff's shoulders. Brunhoff, dependent on an American company but staying in France, struggled against Nazi censorship rules. Both risked their lives in their political opposition to the Occupying Nazi regime. Brunhoff said 'no' to Nazi publication and censorship regulations, deciding to risk crossing back and forth across the Demarcation Line to reach Monte Carlo, whilst Vogel, whose life as a well-known anti-Fascist was threatened from the moment of the Nazi Occupation of France, was forced to flee France before finally working for the France Libre organisation in New York. Neither Brunhoff nor Vogel knew if they would find their place back in post-war France (and in Vogel's case, his citizenship) or re-establish their reputations and their high positions in the fashion press and fashion world at the moment of Liberation.

Finally, Vogel, back in Paris in November 1944, and Brunhoff, (broken-hearted after the Nazi murder of his son, Pascal) decided to resume their work promoting Parisian fashion. Despite the difficulties, especially in finding paper to print on, they aimed to quickly republish *Jardin des Modes* and French *Vogue* to show to the world through the pages of these magazines that French couture still existed. They determined too to re-establish their own careers in the commercial French magazine market, a place that was challenged by a new modern type of magazine which emerged, symbolized by *ELLE*, created in November 1945 by Helène Lazareff. The first issue of French *Vogue* was entitled *Album de la Libération*, published in January 1945, with a cover by Christian Bérard in blue, white and red, and presented a galleon splitting the sea. It was a great success and much approved by fashion and press professionals. 'The Couture, the Government are delighted', wrote Vogel. Alluding directly to the difficult personal situation of Brunhoff and the continuing difficult economic condition of the press, he added that this success represented for Brunhoff and himself 'a personal success of the highest order'.[42]

Brunhoff, in particular, took part in the *Théâtre de la Mode*. Organized after the Liberation by the *'Entraide Française'* and the haute couture, the project took the form of an exhibition of eighty dolls dressed by the French Couturiers (Grès, Lelong, Balenciaga and Balmain, among others), and presented in a miniaturized decor. The exhibition, first shown in Paris at the Pavillon de Marsan in May of 1945, was displayed all around the world to convince everyone, and especially Americans, that Parisian haute couture was still functioning and had lost nothing of its prestige and know-how, despite the Occupation and austerity.

To thank Brunhoff for his courage and his efforts to keep the reputation of French *Vogue* and *Jardin des Modes* intact during the war, Iva Patcévitch, the new director of Condé Nast Publications, offered Brunhoff the position of director of French *Vogue* in 1946. The New York company was very grateful for the commitment of Brunhoff and Vogel to French *Vogue* and *Jardin des Modes*, which dated back to 1920. Their commitment to the promotion of haute couture was also valued by the French state, which presented Brunhoff in 1947 with the title of Chevalier de la Légion d'Honneur.

This honour recognized the long career of Brunhoff, who 'dedicated his life to the publishing and the dissemination of luxurious fashion albums, whose quality helped the development, the prestige and the influence of the French taste', who managed during 'the Occupation, despite the determination of the Occupants, to avoid the publication of *Vogue* under Nazi control and to protect *l'Album de la Mode du Figaro* from the intrusion of the Germans.'[43]

FIGURE 5.8
Paris *Vogue* staff, Brunhoff, Woolman-Chase and four others, 1950. (Getty 533413038.)

References

Archive de la Bibliothèque Forney (ABF), Paris.
Archives du Ministère des Affaires étrangères, série Z Europe (AMAE), Paris.
Archives Nationales (AN), Paris.
Auclair, M. (1978) *Mémoires à deux voix*, Paris: France Loisirs. Condé Nast Archives (CNA), New York.
Bellanger, C. (1972–1976) *Histoire générale de la presse*, tome 4, Paris: PUF.
Brunhoff M., Archives: Private.
Constantini, C. (1980) *La Presse féminine des Années d'Occupation*, Paris: Paris II, 1980.
Dioudonnat, P-M. (1981) *L'Argent nazi à la conquête de la presse française, 1940–1944*, Paris: Jean Picollec.
Dunan, E. (1951) 'La Propaganda-Abteilung de France : tâche et organisation,' *Revue d'histoire de la deuxième guerre mondiale*, no. 4, October.
Eveno, P. (2009) 'Entreprises et marchés de la presse sous l'Occupation,' in *Culture et médias sous l'Occupation : des entreprises dans la France de Vichy*, Paris: Éd. du CTHS.
'French women suffer horrors in Silesia Camp. (1943) *New York Herald Tribune*, 24 August.
'Huge "Fashion Futures" Show Opens Tonight in Effort to Make City World Style Center'. (1941) *The New York Times*, 8 January.
De Holden Stone. (1945) 'French Fashion Survives the Nazis', *Art and Industry*, vol. 39 no. 229: 1–5.
'Gloss Leader'. (2016) *British Vogue*, June: 104.
Kernan, K. (1994) *Horloge de Paris, heure de Berlin,* Montréal: Ed de l'Arbre.

Kurkdjian, S. (2014) *Lucien Vogel et Michel de Brunhoff, parcours croisés de deux éditeurs de presse illustrée au XXe siècle*, Paris: Ed. Varenne.

Kurkdjian, S. 2013. 'Lucien Vogel et Michel de Brunhoff : parcours croisés de deux éditeurs de presse illustrée au XXe siècle,' École doctorale d'Histoire de l'Université Paris 1 Panthéon-Sorbonne (Paris).

Loyer, E. (2005) *Paris à New York, Intellectuels et artistes français en exil, 1940–1947*, Paris: Grasset and Fasquelle.

Martin, L. (2005) *La presse écrite en France au XXe siècle,* Paris: Librairie Générale Française.

Packer, W. (1989) *The Art of Vogue covers, 1909–1940*, New York: Bonanza Books.

'Paris Still Held Center of Fashion'. (1940) *The New York Times*, 25 September.

Picture Post (1943) 'Clothes for Wealthy Collaborators', 7 August, vol. 20 no. 11: 10–11.

Schiaparelli, E. (1954) *Shocking*, Paris: Denoist.

Seebohm, C. (1982) *The Man Who Was Vogue, the Life and the Times of Condé Nast*, London: Weidenfeld and Nicolson.

Sullerot, E. (1963) *La presse féminine*, Besançon: Armand Colin.

Sumner, D. E. (2010) *The Magazine Century: American Magazines Since 1900*, New York: Peter Lang.

'The Fashion Capital Moves Across Seas', (1940) *The New York Times*, 18 August.

Thomas Kernan Papers (TKP), Georgetown: Georgetown University Library, Washington.

Veillon, D. (2014) *La Mode sous l'Occupation*, Paris: Payot.

Ginsburger-Vogel, T. Private Archives.

'What About *French Vogue*?' (1940) American *Vogue*, 15 October.

Woolman Chase, E. W. (1954) *Always in Vogue*, New York: Doubleday.

Yoxhall, H. (1966) *A Fashion of Life*, London: Heineman.

Endnotes

1. Vogel published *The Style Parisien* in 1915 and *The Elegances parisiennes* in 1916 to defend the couturiers' interests.
2. 'The Fashion Capital Moves Across Seas', 1940; 'Huge "Fashion Futures" Show Opens Tonight', 1941.
3. See Kurkdjian, S. (2014) *Lucien Vogel et Michel de Brunhoff, parcours croisés de deux éditeurs de presse illustrée au XXe siècle*, Paris: Fondation Varenne, Part II, chapter 4, p. 365.
4. After the signing of Nazi-Soviet non-agression pact on 23 August 1939, the French Communist party was dissolved by the socialist French government on 26 September 1939 and the French Communist press closed down, though *l'Humanité* continued illegal publication. On 9 April 1940, article 76 of the new *Decree Sérol*, which stated that anyone guilty of 'demoralizing' the French army and nation became liable to the death penalty, aimed more particularly at the French communist supporters of this pact. Marie-Claude consequently thereafter operated in secrecy. (*Amis de la Fondation pour la Mémoire de la Déportation*, http://www.afmd.asso.fr/decret-loi-avril-1940.html; accessed 10 June 2017).
5. The forfeiture of Vogel's nationality was officially announced on 27 January 1941 and then published in *Journal Officiel* on 2 February 1941.
6. Marie-Claude Vaillant-Couturier was a Resistant during the war, whilst Nadine Allégret, Vogel's other daughter, stayed in the South of France. Nicolas Vogel, Lucien's son, managed to join his parents in New York by September 1941.
7. Letter from Michel de Brunhoff to Condé Nast, 1940, CNA 21 July, B2 F22.
8. Thomas Kernan to Condé Nast, 1940, CNA 19 July, *ibid*.

9. Michel de Brunhoff to Condé Nast, 1940, CNA 21 July, *ibid.*
10. Thomas Kernan to Condé Nast, 1940, CNA 19 July, *ibid.*
11. Michel de Brunhoff to Nast, 1940, CNA 21 July 1940, *ibid.*
12. Robert Coutinot to Michel de Brunhoff, Private Archives, 28 May 1945.
13. Iva Patcévitch to Condé Nast, 11 September 1940, TKP. B1F30.
14. Note, 21 August 1940, Archives de la Préfecture de Police, Paris: Michel de Brunhoff file, B5.
15. Lucien Vogel to Nicolas Vogel, 8 January 1941, Private Archives, T. Ginsburger-Vogel.
16. Before war, he financed *La Cagoule*, a radical right-wing group.
17. Lucien Vogel to Condé Nast, 1940, CNA 19 Décember and Kernan 1994: 44.
18. *Ibid.*
19. Under Vichy legislation, the appointment of a temporary business administrator, elected by the Tribunal du Commerce, allowed sequestered goods and property to be protected against German seizure.
20. Michel de Brunhoff to Léone Friedrich, 1940, 27 July, Private Archives M. de Brunhoff.
21. Cosette Vogel to Nadine Allégret, 1941, 17 April, Private Archives T. Ginsburger-Vogel.
22. Nadine Allégret to Lucien Vogel, 1941, 21 October, Private Archives T. Ginsburger-Vogel.
23. Letter from M. Teitgen, 12 April 1945, Folder l'*Album de la Mode du Figaro*, F/41/1017, AN.
24. Nadine Allégret to Lucien Vogel, 1942, 16 September, Private Archives T. Ginsburger-Vogel.
25. *Note technique,*1952 DST, secteur de CE de Toulouse, SN/STA/T1 no. 5106, 10 October, Archives de la Direction de la Surveillance du Territoire, dossier Lucien Vogel no. 659107, sous-dossier 1949–1952.
26. Lucien Vogel to Nadine Allégret, 1941, 28 January, Private Archives T. Ginsburger-Vogel.
27. Lucien Vogel to Nadine Allégret, 1941, 7 February, Private Archives T. Ginsburger-Vogel.
28. Solange d'Ayen to Thomas Kernan, 1941, CNA 20 January 1941, B1F27.
29. Lucien Vogel to Nadine Allégret,1941, 22 July, Private Archives T. Ginsburger-Vogel.
30. Nadine Allégret to Lucien Vogel, 1941, 18 August, Private Archives T. Ginsburger-Vogel. Kostio de War was a designer who specialized in knitwear and crochet. During the war, she was in Cannes.
31. Lucien Vogel to Nadine Allégret, 1941, 22 July, Private Archives T. Ginsburger-Vogel.
32. Lucien Vogel to Nadine Allégret, 1941, 20 May, Private Archives T. Ginsburger-Vogel.
33. Lucien Vogel to Edna Chase, 1941, CNA 12 March, B11F15.
34. Lucien Vogel to Nicolas Vogel, 1941, 8 January, Private Archives T. Ginsburger-Vogel.
35. Lucien Vogel to Nadine Allégret, 1941, 20 May, Private Archives T. Ginsburger-Vogel.
36. Lucien Vogel to Condé Nast, 1941, CNA 19 February B11F15, and from Lucien Vogel to Miss Penrose, 1941, 9 March, CAN, B11F15.
37. Cosette Vogel to Nadine Allégret, 1941, 22 February, Private Archives T. Ginsburger-Vogel.
38. Lucien Vogel to Condé Nast, CNA B11F15, 1941, 10 January and 30 September, and September 1942.
39. *France Forever*, Guerre 1939–1945 Archives des Affaires étrangères, administration centrale, affaires politiques 1914–1944, France libre (CNF, CFLN), London (CNF), see nos. 382, 383, 384 and 385.
40. Lucien Vogel to C. Peignot, 1945, 5 January, Fonds Peignot, Bibliothèque Forney, Box 15, ABF.
41. 'French Women Suffer Horrors in Silesia Camp', 1943, 24 August.
42. Lucien Vogel to Iva Patcévitch, 1945, TKP, 26 February.
43. Légion d'honneur file, Michel de Brunhoff, A.N.19800035/149/18990.

Schiaparelli

SPRING-SUMMER 1940

Chapter 6
New York and Paris fashions during World War Two: a competitive love affair

Sandra Stansbery Buckland

Paris couture long held the reins of fashion leadership. Paris embodied the romance of art and style and craftsmanship, so it was natural for America to fall in love with the élan that was Paris design. But Paris couture was like a beautifully decorated cake from one of her patisseries. The romance of Paris formed the frosting, but the business side of the industry formed its foundation. World War Two forced a shift in the relationship between Paris and the United States more towards business and away from America's love affair with Paris design.

America needed its fashion industry to thrive, despite Paris's Occupation, in order to stabilize its domestic economy. And there were American leaders who wanted to loosen or completely dissolve Paris's grip on fashion leadership. Besides, the romance was one sided, so the American fashion industry concentrated on establishing itself as a leader in its own right.

Before World War Two

The fashion industry in the United States was profoundly different from the Paris industry. In America, ready-to-wear accounted for the majority of the business. Elizabeth King (cited by Lab 1993: 209–210) wrote that, before World War One, America was the greatest rival to Paris because it had both the technology and the workforce to become an international force. King continued, however, that America lacked inspirational, artistic design. Wealthy American women therefore made regular pilgrimages to Paris couture salons for seasonal wardrobes, wedding trousseaus and special-occasion dresses. Regardless of the price point, Paris provided the design leadership for the American fashion industry. America had good designers, but they lacked the celebrity status of French designers. Instead, the majority of the designers worked anonymously for the garment manufacturers who were Americanising Paris designs for the more independent American woman (Milbank 1989: 56).

FIGURE 6.0
Blue day dress, Schiaparelli, Spring-Summer 1940 (the Metropolitan Museum Digital collections, the Thomas Watson Library, the Costume Institute, Bergdorf Goodman Sketches Collection no. i2079650_364).

World War One created hardships in the Paris couture industry, so the American manufacturers were 'plunged into confusion' as they looked for design leadership (Herndon 1956: 58). Perhaps for the first time, those manufacturers featured American designers. In 1914 *Harper's Bazaar* successfully sponsored a fashion show in New York titled 'American Clothes for the American Woman' (ibid.). However, *Vogue* reported that the fashions showed a strong Paris influence because Paris was the master and New York was the pupil (Levin 1965: 211–212). Tobé wrote that America's devotion to Paris design was so strong that during World War One American buyers '[ran] the gauntlet of [German] submarines and mines twice a year in their search for new fashion for the American woman' (Fashion Against the Background 1940: 3).

At the war's end, Paris rebuilt its fashion industry, in part, by targeting the American woman and designing for her needs. The devalued French franc made Paris fashions more affordable for American women, and they willingly bought them. By the 1920s, Paris design once again dominated the American fashion scene, so fashion writers, retailers and manufacturers made regular trips to Paris for the couture openings. Vecchio and Riley (1968: 1) likened them to a flock of migratory birds who traveled to the European couture houses where 'they hope they will learn what the women of America will be wearing next season – or, rather, what they will be able to adapt, produce, promote, and sell to these women'. The *Chambre Syndicale* encouraged the Americans' visits. It prepared press releases for the magazines and newspapers, and it organized the couture openings so that reporters could get to as many shows as their energies would allow. American designer Elizabeth Hawes (1940: 14) described this process as a publicity campaign that promoted the French legend. She said, 'The French legend is a very simple one. All really beautiful clothes are designed in the houses of the French couturiers and all women want those clothes.' The newspaper and magazine writers experienced the romantic side of Paris, and they lovingly articulated that romance to eager American readers.

In 1929 the American stock market crashed and the USA entered into the Great Depression. This economic downturn profoundly influenced both the American and the Parisian fashion industries. The president of the *Chambre Syndicale* reported that Paris experienced a 40 per cent drop in exports from 1926 to 1930 (Milbank 1989: 98) partly because the US government imposed an import duty of 'up to 90 per cent on the cost of [an] original model' (Laver 1969: 246). However, manufacturers could import toiles, with duplication instructions, duty free. Madeline Ginsburg (1972: 92) wrote that in the first season after the stock market crash 'not a single commercial model buyer came to Paris from the U.S.A.' She continued that 'their sudden disappearance was a catastrophic loss to the Paris houses.' Perhaps this loss prompted couture to launch a new marketing initiative: the bonded model. Bonded couture garments received temporary, duty-free admission to the USA, where manufacturers and retailers could duplicate the designs and then return the garments (Palmer 2001: 138).

Despite the Depression, writers and buyers gradually returned to Paris. Nancy White experienced the romance of Paris when she traveled to the 1934 couture shows with her aunt, Carmel Snow, the editor of *Harper's Bazaar*. White (1972: 7) wrote that 'although I approached the great names of Paris with awe and reverence, I instinctively felt an enthusiasm, an empathy and a growing affection.' White became editor of *Harper's Bazaar*, and she remembered lavish luncheons, evening parties and visits to the couturiers' homes. Important writers such as White and Snow enjoyed lavish treatment even though they were not buyers. They, however, generated income for the couturiers through their profound influence over American consumers and, subsequently, the retailers and manufacturers. They also decided which couturiers received the most press coverage. The couturiers created a rarified world for the writers, and the writers lovingly promoted Paris as the ultimate fashion authority.

The manufacturers and retailers were less romantic. Tobé said that hundreds of American buyers in Paris spent millions of francs 'because we got a great deal for our money. It was easy – it was organized – it was fun' ('New York Becomes the Natural' 1940: 18). Manufacturers took their Paris originals back to their factories where their designers adapted the styles for the American market. Manufacturers could even purchase or copy the exact fabrics used by the couturiers. Yet, manufacturers complained that they lost money on copies. The Paris openings came too late for manufacturers to copy couture designs in a timely manner. The designs arrived after the beginning of the season, so retailers often had to mark down the copies in order to sell them ('Paris Style Role' 1945: 22). Still, throughout the Depression, American manufacturers copied or adapted French designs made with economical fabrics and sold at budget-minded price points.

Ginsburg (1972: 107) wrote that during the 1930s 'the big shops like Bendel's, Altman's, Saks, Bonwit Teller and Marshall Field received a regular supply of French models.' These retailers sold some originals, but they copied the toiles and other originals in their custom salons recreating the couture experience. Bergdorf Goodman's salon included a large staff including sixty tailors and eighty-five custom dressmakers (Herndon 1956: 159). Each Paris original or toile came with a reference that listed every item necessary to duplicate the design including vendors where the items could be purchased. The prices were high, but there was little or no profit in the operation. Andrew Goodman lamented that he 'wouldn't mind charging so much in custom if only we could show a little profit . . . But to charge so much and still lose, that I find embarrassing' (Herndon 1956: 165). One anonymous retailer added that 'we keep our custom department open for our old clientele and because it adds distinction to our more profitable ready to wear' (Crawford 1948: 225).

On the eve of World War Two, America had advanced ready-to-wear technologies and talented designers, but Paris was the design authority, because French couturiers enjoyed a celebrity status that American designers had not yet had an opportunity to achieve. The American fashion press lauded the French designers, and the retailers and manufacturers believed that their businesses depended on the inspiration of Paris couture. And Paris needed the American business. So, both New York and Paris watched nervously as war threatened to disrupt their synergistic relationship. The threat of war was not just about the loss of pretty dresses, but about the loss of vital industries for both countries.

1939: the war in Europe begins

New York's fashion industry exerted an enormous economic influence on the city and on the nation. In 1940, fashion manufacturing ranked third among America's industries ('New York Becomes' 1940: 5). *The New York Times* fashion editor, Virginia Pope, reported that fashion was New York's 'ace' industry, and that the city's garment industry dressed 70 per cent of American women (Pope 1941: 11). Sixty percent of New York's workers, over two million people, depended directly or indirectly on the fashion industry for their livelihood ('1898-1948' 1948: 22). This major industry was just beginning to recover from the effects of the Great Depression, so the threat of war and the uncertainty of Paris's future caused great concern among the city's and the industry's leaders.

New York enjoyed a unique opportunity to showcase its fashion industry when it hosted the World's Fair of 1939–1940. The participating countries, including France, competitively displayed their best achievements and provided an opportunity to directly compare Paris and New York designs. Donald Albrecht (2008: 12) concluded that the years between the Paris exposition of 1925 and the New York exposition of 1939–1940 bracketed 'one of the most intense and influential chapters in the love affair between the two cities' and represented 'the shifting balance of influence between them'. He continued 'the interchange between Paris and New York was never simple, comprising in equal measure admiration and

FIGURE 6.1
Poster for New York World Fair, Hall of Fashion, c. 1939. (Miller Art Co., Museum of the City of New York, no. X2011.34.4319.)

envy, respect and rivalry' (ibid.). New York's leaders, including Mayor La Guardia, intended for the fair to give the city a much needed financial boost, and that included turning the spotlight on the American fashion industry. La Guardia believed that New York, and not Paris, was the center of the fashion world. As early as 1937, New York fashion executives began to plan an 'effective and attractive' way to promote American fashion (Silva 2014: 18).

The New York fashion industry came to the fair ready to show off, so the city's department stores exhibited their latest fashions and sponsored fashion shows. By 1940 the World of Fashion building contained 'American fashion [as] an important part of the American culture' (ibid.: 39). Despite the emphasis on New York fashion, the fair organizers 'craved' the support of the Paris couture industry as a way of ensuring the fair's success. Marcia Connor, fashion executor for the fair, wrote to Elsa Schiaparelli in 1938 to encourage her to participate. Connor wrote, 'It is no exaggeration to that [sic] we look to Europe's creative talent to help us set a new keynote in styles that will harmonize with the lofty purpose of this great international spectacle' (ibid.: 19). Silva, however, wrote that 'the European designers were not excited about being part of the New York World's Fair of 1939' (ibid.: 20).

However, the French spent more than four million dollars on a pavilion where they displayed and sold items such as porcelain, tapestries, laces and silks, but no haute couture fashions (Albrecht 2008: 23). Couturier Jeanne Lanvin organized the haute couture group (Picken and Miller 1956: 115). She invited other couturiers to contribute dresses, but they declined. They argued that any dresses that they would show in New York would be outdated by show time and that Americans had bought so many of their dresses that they were on display already. Instead, the couturiers showed pure white bas-reliefs that symbolically displayed the ideals of each couturier (Ginsburg 1972: 112).

The couturiers were mistaken. The majority of Americans had never seen real couture garments. One can only speculate as to why the couturiers snubbed an event that meant so much to New York. Certainly they were concerned with the political unrest in Europe. Perhaps they saw no reason to compete with a nation that had very few known designers. After all, the American manufacturers and retailers already relied on French designs, and the press adored Paris. Paris was already the fashion leader and perhaps thought that it always would be. But this touchy romance was about to change. On 1 September 1939, the Nazis invaded Poland, and two days later England and France declared war on Germany. The Paris couture industry immediately felt the effects of war. Elsa Schiaparelli (1954: 132) wrote of the hardships of producing a collection for the October mid-season openings of 1939 but reminisced that showing her collection was 'a matter of prestige, to prove to oneself that one was still at work'.

Mary Brooks Picken wrote that 'not a single foreign buyer' attended the shows, so the president of the *Chambre Syndicale*, Lucien Lelong, immediately set a plan in motion to encourage the American buyers to return to Paris. After the October shows, Lelong persuaded his business friend, William C. Holmes, to act as an emissary and travel to New York (Picken and Miller 1956: 49). Holmes took a few display models to America in order to show that 'Paris was still her own creative, fertile self' (ibid.). As an incentive to the American buyers to attend the January 1940 spring collections, Lelong arranged for a special train to transport them from Genoa, created a convenient schedule and hosted a special reception for them. One hundred fifty buyers attended the openings (ibid.: 49–50). Carmel Snow (1962: 136) sailed on the *George Washington* with a 'small group' of buyers including Miss Jessica and Miss Frankau of Bergdorf Goodman, Mr. Leon of Henri Bendel, Hattie Carnegie and Nona Park and Sophie Shonnard of Chez Ninon. At Genoa, the group boarded Lelong's special train. Snow (ibid.: 136–137) described the train as bitter cold with no heat, electricity, food or sleeping accommodations. The trip took twenty-four hours to reach Paris with a stop at the border where the travelers waited in the snow while officials checked their credentials. This was not the normal Paris luxury, but these American travelers endured because they were loyal to Paris.

FIGURE 6.2A
French hat, Elsa Schiaparelli, straw, cotton and silk, summer 1940. Brooklyn Museum Costume Collection at the Metropolitan Museum of Art, New York. Gift of Millicent Huttleston Rogers: no. 2009. 300. 1837. (Image copyright the Metropolitan Museum of Art/Art Resource/Scala, Florence.)

FIGURE 6.2B
French dinner dress, Elsa Schiaparelli, silk, ceramic, plastic, summer 1940. Brooklyn Museum Costume Collection at the Metropolitan Museum of Art, New York. Gift of Arturo and Paul Peralta-Ramos, no. 2009.300.1210. (Image copyright the Metropolitan Museum of Art/Art Resource/Scala, Florence.)

FIGURE 6.3
Left, blue dress, Schiaparelli design for Bergdorf. Right, evening dress, Paquin for Bergdorf, 1940. Both sketches from the The Metropolitan Museum Digital collections, the Thomas Watson Library, the Costume Institute, Bergdorf Goodman Sketches Collection. Left: Blue dress, Spring-Summer, 1930, no. i2079650_364. Right: Evening dress, 1940, i2070653_002.

Kathleen Cannell lived in Paris and worked as the fashion reporter for *The New York Times*. In January 1940, Cannell began a series of articles about the Paris openings. She wrote, 'Paris couturiers, determined not to disappoint the intrepid American buyers who risked so much to come over for the January collections, showed them lovely clothes untouched by the shadow of war, and threw in a really new silhouette for good measure' (Cannell 1940: 4D). Meanwhile, in New York, the retailers still promoted Paris originals, but most of those were accessories such as gloves, blouses, hats or leather goods. Many of the New York stores advertised Paris styles that had been copied or adapted from the Paris openings.

In March, 1940, Virginia Pope (24 March 1940: 4D) opened an article on Paris imports with a message about copies. She wrote,

> New York has given a royal acceptance to the Paris imports this season. It is not only a gesture of recognition to the courageous designers of Paris, who despite all the limitations imposed upon them by a country at war have held their standards high, but it is also an acknowledgment that the models sent to this country have been exceptionally beautiful. All the designs shown on this page are taken from couture originals, which are being copied for American women.

Saks Fifth Avenue ran a full-page advertisement suggesting that its Salon Moderne could duplicate the couture experience. The advertisement, titled '*Vive la Vendeuse!*', read, 'Remember the anonymous, black-robed person at your favorite

French couturier?... Indispensable cicerone of your wardrobe, she is not, we are glad to say, indigenous to Paris. You will find her at Saks Fifth Avenue' (Saks 1940: 34). Saks was clearly appealing to those customers who previously travelled to Paris but who were now unable or too afraid to travel to the collections.

As the Nazis marched ever closer to Paris, New York industry leaders feared that they would go out of business without design leadership from Paris since they had made few attempts to promote American designers. They questioned if American women would purchase dresses that were not inspired by Paris. The Nazis occupied Paris on 14 June 1940, and on 16 June, Virginia Pope (16 June 1940: 6D) demonstrated an abrupt about-face in her love affair with Paris when she ran a story in the Sunday fashion section praising American designers. In August, Pope (18 August 1940: 12) wrote, 'With the eclipse of Paris eyes now turn to New York as the focal point for fashions. The couture, which for many years set the pace for style trends, is no more.... Meanwhile, New York is prepared to carry on.'

What shall we do without Paris?

The New York fashion industry was not surprised when Paris fell, but it was not yet prepared. Designer Mary Lewis (1940: 1–9) opened a Fashion Group meeting with the questions, 'Are we mice or designers? What shall we do without Paris?' She concluded, 'Let us get over being lazy, snobbish, dependent – let us be ourselves and go to work.' The New York fashion industry lacked an organizing body, so the industry did set to work, but it suffered, initially, from some chaos (Buckland 2005: 109). Eventually, though, New York asserted itself as a fashion leader to rival Paris. The industry set aside its love affair with Paris and convinced American women that America's designers could produce an American Look that rivalled couture.

A fashion show held at the World's Fair may have been the last Parisian designs that America would see until after the war. On 26 August 1940, *The Times* announced, 'the final fashion communication from Paris shows' ('Fair Today' 1940: 12). This show included gowns by Schiaparelli, Lelong, Molyneux and Balenciaga. These gowns must have been part of the midseason openings held in Paris at the end of May, just days before the Nazi invasion. Times writer Kathleen Cannell submitted reports on these openings dated 31 May and 7 June that included sketches of the couturiers' work. In a rare event (perhaps for the first time), *The New York Times* published photographs of the designs on 9 June, just days after the openings. These photographs violated couture's ban on publishing photographs less than thirty days after an opening. Telegrams sent at the end of the war indicate that *The Times* was very aware of this rule, but it still published the pictures. There was no photographic credit, but the pictures have a very American, very Hollywood, style to them. It may well be that the *Chambre Syndicale* allowed this policy breach as a last message out of Paris before the Occupation. Significantly, the show was held in the American Fashion Pavilion that was intended to promote the American fashion industry, not the French industry. The show, then, appears to have been a farewell homage to Paris.

With Paris in jeopardy, several couturiers brought Paris to New York. American-born couturier Mainbocher closed his Paris salon after the 1939 openings and opened a Fifth Avenue salon 'that was nearly a copy of the old quarters' in Paris (McConathy 1975: 164). Carmel Snow (1962: 140) wrote that 'Mainbocher maintained French standards of elegance in his New York salon.' Mainbocher designed elegant, ladylike dresses, as well as the uniforms for the women of the US Navy WAVES.

FIGURE 6.4
US Navy WAVES uniform, yeoman third class, 1942, designed by Mainbocher, worsted serge, rayon and cotton. (Museum of the City of New York, 46.293.a-d.)

Meanwhile, Italian Elsa Schiaparelli had contracted for a series of lectures across forty-two cities in the United States and Canada during the fall of 1940. She planned to illustrate her lectures with dresses that she had shipped ahead to New York. Whilst Schiaparelli travelled by Clipper from Lisbon in October 1940 (Secrest 2014: 239–242), the ship carrying her collection was torpedoed (Schiaparelli 1954: 137). Bonwit Teller's salon constructed replacement dresses, but Schiaparelli wrote that, 'it is much more difficult to produce an original collection in America than in our country because here we have unlimited materials on approval, whilst in America these materials have to be bought' (ibid.: 142–143). The collection proved to be expensive and, 'in spite of the genuine goodwill and ability of the workers, not what [she] wanted' (ibid.: 143).

Thousands of attendees heard Schiaparelli promote couture despite the German Occupation of Paris, stating that 'it was impossible to replace France in the realm of our particular creative work' (Schiaparelli 1954: 142). She praised the American industry for its sportswear, but she 'prophesied that Paris would again rise to assume the work of dressing women of taste and elegance throughout the world' ('Paris Still Held' 1940: 33). Schiaparelli (1954: 143) wrote that her lecture tour generated great controversies that spawned 'outspoken and brutal directness from a few fanatics'. She added that 'so many times in America' people asked her, 'How can the French work for the Germans?' (ibid.: 150) Schiaparelli ended her tour in New York in December 1940 and sailed to Paris via Lisbon on a ship 'so old that water poured in from every side'. She carried $80,000 worth of medicine and vitamins purchased with monies raised by her joint charity work with the American Quakers and intended for the children in the unoccupied zone of France (ibid.). She returned to the States on 25 May 1941 by Clipper to La Guardia, New York (Secrest 2014: 259–260). Schiaparelli expressed dismay when she found that in New York politics had divided Americans and French refugees into 'two aggressive camps' (ibid.: 158). At a charity auction to support French children, picketers waited outside with rotten eggs and tomatoes (ibid.: 159–160).

The Americans hosted many such relief benefits to aid the civilians in war-torn Europe. One group of socialites demonstrated their love of Paris couture by organizing an exhibition of French couture evening dresses that they had worn on 'Great Occasions' during the five years leading up to 1940. Hosted by Mrs. Ector Munn and Mrs. Harrison Williams, with the sponsorship of Lady Mendl and the Duchess of Windsor, the American branch of Le Colis de Trianon-Versailles held its show at the John Wanamaker Auditorium in New York in May 1940 to raise funds for French relief and to demonstrate the 'supreme and unsurpassed craftsmanship' of the French couture'. The international socialite Aimée de Heeran, famous for her beauty, style and Paris couture clothes (see Chapter 9 and Conclusion), was married by this time to Rodman Arturo de Heeren, the son of Fernando Wanamaker, the owner of Wanamaker department store, where the show took place.[1]

FIGURE 6.5
Evening dress, Madeleine Vionnet, cotton, metallic, Paris, 1939, and shown the following year at the Wanamakers charity fashion show, 1940. (New York, Metropolitan Museum of Art. Gift of Mrs Harrison Williams, C.I.52.24.2a, b. Copyright the Metropolitan Museum of Art/Art Resource/Scala, Florence.)

Despite mixed feelings about the Vichy regime of defeated France, the American press continued to publish any missives about Paris couture sent from Berlin. Manufacturers and retailers, however, did not attempt to follow any of the couture leadings. Instead, the industry focused almost entirely on promoting the American Look for American women. In a rare editorial, fashion publisher Tobé summarized the challenge facing the American fashion industry, saying,

> The fall of 1940 will go down in history as the year in which the whole structure of the fashion business had to be rebuilt. For with the collapse of France . . . went the foundation of the fashion world as we have known it . . . The course we must take lies open before us. The destiny of American fashions lies in the hands of American designers.
>
> ('American Designers' 1940: 15–17)

By 1942 the USA had declared war and its government looked to the apparel industry as one means of providing economic stability. The industry, however, faced multiple challenges as the War Production Board (WPB) took control over most resources, including textiles and paper. In April 1942, the WPB announced Limitation Order 85 that imposed strict styling limitations on women's apparel. Additionally, the WPB limited the amount of paper available to newspapers and magazines. Then, the Office of War Information developed a Retail War Campaigns Calendar that listed specific messages to be promoted through newspaper copy, store posters, window displays and price cards (Tobé Fashion Reports 1942: E). America's newly promoted designers embraced the challenges of the L85 regulations, the newspapers limited their sizes by cutting copy and advertisements and the retailers used their store displays to promote patriotism. The New York fashion industry did not forget Paris, but Paris took a backseat to the pressing needs of America's war efforts.

FIGURE 6.6
US service women window shopping at Saks Fifth Avenue, New York, 1944. (United States Office of War Information. Museum of the City of New York, no. 90.28.22.)

America's austerity measures seemed in sharp contrast to the picture of the Paris couture industry presented by *The Times*. In August 1942, a report from Vichy, France, the capital of the Free Zone, described how couture houses were operating without textile restrictions, charging very high prices and paying their staff members inflated salaries. The evidently hostile article commented that, 'the principal fashion houses have never known such prosperity' ('Fashion Designers' 1942: 14). The story's effect on the New York industry could not have been favourable, especially in light of continued rumors of collaborations and black-market activities.

Ironically, one woman's Parisian-made wardrobe momentarily superseded New York's nationalistic focus. Mme. Dieudonné Costes, the actress wife of the famous French aviator, arrived in New York from Occupied Paris, via South America, in July 1943 with suitcases packed with outfits made in Paris. *The Times* spent some of its precious paper allotment on a photograph and a two-column interview. Mme. Costes described a 'picture of a valiant Paris'. When she shared her couture garments, the writer commented that the styles were much different than the 'L85 controlled garments in this country' ('Mme. Costes' 1943: 14). *Life* magazine, however, shared a different attitude when it published photographs of Mme. Costes. The *Life* writer commented that the Paris designs were made in the Berlin taste. The writer also diminished the importance of this news from Paris, stating, 'in normal times the arrival of a new collection of French clothes in New York would greatly stir the trade and press. Mme. Coste[s]' clothes created barely a ripple' ('New Styles' 1943: 42). *Life* compared two photos of Mme. Costes' garments with two photos of New York designs. One of the Costes photo captions stated, 'Bulky band looks suitable for hefty German frau' (ibid.). *Life* praised the American 'trim styles made according to Government fabric restriction orders' but continued that 'what Madame Coste[s] had to show were vulgar exaggerations of famous silhouettes' (ibid.) that the magazine blamed on the Germans, not on the Paris couturiers.

In the continuing debate concerning New York vs. Paris, some held to the romance with Paris while others took the business approach. These voices often converged at the Fashion Group's monthly meetings. One retailer commented that 'the public was sold on the imported label; now they are beginning to forget it. . . . Right now our domestic designers' clothes are substitutes for Paris designed clothes and . . . to my mind are better' (Elgart 1942: 8). After Stanley Marcus, President of Neiman-Marcus, disputed the claims that New York was the fashion centre of the world, the Fashion Group published a comment on his controversial statement by saying, 'the battle of words, wherever fashion people gather, still goes on, for and against New York as the fashion center of the world with those who agree . . . and those who disagree, equally divided' (Fashion Group Bulletin 1943). By the end of 1943, however, the New York fashion industry anticipated Paris's liberation and worried about the renewed competition. In the spring of 1944, the industry began an almost frantic promotion of American designers and the American Look.

FIGURE 6.7 (left) Peggy Morris of Bergdorf Goodman, New York, draping French satin, August, 1940. (Getty 72399398.) (right) Emmet Joyce of Saks examining his design of Paris silk for an American clientele, August, 1940. (Getty 72399402.)

After the Liberation

The Allies liberated Paris in August 1944 and the American press immediately scrambled for news of Paris fashions. Not everyone, though, welcomed the stories. Internal memos from *The Times* reveal that women's editor Eleanor Darnton was concerned about giving any stories to fashion editor Virginia Pope, stating that, 'she is almost hysterically opposed to Paris at the moment' (Darnton 1945). Leaders in the American fashion industry 'were overjoyed' by the Liberation, but they expressed doubt that Paris would ever dominate fashion as it had before the war ('Clothing Designers' 1944: 16). Still, several voiced their intentions of visiting as soon as possible. Designer Jo Copeland, however, said that she would look to other sources for inspiration as much as Paris including China and South America (ibid.).

As the war continued across France, Lucien Lelong planned a trip to New York City. He announced that Paris was 'out to recapture its position as supreme fashion center of the world', and he 'did not doubt for a minute its ability to do so' (Long 1944: 20). Once news of developments in Paris reached America, it quickly became apparent that the couture industry was not able to immediately resume its prewar activities, though after the Liberation in 1944, Lelong's salon soon picked up business in New York – selling designs on paper to Bergdorf Goodman.[2] Paris held its first post-liberation shows in October 1944 and invited the Allied correspondents ('Paris Opens' 1944: 20). The New York press covered the openings, but the stories often included comments on the shortages in the city and the high cost of the dresses. *The Times* ran several photographic features, but they carried harsh criticisms. One writer commented that 'one thing is clear: The war isn't over yet . . . Present Paris fashions show no definitely new trends' ('From Paris' 1944: 34). Virginia Pope (1944: 44) wrote that the Paris styles seemed 'strangely out of gear with the styles of the days'. Both authors decided that the Paris designs were simply a reflection of the couturiers unrestricted Occupation designs. Though Paris again courted the American market, no buyers attended the shows.

It needs to be remembered that in December and January of 1944–1945, US troops were still desperately fighting Nazi forces across the Ardennes hills and forest of France at the infamous Battle of the Bulge. Fought in the deepest cold of winter at Bastogne, alone, 23,000 US troops, mostly from the 101st Airborne regiment, faced 54,000 German troops. Overall, 10,276 American were killed, 47,493 wounded, and 23,218 missing in the Ardennes fighting.[3]

FIGURE 6.8
US tank at the Battle of the Bulge, France, December 1944.
(Getty 72432865.)

By January 1945, even as this fighting was continuing, the American fashion industry had recovered from its initial fears about the Liberation and had regained its confidence. Jessica Daves, managing editor of *Vogue*, told a Fashion Group meeting that

> Anyone interested in fashion is foolish if they think Paris designs will hurt American design. American women have learned to love the clothes of American designers and to ask for them by name. America will not in future be a fashion stooge for Paris as we were often in the past.
>
> ('Says Dress Trade' 1945: 20)

Lingering hostilities toward Paris are evident in an article carried in *The New York Times* just days after Daves's remarks. In an interview, Lucien Lelong said that the inspiration for couture came from the city of Paris itself. The writer then commented that 'To be inspired by Paris at this time ... might mean reflecting the exaggerated psychoses of a city that is still emerging from the humiliation of defeat with the resentful sensitivity of a convalescent that is plaintively miserable without heat or light and buys its moments of comfort and gaiety on an extortionate black

FIGURE 6.9
Dinner dress, Mainbocher, silk, c. 1945, designed and made in America, worn by Millicent Rogers. (Brooklyn Museum Costume Collection at the Metropolitan Museum of Art, New York. Gift of Arturo and Paul Peralta-Ramos, no. 1945. 2009. 300.172. Image copyright the Metropolitan Museum of Art/Art Resource/Scala, Florence.)

FIGURE 6.10
Roger Worth, Paris, fashion drawing for dress (Eglantine) for the first *Théâtre de la Mode*, Paris, late 1944 to early 1945. (Ms. Nikita Mehta, Brand Development Manager, Akita Brands, SA Designer Parfums Ltd. and Victoria and Albert Museum, E.22247-1957, with thanks.)

market' ('Paris Will Show' 1945: 16). Despite ongoing paper shortages, the New York office did not edit this scathing commentary.

When, on 3 January 1945, the US government announced that it would authorize the shipment of French goods, including gowns for duplicating, manufacturers asked the American fashion press to suppress news of Paris designs until they could have their copies ready to sell ('Paris Style Role' 1945: 22). They wanted to limit their losses on copies. Jessica Daves responded that she could not suppress news of Paris, but that French designs might not be featured as prominently as previously. Spring 1945 brought both news of the latest Paris openings and a stream of French emissaries seeking to restore trade with the United States. In Washington, Mme. Henri Bonnet, the wife of the French Ambassador, told the Fashion Group that design inspiration would remain in Paris. But, she credited America for producing ready-made clothes 'so attractive that great numbers of American women with small incomes managed always to look well-dressed' ('Hails Paris' 1945: 20). The following day, a review of the Paris Schiaparelli show included details of the first restrictions 'ever imposed' by the *Chambre Syndicale* ('Schiaparelli Emphasizes' 1945: 18). The restrictions limited the number of models to be shown, the amount of yardage allowed in a design and the prices charged. Coincidentally, or not, the restrictions addressed several of the criticisms leveled at the couture industry by the American press.

In April 1945, as the war continued, Paris announced that the Paris Office of Art and Creation (OFAC) would send trade emissaries to the USA. *The New York Times* reported that the members' goals were to investigate conditions created by the war, find out the needs of the American market, find out how many French goods the market could absorb, compare prices, study means of distribution and establish contacts with leaders of American industries (Lelong 1945: 20). Emissary Lucien Lelong sought to 'dissipate a number of misunderstandings' about the couture industry, establish opening dates that would benefit both Paris and America fashion, and arrange for the purchase and exportation of couture models (ibid.). Veronique Pouillard (2013: 818), however, wrote that the emissaries also wanted to 'assess the US wartime propaganda detrimental to French Fashions'.

Lelong arrived in New York on 17 May, and by June he told a press conference that there 'was no conflict between American and French creation', because all countries 'must have their own creators of fashion' (Pope 1945: 12). Lelong may have reached this opinion as the emissaries unofficially evaluated the skills of the American designers and the merits of the American Look. They decided that America had only a small number of fashion designers of 'real creative talent', and that, compared to Parisian design, the American Look was 'looking like disaster' (Pouillard 2013: 819). Clearly, they did not see the American designers as a competitive threat and they concluded that couturiers could successfully re-enter the American market (ibid.).

The French emissaries' efforts demonstrated the importance of the US market to France, and they repeatedly stressed that France did not want to compete with the USA but to work in a mutually beneficial manner. Yet, just a week after the press conference, *The Times* published a report from Paris describing the Exposition Française fashion show that was opening in Rio de Janeiro ('Brazil Art Show' 1945: 16). (See Chapter 9.) When Paris was occupied, Rio looked to New York for its design inspiration, but this show appears to be Paris's attempt to regain its leadership position. The Exposition Française traveled to Rio just weeks after the Paris opening of the *Thèâtre de la Mode*.

After the end of the war in Europe on 8 May 1945, the Thèâtre's miniatures traveled throughout Europe for a year before the couturiers refitted them in 1946 designs and displayed them in New York on 1 May 1946 (Pope 1946: 18). Both shows promoted French couture, but both shows traveled for a year before opening in New York. Just as Paris had snubbed New York's World's Fair, challenging New York with these two shows seems to contradict the cooperation message promoted by the trade emissaries. After the New York missions in 1945, the couture industry seems to have dismissed any American competition, felt confident in its future success in the US and concentrated on other markets. America's love affair with Paris appears less than mutual. Yet, in 1949 the Paris couturiers sent a gift of miniature mannequins clothed in French historical dress as part of a Gratitude Train sent 'to the people of the United States by the people of France as a token of their appreciation of American assistance' ('Two Centuries' 1949).

With the promise that trade would soon resume, some American buyers returned to Paris in early 1946. The Couturiers Association courted them by reserving hotel rooms and reserving taxis in a city plagued with shortages and black-market enterprises ('Paris to Send' 1946: 16). American retailer Frederick Knize said that 'Parisian dressmakers [were] eager for American ideas and inspiration' ('Parisians' 1946: 17). On 9 April 1946, *The Times* reported that retailers, including Henri Bendel and Bergdorf Goodman, were showing 'the first post-war fashion imports from France' ('Post War Styles' 1946: 22). The Paris originals [gave] a 'marked appearance of adaptability to the American scene'. The collections included originals that would be sold, but most of the designs were bonded so that they could be copied and returned (ibid).

Thus, it took nearly two years after the Liberation of Paris for French designs to reach New York. By spring 1946, the American fashion industry had been designing without Paris inspiration for almost six years. The American industry used those years to mature, promote its own talents and take a leadership role in the fashion world. Its love affair with Paris continued, but on a more equal footing. America still loved Paris, but it did not need Paris to thrive. Instead of 'Paris Says', the fashion world had become 'Paris Plus New York'.

FIGURE 6.11
Day dress, Claire McCardell, New York, 1948. (With thanks to the Ohio State University, College of Education/Human Ecology Historic Costume and Textiles Collection, no. 1988.318.73.)

References

'1898-1948: Fifty Years of Fashion' (1948). *City of New York Golden Anniversary of Fashion: 1898-1948*, Official Jubilee Edition. New York: The Mayor's Committee for the Commemoration of the Golden Anniversary of the City of New York.

Albrecht, D. (2008). *Paris New York: Design Fashion Culture 1925–1940*. New York: The Museum of the City of New York and the Monticelli Press.

'American Designers and the Future of American Fashions' (16 July 1940). *Tobe Fashion Reports*, 15–17.

'Brazil Art Show Gets Paris Gowns' (14 June 1945). *The New York Times*, 16.

Buckland, S. S. (2005). 'Promoting American Designers 1940–44: Building Our Own House'. In Welters L. and Cunningham P. *American Fashion*. New York: Berg, 99–121.

Cannell, K. (4 February 1940). 'New Paris Silhouette'. *The New York Times*, 4D.

'Clothing Designers Overjoyed at Liberation of Paris, Doubt City Will Dominate Fashions' (24 August 1944). *The New York Times*, 16.

Crawford, M. D. C. (1948). *The Ways of Fashion*. New York: Fairchild.

Darnton, E. to James E. L. (March 1945). Transcript, *The New York Times* Archives, New York.

Elgart, A. (October 1942). *The Fashion Group Bulletin*, 7/8.

'Fair Today' (26 August 1940). *The New York Times*, 12.

'Fashion Against the Background of War' (11 January 1940). *Tobé Fashion Reports*, D1–3.

'Fashion Designers Thriving in Paris' (4 August 1942). *The New York Times*, 14.
Fashion Group Bulletin insert (December 1943). 9/7.
'From Paris' (15 October 1944). *The New York Times Magazine*, 34–35.
Ginsburg, M. (1972). 'The Thirties: Artistry and Fantasy'. In Lynam R., ed. *Couture: An Illustrated History of the Great Paris Designers and Their Creations*. Garden City, NY: Doubleday.
'Hails Paris for Fashions' (15 March 1945). *The New York Times*, 20.
Hawes, E. (1940). *Fashion is Spinach*. New York: Grosset and Dunlop.
Herndon, B. (1956). *Bergdorf's on the Plaza: The Story of Bergdorf Goodman and a Half-Century of American Fashion*. New York: Alfred A Knopf.
Lab, S. J. (1993). 'War'drobe and World War I'. In Cunningham P. A. and Lab S. V., eds. *Dress in American Culture*. Bowling Green, OH: Bowling Green State University Press.
Laver, J. (1969). *A Concise History of Costume*. London: Thames and Hudson.
'Lelong Will Head a French Mission' (11 April 1945). *The New York Times*, 20.
Levin, P. L. (1965). *The Wheels of Fashion*. Garden City, NY: Doubleday.
Lewis, M. (11 July 1940). 'What Shall We Do Now?' Speech to the Fashion Group, Biltmore Hotel, New York, Fashion Group International Archives, New York. Note: These archives are now housed at the New York Public Library.
Long, T. (31 August 1944). 'Paris Fashion Torch Undimmed Despite 4 Years of Nazi Occupation', *The New York Times*, 20.
McConathy, D. (1975). 'Mainbocher'. In Lee S. T., ed. *American Fashion*. New York: The Fashion Institute of Technology, Quandrangle.
Metropolitan Museum of Art, 'Cyclone,' www.metmuseum.org/art/collection/search/82.
Milbank, C. R. (1989). *New York Fashion: The Evolution of American Style*. New York: Harry N Abrams.
'Mme. Costes Pictures Valiant Paris Carrying on Its Famed Couture' (14 July 1943). *The New York Times*, 14.
'New Styles from Paris & New York' (16 August 1943). *Life*, 42.
'New York Becomes the Natural Fashion Center of the World' (3 October 1940). *Tobé Fashion Reports*.
Palmer, A. (2001). *Couture & Commerce: The Transatlantic Fashion Trade in the 1950s*. Vancouver: UBC Press.
'Paris Opens Show of Winter Models' (3 October 1944). *The New York Times*, 20.
'Paris Still Held Center of Fashion' (25 September 1940). *The New York Times*, 33.
'Paris Style Role Problem in Trade' (9 January 1945). *The New York Times*, 22.
'Paris to Send Fashions' (16 February 1946). *The New York Times*, 16.
'Paris Will Show Summer Fashions' (17 January 1945). *The New York Times*, 16.
'Parisians Seeking American Designs' (24 January 1946). *The New York Times*, 17.
Picken, M. B. and Miller. D. L. (1956). *Dressmakers of France: The Who, How and Why of the French Couture*. New York: Harper and Brothers.
Pope, V. (24 March 1940). 'Imports Seen in Shops'. *The New York Times*, 4D.
Pope, V. (16 June 1940). 'Made to American Taste'. *The New York Times*, 6D.
Pope, V. (18 August 1940). 'The Fashion Capital Moves Across Seas'. *The New York Times Magazine*, 12.
Pope, V. (7 December 1941). 'Fashion First Nights'. *The New York Times Magazine*, 11.
Pope, V. (12 November 1944). 'Paris Collections'. *The New York Times Magazine*, 34–35.
Pope, V. (1 June 1945). 'French Delegation Talks on Fashion'. *The New York Times*, 12.
Pope, V. (2 May 1946). 'Fashion Pageant from Paris Opens'. *The New York Times*, 19.

'Post War Styles Here from Paris' (9 April 1946). *The New York Times*, 22.

Pouillard, V. (2013) 'Keeping Designs and Brands Authentic: The Resurgence of the Post-War French Fashion Business Under the Challenge of US Mass Production'. *European Review Of History* 20:5, 815–835.

Saks Fifth Avenue Ad (18 February 1940). *The New York Times*, 34.

'Says Dress Trade Will Not Bar Paris' (11 January 1945). *The New York Times*, 20.

Schiaparelli, E. (1954). *Shocking Life*. New York: EP Dutton.

'Schiaparelli Emphasizes Color in Fashions; Draped Print Dresses Feature Paris Show' (16 March 1945). *The New York Times*, 18.

Secrest, M. (2014). *Elsa Schiaparelli: A Biography*, Penguin and Random House.

Silva, L. (2014). *New York Fashion Industry Goes To The Fair*, unpublished master's thesis, The City University of New York.

Snow, C. with Aswell, M. L. (1962). *The World of Carmel Snow*. New York: McGraw-Hill.

Tobé Fashion Reports (18 November 1942).

Two Centuries of French Fashion (1949). The Brooklyn Museum of Arts and Sciences. New York: The Gallery Press.

Vecchio, W. and Riley, R. (1968). *The Fashion Makers: A Photographic Record*. New York: Crown.

White, N. (1972). 'Introduction'. In Lynam R., ed. *Couture: An Illustrated History of the Great Paris Designers and Their Creations*. Garden City, NY: Doubleday.

Endnotes

1. De Gregorio, W. (2018). 'Hallowed with Memory': The Colis de Trianon Collections of Costume and Haute Couture at the Costume Institute, *Fashion Theory*, Vol. 22, Issues 4–5, pp. 457–484.
2. Lelong salon day dress sketch, 1944, Bergdorf Goodman sketches, the Costume Institute, Thomas J. Watson Library, the Met Digital Collections.
3. Land, G. (2018). 'Battle of the Bulge in Numbers'. https://www.historyhit.com/battle-of-the-bulge-in-numbers/ (accessed April 13, 2019).

Chapter 7
Lisbon as a centre of couture fashion in World War Two and its Paris and international connections

Alexandra Gameiro and Lou Taylor

Introduction

This chapter investigates the world of fashion and couture in wartime Portugal (1939–1945).[1] The starting point is to emphasise that, even though as a neutral country Portugal did not participate in World War Two, there were wartime limitations to the provision of mass clothing and fabrics in Portugal. Women in elite social circles, however, had little problem obtaining fashionable garments and were able all through the war to keep in touch with style developments in Occupied Paris. This chapter explains this situation, building on the work of Margarida Magalhães Ramalho (2012), Valter Carlos Cardim (2013), Isabelle Cantista and Paul Costa Soares (2016), on the dress collection of the Traje Museum in Lisbon[2] as well as on research into fashion magazines of the period, including *Eva*, *Modas & Bordados*, *Jornal Feminino da Mulher para a Mulher*, *Mundo Gráfico* and American *Vogue*.

One might think that war and haute couture are polar opposites, since one represents the destruction of the world and the other the creation of beauty and elegance, but despite the traumas, the couturiers of Paris created a highly extravagant wartime style, proving their autonomy. By 1942, as World War Two took hold, it was obvious that the silhouette of Parisian fashion was changing, with consequent sartorial repercussions for the rest of Europe, including Portugal, as this chapter will show.

Lisbon in neutral Portugal: the great junction of Europe

In Portugal, in 1942, the neutrality that the president of Portugal, Oscar Carmona, and his authoritarian prime minister, Antonio de Oliveira Salazar, maintained with

FIGURE 7.0
Models by Amelia de Morais, Lisbon, *Eva*, New Year, 1944 (with thanks to the Hemeroteca Municipal de Lisboa).

his nationalist philosophy of '*Politica do Espírito*' led to a peace that was lived by the whole population. This was a peace which guarded Portugal's central political location between Old and New Continents. This neutrality turned Portugal, as the most important transport hub in Europe, into the key European stage for both the circulation of goods of all kinds and people of all kinds – politicians, businessmen and refugees of many nationalities and persuasions. This neutral role was marked by the weight of the 600-year-long Anglo-Portuguese Alliance, to which the USA also signed during the war. As de Costa Leite notes significantly 'Portuguese neutrality ... resulted from Allied political and military considerations' (1998: 185–186). Despite this, it needs to be noted that from 1926, following the military coup that ended the First Republic and which led to the establishment of the military dictatorship, censorship had been instituted in Portugal. By 1933 the totalitarian regime, the *Estado Novo*, had been established (Pinto Guimarães 2008: 7).

All through 1939–1946, neutral Lisbon became a city full of diplomats, spies and agents of various nationalities where secret information exchange was widely practiced. Lisbon and its nearby port at Estoril were the only places in World War Two Europe where international passenger shipping and German, English, American, Italian and Spanish planes landed at the same airport. From here, if passengers could afford the price of a ticket, regular sea-landing, luxury Clipper flights flew to the USA.

In 1942, the British photographer Cecil Beaton travelled in the very same Clipper in which Churchill had once flown, noting its 'silk-lined walls, armchairs like Pullmans, various compartments for eating, sleeping, smoking' (1942: 88). At Lisbon airport, pilots of all nationalities ate in the same bars whilst in Lisbon the plane's well-off international passengers frequented the same hotels, restaurants, clubs and casinos, met at the same official diplomatic functions and exchanged, in the words of American *Vogue* reporter Marya Mannes, 'eternal social reciprocities' (Mannes 1944: 132).

FIGURE 7.1
Pan-American Clipper, moored on the Tagus River, Lisbon, unloading passengers, 1940. (Getty 50612043.)

During the war period, Lisbon thus gained increasing political importance as an international meeting centre at the southwestern tip of Europe. Not directly involved in the European conflict, it became the city of call for many European and American personalities, including fashion leaders, as this chapter will show. As for spies, also for refugees – and of all kinds stranded in Europe by summer 1940. These included thousands of Jews fleeing persecution from all across Europe. Costa Leite confirms that an important consequence of Portuguese neutrality was that 'it opened the way for many people to escape annihilation' (1998: 193). For refugees, Lisbon was a paradise where risk was reduced and the hospitality was excellent. In 1942, Beaton, en route to gather wartime information in the Middle East for the British government, passed through Lisbon, photographing the president and military and social leaders. He noted that they all felt strongly that their country was being misinterpreted by 'passing journalists, who have written of their capital city as a melting pot of spies, adventurers, gambling refugees and . . . shady characters'. For his influential sitters, a truer view was to see Portugal as 'the partner of the Allies' and of the 'Alliance formed in 1386 and renewed many times since [which] has not been revoked by us in this war' (Beaton 1942: 88).

Arriving to 'another world': Portugal 1940–1944

Journalists emphasised the stress involved in reaching the borders of Portugal during the war. In the period before America joined the fight against Hitler, the American journalist Tim Treanor arrived by slow train from across Franco's Spain. Shortages of hotel rooms and train tickets meant that refugees, whether wealthy or poor, once they had passed through the French border with Spain, could only move on towards Lisbon if hotel rooms and rail tickets became available – 'a nice little final touch of democracy [which] makes celebrities and nonentities alike in this respect' commented Treanor (1940: 132). Another journalist, Roderick Cameron, travelling from Madrid to Lisbon in 1942, observed that new arrivals were entranced by 'the strange fascination, the unexpected beauty of Portugal itself'. He found the country 'clean and peaceful' and was touched by 'the kindness of the people; the pleasantness of the country . . . there was no war . . . another world' . . . even though 'always lurking in the background [were] the grim realities of war' (1942: 113–114). Treanor too wrote that in the summer of 1940,

> Lisbon has sparkled with unexpected encounters, with amazing little parties that are gotten up between cocktails at the Avia and dinner at Negresco . . . the maddest whirl of seeing people whom you least expected to see. They pop out at every corner. At the Palacio Bar in near-by Estoril, you could see anybody, everybody and the night life lasted till seven am.
>
> (1940: 82, 132)

FIGURE 7.2
Women at a beach bar in Estoril, 1936. (Photo by Eric Borchert/ullstein, Getty 548787407.)

All the journalists commented on the extraordinary mix of people. Cameron was very aware, for example, of 'Germans at the next table to you at luncheon' (1942: 114). High society circles in Lisbon, as elsewhere, included diplomats, politicians, businessmen and military/naval leaders, often accompanied by their well-dressed wives. Other famous international personalities were to be seen passing through the city, now joined socially by a throng of well-off refugees. Mixing with journalists, all moved easily from Embassy functions to the best restaurants, the opera and the sunny beaches of Estoril. Elegant foreign visitors, mostly conversing in French, were not a new phenomenon. Since the early twentieth century with the opening of Estoril's thermal springs as a health cure, Lisbon and Estoril had become elegant, international leisure spaces.

Carvalho writes that by the 1930s, the elegant Chiado district of central Lisbon featured smart hotels and its shopping arcades included couture salons that 'resembled Parisian shops' selling the latest French fashions. By the 1930s, leisure activities for sports-conscious, wealthy visitors included sunbathing, swimming, golf, riding and car racing, with evenings spent at theatres, restaurants and the famous Estoril Casino (2015: 379). The grand department store Loja das Meias declares today that Primo de Rivera, the Spanish prime minister in the late 1920s, the Duke of Windsor, Guilhermina Suggia, the famous Portuguese cellist, Baron de Rothschild, King Humberto of Italy, King Carol of Romania, Elsa Schiaparelli and Jean Renoir were all to be seen shopping there (www.lojadasmeias.pt). Beaton, arriving in early 1944 from bomb-blasted, austerity London, reflected that 'one has forgotten the pleasure of merely looking into shop windows filled with goods that one would like to possess, even if one had the necessary money: Swiss watches, German cameras, American silk stockings, crystallized apricots and nougats' (1944: 78).

The Portuguese fashion press eagerly reported the social and fashionable comings and goings in Lisbon, Estoril and Portugal's second city, Porto. Eve Curie, the beautiful pianist French daughter of Marie Curie, passed though Lisbon a few times by air from London en route to lecture in the USA on behalf of General de Gaulle and the Free French Forces. American *Vogue* reported that she arrived in Lisbon from Paris in early 1940 with an entire Schiaparelli wardrobe for her US lecture tour (American *Vogue* 5 March 1940: 128–129). By February 1941, by when she had herself joined the Forces Françaises Libres in London, her US lecture tour clothes were designed by Molyneux in his London salon (American *Vogue* 15 February 1941: 40–41).[3] Eve Curie's elegant couture clothes and her personal Parisian sense of simple couture chic thus caused a stir both in the Lisbon and in the international women's periodical press, where the couture clothes of other refugees were also often noted. Treanor met Salvador Dali's wife, Gala, in Lisbon in 1940, commenting that after her struggles to reach Lisbon, she was dressed in 'remnants of Schiaparelli' (1940: 82). Schiaparelli herself flew by Pan-American Clipper to and from New York via Lisbon several times in the 1940–1942 period (see Chapters 5, 6 and 12). In 1941, the Lisbon fashion magazine *Eva* (1 February: 8–9) reported that 'the great fashion designer of France, had recently arrived from America. Schiaparelli, in an *Eva* interview, offered her opinion on the future of European elegance.'

The Duke and Duchess of Windsor, having fled Paris at the time of the Nazi Occupation, also passed through Portugal. They lived outside Lisbon from early July 1940 in the grand villa of the Portuguese banker Ricardo Espírito Santo Silva, before being ordered out of Europe by the British government, who suspected that both had pro-Nazi sympathies. They travelled on reluctantly to eventual isolation in Bermuda, where the Duke became Governor General and where they remained until the end of the war (Bloch 1984). Treanor spotted that 'in the little restaurants overlooking the sea at Cascals . . . you could see the Duke and Duchess of Windsor while they were here playing their latest peculiar role – refugeeing' (1940: 82).

Leaving

For all the refugees and travellers, the anxiety that hung over their lives in Lisbon was how to leave as they waited for tickets for ships and Clippers, and struggled to get entry visas for South America or the USA or anywhere that would take them. Cameron, like others, had expected to stay only for three days before leaving on his pre-booked Clipper flight home to the USA. He ended staying six weeks in a state of constant suspense 'waiting, expecting each day to hear about the "Clipper" . . . the waiting list is long' (1942: 116). Refugees sold whatever they could not take with them or whatever was necessary to obtain tickets. Treanor observed in 1940 that 'half the population seems to be trying to sell a Rolls Royce, which does not pack well into a Clipper' (1940: 132).

The American journalist William Shirer, who worked with Edward Murrow, the head of the American news service CBS, experienced this reality himself. Leaving from Berlin and Vienna in 1941, Shirer waited in Estoril for his American Export

Lines passenger liner, the *SS Excambion*, to sail to New York,[4] spending a last evening in the elegant casino at Estoril. Shirer wrote on 10 December 1941 that

> The gaming rooms were full of a weird assortment of human beings, German and British spies, male and female, wealthy refugees who had mysteriously managed to get a lot of money out and were throwing it about freely, other refugees who were obviously broke were trying to win their passage money in a few desperate gambles with the fickle roulette wheel and the usual international sharpsters you find in such places.
>
> (Shirer 1941: 471)

Shirer was moved by the desperate refugees besieging the dockside and jamming the Offices of the Export Lines. He described them as

> a mob of refugees – jittery, desperate, tragic victims of Hitler's fury – begging for a place – any place – on the next ship. But one of the company officials explained to me, there are three thousand of them in Lisbon and the boats only carry one hundred and fifty passengers and there is only one boat a week
>
> (Shirer 1941: 471)

Treanor observed that in Lisbon, 'American visas are like pearls' (1940: 82). He watched the struggles at the American Consulate: 'There are scenes, as women wearing all their jewels, not knowing what to do with them, fly into passions at being denied visas after warming a hardwood bench for days' (1940: 132). Peggy Guggenheim, an American, Jewish, well-off and famous modernist art collector, who had been sheltering in Marseilles in the spring of 1941 with her family, also struggled too to find a hotel in Lisbon. She found herself obliged to fill time with 'long meals, days at the beach and excursions'. Vial writes that 'Finally on July 18th, after an agonising wait for various legal papers, eleven people, one husband, two ex-wives, one future husband [Max Ernst] and seven children boarded the Pan American Clipper to New York' (1998: 49).

Thousands of refugees were Jewish, escaping out of Europe. Salazar's regime, whilst refusing them permanent settling rights, had no anti-Semitic legislation and thus Milgram writes that 'the policy of neutrality, authored in the main by Salazar, enabled thousands of Jewish refugees to enter [Portugal] after the fall of France in the summer of 1940'. Portugal itself had a tiny Jewish population 'that did not exceed one thousand' (1999: 4). Fleeing by land, refugees required an exit permit from Vichy France, a Spanish transit visa, an entry permit into Portugal and could only leave from there by ship or plane with an overseas entry permit. The key document was the Portuguese entry visa. Milgram stressed that there is 'no evidence of any anti-Semitic prejudice . . . on the part of Portuguese Consuls abroad.' It was they, in fact, who issued fleeing Jews from all over Europe with many thousands of vital entry visas to Portugal (1999: 30).[5]

To give just one example of the desperate measures taken, and unlike Shirer's direct passage from Estoril to New York, a group of 317 refugees, including over a hundred European Jews – amongst them families with children and the French Jewish actor Marcel Dalio and his wife Madelaine Lebeau[6] – went to the length of chartering their own ship. Thus the *SS Quanza*, a Portuguese coal-burning passenger cargo ship, left Estoril harbour on 9 August 1940, bound for New York and Vera Cruz.

Two hundred passengers disembarked in New York but on arrival at Vera Cruz, on 30 August 1940, the final destination of the ship, the Mexican government declared that many of the entry visas of the remaining Jewish passengers were false and only allowed entry to thirty-five refugees. The ship then set out to return to Lisbon with many Jewish passengers still on board. A refuelling stop at Norfolk, Virginia, however, allowed time for local American Jewish lawyers to trigger legal discussions at the presidential level involving Eleanor Roosevelt. Finally, around eighty US visas were issued on 12 September 1940 to Jewish passengers who disembarked on their return to New York (Brown 2008: 20–31, 35). The remaining Jewish passengers were forced to return to their differing fates in Europe.

FIGURE 7.3
Refugee passengers still on the *SS Quanza* at the dockside in Norfolk, Virginia, 11 September 1940 (photograph by Charles Borjes, the *Virginian Pilot* Photograph Collection, Sargeant Memorial Collection, Norfolk Public Library).

Fashion leaders in Lisbon

This large movement of people, including many members of the international fashionable and cultural elite, has been detailed here because one unexpected consequence of this was that Lisbon's couture world greatly expanded. It became a consumption target for well-off women travellers and refugees from all over the world. By 1944, for example, just after the Liberation of Paris but well before the end of the war in France, Mannes reported that Countess Erica Hoyas, 'a young Austrian beauty', had been seen in Lisbon in an afternoon dress by Schiaparelli of 'sheer grey fabric that is half cloud and half pussy-willow'. The Countess also had 'an Alix evening dress of heavy oyster-white silk striped in black' (1944: 141). Mannes noted other elegant diplomatic foreigners in Lisbon, including

> two fair Italians, Madame Prunas, the wife of the former Italian Minister to Portugal, who is now with the Rome government, and Marchese Lanza d' Ajeta, wife of the Italian *Chargé d'Affaires* and two elegant Americans – 'Mrs Hendry Hopkinson and Mrs Wilson-Young, wives of high-ranking British diplomats', as well as Mrs Judith Symington, the wife of an English business man.
>
> (1944: 198)

Mannes was also impressed by 'outstanding, internationally-minded [Portuguese] families' – the Pinto Bastios, the Castro Pereiras, and the Espirtia Santos families – 'graced with beautiful women who can wear [Paris] clothes with style and restraint' (1944: 198).

Beaton admired the Anglophile and 'dashing' Madame Ulrich, formally in London as the wife of the Portuguese Ambassador (1942: 88). Mannes was more cautious however, concluding her *Vogue* report of 1944 critically – comparing the lives of wealthy American woman back home wearing 'ready-made cotton, halving her time between cooking for her servant less household and acting as a nurse's aide', with that of some fashionable women in European 'neutral, satellite and even Occupied capitals with their endless social programmes'. Mannes declared that 'It might be felt that the nearer one got to war, the deeper one felt' [about the horrors of war] but to Mannes, 'fashionable ladies seemed to belie' this idea (1944: 199).

Fashion in Portugal in World War Two

The journal *Vestir* observed as early as December 1940 that the many foreigners who passed though Lisbon had 'influenced the habits and dress of many Portuguese'. With some astonishment, *Vestir* commented on the imitation Paris styles worn by both men and women, who were copying the dress of some of the smart refugees seen in the streets of the city (Ramalho 2012: 14).

Vestir also astutely noted in an article titled 'Chronicle of foreigners in Portugal' that by December 1940, Lisbon women were copying styles that only shortages and

FIGURE 7.5
Left: 'Morning walk on Avenida da Liberdade'. Centre: 'The Portuguese have become accustomed to walking without a hat'. Right: 'A French refugee in her white dress with geometric lines and no hat'. (*Mundo Gráfico*, no. 1, 15 October 1940: 7, with thanks to the Hemeroteca Municipal de Lisboa.)

FIGURE 7.4
'Lisbon the capital of fashion': An elegant Lisbon woman as graceful as a Parisian woman dressed in Rue de la Paix. (*Mundo Gráfico*, no. 1, 15 October 1940: 7, with thanks to the Hemeroteca Municipal de Lisboa.)

tough necessity had forced French women to adopt. Thus Portuguese women too wore thick, open, cork-soled shoes, though there was no leather shortage in Portugal. *Vestir* further advised on updating a suit. 'To give a certain elegance and originality to the toilette, wear a hat with a feather, a current [Paris] trend' (December 1940 no. 14: 36–37). (See also Figure 3.10B.) Refugees were passing on a more modern casual style of dressing to the more formally dressed Portuguese woman. By the end of the war some even dared to go bare-legged whilst others began to frequent the esplanades and the cafés for the first time in their lives. The new styles were sometimes seen as scandalous. The swimsuits worn by refugees were judged, for example, as far too bold. The Portuguese authorities were attentive to such developments, trying whenever possible to stop these modernities but always without success (Ramalho 2012: 41).

Amongst imported goods, Mannes reported on the excellence and profusion of fashion fabrics in 1944: 'The silks available in Lisbon are delectable: a limitless variety of small patterned prints in the purest of colours' (Mannes 1944: 141). Two silk couture day dresses in pretty floral prints made by Beatriz Gomez at her Porto salon in about 1940 confirm Mannes' opinion. In the collection of Lisbon's Museu Nacional do Traje e da Moda, one such print, with a centre front-buttoned opening, features a small repeat berry-and-twig print in dark blue on a white ground (no. 35603/1) and another, a bolder floral pattern in cream colour on a mid-blue ground, with a centre front opening fastening with small, self-covered buttons (no. 35602/1), was made with a knife pleated skirt. Both dresses are labelled in French: '*Robes et Manteaux/Beatriz Gomez/Porto*' and show the fashionable padded shoulders of the period. In their simplicity, both garments have, however, also a London style about them, which is not surprising because London *Vogue* was available in Lisbon and *Eva* too reported regularly on '*Moda Inglesa*'.

FIGURE 7.6
Top: Silk day dress with small, navy blue, floral print on white ground, Gomez, Porto, 35603/1 Bottom: Silk day dress, with larger floral print, white on a mid-blue ground, Gomez, Porto.no.35602/1 (Both from the Museu Nacional do Traje, with thanks to the Directorate-General of Cultural Heritage/Documentation Archive, Lisbon. Photographer, Luisa Oliveira.)

Paris couture in Lisbon

The concept of fashion in Portugal before and after World War Two continued to be firmly based on the matrix proposed by Paris, though press reports on the simpler London Utility fashions were indeed also published. In October 1940 *Mundo Gráfico*, reporting on Britain and on the progress of the war, declared proudly that already 'Lisbon with the war has become the fashion capital. Styles taken from all the covers of women's magazines now parade in the streets of the city.... There is no longer any need to go and get dresses in Paris.' *Mundo Gráfico* described Lisbon as a city where fashion designs from all the centres of European elegance – France, Italy, Spain and more – were paraded: 'This contact with the international world of female grace, its wild fantasies, its complicated outbursts, gives the Portuguese woman, so sensitive to taste and so demanding, an exquisite harmony of dress' (*Mundo Gráfico* no. 1, 15 October 1940: 7). Treanor too confirmed that refugees were wearing 'clothes from the best Paris dressmakers', adding though that these were 'a little messed by Portuguese dry cleaners who are not the best of all' (1940: 82). Mannes noted in September 1944, shortly after the Liberation of Paris, that 'many smart Lisbon women wear the actual French models brought back to them by friends who cross the border regularly. Others have their own couturiers make copies.' She added significantly, that 'communication with Paris has never been a problem here.' Mannes noted too the names of the most influential Paris haute couturiers in Lisbon, observing that 'the rising star is Jacques Fath. Balenciaga, working from Madrid, is a great influence here' (American *Vogue*, 1 September 1944 : 141).

Original Paris couture garments could be also bought in Lisbon's couture salons. Mannes reported in September 1944 that the 'best evening dress I saw was a Paquin model, shown at *Bobone* with a pale pink bodice embroidered in black, with a long "narrow and complicated" sarong skirt in black crepe' (1944: 141). The illustrations in Portuguese wartime fashion magazines clearly reflect the close attention paid to Paris couture style development. By September 1944, only a few weeks after the liberation of the city, Mannes noted that in Lisbon as in Paris, 'the shoulders are all round with curved pads.... The general effect is one of voluminous grace' (1944: 141). In October 1944, just a month later, *Eva* magazine published a series of Janine fashion drawings illustrating that just such Paris haute couture garments were by then available at the usual Lisbon couture outlets.

The journal noted that new garments from other haute couturiers were also available at Mme. Valle, including Piguet, Ricci, Callot Soeurs, de Rauch, Carven, Bruyere, Schiaparelli, Worth and Rouff. Janine's drawings show that this salon was also selling exaggerated high-hat Paris couture millinery.

This Paris focus was far from new. The salon Madame Valle was one of the first to import Paris couture into Lisbon in the late 1920s. In 1937, a grand haute couture show was organised by the fashion magazine *Eva*, which presented fashions by the leading Lisbon and Porto couturiers in a magnificent state room in Palácio Foz. 'Tea

FIGURE 7.7A
Designs by Paquin, Lecomte and Lanvin available in Lisbon; drawings by Janine, *Eva*, October 1944 (with thanks to the Hemeroteca Municipal de Lisboa).

FIGURE 7.7B
Obtainable from Mme. Valle in Lisbon, left to right: Legroux hat, Jane Laforie draped silk dress and Lecomte dress with large *broderie anglaise* collar trim (with thanks to the Hemeroteca Municipal de Lisboa).

was served, a jazz band played and dancing went on until 9pm'. Maria Luisa Silva Teixeira, owner of Casa Bobone in the Chiado, and Maria da Piedade do Valle, who opened Madame Valle, near Praça Marques do Pombal, 'would go to Paris twice a year on exhausting forty-eight-hour train journeys' to see the seasonal couture shows (Teixeira 2015: 7–10).

Lisbon and Porto couture in wartime

From the early twentieth century, influential Portuguese dressmakers included Judith and Amélia de Morais, who both trained in Paris, then worked as seamstresses at Casa Bobone and finally opened their own salon with a small and elegant urban clientele (Paiva Boléo 2004: 71). Mannes explained to American readers that

> the smart women of Lisbon – and many of them are in the diplomatic corps – have every stitch they wear made to order. . . . The town is full of able little dressmakers who, with guidance and a few copies of French magazines and British *Vogue*, can turn out charming clothes.
>
> (1944: 140)

Above these in the Portuguese fashion hierarchy came the Lisbon couturiers. Although these never reached the international fame of the great Paris haute couture houses, there was nevertheless a group of well-known Portuguese couture designers, headed by Maria Luisa Teixeira of Casa Bobone, who trained many of the designers and seamstresses who later opened their own salons (Cantista and Costa Soares 2016: ch. 3) They continued, as before the war, to base their work on seasonal Paris couture style, legally copying from toiles purchased from the Paris salons (Carvalho 2015: 8).

Two examples from the collection of the Museu Nacional do Traje e da Moda in Lisbon serve to illustrate this point. The first is an evening dress in pink silk and tulle with short, puffed sleeves and a fully flared skirt from the salon of Albertina Naar, Lisbon, from the early 1940s. The second example, probably made in the 1943–1946 period, is a finely tailored, black jersey suit by Beatrix Gomes, Porto, with scalloped edging and the typical Paris Occupation style with narrow waist and long peplum.

The designer Ana Maravilhas, in an interview, usefully clarified that when working at Bobone, she went to Paris to buy toiles and original fabrics in order to reproduce legally the creations of the great French dressmakers: 'We simply copied, there was no creation.' Soares and Cantista notes that Maravilhas 'boasted that, thanks to her excellent memory, she could remember every detail of what she saw, which would set the tone for the next season' (Costa Soares and Cantista 2016: ch. 3). Other well-known couturiers included Napoleāo, Sérgio Sampaio, Mário Remédios (well known for his tailored designs such as the trim winter coats worn

FIGURE 7.8
(above) Evening dress, in pink, about 1940, Albertina Naar, Avenidia de Liberdade, Lisbon, no. 35036. (top right) Close up of its gold, floral, appliqué neck trimming, no. 35036. (bottom right) Black jersey jacket, Beatriz Gomez, 1940–1945, no. 35610. (From the Museu Nacional do Traje, Lisbon with thanks to the Directorate-General of Cultural Heritage/Documentation Archive. Photographer, Luisa Oliveira, 2017.)

with early wartime styled small hats published in *Vestir* no. 14, December 1940: 26) as well Beatriz Chagas and Rosy Pollak, a Polish refugee, who settled in Portugal, became famous for her couture jersey and knitwear and 'was admired by the upper classes and by the various royal families living in exile in Portugal' (Cantista and Soares 2016: ch.3). In 1944, Mannes was impressed by some of Bobone's in-house designs: 'Among Bobone's own models, was a wool tricot evening dress with a bell-skirted Gibson girl shape. This had definite originality' (1944: 141).

FIGURE 7.9
(top) Evening wear by Bobone, Mme Valle and Amélia de Morais and (bottom) models by Amelia de Morais, Lisbon, both images from *Eva*, New Year, 1944 (with thanks to the Hemeroteca Municipal de Lisboa).

Couture millinery from Paris to Lisbon

As with dress designs, so with couture millinery as Lisbon and Porto milliners copied the latest Paris hat styles. The Traje Museum has a small, smart, black felt hat of 1939, with black veil, that would have been worn tipped over the forehead – much influenced by Schiaparelli.

As styles moved on, Mannes reported in 1944 that the exaggerated high, wide hat styles from Paris were flourishing in Lisbon. She noted that 'the most popular Paris milliners are Paulette, Legroux, a new house called Albuyes [Albouy], Janet

FIGURE 7.10
Four Lisbon hats. (top left) Hat, black felt, 1939, no. 7821, Museu Nacional do Traje, Lisbon. (With thanks to the Directorate-General of Cultural Heritage/Documentation Archive, Lisbon. Photographer Luisa Oliveira, 2017.) (top right) Hat by Bobone, *Eva*, May 1944. (bottom left) Hat, with violets, cover, *Eva*, January 1945. (bottom right) Hat by Amelia de Morais, *Eva*, New Year, 1944: 24. (With thanks to the Hemeroteca Municipal de Lisboa.)

176 Paris Fashion and World War Two: Global Diffusion and Nazi Control

Colombier and the ever resourceful Suzy' (See Chapter 3.). As *Eva* magazine illustrated and Mannes reported, 'Bobone and Mady here show originals and copies of all of them, including their own models.' Three basic fashionable hat forms were the most popular: 'the enormous, intricately draped Arabian Nights turban; the poke-bonnet type jutting upwards and forwards, weighted down with flowers . . . and the peach basket type, thick brimmed, thick crowned, invariably laden'. Mannes illustrated her text with drawings, including one of a high, white satin turban by Balenciaga and a scarlet straw boater-style hat by Suzy, with a wide, high crown trimmed with a dark purple velvet band and a large bunch of violets standing proudly upwards on the left side of the brim (1944: 198). Beaton, in Lisbon in early spring 1944, also noted the astonishing hats: 'Here even the most nondescript housewife wears a most exaggerated hat. On trains, in cars, in the street, one sees hats like enormous fans, like the "Fantouches" worn by the women in Restoration comedies' (1944: 78). Mannes was however critical of some Portuguese versions, feeling that 'the local adaption of the Paris hat is still quite horrible. . . . Women stump along under huge top heavy structures overburdened with flora and fauna' (1944: 141).

Portuguese fashion magazines

The dictatorship in Portugal did not try to create a national fashion style as in Germany and Italy (Cardim 2013: 133) but nevertheless from the 1930s all journals passed through the Portuguese censorship system before publication. From the early years of the twentieth century, magazines and newspapers reported regularly on the latest fashion models in Paris, including all the major circulation periodicals, such as *O Século* from early 1905, *Diário de Notícias* in Lisbon and Porto's *Jornal de Notícias* and *Portuguese Illustration* (Guinote 2001: 136). Fashion magazines became a key means of transmitting seasonal design style to Portuguese women at all social levels, as this chapter has already shown, including *Eva, Modas & Bordados, Vestir, Jornal Feminino da Mulher para a Mulher* and *Mundo Gráfico. Eva* magazine, as shown here, consistently reported on couture design in Paris, Lisbon and occasionally London through elegant fashion drawings by Janine. Its May 1944 edition, for example, before the Liberation of Paris, discussed both Paris and Portuguese style, featuring the work of Madame Valle and the House of Bobone. The Valle's collection was described as inspired by designs by Nina Ricci, Patou and Lecomte – legally copied designs made up in the Valle atelier (*Eva* May 1944: 20–21).

Almanak Silva in an article title '*Notre Janine*' notes that in 1941 *Eva* magazine first employed the fashion illustrator known as 'Janine', who was 'professional in the sinuosity and precision of her drawings, which enhanced the styles of fashionable garments of Lisbon designers and also those of leading fashion houses in Paris'. Janine drew her 'bold compositions in watery two tones and black, either in pencil or China ink. These were often reproduced in full pages in the magazine.' Janine was Guida Ottolini (1915–1992), the third generation of the Roque Gameiro family of artists, and she continued to work for *Eva* until 1953 when photographs gradually came to replace her illustrations (*Almanak Silva* 6 November 2013). *Eva* regularly featured Janine drawings of Paris couture as Figure 7.7A has shown. Cardim notes significantly however that magazines gave 'greater importance to models made by Portuguese houses and dressmaking establishments' than they had before the war (2013: 157).

As well as reporting on couture worn by the wealthy, fashion magazines also responded to wartime shortages that were impacting on the lives of their readers. Women treasured whatever garments they owned and recycled them, with advice from the magazines. It needs to be noted here that most everyday Portuguese women turned the old into new and followed advice on how to turn curtains into clothes, men's overcoats into ladies coats and curtains into wedding dresses.

The Liberation of Paris draws near

The availability of regular monthly Paris couture information continued on throughout the war without a pause. In July 1944, just before the Liberation of Paris, *Eva* magazine reproduced Janine drawings of designs inspired by Paquin, Charles Montaigne, Nina Ricci, Madelaine Rauch, Vera Borea, Maggy Rouff and Jacques Fath. The October 1944 edition, as already noted above, just two months after the Liberation, offered the full range of garments from the Paris couture salons. (See Figures 7.7A and B.) Portuguese collections were emphasised in the November 1944 edition with designs by Bobone, Amelia and Madame Valle. This emphasis was repeated in *Eva* in January 1945, coupled with an article on London couture fashions. Lelong, Fath and Molyneux were the three Paris couturiers highlighted

FIGURE 7.11
Fur fashions from Paris, October 1946, *Eva*, drawn by Janine (with thanks to the Hemeroteca Municipal de Lisboa).

in November 1945, the first Paris autumn collections after the final ending of World War Two. All the designs of 1944–1945 in *Eva* magazine featured the Paris Occupation style and indeed the Paris fur coat styles published in *Eva* in October 1946 still showed the same very broad shoulders, tiny waists and full skirts of this style.

Conclusion

In 1942 Shirer remembered as he waited for his ship, the *SS Excambion*, overflowing with refugees, to leave Estoril harbour,

> a full moon was out over the Tagus and all the million lights of Lisbon and more across the broad river on the hills sparkled brightly as the ship slid down to the sea. For how long? Beyond Lisbon, over almost all of Europe, the lights were out. This little fringe on the south-west corner of the Continent kept them burning. Civilization, such as it was, had not yet been stamped out here by the Nazi boot. But next week? Next month? The month after? Would not Hitler's hordes take this too and extinguish the last lights?
>
> (Shirer 1941: 473)

Portugal however remained free of Nazi Occupation throughout the war, though economic consequences were biting by 1944. During his early 1944 stay in Lisbon, Beaton noticed that 'many changes have taken place in Lisbon during the last year' with basic shortages of petrol, coal and electricity and that 'a German visitor is seldom seen in his former aggressive attitude. Only a few stragglers linger in front of the Nazi Propaganda Bureau windows. Portugal is now 100% pro-Ally' (1944: 78).

Portuguese wartime neutrality had opened many doors to the global diffusion of information, people, goods and fashion, as stated at the start of this chapter. Crucially, Da Costa Leite emphasises that Portuguese neutrality also 'opened the way for many people to escape annihilation' (1998: 193), including thousands of Jewish families. In fashion business terms, the constant to and fro of information, garments, hats, patterns and designs from Paris helped keep Paris couture salons operating through the war as well as keeping Lisbon and Porto couturiers completely up to date on new seasonal Paris styles, as this chapter has shown. Fashion news was passed on to the public by Portuguese fashion magazines and by elegant international travellers, whilst wealthy Portuguese couture clients could still order close copies of seasonal Paris couture from the skilled workshops of Lisbon's famous couture salons or even purchase Paris originals. The world of fashion in Portugal therefore never wavered in its continuing allegiance to Paris couture style and had no difficulty in obtaining detailed seasonal information, month by month throughout the duration of World War Two.

References

Almanak Silva. (2013). *Notre Janine*, 6 November. https://almanaquesilva.wordpress.com/tag/janine/ (accessed 12 June 2017).

'Anna Maravilhas, the Magical Name of Portuguese Couture'. (2011). *https://ivanirfaria.wordpress.com/2011/09/19/ana-maravilhas-alta-costura-em-portugal/* (accessed 25 May 2017).

Beaton C. (1942). 'All of this I saw', American *Vogue*, 15 November: 88.

Beaton C. (1944). 'London to Lisbon, Cairo to Delhi – A flight journey to the Orient on a mission for Britain's Ministry of Information', American *Vogue*, 19 May: 78.

Bloch, M. (1984). *Operation Willi: The Nazi Plot to Kidnap the Duke of Windsor, July 1940*, London: Weidenfeld & Nicolson.

Brown, F. O. Jr. (2008). 'Jacob L. Morewitz, Eleanor Roosevelt and the Steamship Quanza', *Virginia Lawyer,* Senior Lawyers Conference, April: 20–31, 35. http://www.vsb.org/docs/valawyermagazine/vl0408_quanza.pdf (accessed 30 July 2017).

Cameron, R. (1942). 'Release – Flight to Lisbon – and then the waiting', American *Vogue*, 1 October: 113–114, 116.

Cardim, V. C. (2013). *A Moda em Portugal 1914–1959*. Lisbon: Iade Ediçoes.

Carvalho, C. (2015). 'The Shifting Shades of Elegance and Display in 1930s Estoril', *International Journal of Arts and Sciences*, vol. 68: 375–386. http://www.universitypublications.net/ijas/0808/pdf/U5K11.pdf (accessed 14 April 2019).

de Costa Leite, J. (1998). 'Neutrality by Agreement: Portugal and the British Alliance in World War II', *American University International Law Review*, vol. 14, issue 11: 185–192. digitalcommons.wcl.american.edu/cgi/viewcontent.cgi?article=1305&context=auilr (accessed 15 May 2017).

Cantista, I. and Costa Soares, P. (2016). 'Portuguese fashion in the 20th century', in Cantista, I. (ed.) *Fashion Spaces, Geographical, Physical and Virtual*, chapter 3, Porto: Leya.

Guinote, P. (2001). *Quotidiano Feminino – 1900–1940*, Lisbon Departamento do Património Cultural.

Mannes, M. (1944). 'In Lisbon – Dressed for Reaction', American *Vogue*, 1 September: 140–141, 198–199.

Mannes, M. (1940). 'Lisbon Fiddles', American *Vogue*, 1 October: 82, 132.

Milgram, A. (1999). 'Portugal; the consuls and the Jewish refugees', *Yad Vashem Studies* vol. XXVII: 123–156. Jerusalem: Shoah Resource Centre, the International School for Holocaust Studies.

Mundo Gráfico. (1940). 'Lisbon the capital of fashion', no. 1, 15 October.

Paiva Boléo, L.V. (2004). *Casa Havanesa, 140 anos à esquina do Chiado*, Dom Quixote: Porto.

Pinto Guimarães, M. A. (2008). *Saberes, Modas & Pós-de-Arroz – Modas & Bordados. Vida Feminina (1933–1955)*, Lisbon: Livros horizonte.

Ramalho, M. M. (2012). 'Lisbon, a city in the time of war', Lisbon: INCM National Print Mint Edition.

Shirer, W. (1941). *Berlin Diary – the journal of a Foreign Correspondent 1934–1941*, London: Hamish Hamilton.

Teixeira, M. B. (2015). 'Amália, a grande figura do fado' in *Amália em Palco, s.n.*, Estoril: Ilda Aleixo, 7–10.

Vail, K. P. B. (1998). *Peggy Guggenheim: A Celebration*, Venice: Guggenheim Museum.

Vestir. (1940). 'A Chronicle of Foreigners in Portugal', no. 14, 3 December.

Endnotes

1. With many thanks to Giulia Bonali and Dr. Marie Mcloughlin for generous help and advice given for the development of this chapter.
2. We are most especially grateful for the generous help of Clara Vaz Pinto, Director, Museu National do Traje, Lisbon, in obtaining the permission to use photographs from her museum collections.
3. See also Curie, E., 1943 'I saw the Nazis fall back', American *Vogue,* 15 July: 38–39.
4. The *SS Excambion* became an Amercian troop ship, the USS *John Penn*, in 1941. www.ssmaritime.com/Excalibur.htm (accessed 23 June 2018).
5. Milgram writes that the numbers of displaced Jewish refugees who left Europe via Lisbon/Estoril is estimated at 10,500 to 40,000 in the period 1940–1942 (4/31 footnote 13) with a peak in the summer of 1940 (5/31). Portuguese entry visas were only issued for thirty days, hence the desperate scramble for tickets on boats and planes (10/31 Milgram 1999).
6. Dalio and Lebeau found their way to Hollywood and both appeared in the 1942 film *Casablanca*, directed by Michael Curtiz. http://www.cineartistes.com/fiche-Marcel+Dalio.html (accessed 26 November 2018).

Chapter 8
Fashion in Denmark in the 'Five Dark Years'
Kirsten Toftegaard

Introduction

On 9 April 1940, Germany invaded Denmark. At first, the Occupation remained relatively peaceful. The government stayed in office and parliament continued its work. The Germans, who had an interest in maintaining existing levels of imported Danish food provisions, had no desire to rule Denmark with an iron fist. Although the Danish population was against the Occupation, there was a political desire to handle the situation pragmatically. However in August 1943, increasing dissatisfaction with the German occupiers led to widespread strikes, civil unrest and disobedience, and Germany declared Denmark to be in a state of emergency. Thereafter Denmark was ruled by direct orders from the German Foreign Ministry. As resistance grew in Denmark and general strikes were resumed in the summer of 1944, the last year of the German Occupation of Denmark turned out to be a savage finale to World War Two, with severe casualties.

The lack of materials available during World War Two influenced both the textile and clothing industry from the very beginning. The sense of insecurity pervading Europe before and during the war caused fashion, and also patterns and textiles, to revert to styles that typified earlier times, and many fashion photos demonstrate this retrospective tendency. Every museum with a dress collection knows about difficulties of tracing and collecting surviving clothes from the World War Two period because the shortage of textile materials led to the altering of many garments before they were finally worn out. However, a couple of dresses in the collection of Designmuseum Danmark, discussed in this text, convey stories of styles worn in Denmark in this period, of shortage of textile supplies, of quiet and sometimes downplayed resistance communicated through the dress code and finally the joy of the Liberation in May 1945.

FIGURE 8.0
Marie Gudme Leth, 1943, 'Friendship', a print in five colours on twill woven cellulose fibre fabric. (Designmuseum Danmark, no. 198, 1999. Photo by Pernille Klemp.)

The main source for this chapter is the weekly women's magazine *Tidens Kvinder*.[1] The magazine's overall approach was cultural and aesthetic, and it was aimed at the active, wealthy woman who could afford to follow the lead of fashion dictated from Paris and who could afford to travel the world. The magazine reported on the latest fashion from Parisian fashion houses as well as Danish fashion designers and department stores, and it offers an insight in the increasingly limited access to fashion news from Paris during the first three war years and once this ceased from 1943. The sources of Danish fashion news coverage significantly changed from direct contact from Paris (which at that time was considered the fashion capital of the world) to indirect contact via other countries, for instance Sweden. Thereafter fashion news started to flow instead from what was suggested as other fashion centers. This continuous, if limited, flow of information on seasonal fashion change from Paris did however provide Danish department stores, smaller dress-makers and fabric shops with a momentum, as well as proclaiming other countries and cities as fashion centers.

Whilst Paris was liberated on 19 August 1944, the Liberation of Denmark did not come until 5 May 1945. Fashion readers, couturiers, dressmakers, designers and their customers longed for news from the Parisian fashion houses. Two major events contributed to restoring Paris couture as the leading international fashion design source in Denmark. In November 1945, a fashion show with the participation of several Parisian fashion houses was held in Copenhagen as a part of a big charity event for France, and in January 1946, eight months after the Liberation, the cultural and fashionable elite in Copenhagen celebrated the opening of the traveling exhibition '*Thèâtre de la Mode*' in Denmark called '*La Mode Française*', hosted by Designmuseum Danmark (then the Danish Museum of Decorative Arts (Kunstindustrimuseet)). For both events, the press coverage was extensive.

The influence of Paris

Many Danish women had followed the lead of Paris fashion style in the pre-war period in their own way, adapting style to their own tastes, but this became increasingly difficult as the war progressed and less and less style news reached Denmark. The international system, whereby a department store bought the right to copy a selected group of models from chosen Parisian fashion houses, was also applied to bigger department stores in Denmark. In 1938, Westerby advertised models created through after this system, with the resulting garments being most acceptable to the more modest customer: 'Perhaps some rational female teacher may consider her budget insufficient for this tempting luxury. But one has to remember that Westerby has a special system, whereby the original model is adapted to the usual Westerby prices' (*Tidens Kvinder*, 1938, 14: 29). However, the system was not always clarified so clearly in advertisements and with today's view on copying in mind, the line between inspiration, legal copying or rip-off is blurred and sometimes rather difficult to determine from the provided texts.

Already in 1939, the sense of fashion insecurity that was pervading Europe, caused by the war, created a return to styles that typified previous periods. The journalists were at a loss and statements such as 'Insecurity Regarding Future Styles', 'In Search of Lost Time' and 'Is the Wasp-Waist Returning?' hit the headlines (*Tidens Kvinder*, 1939, 41: 26–27; 43: 12–13; 50: 14–15).[2] From the outbreak of the war, fashion news from Paris became increasingly scarce. Sometimes it reached the Danish readers through complicated and indirect channels: 'It sounds unbelievable, but it is nevertheless true that ideas and indications of Parisian fashion have reached the department store Jac. Olsen through America together with news of American fashion and the solid fashion houses in Vienna' (*Tidens Kvinder*, 1940, 39: 30–31). In 1942, despite the German Occupation, more and more reports from Paris were reproduced from French fashion magazines, especially *La femme chic* and *l'Officiel* (*Tidens Kvinder*, 1942, 11: 28–29; 18: 18–19; 24: 14–15). Then suddenly in the late summer the same year, as a rare incident: 'Just arrived from Paris a collection of original fashion photos of delightful summer dresses'. Unlike some of the photos and drawings from Paris, which had become increasingly anonymous and without any information on designer or fashion house, these fashion photos had full details, although the designers were from lesser-known fashion houses, among others Germaine Lecomte, Jeanne Lafaurie and Charles Montaigne (*Tidens Kvinder*, 1942, 32: 30–31).

However, around even months later, the frequency of fashion news from Paris was reduced to point zero in February 1943, due to the fact that news items became rarer and photos of fashion designs were no longer printed in French newspapers and magazine, as the Germans banned the distribution of photos of French fashion (Veillon 2002: 116–119). Instead, the number of fashion news reports from Nazi Berlin and Vienna grew in number, though information on designers or fashion houses remained unknown to the Danish reader. Whether this was a deliberate strategy from the magazine editor or actual lack of information, is difficult to determine. Often behind the promotion of Nazi fashion were the two organisations Berliner Modelle Gesellschaft and Haus der Mode from Vienna (see Chapter 10).[3]

Although *Tidens Kvinder* saw Paris as the most important fashion centre before the war, already other cities and countries were named as important fashion centres for the benefit of the Danish readers, for instance America and especially Hollywood, but also London (*Tidens Kvinder*, 1938, 14: 29). By 1941, Sweden had become a country to which the Danish fashion-conscious woman turned her eye for inspiration. However in 1943, as the war took a severe turn for several occupied countries, Sweden finally became the one main fashion centre for Danish fashion consciousness and the main fashion source for Danish fashion magazines. Reports from Sweden included fashion photographs carried out by the Danish journalist and photographer Ketty Selmer (1915–1989) who was married to a Swede.[4] A growing number of fashion photos were replaced by fashion drawings, which were most often executed by Swedish textile artist Göta Trädgårdh (1904–1984).[5]

Later in the war, other countries were proclaimed as fashion centres too, for instance Switzerland, because of a never failing supply of fabrics (*Tidens Kvinder*, 1944, 52: 21). At one point, late in 1945, after the end of the war, perhaps the magazine's editors became too generous with the label 'Fashion centre', as the Swedish town of Malmø was also declared a fashion centre after a big fashion show at the local theatre (*Tidens Kvinder*, 1945, 44: 22–23).

Momentum for Danish couture

This continuous, if limited, flow of information from Paris on seasonal fashion change did however provide Danish department stores with their model salons, as well as dressmakers with their individual salons, and smaller dressmakers and shops selling dress materials with momentum. Already from the second half of the 1930s, one of the so-called Three Bs, Holger Blom (1906–1965) – the other two were Preben Birck (1906–1992) and Uffe Brydegaard (1901–1962) – already had his individual couture salon in Copenhagen.[6] Furthermore, several Copenhagen department stores had long-established couture departments, the earliest being the fashion salon in Magasin du Nord from 1913. Among others were Illum, Fonnesbech, Jac. Olsen, Westerby and Modepalæet.

The department store Crome & Goldschmidt addressed the problem of customers who were no longer able to shop in celebrated foreign fashion houses: '[This dress is] a find for the elegant customer with the discerning taste, who bought her clothes in the finest foreign fashion houses before the war' (*Tidens*

FIGURE 8.1
Exhibition of synthetic fabrics arranged by the National League of Danish Manufacture, 1942 (with thanks to the *Magasin du Nord* Archive).

Kvinder, 1943, 19: 4). During all five years of the war, the increased numbers of press advertisements and fashion reports from local suppliers was significant, including those by the couture salons of department stores and from their own ready-made women's wear departments. A well-known fabric store in the center of Copenhagen, Per Reumert, extended its activities to include a 'dress salon' where the shop also sold ready-made clothes. Some stores and shops offered fashion presentations and tea in an exclusive environment. A number of apparently small dressmakers advertised few times before disappearing from the magazine's columns after the war (*Tidens Kvinder*, 1941, 14: 37; 17: 33; 37: 32–33, 35; 40: 41; 1942, 10: 33; 1943, 11: 33; 15: 33; 16: 33).

Home diligence sweeps across the country: shortage of materials and the use of alternative materials

Already in 1940, *Tidens Kvinder* reported: 'The spirit of home diligence sweeps across the country . . . We have to adjust to use alternative materials', for instance to make dance dresses out of sheeting and even using cretonne curtains. Readers were encouraged to show ingenuity or resourcefulness in utilisation and nothing, even the smallest piece of fabric, was allowed to go waste. Amongst clothes and accessories, shoes were first to make use of substitute materials. Platform shoes with cork soles and skin from catfish, plaice and pigskin became commonly used as shoe material (*Tidens Kvinder*, 1940, 13: 30–31; 19: 12–13; 20: 28–29). The department store Illum had apparently been hoarding woolen fashion fabrics, because they announced that they were able to avoid the use of fabric alternatives and that, despite the fact that wool cloth was by then almost impossible to procure, 80 per cent of all their models were still in wool (*Tidens Kvinder*, 1940, 37: 26–27).

In 1942, another department store advertised with the headline: 'From fustian to tulle and taffeta'. The department store, Crome & Goldschmidt, suggested that the fabric fustian, in Denmark normally used for bolster covers and bed ticking, now served a different function as dress material (*Tidens Kvinder*, 1942, 38: 4–5). In 1945, the department store Jac. Olsen, which was known for its excellent fur department, advertised fur coats made of pony skin – they even printed an image of a cute newborn foal together with photos of the these coats (*Tidens Kvinder*, 1945, 4: 5). Frequently, *Tidens Kvinder* reported on clothes and accessories seen at Danish society weddings, such as a double-page report from an early summer wedding in 1943. For the wedding, fabric printed by the Danish textile printer Marie Gudme Leth (1895–1997) was made up into dresses for the six bridesmaids. In the 1930s to 1940s, Marie Gudme Leth's classic and narrative flora-and-fauna patterns were immensely popular, and although her printed textiles were mostly used for upholstery and curtains, her printed fabric design featuring a pair of doves carrying sprays in their beaks was employed for the six bridesmaids' dresses (*Tidens Kvinder*, 1943, 22: 14–15).[7]

To gamle Adelsslægter forenes

Komtesse Drude Ahlefeldt-Laurvig vies til Baron Rosenørn-Lehn

9) Brudeparret.
10) Komtesse Karin von Rosen, Komtesse Margit von Rosen, Grev Bobby Moltke, Komtesse Helle Danneskiold Samsøe.
11) Grev Claus Ahlefeldt-Laurvig og Grevinde Fritze Ahlefeldt-Laurvig.
12) De smukke Brudepiger, Komtesserne Beke Ahlefeldt, Caritas Bernstorff, Helle Danneskiold-Samsøe, Baronesse Elisabeth Blixen-Finecke, Frøken Hasselbalch og Frøken Doreen Wessel.
13) Prins Flemming, Baron Otto Rosenørn-Lehn, Komtesse Caritas Bernstorff, Prins Axel, Lensgrevinde Irene Kragh-Juel-Vind-Friis og Baronesse Ulla Rosenørn-Lehn.
14) Brudepigerne, Bruden og hendes Broder Grev Claus, Grevinde Ahlefeldt og Baronesse Rosenørn-Lehn.

FIGURE 8.2
Six bridesmaids wearing dresses, in printed fabric, 1943, by Marie Gudme Leth, titled 'Birds'. (*Tiden Kvinder*, 1943, 22: 15, photo by Pernille Klemp.)

FIGURE 8.3
Tailored *culotte* suit for cycling in Copenhagen during World War Two (with thanks to the *Magasin du Nord* Archive).

Because of the shortage of quality fabric available for printing during the war period, the regenerated cellulose fibre called 'Vistra' became commonly used both for curtains and dress fabric because of its natural hang. Again the same year, another summer wedding made use of fabric printed by Marie Gudme Leth for the bridesmaids, this time the four-colour floral print design 'Hydrangea' (*Tidens Kvinder*, 1943, 29: 27).

Inhabitants in Denmark as in several other war-afflicted countries had to adjust to more practical styles and dresses became simpler and stripped of excesses. Customers tried to adjust to wartime reality and at *Magasin du Nord*, the fashion salon reported that 'times have changed, and the great gown belonging to the glittering evening party has disappeared' (*Tidens Kvinder*, 1944, 47: 25). In 1944, indeed, a restriction against long dresses was enforced because it was considered to be an unnecessary waste of fabric, though it was noted that 'perhaps Sweden is the only country in Europe where long evening gowns are still allowed to be worn' (*Tidens Kvinder*, 1944, 51: 20). The culotte or a divided skirt became fashionable as in many other countries where the bicycle became a widespread means of transportation because of a shortage of fuel.

In the last month of the Occupation in 1945, the readers of *Tidens Kvinder* also had to embrace the ever-more-profound seriousness of the shortage of supplies and materials. The magazine featured one article explaining the role of a clothing exchange centre, under the title 'Swopping is today's slogan' – with a double-page spread discussing the work of just such a centre (*Tidens Kvinder*, 1945, 11: 12–13; 16: 8–9).

Silent resistance

For modern readers today, the texts attached to the Danish fashion photos in the weekly reports in *Tidens Kvinder* can be complicated to decode for several reasons. Firstly, today's readers need to understand that the fashion reports in general in wartime Denmark were intended to be more inspirational rather than providing commercial examples of available ready-made or couture garments. This had also been the case before the war, but was reinforced especially after 1943 through the increasing use of fashion drawings instead of fashion photographs of actual garments. Secondly, we must realise that in the written press, in songs and theatre as well, and particularly in fashion reports, a new subtle Danish language with implied meanings evolved during the war years. The significance in the texts was not only to be found in the actual printed words, but in what lay between the lines, encouraging readers (or listeners) to reflect on what was left out, that is to say, what was not written. Thus, every photograph of a fashion garment from Sweden or of one of the rare original Parisian fashion photos, was followed by a detailed style description, including the name of the designer where known, whereas the much less favoured garments from Germany, Austria or Italy were only identified by country of origin and the words, for example, 'a Vienna model' or 'a Berlin model'. Was this a deliberate omission of words or just lack of available information? We do not know.

On 7 February 1943, the German Chamber of Commerce hosted a major fashion show in the Palm Court at the Hotel d'Angleterre at the Kgs. Nytorv in the centre of Copenhagen. The show of 230 German and Austrian dresses was arranged by Berliner Modelle Gesellschaft and Haus der Mode in Vienna and presented spring and summer fashion for 1943.[8] The event was officially attended by the Italian and Finish legations and representatives from the Copenhagen fashion industry. A press report commented, 'For once, more men than women attended a fashion show', adding that 'consequently it was a very business-like audience'. The fashion journalist was however not impressed because 'the "new" line turned out to be the "old" line'. Before Copenhagen, the export show had visited Stockholm and afterwards the show went on to Zürich and Budapest (*Politiken*, 1943, 8/2: 5; *Nationaltidende*, 1943, 8/2: 6; *Tidens Kvinder*, 1943, 8: 16–17).

Though much more visible during the first ecstatic period after the Liberation, as we shall see later, the use of the colours of the Allies – red, white and blue – in clothes during wartime was a way to mock the Germans and a subtle way to demonstrate ones political and national affiliation. Other ways to show affiliation were to wear small badges showing the Danish colours of red and white or with images of the king and to participate in reunions for community singing.[9] An elegant dress of 1944 with matching jacket in dark blue serge in the collection of the Designmuseum Danmark seems to be, and can perhaps today be judged as, an example of this discrete demonstration. The upper part of the dress and parts of the jacket are made of skillfully stitched together cords in blue, red and white. The ensemble is an excellent example of the use of the Allied colours, or, as they were also called in Denmark, Royal Airforce colours. The sculptor Kirsten Rose (1909–2001) apparently bought this dress and jacket at the department store Fonnesbech in the centre of Copenhagen.[10]

The five-colour printed, twill woven cellulose fibre fabric 'Friendship', designed by Marie Gudme Leth in 1943, is not unambiguous at all in its motives – so it seems for the contemporary viewer. The design features sprays of roses and lilies-of-the-valley, butterflies, swans, a book with flowers, a couple of Staffordshire spaniel dog figurines, a balloon decorated with flowers carrying a letter, a heart decorated with a garland of flowers and a garland with a man and a woman's hand joined in a handshake underneath the word 'love'. This design leaves no doubt – the friendship referred to in the design is not to Germany, but rather to the United Kingdom, hence the word 'love' and the ubiquitous English Staffordshire dogs.[11]

FIGURE 8.4
Dress and jacket in Allied colours, from the Fonnesbech department store, Copenhagen. (Designmuseum Danmark, no. 179 a-b/1987. Photographs by Pernille Klemp.)

FIGURE 8.5
Marie Gudme Leth, 1943, 'Friendship', a print in five colours on twill woven cellulose fibre fabric. (Designmuseum Danmark, no. 198, 1999. Photo by Pernille Klemp.)

The Liberation

In May 1945, the Liberation came and it was celebrated at every occasion. The couturier Pierre Balmain recalled: 'Meanwhile the Normandy Landing [6 June 1944, D-Day] had taken place. We all felt so sure about the impending victory that we [at Lucien Lelong, where he and Dior worked during the Second World War] had prepared a so-called Liberation Collection long before the Allied troops entered Paris' (Balmain 1964: 83). Fashion readers, couturiers, dressmakers, designers and their customers longed for news from the Parisian fashion houses.

However, although news from Paris soon after the Liberation became much more accessible, other sources, which had been so useful during wartime, continued to flow too for the benefit of the thirsty audience, for instance news from Sweden. Moreover, the magazine *Tidens Kvinder* established a correspondent in Hollywood and one in New York who regularly reported from the two cities. The magazine succeeded in printing several drawings of fashionable Hollywood film costumes

FIGURE 8.6
General Montgomery and British forces welcomed in Copenhagen's Straget Street on 12 May 1945. (Getty 514704308.)

made by the American costume designer Edith Head (1897–1981) (*Tidens Kvinder*, 1945, 21: 19; 23: 14–15; 24: 19).[12]

The language used in the press was often nationalistic and the most popular colours seen in the dresses played an important part in the celebrations. The blue, red and white colours of the Allies no longer had to be hidden or excused. They were used proudly after the Liberation:

> Victory fashion thrives … this summer of course, every young woman must have a festive dress in the Allied colours – Modepalæet (the Fashion Palace) displays an enchanting fantasy in combining these three bright colours which beautifully matches the green leaves of summer and a suntanned complexion.
>
> (*Tidens Kvinder*, 1945, 25: 27)

An example of such a Victory dress was a white summer dress with the Allied flags placed on the full skirt and with a blue and white belt. Another was a 'stars and stripes' dress, the skirt with red-and-white transverse stripes, the blue top appliquéd with white stripes at the waist and around the armhole.

In Denmark, a new fashion colour 'Victory blue' was launched: 'Think of the clear blue colour in the Tricolour and picture yourselves the colour a shade more bright and vivid –and you have got "the Victory blue"' (*Tidens Kvinder*, 1945, 27: 25). From the department store Crome & Goldschmidt, fashionable versions of the French police and military hat, the *kepi*, were introduced made in straw with a cockade in the colours of the tricolour (*Tidens Kvinder*, 1945, 26: 5).[13] In September 1945, the sports section of Crome & Goldschmidt offered a man's 'Monty-Jacket', referring to the classic British military uniform worn by General Montgomery. Worn inside the trousers, this 'Monty-Jacket' was more comparable to a military shirt with two chest pockets with flap closures (*Tidens Kvinder*, 1945, 39: 5).

A few years ago, the Designmuseum Danmark purchased a red and whitish dress made in a poor quality of linen. Today, the fabric would be considered to be unfit for use as a dress material as it is quite scratchy. In addition, the linen looks as it would disintegrate on contact with water. However, the design of the upper part of the dress shows unmistakable references to the Danish red and white flag. Although suffering still from shortages of material for clothing, it can be safely assumed that this dress was sewn in order to celebrate long-awaited Danish freedom in the spring of 1945.[14]

In the summer of 1946, it was announced that Denmark had improved the quality of its linen, and eight beach dresses were photographed in a fashion report supporting this statement. Again Marie Gudme Leth had created and printed a linen design for one of the dresses, this time the pattern titled 'The Frederiksberg Gardens' (*Tidens Kvinder*, 1946, 25: 22–23). That same year, in the autumn, Westerby launched a collaboration between fashion designers and Danish hand-weaving

FIGURE 8.7
Liberation flag dress, 1945. (Designmuseum Danmark, no. 228/2013. Photo by Pernille Klemp.)

workshops whilst the store waited for fashion fabric supplies from abroad (*Tidens Kvinder*, 1945, 40: 29). Sadly enough, this positive Danish collaboration did not establish itself successfully or stably enough and the use of Danish hand-woven fabric as dress materials remained a niche production.

Two events relating to France and Parisian fashion are notable within the months after the Liberation. On 9 November 1945, seven months after the Liberation of Denmark, a charity event was launched for the benefit of the people in France. Under the headline 'Paris in Copenhagen', the widely distributed Danish newspaper *Politiken* declared the arrangement to have been a great success, raising enough money to enable a convoy of eighteen food lorries to leave Copenhagen for Paris. The event included a book market, with an open-air service of coffee, with cabaret singers at restaurants and in trams and finally two days of fashion shows held at the Copenhagen Town Hall. This was a landmark within the Danish fashion world as it was the very first live glimpse of Parisian fashion in Copenhagen since 1939. Danish actor and active participant in the Resistance Movement Mogens Wieth (1919–1962) opened the event by singing the national anthem of France, '*la Marseillaise*'. Around seventy dresses were on parade, including among others, dresses by Worth, Schiaparelli, Molyneux, Jacques Fath, Jean Dessés, Lanvin, Nina Ricci, Madeleine Carpentier, Agnès-Drecoll, Lucien Lelong and Paquin. The newspaper noted however, that husbands did not have to worry about the content of their purses because nothing at the fashion show was for sale (*Politiken*, 1945, 9/11: 5; 10/11: 1; *Nationaltidende*, 1945, 9/11: 2, 3).

Two months later, still without the means to create garments for actual sale, in January 1946, the Designmuseum Danmark (then the Danish Museum of Decorative Arts) hosted one of several versions of the travelling exhibition *Thèâtre de la Mode*, put together by the *Chambre Syndicale de la Couture Parisienne*, featuring scenes of small wire figures dressed in the latest Paris models, with tiny hats, shoes and handbags. In Denmark, the exhibition was called '*La Mode Française*'.[15] Accompanied by Danish royals – the Crown Prince, Frederik (1899–1972), and his mother, Queen Alexandrine (1879–1952) – the cultural and fashionable elite of Copenhagen celebrated the exhibition's opening with official speeches, supper, wine specially imported from France and finally a ball.

Press coverage was extensive. Dresses from thirty-nine fashion houses were shown, including all the great Parisian couturiers: Balanciaga, Madame Grès, Jacques Fath, Jean Patou, Jeanne Lanvin, Lucien Lelong, Maggy Rouff, Molyneux, Schiaparelli and Worth. Six houses showed fur coats and all possible accessories were included, such as lingerie and jumpers.[16] The leading Danish couturier Ejnar Engelbert, head of the fashion salon in the department store Magasin du Nord, lectured at the museum about the new inspiration from Paris fashion. *La Femme*, published in Paris, reported on 20 February 1946 that one of the features of the

FIGURE 8.8
Front cover of *La Femme*, no. 36, 20 February 1946 (with thanks to the Dress History Teaching Collection, University of Brighton).

display was a large promotional mannequin figure created by Saint-Martin from chicken wire, kindly donated by an ironmonger who pulled down his chicken coop to provide the necessary raw materials, and that 'three of the twelve sets were presented by Jean Saint-Martin, Eliane Bonabel and members of the Chambre Syndicale de la Couture Parisienne . . . in gratitude for the 15,000 daily meals provided by Denmark to Paris school children'.[17] Half of the entrance fee was donated to the provision of meals for starving Parisian children.

The exhibition of the very latest Paris couture styles was open for one month and was an immense success, with around 40,000 visitors. For many future Danish fashion designers, the exhibition was a revelation, something they remembered for many years afterwards. The number of visitors to the exhibition at the museum has never, before or ever since, been surpassed and this massive success spoke for itself. Paris couture had re-asserted itself again as the leading fashion design inspiration in Denmark.[18]

FIGURE 8.9
Chicken wire figure made in Copenhagen by Jean Saint-Martin to promote the showing of the *Théâtre de La Mode, La Femme*, 20 February 1946 (with thanks to the Dress History Teaching Collection, University of Brighton).

Conclusion

Examination here of the woman's magazine *Tidens Kvinder* has shown that it has offered a useful, if limited, context in order to understand that it was wartime. In 1943, its regular fashion reporter Madame Tildi wrote: 'One speaks so much about problems of obtaining fabrics and materials, and all that tediousness, and then it turns out that fashion has an immense flexibility to make things happen' (*Tidens Kvinder*, 1942, 19: 18–19). Although women wanted a strong lead from the fashion magazine in the 1940s, the consequences of the war became unavoidable for the readers of *Tidens Kvinder* in 1943. First, fashion photos of French fashion were banned from being distributed and printed. When news did reach the magazine, it was as verbal reports accompanied by fashion drawings. French news was replaced instead by an increase in the number of fashion photos from Berlin and Vienna. In general, fashion reports and advertisements for clothes became noticeably rarer and rarer in the last year of the war. The small dressmakers, who had their heyday in wartime, played an important role in disseminating fashion trends. However, it is important to stress that during the war the revival of fashion drawings must not be underrated. This was of significance because it was a vital way to disseminate fashion trends, whilst avoiding the radar of German censorship.

In the first period after the Liberation, Paris once again became one of the leading sources for fashion news in Denmark, but Sweden, Hollywood, New York, and London also contributed to the dissemination of news for the benefit of the readers of *Tidens Kvinder*. In the summer of 1945, the American photographer and war correspondent Lee Miller (1907–1977) visited Denmark for a month. For the readers of *Tidens Kvinder*, she made every effort to promote the reinstatement of Paris as the leading international fashion city. However, after her many months of photographing and reporting all over war-decimated Europe, what intrigued and impressed her above all in Denmark, and finally led her to proclaim the country to be a paradise, was the abundance of food compared to other European countries (*Tidens Kvinder*, 1945, 27).[19] In Denmark, as discussed, the usual natural fibres such as wool, silk, linen and cotton were in short supply whilst manmade fibres prospered. In 1943, the Carlsberg Foundation donated a grant to the designer-printer Marie Gudme Leth to undertake research into the development of manmade fibres for textile print.[20]

Regarding fashion in France, Dominique Veillon's comment that 'Creative couture was growing ever closer to the fashion of everyday living' is open to discussion even regarding French fashion (Veillon 2002: 116). Whether this was true depends on region, period of the war and whether it applies to haute couture, ready-to-wear or fashion accessories. For instance, in many European countries, hats were one of the few fashion items sold without rationing. Hats became popular in fashion reports and the creation of hats exceeded in fantasy and crazy whims as the war years went by. During wartime, in Denmark, colours were played down and in general, clothes became simpler, stripped of excesses and with an overall expression that was much more serious than before the war. The little black dress in wool was the safe and appropriate choice for evenings. Re-use, altering and remaking became the order of the day. Cupboards and drawers were searched for every piece of fabric to use as dress material, cut-away or unused old embroideries were brought to light in order to decorate an otherwise dull dress. Although not applicable in some European countries, it became a reality in Denmark that creative couture grew closer to the fashion of everyday living.

Sources

Designmuseum Danmark, Accession Protocol
Marie Gudme Leth Archive, Designmuseum Danmark
Nationaltidende, 1943, 1945
Politiken, 1943, 1945
Tidens Kvinder, 1938–1947

References

Balmain, Pierre (1964): *My Years and Seasons*, London: Cassell.
Christensen, Claus Bundgård et al. (2005): *Danmark besat*, Copenhagen: Høst.
Guenther, Irene (2004): *Nazi Chic? – Fashioning Women in the Third Reich*, Oxford and New York: Berg.
Howell, Geraldine (2012): *Wartime Fashion – From Haute Couture to Homemade 1939–1945*, London: Bloomsbury.

Jensen, Klaus Bruhn, ed. (1996–2003): *Dansk mediehistorie*, 4 bd., vol. 2, Copenhagen: Samleren.

Jensen, Sigurd (1971): *Levevilkår under besættelsen*, Udgiverselskab for Danmarks Nyeste Historie, Copenhagen: Gyldendal.

La Femme, 20 February 1946: 3–6.

Møller, Viggo, ed. (1943): *Krisebestemmelser for Textilhandlere 1942–43*, Copenhagen: Dansk Textil Union.

Normann, Henning, ed. (1944): *Krisebestemmelser for Textilhandlere 1943–44*, Copenhagen: Dansk Textil Union.

Richard, Anne Birgitte (2005): *Køn og kultur, 1930ernes og 1940ernes kamp om køn, kultur og modernitet læst gennem kvindernes tekster,* Copenhagen: Museum Tusculanums Forlag.

Sladen, Christopher (1995): *The Conscription of Fashion – Utility Cloth, Clothing and Footwear 1941–1952*, Aldershot and Brookfield: Scolar Press.

Summers, Julie (2015): *Style in the Second World War – Fashion on Ration,* London: Profile Books.

Taylor, Lou (1995): 'The Work and Function of the Paris Couture Industry During the German Occupation of 1940–44', in *Dress – The Annual Journal of the Costume Society of America*, Vol. 22.

Textil (1935): Vol. 7, Copenhagen: Dansk Textil Union.

Thing, Morten (2008): *De russiske jøder i København 1882–1943*, Copenhagen: Gyldendal

Tidens Kvinder, Volume 1938–1947.

Tscherning, G, ed. (1965): *Dansk Textil Union 1915–1965, 50 års Jubilæumsnummer,* Copenhagen: Dansk Textil Union.

Veillon, Dominique (2002): *Fashion under the occupation*, Oxford and New York: Berg.

Wassilitchikoff, Marie (1989): *Dagbøger fra Berlin 1940–1945*, Copenhagen: Gyldendal.

Endnotes

1 *Tidens Kvinder*, published from 1919 to 1969, was established by the Danish Women's National Council. In this period, the magazine differed from other women's magazines aesthetically and in content and price. *Tidens Kvinder* (the Age of Women) was around 40 per cent more expensive than family-oriented magazines, for instance *Hjemmet* (the Home) and *Hus og Frue* (House and Wife). Every volume had features about royalty and celebrities, foreign or Danish, and the magazine wrote about beauty products and interior design. The role of the woman in *Tidens Kvinder* was staged and idealized, and neither housework nor paid employment were expected to be of any interest to the reader. In the 1950s, the magazine changed content and target group. Richard, Anne Birgitte (2005): *Køn og kultur, 1930ernes og 1940ernes kamp om køn, kultur og modernitet læst gennem kvindernes tekster,* København: Museum Tusculanums Forlag.

2 'In Search of Lost Time' is a reference to the French author Marcel Proust's (1871–1922) novel cycle 'À la Recherche du Temps Perdu' from 1913–1927.

3 Berliner Modelle Gesellschaft (BMG) was established in 1940. The members were top fashion designer salons in Berlin. By 1941, the number of participating salons in the organization had grown to eighteen. Vienna was the leading fashion centre in Austria, which was incorporated into the Greater German Reich in 1938. BMG and Haus der Mode in Vienna, which was established to promote Viennese fashion, remained separate entities, although both organizations were closely linked to Deutsches Mode-Institut (DMI).

4   Ketty Selmer was a controversial woman. As a young woman, she lived an agitated life as a waitress and a dancer. During the war, she moved in shady circles. She entered into a pro forma marriage with a somewhat older Swedish man. The marriage secured her free passage between Sweden and Denmark. Apparently she acted as a courier for the Danish National Police at the same time as having contacts with the German Occupiers. On top of this, she worked as a reporter and photographer for Danish women's magazines.

5   Göta Trädgårdh was educated at Beckmans College of Design in Stockholm and besides being a textile artist, she taught pattern and fashion drawing.

6   Before the heyday of Danish couture in the 1950s and 1940s and during the war, all 'Three Bs' worked with costumes for film and theatre.

7   'To gamle Adelsslægter forenes – Komtesse Drude Ahlefeldt-Laurvig vies til Baron Rosenørn-Lehn'. Marie Gudme Leth was one of the pioneers who revived textile printing as an artisanal craft in Denmark around 1930. The pattern with two couple of birds was titled 'Birds', designed in 1941–1942.

8   Berliner Modelle Gesellschaft organized export fashion shows sponsored by Deutsches Mode-Institut. Sometimes Haus der Mode in Vienna participated.

9   Throughout the country, one-fifth of the Danish population (around 740,000 Danes) were gathered to sing together on 1 September 1940.

10 Serge is self-coloured suiting, twill woven in wool and in this case a mixture of wool and synthetic wool. The fabric was popular for dark blue suits for men. The department store Fonnesbech was established in 1847 and closed down in 1970.

11 Designmuseum Danmark, Accession Protocol 198/1999, Vistra fabric, screen print in five colours, 'Friendship'.

12 Throughout her entire carrier, Edith Head won a record of eight Academy Awards (Oscars) for Best Costume Design.

13 Confusingly in the advertisement, the hat is called a 'Sergot'.

14 Designmuseum Danmark's Accession Protocol 228/2013. Unfortunately, there is no provenance to the dress.

15 The precise title of the exhibition was '*La Mode Française*' – with the famous dolls from '*Théâtre de la Mode*' dressed by '*la Couture Parisienne*'.

16 *Udstillingen La Mode Française – med de berømte dukker fra 'Théatre de la Mode' klædt paa af La Couture Parisienne*, København: Kunstindustrimuseet, 1946.

17 *La Femme* was published bi-monthly, with the first edition printed in Paris on 15 March 1945, seven months after the Liberation of Paris and two months before the final end of World War Two in Europe. It existed for less than two years, with just sixty editions published in 1945–1946. It was attached to the Resistance Movement de Liberation National (MLR), one of whose founders was the war heroine Lucie Aubrac. She was director of this journal through its two-year life. It featured two regular sections on fashion – one on day-to-day styles and another on Paris couture (*Biblioteque National*, Paris, gallica.bnf.fr (La Femme Paris 1945)).

18 Press release from the museum archive, Designmuseum Danmark, Box 39, amongst others, *Børsen*, 19 January 1946, *Berlingske Tidende*, 24 January 1946, *Nationaltidende*, 25 January 1946.

19 In her reportages for both *Vogue* and *Harper's Bazaar*, Lee Miller spanned a wide scope from fashion to being a war correspondent.

20 The Marie Gudme Leth Archive, Designmuseum Danmark.

Chapter 9
The diffusion, reception and use of Paris style information in Brazil and its couture salons: 1939–1946

Cláudia de Oliveira

FIGURE 9.0 (opposite) Fashion drawing from the collection 'Brazilian Beige' by Worth and Hermès, *Sombra*, May 1941 (with thanks to the Biblioteca Nacional, Rio de Janeiro).

FIGURE 9.1 (right) Walking on the famous mosaic pavement at Copacabana Beach, Rio de Janeiro, 1941. (Getty 50453673.)

This chapter builds on the thorough research undertaken by Maria Cristina Volpi and Cristina Seixas since the 1970s, and on the archives of Casa Canadá, the first Brazilian couture salon, which opened its doors in 1940. It parts from the accepted dress history hypothesis, which states that during World War Two Paris haute couture became isolated from its international markets and retreated into a luxury world of its own. In fact, this research will show that despite the Nazi Occupation of Paris from 14 June 1940 to 25 August 1944, and German restrictions imposed on Parisian haute couture, French fashion continued to be appreciated and consumed in Brazil throughout the war.

The focus in this text is on purchases by the wealthy Brazilian elite, who understood that such clothing acted as a demonstration of their taste and class distinction, as Bourdieu notes (2011: 264, 241). This research has drawn on oral history interviews, the archives of Casa Canadá and analysis of reports from the Brazilian social and fashion press between 1939–1945.

It needs to be clarified that Brazil in the 1930s was an important theatre of political, economic and cultural rivalry between Nazi Germany, the USA and Britain. McCann writes that 'there was intense competition' amongst

FIGURE 9.2
The Brazilian Expeditionary Forces marching past Castel Nuovo, Naples, 1944. (Getty 82031815.)

these countries over access to Brazil's resources: 'cotton, coffee, cocoa, tobacco, rubber, wool, woods, tropical fruits, hides, butter, iron ore' and steel. When World War Two erupted, Brazil remained neutral until 22 August 1942, when President Vargas, head of the dictatorial '*Estado Novo*', declared war on Germany and Brazil joined with the Allied forces. McCann notes that 'Brazil took an active part in World War Two as a supplier of strategic raw materials, as the site of important [US] air and naval bases,... as a contributor of naval units, a combat fighter squadron and a 25,000 strong infantry division', which fought in Italy in 1944. McCann notes too that when the war started, 'of the $2,242,200,000 foreign investment, the British held 48%, the Americans 25%, the Canadians 18%, and a mix of others 9%' (McCann 1995 : 50, 70).

French business interests were embedded too in this economic rivalry as Paris fashion continued to be appreciated and consumed in Brazil throughout the years of World War Two, a contention based here on two explanatory axes that confirm this hypothesis. The first refers to the sale of Paris couture, and the making of legally agreed copies, for a Brazilian and Latin American clientele through elegant new fashion houses that emerged in Rio de Janeiro in the 1930s, catering to the habits of a socio-economic elite of the New World who, since the late nineteenth century, divided their time between Paris and their countries of origin (Bueno 2012: 23).

Indeed, ever since the arrival of the Portuguese court to its colony in Brazil in 1808,[1] France was always seen by the Crown and Brazilian elites as a great symbol of civilization, with French fashion as one of the foremost symbols of this. In 1826, Brazil signed a Treaty of Friendship and Commerce with France,[2] which was followed by a large wave of French immigrants, including fashion tradesmen and salesmen, seen as symbols of modernity, arriving in the tropics (Medeiros 2007:

13). Rio de Janeiro became a city where the elites spoke French and Paris fashions allowed a sophisticated lifestyle to be reinvented (2007: 15).

In the twentieth century, whilst the weight of Brazilian business lay with England, this French preference remained intact. Andrade comments, for example, that from 1913–1940, fashion advertisements for the famous English department store Mappin, in São Paulo, emphasised 'the praised Parisian fashions of *Vogue* magazine' (Andrade 2005: 184–186). Bueno confirms that amongst the principal buyers of new French trends in the early twentieth century, secondly only to US department stores, were stores from Argentina and Brazil (Bueno 2011: 23). In 1914 the House of Paquin opened an Argentinian branch in Buenos Aires (Sirop 1989: 3). Davis notes that even with the outbreak of World War Two in 1939, the large stores in the New World continued to sell French luxury articles, especially Parisian couture (Davis 2006: 6), which became one of the most popular luxury items in the New World during the first half of the twentieth century according to Bueno (2012: 23).

Kauffman comments that Brazilian clients included, for example, one of the most famous international beauties of '*Tout Paris*' international social circles in the late 1930s: the wealthy Aimée de Heeren. Rumoured to be the former mistress of Brazil's President Vargas, she had moved to New York in the late 1930s, living often in Paris and patronising the salons of Rochas, Schiaparelli, Fath, Vionnet, Givenchy, Molyneux and Alix, amongst others. In 1941 she married Rodman A. de Heeren, son of the Wanamaker department store family (see Chapter 6). She lived in New York through the war (Kauffman 2012: 2–7).

Related to these developments was the active sending of Paris couture fashion shows directly to Brazil during World War Two, a process that also highlights the complex competition between Paris and London couture. In August 1940, for example, the British government, struggling to keep its political and economic contacts with Brazil alive, asked its Board of Trade to organize a non-selling, propaganda fashion show to be titled 'The London Fashion Collection for South America'. Leading British textile companies and nine London couturiers showed in Buenos Aires, São Paulo, Rio de Janeiro and Montevideo between April and May 1941, at a time when Brazil, significantly, was still politically neutral (Education-Hansard - UK Parliament, 30 Jan. 1941).

The second axis in these developments from the late nineteenth century onwards, was the role of the press, both local and international, which served as an important channel of dissemination of new Paris. From 1850, French seamstresses in Rio de Janeiro copied designs taken from these magazines for their wealthy clientele (Medeiros 2007: 18). Fashion and social gossip magazines (Brazilian and French) took a pioneering approach towards fashion as an expression of the new lifestyles that evolved alongside the changing place of women in modernity (Bueno 2011: 88).

Based on research carried out in four weekly magazines and eight major daily newspapers between 1939 and 1945, this chapter will show that such was the importance attached to news of Paris styles, that Brazilian periodicals continued to report on Paris seasonal collections throughout World War Two. The eight newspapers examined are *A Manhã, O Jornal, Correio da Manhã, A Noite, A Batalha, Jornal do Brasil, Diário Carioca* and *Correio Carioca*; and the magazines *Granfina, Revista Rio, Sombra* and *O Espelho*. Some 300 news reports on French fashion were found, including around 200 images of Paris couture. Fashion journalism was thus not interrupted in Brazil through the war. This survey confirmed unequivocally that these reports continued to be published in Rio de Janeiro during World War Two, demonstrating the war time success of the Paris salons in maintaining their place in the Brazilian market.

Casa Canadá

One of the key fashion houses to invest in Parisian haute couture in Rio de Janeiro in the 1930s was Casa Canadá. The store was first opened as a furriers in 1928. Its owner was Jacob Pelicks, a Jewish trader from Minsk in the Russian/Polish 'Pale of Settlement' Poland. Born in 1896, he emigrated to Rio de Janeiro in 1908 and died in 1957. His wife, Helen, had no children. Pelicks began working in the fur trade and in 1928 opened Casa Canadá, selling furs purchased from Canada (*O Paiz* 1929: 5). In the early 1930s Pelicks invited the milliner Filomena Fiala – owner of a hat shop in the fashionable Rua do Ouvidor and known as Mena Fiala – to work at Casa Canadá as sales director. Following her arrival, Casa Canadá began to sell not only furs but also Parisian couture. In 1938, Jacob Pelicks invited Mena Fiala's sister, Cândida Gluzman, to join the store team. Cândida became head buyer for Casa Canadá, traveling to Paris to buy couture (Seixas 1977). After the German occupation of Paris on 14 June 1940, Cândida's and also Pelicks' travels to Paris were interrupted and instead, Pelicks began travelling to New York to access information on French fashion in American department stores (Oliveira 2015). Significantly for this study, after his last purchasing visit to Paris, probably in May 1940, just before the Nazi occupation of Paris, Jacob Pelicks published, in the *Jornal do Brazil*, on 2 June 1940, an open letter to clients of Casa Canadá. He wrote:

> It was my intention to write directly to every customer sending you news about my visit to Paris. But it is impossible to do so. So I turn to this open letter which I hope will answer many of the questions that are being asked of me.
> PARIS – War.
> Many ancient sites. Maxim Café de Paris, Ritz, George V.
> FASHION – There have been major changes in this domain. Some establishments – whose light was shining bright a year ago – have been extinguished. Glories of the past. After visiting a number of fashion-houses I only concentrated on five in the end. And I keep their names secret.

> The dresses – are they shorter?
>
> The silhouettes – are they finer?
>
> I will answer all this soon. I promise you novelties – and great ones.
>
> HATS – Charm in the first place.
>
> FABRICS – Have you ever heard of velvets and satins . . . Brochés. Striped velvet? They are charming indeed . . . but a bit expensive.
>
> FURS – In this, Paris shines less than New York. Prices are much higher than in Rio. For a long mink coat Paquin asked me for many, many francs! I advise, therefore, all my customers from Rio and Sao Paulo to buy their skins in Brazil before traveling to France.
>
> In the street, Astrakhan and Mink are the most appreciated. Beaver is a great success.
>
> I hope soon to do a very special show – a gala show –in both Rio and in Sao Paulo to present an unforgettable collection of models now in fashion.
>
> And in this expectation, I present my most sincere greetings.

It is important to note here that the 1930s and 1940s also marked the peak point for the importation of American high-quality ready-to-wear fashion into Brazil. This had started in the 1920s but despite its popularity, Casa Canadá determinedly never accepted the business lure of this American ready-to-wear market. On the contrary, the store chose to invest in Parisian design and Casa Canadá remained a temple to French haute couture. According to Maria Cristina Volpi, the importance of Casa Canadá during World War Two was thus its pioneering work in creating the first Brazilian-owned haute couture salon run on Parisian artisan-craft lines (Volpi 1996). Even with all the restrictions imposed by the Nazis on Parisian haute couture in France, Casa Canadá was still able to expand its consumption of French fashion in Rio de Janeiro.

Mena Fiala as sales director of Casa Canadá

Although Mena Fiala, the sales director for Casa Canadá, and her sister Cândida Gluzman, in charge of purchasing for the store, were in fact of Italian descent, they followed in the tradition of the French seamstresses and tradesmen of nineteenth century Rio de Janeiro. Mena Fiala, as the person responsible for expanding sales at Casa Canadá, showed special concern over discipline in the creative couture process. As sales director, her function was to understand how the imported Parisian models were made – unstitching the dresses to see how they were constructed, in order to teach the process of fabrication to the dressmakers in her own workrooms. She also supervised the presentation of the collections themselves and the formation of a team of couturiers. Thus Casa Canadá represented an extremely important moment in the history of the development of a haute couture manufacturing tradition in Brazil. In an interview with Cristina Seixas in 1977, Mena Fiala explained how, soon after being appointed sales director, she had the idea of showing imported furs and fashions to her local customers using young mannequins specially hired and trained by her (Seixas 1977).

Casa Canadá reigned as a source of elegance and glamour in Brazil in the 1930s, 1940s and 1950s, meeting the fashion aspirations of the wealthy female elite for whom appearance was synonymous with cultural and social status and for whom the luxury of couture clothes was a required refinement amongst the Brazilian upper classes. Mena Fiala stated in interview that her clients would commission four to five outfits per year from Casa Canadá for the key events of the Brazilian social season, such as the occasion of the Sweepstake – the Grand Prix of the Brazilian Jockey Club – an annual ritual that mobilized the upper classes of Rio de Janeiro, which began with a cocktail party for foreign diplomatic and business delegations, followed by a Saturday night ball at the Hotel Copacabana Palace, the race itself on the Sunday and finally on the Monday, a gala dinner: *Nuit de Longchamps* (Volpi 1996).

Mena Fiala and Cândida Gluzman thus became mentors for the reproduction and interpretation of original Paris couture in Brazil. This transformed the workshops into major laboratories of creation, as Mena Fiala confirmed herself (Seixas 1977). Customers had the option to purchase originals from Paris or interpretations made by Casa Canadá. In an interview with Maria Cristina Volpi, Mena Fiala explained: 'We would buy the collection from Paris . . . so we had to adjust it to suit the climate of Rio de Janeiro and Brazil, following the trend set in Paris' (Seixas 1977).

Casa Canadá, with Mena Fiala as director of sales, Cândida Gluzman as buyer and Jacob Pelicks in charge of the management of the store, became a central focus of Brazilian fashion refinement. Mena Fiala also introduced unique characteristics to the store, such as service-by-appointment and delivery-date, a bespoke service with the permanent presence of mannequins to parade models (Seixas 1977). There was fierce competition amongst its clientele to acquire the new seasonal models launched in the elegant 'L'-shaped showroom, Canada de Luxe, opened in 1944, where the most significant names of the elite in the country would gather (Seixas 1977).

Fashion press and social reportage in Brazil during World War Two

It is clear from interviews that the sisters, Mena and Cândida, and Jacob Pelicks were highly influenced in their perceptions about Paris fashion by Brazilian and international fashion press reports and images from the social pages. According to Maria Lúcia Bueno, up until the mid-nineteenth century the international circulation of French haute couture was slow, restricted mainly to word-of-mouth or standardised images in fashion magazines (Bueno 2011: 74). In the early twentieth century, however, the channels for fashion publication expanded, resulting in an analogous development of the French fashion industry. Bueno confirms that the magazines rapidly found a captive audience amongst both French and international elites (2011: 82).

In Rio de Janeiro in the early twentieth century, Brazilian fashion journalism emerged in the local press, together with social reportage portraying the worldly life of the upper classes. Importantly, these commentaries contained detailed descriptions of the imported Paris seasonal fashions flaunted by women of the local elite. By the 1930s in Brazil, a system for the diffusion of fashion information had been firmly established. (During the period of World War Two, however, no evidence has been found that international fashion magazines were commonly available on the newsstands of Brazilian cities, though there is no doubt that they were still read by society women, as well as by Mena Fiala, Cândida Gluzman and Jacob Pelicks.)

In general, most of the foreign news coverage of Parisian fashion was sent to Brazil by European news agencies and translated for the local audience. The best known source was the French news agency Havas,[3] as Lefébure notes (1992: 46). In World War Two, Havas had as its own fashion reporter, the journalist Rachel Gayman, who attended all the Parisian couture shows and sold her reports around the world through Havas. These reports were circulated in the Rio de Janeiro press and in this way, as this text will now prove, reports of Paris couture continued to arrive in Brazil during the war.

Throughout this entire period a group of Brazilian reporters wrote about the uniqueness of French haute couture which, they declared, differed from that of other countries because of its extreme refinement. Reports did point out how, despite the difficulties, Parisian women were successfully replacing products missing in order to continue wearing their fashions as emblems of French cultural sophistication. As early as October 1939, just one month into the 'Phoney War' period, the Rio newspaper *O Imparcial* published, in its column 'Parade of Elegance', details of Elsa Schiaparelli's 'Cash and Carry' collection of bags and the dress collection 'La Lavense'. In the same publication Brazilian readers could find out about Molyneux's Paris collection, named 'Double Swing'.

It is of key importance to note here that even after the occupation of Paris by the Nazis in June 1940, the Brazilian press continued to report on the new Parisian collections. Significantly, the *Correio da Manhã*, on 22 January 1941, reiterated once again that in the eyes of Brazil, 'Paris is still the only creative center of all that relates to women's fashion'. Also of much interest was the arrival in Rio de Janeiro in April and May 1941 of the British government's Board of Trade–sponsored couture collection, noted above, designed to promote British interests, both in Brazil and Argentina, through its fashion textiles ('Parliamentary Oral Answers' 1941). The debutante models for this fashion show left London on 18 March 1941, posing for a press photograph with British sailors at the station. This show opened over three months later to much acclaim at the Copacabana Palace Hotel in Rio.

FIGURE 9.3
London fashion models leaving for South America on 15 March 1941 to exhibit British fashions, posing with British sailors at the railway station en route the docks to catch their ship. (PastPix/TopFoto.)

FIGURE 9.4
London model at the Copacabana Palace Hotel dressed in a design by Worth, London, in striped Moygashel from the British collection. *Correio da Manhã*, 7 July 1941 (with thanks to the Biblioteca Nacional, Rio de Janeiro).

The London fashion models showed seventy-seven garments by nine leading London couturiers, including Molyneux, Worth, Paquin and Creed. These four Paris couture houses also had long-established salons running in London as well as in Occupied Paris. It was these four salons that clearly received the most press coverage, even though their specific couture collections would in fact have been made in London and not Paris. In April 1941, *Sombra* reported on this London fashion show, noting, as Andrade highlighted, this particular interest in Paris style and the designs of these four Paris-based salons. By May 1941, *Sombra* reported on designs by Maison Hermès together with Maison Worth, who were showing a special collection titled 'Brazilian Beige'.

The success of this collection was in its colour palette, which astutely alluded to Brazilian nationalism. 'Brazilian Beige' was a reference to 'coffee and milk' – *'café-com leite'*, the nickname for the period of Brazilian constitutional democracy of 1889–1930. In May 1941, *Sombra* noted 'the fashion evokes South American lands with Brazilian coffee and milk inspiring the "Brazilian-beige" by Hermès and Worth. This tone of "latte" has achieved immense success and is found at Casa Canadá'. Where this collection came from remains a mystery, but it was most probably, again, via New York and possibly made up from designs sent from London and created there in a leading department store.

Brazilian society women were regularly pictured wearing French couture. One of many of these images is found in *Sombra*'s February–March 1942 article 'White

FIGURE 9.5
'Brazilian Beige' collection, fashion drawings of designs by Worth and Hermès, *Sombra*, no. 4, May 1941 (with thanks to the Biblioteca Nacional, Rio de Janeiro).

FIGURE 9.6
Brazilian socialite Sylvia Regis de Oliveira in dress by Maggy Rouff, *Sombra*, no. 2, February–March 1942 (with thanks to the Biblioteca Nacional, Rio de Janeiro).

is to summer as black is to winter'. This article featured the Brazilian socialite Sylvia Regis de Oliveira – daughter of a prominent Brazilian diplomat, later to become Princess Sylvia Amelia Laura Faucigny-Lucinge – draped in a white jersey dress by Parisian designer Maggy Rouff, whose couture house remained open in Paris throughout the war.

Allied from August 1942, Anglo-Brazilian diplomatic and cultural contacts, set in place by the April 1941 British Board of Trade fashion show held in Rio de Janeiro, also continued as best they could. The highlight of this Brazilian-British political alliance was a major exhibition of the work of seventy Brazilian artists. Planned through 1943, it was held at the Royal Academy and the Whitechapel Gallery in London, then toured six other UK cities. Under the auspices of the Brazilian government, it raised funds for the British war effort. (The exhibition was re-created at the Brazilian Embassy's Sala Brazil in London in April 2018, titled 'The Art of Diplomacy: Brazilian Modernism Painted For War' ('Art of Diplomacy' 2018). As cultural and trade contacts across the Atlantic between Brazil and France grew more difficult between 1942 and 1943, news of Parisian haute couture became rarer in the Brazilian press and only three press reports were found from this period. The first, in *Sombra* magazine in October 1942, noted how Paris women were dressing in times of war; the second, also in *Sombra*, in April 1943, described trend changes in Parisian fashion, whilst the third, of May 1943, is discussed below. The social and

FIGURE 9.7
From right to left: Sras. José Lima Guimarães, Silvio Matos, Mario Ipanema Moreira and Abel Ribeiro attending a cocktail party in Rio de Janeiro, *Sombra*, no. 2, May 1943 (with thanks to the Biblioteca Nacional, Rio de Janeiro).

gossip reports continued to show society women at their parties or at the Jockey Club of Rio de Janeiro. In these images, we can see how they continued to dress according to the rules of Parisian fashion.

In Figure 9.7, we see at a cocktail party offered by the Minister of Education and Health, Gustavo Capanema, in May 1943, from left to right: Sra. Isaura José Guimarães Lima, wife of the president of the Pitanguy Textiles Company; Sra. Silvio de Matos; Sra. Otavio Moreira de Ipanema, wife of the son of the Baron of Ipanema; and Sra. Abel Ribeiro Filho, wife of the Minister of Labour, Industry and Commerce in the Vargas government. Their clothing follows the styles from Paris: dresses and coats with padded, angular shoulders, skirts shorter with fine pleats, shoes heavier and hats, again as in Paris, very creative, with flowers, feathers and veils. Even in 1943, readers in Rio de Janeiro could therefore still find out about the latest Paris trends, which included extravagant use of yardage in full skirts and the start of a new fashion for exaggerated sleeves. In May 1943, the *Sombra* reporter Hortênsia Redig de Campos described how the couturiers in Paris continued to create in the face of adversity:

> The elegant woman will be surprised to know that the Parisian couturiers continue to work against all the odds! Paris continues to create delicate and exciting things! The lack of buttons has motivated ties, '*fermature à lacets*'; and who knows if the shortage of thread does not inspire bodices with few seams … and is that not also the reason for the kimono sleeve and 'dolman' sleeves? Despite the lack of materials, the couturiers still launch new silhouettes.

Once Paris was liberated in August 1944, there was an explosive return of articles on the seasonal Paris couture collections in the Brazilian media, including details of accessories such as hats, jewellery, scarves, perfumes, shoes and handbags.

By 1945 the number of articles and images on French fashion doubled and many designs by famous French couturiers were presented in the magazines. The reports celebrating the liberation of France noted the delegations representing the Paris couture industry that soon began to arrive in Brazil seeking to prove that Paris couture was once again open for business. In May 1945, for example, the very month of the unconditional surrender of German forces in Europe, *Sombra* reported the first post-war Parisian fashion embassy and fashion show, presented by Casa Canada in São Paulo.

The reports selected here, out of hundreds of others surveyed, show clearly that demand from the Brazilian elite for Parisian haute couture did not diminish during World War Two – and neither did direct contact. This study has noted the comment in *Sombra* that by May 1941, inspired by Hermès and Worth designs, garments made up in their exclusive tone of 'latte' could be purchased at Casa Canadá. This continuous demand enabled Casa Canadá in 1944 to inaugurate its famous salon, Canadá de Luxe. This salon continued the tradition of supporting French couture in Brazil by presenting actual Paris garments and accessories as well as Casa Canadá couture to the press and to the wealthy consuming public alike, although, as this study has shown, the years 1941–1944 marked an anguished break from direct contact with Paris haute couture. Nonetheless, Canadá de Luxe became the key focus for information on the newest Paris seasonal styles right through World War Two.

McCann has shown that World War Two stimulated Brazilian industrial manufacturing and agriculture (1995). Durand confirms too that with considerable US financing, growing industries including the Brazilian textile industry were able by the late 1940s to export Brazilian fabrics and cotton to France and other markets (Durand 1988: 78). Unlike the ruined economies of Europe, Brazil's was flourishing and its wealthy, fashionable class remained in place, leading French couturiers put their energies and what means they had into organising a major fashion export show for Brazil. They chose to mark their post-war return, as early as April 1945, one month before the ending of the war in Europe, by showing collections at Casa Canadá's new elegant salon. As noted above, in May 1945, *Sombra* magazine described these fashion shows at Canadá de Luxe in São Paulo, including designs by Balenciaga, Paquin, Creed, Molyneux and many others from the spring Paris couture collections of 1945 as a 'sensation'. This text is cited in full since it is of fundamental importance in understanding the hypothesis of this chapter.

Impressions of a fashion show

The 'Mannequin Parade' staged by Canadá De Luxe in São Paulo last month was a truly sensational event. For the first time after so many years, *Paulista* society was presented with authentic models by the great French couturiers.

A never-before-seen collection of Molyneux and Creed was presented, with great success. A new color was launched for tailored suits and coats – and also for hats – 'Vin Blanc', the great success of the season. The new trends from the great French masters are clear: dresses with many charming details and showing Russian influence – like metal embroidery. Most successful were the '*Tunique-Ville*', where the spirit of Balenciaga, Patou and Piguet can be clearly seen. New hats – captivating and different – were also on show. Amongst the American salons, the most successful were: Hattie Carnegie, Philipe Mongone, Vivian Davis, Florence May, Adele Simpson, Monte Sano, Rose Barrack, Capri Original, D.W. Coppola, La Balbo, Herbert Sondheim, Pauline Trigère and Maurice Rentner.

(*Sombra*, May 1945)

This *Sombra* fashion report, published one month after the show in São Paulo in April 1945, raises two important issues. The first is the fact that 'original' Paris couture garments were shown at Casa Canadá together with garments from top American fashion houses, indicating that the garments arrived in Brazil via New York. This suggests that these 'Paris' clothes may well have been made up in the couture dressmaking salons of department stores such as Bergdorf Goodman, New York, from original designs sent from Paris. The Metropolitan Museum's Digital Library contains many examples of such *croquis* designs sent in 1944–1946 directly from Paris, including many from Lelong, Paquin, Balenciaga and Molyneux[4] (see Chapters 6 and 11).

The second issue involves the emphasis in the picture captions on a select group of couture clients from the São Paulo elite who were amongst those who attended this parade, including Countess Honório Penteado and Sra. Yolanda Penteado. Countess Honório Penteado and Sra. Yolanda Penteado were from one of the most traditional families of the Brazilian aristocracy. Yolanda Penteado – known as the 'coffee princess' – was a niece to Olívia Guedes Penteado, the great *mecenas* of Brazilian modernism. She became the wife of the Italian-Brazilian industrialist Francisco Matarazzo Sobrinho, owner of Latin America's biggest industrial conglomerate in the early twentieth century, Matarazzo Industries, which included the Matarazzo Cloth Company, one of Brazil's leading textile firms. Yolanda and Ciccilio (as Francisco Matarazzo Sobrinho was nicknamed) played distinguished roles in the history of Brazilian art as great patrons founding the Museum of Modern Art in São Paulo in 1949 (Miceli 1996: 30).

This parade by Casa Canadá in São Paulo in April 1945 was the first in a series of events that year that demonstrated the strenuous efforts made by the Paris haute couture to re-conquer its valuable pre-war Brazilian market. On 21 November 1944, just three months after the Liberation of Paris and six months before the end of the War in Europe, General François D'Austier de La Vigiere[5] was appointed as French Ambassador to Brazil. In February 1945 he gave a significant interview to the Brazilian newspaper *A Manhã* in London highlighting the economic importance to France of its exports in luxury goods and especially in fashion. He declared that 'France continues to maintain and develop its primacy in the field of fashion. Despite our present poverty, we are already in a position to export to our allies certain luxury goods.' The general was one of de Gaulle's closest confidants and the focus deliberately made here by this distinguished ambassador confirms the urgent importance the new post war French government attached to its markets in Brazil, including valuable sales of couture clothes and accessories. By May 1945 *Sombra* had already reported that the *Thèâtre de la Mode* was going to be exhibited in Brazil's capital city.

In July, August and September of 1945, commemorations to mark the end of the war in Europe exploded all over Rio de Janeiro. In July 1945, the most prominent of the many galas, balls and receptions portrayed in *Sombra* were those of the Brazilian imperial family: Prince Pedro de Alcântara de Orleans e Bragança e Bourbon and his wife, Princess Maria Isabel de Wittelsbach, the former princess of Bavaria. A celebratory ball was held at General D'Austier de La Vigiere's French Embassy to mark these events, attended amongst others by Aimée Rodman de Heeren (see Figure 14.6).

On August 1945, *Sombra* also reported on that a major show of Paris couture had been organised by the French Ambassador's wife, Baroness D'Astier de La Vigiere, together with the wife of the French Consul, Mme. Monique Saint de Wallerstein, hosted by Mme. Dourdin. The audience was entertained by the Parisian singer Roberta. Seven top French mannequins modelled the designs, with their hair arranged by the famous Paris stylist Louis Gervais. The models were photographed for the press wearing these latest post-Liberation Paris designs – including a clear example of the continuation of 'Occupation style', a dress with huge sleeves, tiny waist, full skirt with an exaggerated peplum, very wide shoulders and a high fanciful

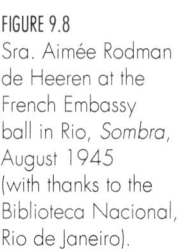

FIGURE 9.8
Sra. Aimée Rodman de Heeren at the French Embassy ball in Rio, *Sombra*, August 1945 (with thanks to the Biblioteca Nacional, Rio de Janeiro).

hat. Mme. Wallerstein opened the show wearing a '*robe-de-soir*' by Lelong. The parade was considered a great success:

> Marvellous models crafted by the brilliant hands of the great Paris couturiers. An incredible world full of grace, lightness and elegance – all this was seen by *Carioca* society at the Golden Room of the Copacabana Palace, with the presentation of the latest French fashions recently arrived in Rio de Janeiro. This fabulous collection of '*robes-de-soir*' – the richest and most luxurious we have yet seen – deservedly won the most enthusiastic applause.
>
> (*Sombra*, August 1945)

Also in August 1945, and almost certainly connected to this very same display, *Sombra* reported another Rio fashion show, a commercial show held unsurprisingly at Casa Canadá, where 'authentic models by the greatest Parisian couturiers were shown: Lelong, Molyneux, Paquin and Balenciaga'. Then, on 28 August 1945, the newspaper *Correio Carioca* announced on its front page the arrival in Brazil of the 'Great Exhibition of French Art' and its forthcoming opening on 14 September. This was organised by the French Ministry of National Economy's department of '*Metiers d'Art et de Creation*'. Six thousand artefacts were displayed at the Brazilian Ministry of Education's spectacular 1943 construction, Rio's Capanema Palace, the first modernist public building in the Americas, designed by some of Brazil's exciting new architects including Lúcio Costa and Oscar Niemeyer. *Correio Carioca* announced that this show was

> a great message celebrating the creative spirit of immortal France . . . [with] one objective – to show Brazilians that the Spirit . . . of French intelligence neither died nor slept under the boot of the Nazi occupation; on the contrary, it sought new stimuli and new creative motifs in its struggle against the invader. In truth, all the exhibits have one common characteristic: they were produced during the past five years, under War and Occupation, as an example of this Spirit's defiance of those who tried to eliminate it from France and from the world.[6]

Twenty French films made during occupation were screened and thousands of commercially desirable luxury decorative arts products were put on display, including porcelain, crystal glass, wines and perfumes, textiles and fashion. The impressive fashion section presented the latest designs by twenty-seven Paris couture salons, all members of the *Chambre Syndicale de la Couture Parisienne*, as cited in the press reports. *Correio Carioca* published a photograph of the Paris couturiers' models arriving in Rio on 22 August 1945 on board the passenger liner *SS Serpa Pinto*. This ship, belonging to the Portuguese shipping company Companhia Colonial de Navegação, had made regular transatlantic crossings to and from from Lisbon to New York, Baltimore and Philadelphia to Rio de Janeiro, all through the

FIGURE 9.9A
French models arriving in Rio de Janeiro from Paris, 22 August 1945, *Correio Carioca*, ano XVIII, no. 5271, August 1945 (with thanks to the Biblioteca Nacional, Rio de Janeiro).

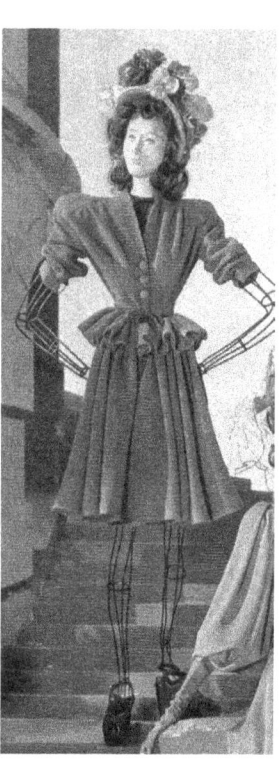

FIGURE 9.9C
Dress with fashionable full-frilled peplum, from the 'Port of Nowhere' scene by Georges Wakhévitch, from the *Théâtre de la Mode* catalogue for London, printed in Paris, autumn 1944 (with thanks to the Dress History Collection, University of Brighton).

FIGURE 9.9B
Paris couture dress with frilled peplum shown at the fashion show during the Great Exhibition of French Art in Rio de Janeiro, *Sombra*, August 1945 (with thanks to the Biblioteca Nacional, Rio de Janeiro).

war.⁷ *Sombra* photographed a couture outfit with full sleeves and skirt, with a deeply gathered peplum. This design was close indeed to the garment worn by a little figure in the *Thèâtre de la Mode's* 'Port of Nowhere' scene, by Georges Wakhévitch.

A few weeks later, in September 1945, *Revista Rio* magazine finally reported the long-awaited arrival of the *Chambre Syndicale de la Couture Parisienne*'s *Thèâtre de la Mode* itself ('arriving via Madrid') and yet another fashion show. Photos in an article titled '*Alo Rio*' show dolls from the *Thèâtre de la Mode*. This was a highly successful Paris couture promotion exhibition consisting of twelve small-sized stage sets of scenes of life in Paris. These were filled with quarter-size dolls dressed in the latest styles for the spring/summer 1945 season, by forty-one of the great fashion houses and the accessory makers of Paris (except Chanel, who was not invited). The *Thèâtre de la Mode* was first shown in Paris from 25 March to 6 May 1945.⁸ Then, via Spain, it opened in London on 12 September with, as Susan Train significantly notes, 'portions' showing through the winter of 1945–1947 in Sweden, Copenhagen and Vienna (Train 2002: 190). Photographs in the '*Alo Rio*' article of September 1945 offer convincing evidence that indeed as Train indicated, 'portions' of the *Thèâtre de la Mode* were shown in Rio and São Paulo from late August 1945, probably over a few months. One *Revista Rio* photograph shows dolls being passed around high society diners at a grand *soirée* in São Paulo.

Figure 9.10 offers a close up of some of the dolls shown in Brazil. Figure 9.11A shows photographs from *Revista Rio* of three specific dolls from the 'Rue de la Paix' scene by Touchagues, which were shown in Rio and São Paulo. The very same

FIGURE 9.10
Figures from the *Thèâtre de la Mode* shown in Brazil from late August into September 1945, *Revista Rio*, no. 75, September 1945: 88 (with thanks to the Biblioteca Nacional, Rio de Janeiro).

scene with dolls wearing exactly the same clothes was featured in photographs in the London catalogue of the Théâtre de a Mode printed in Paris in August 1944 for the London showing. Thus, whilst the 'Rue de La Paix' scene was intended in autumn 1944 to be shown in London, and was therefore included when the London catalogue was printed in Paris, it seems highly probable that the scene never did get to London but was was sent instead to Brazil.[9]

Related Paris fashion shows were also held in São Paulo. *Revista Rio* magazine reported, with photographs, in November 1945 that São Paulo society had received a visit from Paris, 'the Paris re-born from the chaos, Paris the immortal phoenix of art, grace and beauty. In these pictures we can see the very "*grande monde*" as they assembled to watch the fashion parade. . . . This manifestation of the innate taste of Paris was unveiled during a dinner.' No more details are given about which designers' clothes.

FIGURE 9.11A
Four *Théâtre de la Mode* figures in the '*Rue de la Paix*' scene by Touchagues, shown in Rio and São Paulo, late August–September 1945, *Revista Rio*, no. 75, September 1945: 89.

FIGURE 9.11B
Four *Théâtre de la Mode* figures in the '*Rue de la Paix*' scene by Touchagues from a photograph in the London catalogue of the exhibition, printed in Paris in August 1944 (with thanks to the Dress History Teaching Collection, University of Brighton).

Conclusion

When the reporter from *Diário Carioca* wrote that the 'Great Exhibition of French Art' of September 1945 aimed to 'show Brazilians that the Spirit – the art and creative force – of French intelligence "neither died nor slept under the boot of the Nazi occupation"', this also included of Paris couture, which continued to offer a global standard to be emulated. The emulation of Paris couture had continued through the war to be one of the most significant marks of the representation of Brazilian civility as it had been before the war. Jacob Pelicks, Mena Fiala and Cândida Gluzman played significant roles in this emulation tradition. Despite the adversities imposed by the Nazis during those long dark years, Casa Canadá never stopped offering its clientele access to French haute couture style. All three understood that for their clients, dressing Paris-style from head to foot was synonymous with elegance and, especially, civility in Brazil. The inauguration of Canadá de Luxe in 1944 was to transform Casa Canadá in the 1950s into the most successful fashion salon in Brazil. It became the one reference point for elegance, luxury and social distinction, presenting Paris couture in spectacular seasonal shows and eventually sponsoring the visits to Brazil of French couturiers such as Jacques Fath (Oliveira 2014).

The wide range of available information in the Brazilian fashion periodicals analysed here, as well as the holding of Paris couture fashions shows and the arrival of the *Thèâtre de la Mode* by late August 1945, confirm, finally, that Parisian haute couture did not lose its position of fashion leadership in the universe of the Brazilian elite throughout World War Two and, further, that it made dramatic and successful efforts in autumn 1945 to re-invigorate its important export trade with Brazil.

Acknowledgments

With thanks to Ana Carolina Azevedo, Marina Duarte and Marina Ginefra.

References

Andrade, R. (2015), 'Mappin Stores: Adding an English Touch to the Sao Paulo Fashion Scene', 176–187, in Root. R. ed. (2015), *The Latin American Fashion Reader*, Oxford: Bergs.

'Art of Diplomacy'. (2018). http://theartofdiplomacy.com/about/ (accessed 23 April 2018).

Bueno, M.L. (2001), *Artes Plásticas no século XX. Modernidade e Globalização*, Campinas/São Paulo: Editora da Unicamp/Imprensa Oficial/Fapesp (2nd edition).

Bueno, M.L. (2011), 'Alta-Costura e Alta Cultura. As revistas de luxo e a internacionalização da moda (1901–1930)', in *Moda em Ziguezague. Interfaces e expansões*, São Paulo: Estação das Letras e Cores.

Bueno, M.L. (2012), 'Les femmes de la haute-couture. Mode et Genre au début du XX siècle', in *Créations. Le Genre l'oeuvre* (vol. 2) (org. Buscatto, M., Leontsini, M., Maruani, M., Pequinot, B. and Ravet, H.), Paris: L'Harmattan.

Durand, J.C. (1988), *Moda, Luxo e economia*, São Paulo: Babel Cultural.

Kauffman, M. (2012), *The Couture Client*, http://process.arts.ac.uk/content/couture-client-patron-art-fashion (accessed 4 August 2016).

Lefébure, A. (1992), *Havas: les arcanes du pouvoir*, Paris: Grasset.

London Fashion Collection (South America), Hansard , 30 January 1941. vol. 368. no 85. Education - address: Hansard - UK Parliament https://hansard.parliament.uk/Commons/1941-01-30/debates/695dc302.../Education. Accessed May 16th 2019

McCann, F.D. (1995), 'Brazil and World War II: The Forgotten Ally. What did you do in the war, *Zé Carioca?*', *Estudios Interdiscipliarios de America Latina y el Caribe*, 6, no. 2, 9 July–December 1995: 35–70.

Medeiros, L. (2007), 'Francesas no Rio de Janeiro: modernização e trabalho segundo o Almanak Laemmert (1844-1861)', Revista do Instituto Histórico e Geográfico Brasileiro, v. 423: 11–32.

Miceli, S. (1996), *Imagens Negociadas. Retratos da Elite Brasileira (1920–40)*, São Paulo: Companhia das Letras.

Oliveira, C. de. (2014), 'Moda, arte e sociedade: o pioneirismo da *Maison* Canadá-de-Luxe e a emergência da indústria fashion nacional nos anos 1950', *Revista MODAPALAVRA*, vol. 7, no. 14: 28-50. www.revistas.udesc.br/index.php/modapalavra/article/view/5098

Oliveira, C. de. (2015), interview with Shimon Pelicks, 8 August.

Parliamentary Oral Answers to Questions – London Fashion Collection (South America) (30 January 1941), https://www.theyworkforyou.com/debates/?d=1941-01-30 (accessed 2 August 2016).

Seixas, C. (1977), personal interview with Mena Fiala, 5 August.

Seixas, C. (2015). *A questão da cópia e da interpretação no Contexto da Produção de Moda da Casa Canadá, no Rio de Janeiro da década de 1950*, Rio de Janeiro: Editora Cassará.

Seixas, C.A. (2002). A questão da cópia e da interpretação no contexto da produção de moda na Casa Canadá, no Rio de Janeiro. Dissertação de mestrado do Programa de Mestrado em Design, Departamento de Artes & Design, PUC-RJ, 2002. http://www.puc-rio.br

Sirop, D. (1989), Exhibition catalogue for 'Paquin, Une Retrospective de 60 ans de Haute Couture. Dec 1989–March 1990', Lyon/Paris: Adam Biro and Musée Historique des Tissus, Lyon.

Train, S. (ed.) (2002), *190, Theatre de la Mode, Fashion Dolls and the Survival of Haute Couture*, 2nd edition, Portland: Palmer/Pletsch.

Volpi, M.C. (1996), interview with Mena Fiala, 14 November.

Volpi, M.C. (2002), 'Rio, cenário da moda', in Wajman, S. and Jose de Almeida, A. (eds.), *Moda, Comunicação e Cultura; um olhar acadêmico*. São Paulo: Arte e Ciência.

Volpi, M.C. (2002), 'Apparel manufacturing and workmanship in Rio de Janeiro, in the first half of the 20th century', 58 Congresso Brasileiro de Pesquisa e Desenvolvimento em Design, P&D, Universidade de Brasília – UNB, de 10 a 13 de outubro.

Volpi, M.C. (2006), 'Dressmaking and handwork in Rio de Janeiro, in the first fifty years of the twentieth century', in Villaça, N., Castilho, K., and Castilho, K. (eds.) *Plugados na moda. Plugados in fashion*. São Paulo: Editora Anhembi Morumbi. São Paulo: Anhembi Morumbi Publishing House.

Sources

Newspapers

A Batalha, 10/4/1939
Correio da Manhã, 22 January 1941 and 7 July 1941
O Jornal, 5/3/1934 and 1/9/1936
A Noite, 1939, 1943, 1945
O Imparcial, 10/2/1939
Jornal do Brasil, 21/11/1940
Correio Carioca, 22/8/1945; 30/8/1945; 31/8/1945
O Paiz, no. 145, 13 December 1929, p. 5

Magazines

Granfina, August 1940
Revista Rio, December 1944 to October 1945
Sombra, April, May and July 1941; Febuary, March, May and October 1942; April and May 1943; May and August 1945
O Espelho, March 1940

Endnotes

1   The Portuguese royal family – *Bragança* – together with their court of nobles, bureaucrats and other domestic servants, fled to Brazil escorted by a fleet of British warships to escape the Napoleonic troops that invaded Portugal in 1807. The Portuguese court arrived in Rio de Janeiro in January 1808 and remained in Brazil until 1821. Overnight, Rio de Janeiro became the capital of the kingdom of Portugal, transformed from a mere colonial port into capital of the Portuguese Overseas Empire, and later, in 1816, capital of the United Kingdom of Portugal, Brazil and Algarve. The arrival of the court brought a complete change of habits among the elite of Rio de Janeiro, including ways of dress, as the local elite adopted French fashion, imitating the Portuguese Court.

2   The Treaty of Friendship, Navigation and Commerce was ratified by France on 19 March 1826, and by Brazil on 6 June 1826. FUNAG: Fundação Alexandre de Gusmão, Centro de História e Documentação Diplomática (CHDD), http://funag.gov.br (accessed 16 August 2016).

3   The agency Havas was founded in 1835 by Charles-Louis Havas. Headquartered in Paris, it sent information and news by telegram to newspapers around the world who paid for this service. In 1851, British journalist Julius Reuters left the company to found Reuters News Agency in London. Havas would become what is today Agence France-Presse (AFP). See Lefébure, A. (1992), *Havas: les arcanes du pouvoir*. Paris: Grasset.

4   The Digital Collections of the Thomas Watson Library, Costume Institute Collections Metropolitan Museum, New York. No i2079678 001. Watson online record number: b117508952. http://libmma.contentdm.oclc.org/cdm/compoundobject/collection/p16028coll1/id/15013/rec/5 (accessed 12 June 2018).

5   François Astier de la Vigerie was appointed Ambassador to Brazil between 1944–1946. Between 1942–1944 he was Inspector of the Free French Air Force. http://www.fgv.br/cpdoc/acervo/dicionarios/verbete-biografico/francois-d-astier-de-la-vigerie (accessed 27 August 2016).

6   *Correio Carioca*, 22 August 1945.
7   See 'The Story of the Serpa Pinto', https://www.chabad.org/therebbe/article_cdo/aid/2623573/jewish/The-Story-of-the-Serpa-Pinto.htm and 'Sailing on the SS Serpa Pinto', https://www.scribd.com/document/282708420/Sailing-on-the-SS-Serpa-Pinto (accessed 14 April 2019).
8   Catalogue: August 1945, 'The exhibition of the Théatre de la Mode in London', Paris: Aljanvic Publicité, Dress History Teaching Collection, University of Brighton.
9   The display was refitted in Paris by the couturiers for the spring/summer season of 1946 and sent off again, opening in New York (see Chapter 5) and in Montreal and Los Angeles, ending in San Francisco in 1946. See Maryhill Museum, http://www.maryhillmuseum.org/ongoing-exhibitions/theatre-de-la-mode (accessed 14 April 2019).

Chapter 10
Annexed, neutral and occupied: the worlds of couture in Austria, Switzerland and Belgium and their relationships with Paris couture, 1939–1946

*Lou Taylor**

FIGURE 10.0
Swiss design, Paris style: 'New designs for spring suits', *l'Illustré*, Swiss French edition, Lausanne, 5 March 1942. (Dress History Teaching Collection, University of Brighton with kind permission from *l'Illustré*.)

Introduction

This chapter examines wartime couture in countries not yet discussed in this book: annexed Austria, neutral Switzerland and occupied Belgium. It draws on the work of Gloria Sultano, Irene Guenther, Veronique Pouillard and Nele Bernheim and uses museum collections and wartime fashion magazines, such as *l'Illustré* (Lausanne edition), *La Semaine de la Femme*, *Aujourd'hui* and *Annabelle* as additional sources.

Austria

The history of European Jewish communities is wrapped into this story because they were so closely involved in the fashion trades, including many of the estimated 192,000 strong Austrian Jewish community, of all social classes, who lived in Vienna.[1] Vienna's couture trade was flourishing by the 1880s, catering to the demanding sartorial formalities of the Imperial court in Vienna until 1918 and to the city's wealthy, sophisticated bourgeoisie. Viennese fashion embraced too the independent designs of Emilie Flöge in the avant garde Wienna Werkstatte style. Loschek confirms that 'fashion in Vienna was characterised by individual salons . . . [which] adapted Paris fashion to the tastes of the Viennese' (2007: 72). Famous couture salons included the Mode Salon of Gertrude Hochsmann, with hats by Adele Lister,

---

*Translations from French by the author.

and the salons Jerlaine and Tailors Stone and Blyth, the latter owned by Ignazy and Stephanie Sass from the 1920s. This company was housed in the Esterhazy Palace and also re-created 'the fashion consciousness of Paris' (Sultano 2007: 118–119).

On the night of 11 March 1938, Austria's own Nazi party activists and stormtroopers opened the way to the overthrow of democracy in Austria. By the evening of the next day, Hitler's troops and tanks were on the famous Viennese *Ringstrasse*. Immediately after this *anschluss*, Austria was annexed and incorporated into Germany amidst the jubilation of much of the population. William Shirer, European correspondant for American CBS News, wrote in his diary on 20 March 1938 that 'Vienna has been completely Nazified in a week – a terrifying thing' (1941: 93). Nazi anti-Semitic legislation was immediately set in place. G.E.R. Gedye, reporter for *The Times* of London, also watched every move. He wrote too of the horrors to which Austrian Jews, patriots and democrats – in fact all non-Nazis – were subjected: 'Viennese Jews were pariahed over-night, deprived of all civil rights, and subjected to public humiliations of every kind.' Gedye continued,

> The sweep of the Nazi scythe continued to cut down ruthlessly the flower of the intellectual and professional life of Vienna, impatient to destroy the last traces of that cultured civilation which for five years had marked out the distinction between Austria and the barbarous Germany of Adolf Hitler.
>
> (1939: 305, 313)

FIGURE 10.1
Hitlerjugend forcing Jewish women and men to scrub a street, Vienna, Austria, 1938. (Getty Images 566465051. Photo from Universal History Archive/UIG.)

As in Germany and all annexed and occupied countries, precious Jewish art collections were listed, looted and wrecked at the great homes of the wealthiest Jewish families. Shirer and Gedye both witnessed the pillaging of the palace of Baron Louis Rothschild (Shirer 1941: 93; Gedye 1939: 303) whilst De Waal has detailed the same process at the home of his own Ephrussi family (2011: 248–252). Gedye felt that 'far worse was the plundering of the humbler Jews' who were left with nothing at all. Gedye had witessed for himself the looting of a big Jewish store in the *Tabostrasse*, the Jewish quarter of Vienna, where he saw 'a long string of lorries into which stormtroopers were pitching all kinds of millinery goods as they took them from the shop'. There was 'nothing remarkable in this incident', he wrote. It was 'one amongst thousands' (1939: 304). Of the 192,000 Jews in Vienna, by 1939 emigration cut the figures to 57,000. By the end of the war, 8,000 survived, mostly those married to non-Jews. Many thousands did not survive the concentration camps.[2]

Austrian fashion and couture

The impact of all of this on the Austrian fashion industry, including couture, was immediate and profound. Austrian Aryanisation laws were applied rapidly under orders from Josef Bürckel, who became the Gauleiter of Austria (Sultano 20017: 115–116). Regina Karner, dress curator at the Wien Museum, writes that 'most of the well known fashion houses were aryanized but operated under the name of their old owner' (Karner 2017). Sultano notes, however, that the new company owners could 'seldom carry on the businesses they had bought at thief prices, in the old and tested way' due to lack of professional skills, often leading to financial difficulties (2007: 116–117). Jewish fashion company owners and designers fled to Britain, North and South America and later to Australia (Sugarman 2012). Sass and his wife, owners of Tailors Stone and Blyth, for example, left for London over the winter of 1938–1939 (Sultano 2007: 119).

Control of the entire Austrian fashion industry fell under direct Nazi legislation. Guenther details that after 1 March 1938, Austrian fashion companies were incorporated into the National German Fashion Institute (the DMI; see Chapter 1) through the creation of an all-encompassing Austrian House of Fashion, *Haus der Mode* (2004: 184). Karner (2017) confirms that this was 'located in the Palais Lobkowitz', a grand baroque palace built in the 1680s. Thus, in 1943, Schuler Wien produced a tailored coat with opulent lengths of silver fox fur running down the skirt (Figure 10.2).

Sultano illustrates Elégance Wien's modernised dirndl dresses for summer 1943 as well as designs that clearly show Paris influence. These include a long-jacketed suit from the salon of Stone and Blythe of 1942–1943 with large sophisticated, matching polka dot hat and gloves (Sultano 1995: 186, 197). The Salzberg Museum collection includes a short day dress in brown and yellow ochre with large patch pockets, dated to 1940–1944 (Figure 10.3).

FIGURE 10.2
(left) Silver fox fur coat by Schuler Wien (Getty 548144067). (right) Elégance Wien showed a slim evening dress with jewelled belt and flowing cape displayed at a fashion show at the Palais Lobkowitz in 1943, Vienna (Getty 548791963).

FIGURE 10.3
Day dress in rayon crepe de chine, Austria, 1940–1944, which is very similar to Molyneux's day dress photographed in *Marie Claire* shown in Figure 12.11. (© Salzburg Museum, no. 22539.)

Guenther highlights too that although obliged to be closely linked to the Nazi fashion industry policies and despite German efforts, 'the German and Austrian branches of the DMI remained separate entities' (2004: 185). Karner (2017) adds that the Austrian House of Fashion took part in many fashion shows held across Europe and that there was 'always rivalry with the House of Fashion in Frankfurt, München and Berlin'. Both, however, joined together in export drives. Kirsten Toftgaarde has already noted in Chapter 7 that on 7 February 1943, the German Chamber of Commerce hosted a major fashion show at the Hotel d'Angleterre in Copenhagen with 230 German and Austrian dresses arranged by the Berliner Modelle Gesellschaft and the Haus der Mode, Vienna, presenting spring and summer seasonal fashions for 1943. Stone Blyth were one of the few Viennese couture companies to survive the war intact. Sultano writes that although Aryanised for a derisory sum in 1938, they were able to leave their business in the hands of Fred Adlmüller, their manager and also a talented designer. He held two fashion shows a year, despite fabric shortages, and kept the business intact, albeit in a diminished condition (Sultano 2007: 119–120). Most Jewish fashion companies did not survive.

Switzerland, the setting for Swiss fashion and textiles, 1939–1945: neutrality and relationships with Berlin and Paris

Switzerland's geographical position makes it a particularly interesting study through which to assess the trans-border diffusion of its own luxury fashion textiles products and the inward importing of Parisian haute couture style during World War Two. Its story is very different from that of Nazi-annexed Austria. Switzerland had its own distinguished textile manufacturing history producing luxury fabrics often used by Paris couturiers – sales that were threatened by World War Two.

Once France was defeated, Switzerland, with its policy of armed neutrality, was completely surrounded by Axis powers. Petropoulos writes that the neutrality of Switzerland shared with Portugal, Sweden and Spain, 'the common objectives of preserving relative independence in foreign policy and resisting encroachment into domestic affairs' (1995: 15). However all of this hung on a fine thread because, as Hayes believed, 'Once Nazi Germany had reached the height of its power during World War 2, there was no nation as vulnerable to a sudden surprise attack as Switzerland' (Hayes 2004: xiii). Elwyn Jones had noted in 1938 that 'the liberties of the Swiss people [were] being encroached upon' through an active Swiss Nazi party and that and the Gestapo was already 'reputed to have at least five hundred secret agents in Switzerland' (1938: 199–202). As to the situation of Jewish refugees trying to flee from Nazi Germany, in 1999 the Independent Commission of Experts charged with examining 'Switzerland and Refugees in the Nazi Era' stated that in the summer of 1938, it was Switzerland that pushed for the passports of German Jews to be marked with the 'J' stamp. By August 1942, Switzerland had closed its borders to 'racially' persecuted refugees, who the Commission described as being in 'mortal danger', declaring that a more humane policy might have saved thousands of refugees from being killed by the Nazis and their accomplices (ICES 1999: 270–272).

Switzerland was dependent on both Nazi Germany and, increasingly towards the end of the war, on trade with Allied countries for its survival, seeking always to keep all trade doors wide open. Golson's research shows that 'with only 58% of its energy produced domestically', Switzerland, with its four languages and large German speaking population, 'was dependent on Germany for its long-term fuel supplies and by 1944 for 16% of its imported foodstuffs and drinks' (Golson 2011: 297, 299).

Swiss fashion textile exports

High amongst Swiss money-earning exported goods were textiles. In 1939, Switzerland exported 21 per cent of these to Germany, a figure which fell to 11 per cent in 1944 (Golson 2011: 262). By the 1930s its reputation as a supplier of the highest quality, *nouveauté* fashion textiles to the Paris couture trade was firmly established. Silk manufacture was based in the Canton of Zurich. A characteristic Swiss specialism was innovative machine-made embroidered and lace fashion textiles of silk, rayon or cotton, an internationally famous industry that was based around St. Gallen.

High-quality cottons were sold all over the world. American *Vogue* featured two examples of Swiss cottons as 'important types for the summer' in its edition of 15 January 1940, illustrating a 'sheer crepe organdie imported from Switzerland'

FIGURE 10.4
Machine embroidery by Els Bossard for C. Forster-Willi, St. Gallen, 1943 (Schweizerisches Nationalmuseum, Landesmuseum Zürich, no. LM 118929).

patterned with bunches of field flowers tied with bows. Swiss cottons were available in quantity in Lisbon during the war. Mannes reported to American *Vogue* in 1944 that 'the freshness of the patterns is noticeable, especially in the cottons, both Swiss and Portuguese' (Mannes 1944: 140).

Swiss wartime fashion textiles

Swiss silk exports doubled between 1939 and 1942 with 'a new high of 100 million Swiss francs' by 1944 (INSEE 1950: 939). Real silk played a small, though not insignicant role in these sales because the industry had 'for the most part switched to artifical silk by then'. Germany was the Swiss silk industry's biggest customer in 1942, the fabric probably being used for parachute manufacture (*Soie Pirate* 2011: 36). One of the most successful international Swiss fashion textile companies was (and still is) that of Abraham and Co., with close business links to Paris couture salons and with sales offices around the world well established by the late 1930s. The founding families of the company were the Jewish family of Abraham and their colleagues, the Brauchbars. From 1935 to 1940 the designer and manager of the Paris branch was Ludwig Abraham, friend of Braque, Leger, Chagall and Miro.

As war broke out, by 1940 these founding families had split. Ludwig Abraham moved to New York and from there in 1943 opened his own company, Abraham and Co. Seiden Ag of Zurich. The Swiss company was left in hands of his brother-in-law, Erwin Stiebel (*Soie Pirate* 2011: 36). In an interview, the grandson of one of the company founders, Hans George Rhonheimer, remembered fabrics sold during the war. 'Silks of course!' he declared, 'plain and printed. In addition to silk, the company also sold artificial silk and cotton.' He confirmed that

> even before the war Abraham had sales representatives all *over* the world. And don't believe that exports dried up during the war. There was air freight even in those days, and that's how we reached our markets in South America and the United States. Sweden became our most important market towards the end of the war.
>
> (*Soie Pirate* 2011: 2)

News of design developments in Lyon luxury silks still reached Switzerland during the war. In April 1942, the Palais de Congrès in Zurich received the *haute nouveauté* fashion textile section of the Paris, 1942, Palais de Tokyo exhibition (noted in Chapter 2). In Zurich, this was entirely laid out around the key tenets of Vichy cultural policies and once again the same huge Pétain *mise-en-carte* portrait was the centre of the show (see Figure 2.5). The Swiss journal *Semaine de la Femme* featured a double page spread showing some of the show's 150 pure silk fabric lengths, stressing that these had been 'designed according to the suggestions of Maréchal Pétain himself'.

The article detailed that the impressively laid out commercial show was attended by Brochier, President of the Syndicat de Fabricants de Soieries Lyonnais (see Chapter 2) and noted that the exhibition displayed current high-fashion silks in sections lauding Pétains's ideologies of *Travaille, Patrie, Famille* and *Retour à la Terre* – with scenes of bucolic farms, oxen and villages. It noted too that colours were restricted largely to red and blue on a white ground, colours that the Swiss reporter found limiting, even though their patriotic function was well understood. Questions were then raised about why only silk fabrics were shown and no synthetics, but no mention was made of the desperate conditions under which these silk samples had been made (see Chapter 2). Finally the *Semaine de la Femme* reporter asked a Swiss 'textile specialist' whether or not this exhibition would inspire the next season of Swiss textile designs. The swift reply was 'not at all – we will show designs based entirely on Swiss originality' (*Semaine de la Femme* issue 2, 9 January 1943).

FIGURE 10.5
Lyon *haute nouveauté* silk exhibition, Palais de Congrès, Zurich, April 1942. (*La Semaine de la Femme*, Issue 2, 9 January 1943, with thanks to Musée Suisse de la Mode, Yverdon-les-Bains.)

Album: *Étude 1, Textiles Suisses pour la Mode/ÉTÉ 1943*

The Swiss did indeed soon exhibit their own very different fabrics and at the very same venue – the Palais de Congrès in Zurich. In 1943, as if in riposte to the Vichyist display, an especially creative project of Swiss *nouveauté* fashion and interior design textiles was developed by the Swiss Centre for Trade Promotion 'to publicise creative textile design in Switzerland, with the aim of planning for post war reconstruction' (Pallmert 2012: 215, 219). The exhibition text concluded by stressing the show's important export role, highlighting the elite *nouveauté* market level of the displayed fabrics and noting that in 1939 there were 107,000 workers in the Swiss textile industry needing support (2012: 222). To create this brand new fabric collection, the Swiss craft textile organisation, textile companies, fabric designers and couturiers all worked together. The basic aim was to produce a collection of fashion and interior design prints, weaves and knits demonstrating the technical and contemporary creative prowess of the Swiss trade. A few of these fashion fabrics were selected and made into couture garments.

This entire developmental programme was recorded in a large beautiful album, *Étude 1, Textiles Suisses pour la Mode/ÉTÉ 1943*, which included paper designs, fabric samples and photographs. All the fabric designs were based on a shared theme – 'the world of water' – used by all participating companies. This in turn was subdivided into four sub-themes, each to be created created with a specific and restricted colour palette. One sub-theme was 'ropes and nets', another, 'shells', used rose, beige,

FIGURE 10.6
Album *ETUDE I/ETE 1943*. Left: watercolour design on paper by Cornelia Forster. Right: the same design, printed linen by Langenthal AG. (Schweizerisches Nationalmuseum, no. LM 118929.)

lavender blue, *bois de rose* and water green tones. A 'Néiriédes' theme was selected for evening dress design, which resulted in fabrics described as reflecting 'the myth of the waves and Neptune and his entourage' (2012: 217).

The resulting album survives today in the collection of the National Museum in Zurich (Pallmert 2012: 215).[3] Photographs in the album also show summer fashions designed by top Swiss fashion designers, clearly based on 1942–1943 Paris fashion. The difference between the Swiss and French designs lies in the use of the album's large-sized fabric designs, the very opposite of the small-size repeat prints found in French wartime fashion fabrics (see Chapter 3). Pallmert writes that a fashion show featuring these garments created a sensation at Swiss Fashion Week in Zurich in 1943, as did the displays of the scheme's fabrics. The Swiss magazine *Textiles* declared in March 1943 that 'a glorious and charming fashion had "grown out of the gloom of the time"' (Pallmert 2012: 219). In August 1943, *Annabelle* highlighted a summer evening dress with ankle-length skirt and full sleeves designed by Scheidegger-Mosimann (whose name was cited in the original album) and made up in a large-sized print by Strub et Cie. This featured starfish, mermaids and sea creatures.

A second project, *ÉTUDE II/ÉTÉ 1944*, again with its own album,[4] involved thirty-two manufacturers and the theme of 'Music'. This produced a hundred textile samples which were far more abstract but no less popular than *Album 1* (Pallmert

Chapter 10: Annexed, neutral and occupied 233

FIGURE 10.7
Summer dress by Scheidegger-Mosimann in Strub fabric, *Annabelle*, August 1943, Swiss French edition, Lausanne (Dress History Teaching Collection, University of Brighton, with kind permission from *Annabelle*).

2012: 223). The names of all the textile designers and companies involved were listed in the texts[5] of both albums, reflecting the textile focus of these projects whilst the couturiers' names were placed only at the end of the books[6] (2012: 213).

The world of couture in wartime Switzerland

Both Paris and Swiss couture were featured in Swiss fashion magazines such as *Semaine de la Femme, Annabelle* and *l'Illustré*, which were published in both German and French editions. The Swiss couture fashions shown in these journals were designed, made and shown in Zurich, Geneva, Berne and Lausanne and all reflected Paris style. The salon of Gaby Jouval, for example, was already internationally known before the war and throughout 1939–1945 was able to keep up some of its business abroad, as noted in Chapter 8.

Swiss ski and winter sports wear had long had a high profile in the French fashion press. *Marie Claire*, for example, on 11 October 1941 featured a white ski outfit with knee-length waterproof linen culottes and a hand knitted cardigan under the banner 'New Winter Fashions – the Swiss eye view on sportswear'.

FIGURE 10.8
Hat with lace veil, Gaby Jouval, cover of *l'Illustré*, French edition, 5 March 1942, published in Lausanne (Dress History Teaching Collection, University of Brighton, with kind permission from *l'Illustré*).

FIGURE 10.9
Swiss winter fashions for sportswear, *Marie Claire*, 11 October 1941. (Photograph by Werner Bischof, with the kind permission of the Bischof Estate, Lausanne and the Dress History Teaching Collection, University of Brighton.)

The first ever Swiss Fashion Week was held in 1942 with exhibitions and shows in the fashion cities of Zurich and Geneva. *L'Illustré*, featuring this major commercial event on 5 March 1942, noted that it was organised by the Swiss Bureau for Commercial Expansion and aimed at publicising the vitality of the Swiss fashion textiles industry rather than the work of individual couture salons. An impressive promotion fashion show was held both at the Hotel Metropole, Geneva and then in Zurich from 28 February to 15 March 1942. Swiss lace and embroidery was heavily featured in *l'Illustré*'s accounts of these events. A summer dress collection by Gaby Jouval promoted Strub and Co's new synthetic floral printed 'Ticinella' fabric, including one group of modernized dirndl dresses.

In Geneva, static mannequins also displayed couture designs by Gaby Jouval from Zurich and Andre Weigandt, Leon Fischer and Paul Daunay from Geneva – designers who were listed in the 1943 and 1944 fashion textiles albums. Paris influence is clear here.

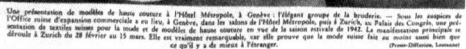

FIGURE 10.10A (above left) Fashion show of Swiss lace, Swiss Fashion Week, spring 1942, l'Illustré, 5 March 1942, no. 21 (Dress History Teaching Collection, University of Brighton, with the kind permission of l'Illustré).

FIGURE 10.10B (above right) Gaby Jouval's collection made in Swiss 'Ticinella' fabric by Strub and Co, l'Illustré, 5 March 1942, no. 21 (Dress History Teaching Collection, University of Brighton, with the kind permission of l'Illustré).

Paris couture in Switzerland

Before the war, many of these exclusive Swiss salons sold Paris couture garments alongside their own creations. *Officiel de la Mode* of 1939, for example, stressed that Paris models could be bought from Schwyzerli de Picard at St. Moritz and Lausanne (1939, no 20: 88–89). Ulrika Kyaga has confirmed in Chapter 4 that 'original models' from Switzerland, as well as from Paris, Vienna and Prague were available in wartime Stockholm. Swiss journals thus offered up a continuous stream of news on style developments in Paris alongside their allegiances to Swiss national couture, with almost no reports on German fashions. Information leaked across the Franco-Swiss borders seemingly with impunity. For example, *l'Illustré*, 5 March, published a double page of fashion drawings of designs by Mme Grès, Piguet, Fath, Lelong, Rouff, Vrament, Bruyère, Dormoy and Balenciaga, under a banner that read '*Les Parisiennes Toujours Élégantes*'.

The Piguet design, described as an 'Ensemble Surprise', was a tailored in black wool cloth with a surprising pink sequinned waistcoat beneath. (The wartime career of Piguet, a leading Paris couturier – and Swiss – is discussed in more detail in Chapter 12.) Swiss fashion ilustrators had long been tuned into Paris style. One young illustrator for *Semaine de la Femme* was Jacqueline Jonas, a Swiss Jewish artist from Lausanne, whose pseudonym was 'Line'. She drew the long line, slim, tailored jacket line and high hat Paris styles in the magazine's edition of 9 October 1943. Her lifetime of fashion drawings survive in the Archives Cantonales Vaudoises, Lausanne. Photographs of Paris couture were freely published in Switzerland, as can be seen for example, in *Semaine de la Femme* of 15 May 1943. One double-page spread on summer prints – *Imprimés Parisiens* – highlighted a Lucile Manguin summer coat in piqué cotton with white, red and blue flower heads on a lavender ground, shown with a very high-crowned straw hat (Figure 10.12).

FIGURE 10.11A
(near right) Swiss design, Paris style: Swiss lace skirt and bolero over black dress. *Annabelle*, August 1943. (Dress History Teaching Collection, University of Brighton, with thanks to *Annabelle*.)

FIGURE 10.11B
(far right) Fashion drawing, 'Les Parisiennes Sont Toujours Élégantes', *l'Illustré*, 13 January 1944 (with thanks to the Musée Suisse de la Mode, Yverdon-les-Bains and with kind permission from *l'Illustré*).

FIGURE 10.12
Lucile Manguin summer coat, *Semaine de la Femme*, 15 May 1943 (with thanks to Musée suisse de la Mode, Yverdon-les-Bains).

One way or another, Swiss fashion magazines found their way around the world, even through the war. On 15 May 1944, just before the Liberation of the city, when Paris fashion news was rare in New York, American *Vogue* marvelled at the detailed news of the exaggerated style of Paris couture hats, which had reached its offices in New York through the pages of an 'unsolicited' Swiss fashion magazine ('Much Ado About Hats' 1944: 103).

Switzerland: Conclusion

What is clear here is that throughout the war, neutral, unoccupied Switzerland energetically and creatively sought home and export markets in order to maintain markets for the products of its own *haute nouveauté* textiles and couture industries, whilst at the same time maintaining allegiances to Paris couture. Whilst retaining its own character, Swiss fashion style in the 1939–1945 period reflected Paris Occupation styles but largely rejected Lyon's Vichyist fabric designs. Swiss lace was often promoted, as for example, in *Annabelle* in a short full-skirted Occupation-style skirt in August 1942 (Figure 10.11A).

FIGURE 10.13
Swiss design, Paris style: 'New designs for spring suits', *l'Illustré*, 5 March 1942 (Dress History Teaching Collection, University of Brighton, with kind permission of *l'Illustré*.)

Belgium

Wartime couture in Brussels

The position of the couture trade in occupied Belgium was totally different from that in annexed Vienna or neutral Switzerland. It managed under extreme difficulty to maintain its business contacts with Paris couture through the war. Pre-war, a complex legal system had been established for purchasing Paris couture garments, toiles and designs on paper. First came the formal, legal purchase of original garments selected in situ in Paris salons by wealthy private clients. The most exclusive fashion salons and department stores came next, paying for original garments, toiles and copying rights. Next were the top levels of international ready-to-wear trades, making legal purchases for manufacturing copy garments. Then came layers of copy garment manufacturers, often functioning illegally around the world. A parallel system existed for fashion illustrators and journalists.

Belgium's position within this ranking lies at the heart of its wartime fashion story. Its couture trade functioned in pre-war years like a little sister dependent on copying the actions of her older more experience sibling – the Paris couture trade. Veronique Pouillard and Nele Bernheim both confirm the Paris copyist base of Brussels couture and its consequent lack of originality. In truth, it was proud to be a

FIGURE 10.14
Dress with frilled cape, in floral print, Belgium, late 1930s (Hasselt Fashion Museum, no. 2011.0027.01, photo by Frank Gielen © Modemuseum Hasselt/Frank Gielen).

FIGURE 10.15
German soldier reads *West-Front*, a German propaganda newspaper in a café in Brussels, 1940. (Getty Images 542367797.)

copyist trade. Both state that Paris Occupation styles were still to be seen in Brussels and in the Belgian fashion press all through the war, though Pouillard details the increasing difficulties in keeping Paris links alive (2005: 185).

The Nazi Occupation of Belgium lasted from 28 May 1940 until 4 February 1945. Brussels itself was liberated by Allied forces on 4 September 1944. As in all occupied countries it had been a fearsome, deeply divided five-year period in Belgian history. With its French borders, Belgium was geographically easily incorporated into the 'Military Administration of Belgium and Northern France' (the departments of Nord and Pas de Calais and the *zone interdite*, a narrow strip of territory running along the French northern and eastern borders (see the map in Figure 1.6). Hitler installed a military government headed by a military commander, Alexander von Falkenhausen and a civil administrator, SWKI SS Gruppenführer Eggert Reeder.

Whilst King Leopold remained in Belgium under house arrest, a Belgian government in exile was based in London. Fascist Flemish, Walloon and French collaborators formed regiments in the *Wehrmacht* (Geller 1999: 99, 108) whilst estimates suggest that 5 per cent of the Belgian population joined the Resistance movement in one way or another; 19,000 of them died.[7] The German occupiers imposed Nazi anti-Semitic legislation, from Aryanising Jewish businesses to the wearing of yellow stars. Twenty-five thousand Jews, mostly refugee foreigners, were deported to Auschwitz. A futher 25,000 avoided deportation, with many sheltered by Belgian families, whilst the Belgian civil administration refused to cooperate with the deportations.[8]

Belgian couture

From May 1940, under German control, Belgian couture continued functioning. As in France, companies struggled to keep their highly skilled staff in employment and were in constant fear that if forced to close, businesses would never re-open. Belgium's flourishing fashion industry was owned in part by Jews as elsewhere in Europe. Véronica Pouillard's detailed and fascinating research into the archives of the Jewish-owned Hirsch luxury department store in Brussels offers precise details of how Belgian couture, and Jewish companies in particular, survived the Nazi occupation of Belgium.

Jean-Paul Hirsch, as the store's Jewish director, had been a key figure in setting up close business relationships between the couture worlds of Paris and Brussels in the interwar years. By 1936, he had successfully established the *Chambre Syndicale de la Couture Belge*, which placed Belgian couture on an advantageous commercial footing with its older sister Chambre in Paris (Pouillard 2006: 422, 426). The Paris salons were well aware that Belgian specialists acted as 'privileged intermediaries', selling their legal Paris copy designs 'made with great discernment' not only in Belgium but onwards to the Netherlands and Germany (2006: 446; 2005: 184; 2004: 411).

The couture salons of Hirsch and Norine

Established in the late nineteenth century, by 1939, the Hirsch department store was owned by the grandsons of the founder, Lucien, Robert and Jean-Paul, whose father was Jewish and whose mother was Catholic. This, as Pouillard confirms, gave them for a while some protection against German imposed anti-Semitic legislation, though in 1939, Lucien left for Brazil and Robert for London. Jean-Paul Hirsch ran the store in Brussels until 1942 when it was forcibly Aryanised (2005: 175, 177). The company was, like all Aryanised businesses, forced to adapt to German-imposed legislation in order to stay open. The elegant fur workshop was thus obliged to make fur waistcoats for the German army – seven a day in 1942 – which were sold by an intermediary (2005: 182). By then, as Nazi control grew tighter, Robert Hirsch too fled, reaching safety in Switzerland as direct staff links to Paris grew weaker and weaker. Hirsch's sister store in Amsterdam had been founded by the family in 1882. In the Netherlands, anti-Semitic laws were even more savage than in Belgium and having been Aryanised, the store was liquidated and all stocks stolen and sent to Germany.[9]

Pouillard found that 'as did Hermès or Fath in Paris, the Hirsch store was still able to sell luxury products to Germans as they passed through the city even though the precious and long-established couture supply routes had closed down'. She notes that to get around the shortages of fabric supplies, Hirsch couture clients brought in their own fabrics (2005: 183–184). Again, as in Paris, the salons had to find different raw materials, 'lowering standards and using "rabbit fur, rayon for dresses, wood shavings for hats" and struggling' even to find 'linings and sewing thread' (2005: 183–184). The Hirsch archives, as Pouillard carefully notes, contained a small amount of information on Paris and even Lyon visits made by Hirsch staff. However, these trips, were rare, deliberately made difficult to organise and 'discouraged by the occupiers' (2005: 183-184). In 1941, for example, Hirsch applied for four members of staff to go to Paris but permission was granted only for one. Thus 'trying to follow Paris fashion became a source of perpetual anguish even though the countries were neighbours' (2005: 183-184).

However, fashion shows of Hirsch's own couture designs were still put on at the store alongside the Paris copy designs. By comparing surviving 'bills, invoices and clients' dossiers, [and] lists of garments', Pouillard could even 'track what [Paris] couture garments were bought and copied during the Nazi occupation of Belgium' (2005: 185). Thus, whilst no examples of Hirsch occupation-period clothes survive in museums in Belgium and Holland, detailed files exist naming specific models purchased, with fabric samples, paper designs and photographs attached (2005: 174). She notes that the Paris styles 'copied at P.A. Hirsch during the Occupation, were above all practical, such as suits, coats in dark classic colours, whilst for winter wear the colour black and warm fabrics dominated.' The tricolour dress designs seen in Paris at the Liberation in August 1944 were not however followed at Hirsch (2005: 185).

Other couture salons also stayed open in Brussels, including Chez Nathan and Maison Borgeaud (which dressed the Belgium royal family) and the avant garde studio Norine. Nele Bernheim writes that this salon did use the Allied colours and in a deliberately coded manner. The journal *Mode de Pringtemps* of 11 May (a day after the Germans entered Brussels) described a Norine design: 'The dress is blue and white but would be just a perfect with a plain white, red or blue ground' (Bernheim 2017). Bernheim states that Norine was run by a charismatic couple: the cultural and intellectual polymath Paul-Gustave Van Hecke and the *grande couturière* Honorine 'Norine' Deschrijver. They established their couture business during World War One.

> For the first time, a Belgian couture house created its own designs instead of buying them from Paris. . . . After the war, they became the most important couture house in the country. Their avant-garde designs boldly transcended the modest conventionality of Belgium. The national and, to some extent, international artistic intelligentsia were their customers. The history of Belgian avant-garde fashion begins with Norine . . . a hub of Surrealism and Expressionism.[10]

Bernheim found many other press reports on this company, such as one in the May 1942 issue of the collaborationist women's magazine *Anne-Marie*. This featured original photographs taken by the German press agency, and showed typical 'Paris' styles 'with broad shoulders and elaborate hats' (Bernheim 2017). It is clear too that many young women either made their own Paris-style clothes following patterns available from magazines, as in France and elsewhere, or ordered them from local dressmakers. Alison Settle, Britain's leading fashion journalist, reached Brussels in her capacity as a war reporter in autumn 1944, meeting up with her old friend Hardy Amies, the well-established London couturier, who was serving as a Lt. Colonel, and Head of the Belgian Section of Special Operations Executive. She remembered that

> in Brussels, I had been staggered by the French women whom I saw in huge over decorated hats, vast sleeves, tight belts above wide skirts with padded hips, wedge shoes, (true of wood) carrying long handled parasols or umbrellas decorated with huge ribbon bows 'to keep up the spirits' they said.
>
> (Settle Archives BO 405.6)

For most women, finding clothes and fabrics of any sort was a constant struggle. Parachute fabric, as in every war-torn country, was much sought after and never wasted. Hasselt Museum owns a short, elegant, parachute silk dress with its deeply gored Paris-style skirt created from the pattern of the parachute.

The Allied battle to free Belgium was led by Canadian forces, and Brussels was freed by British troops on 3–4 September 1944.

FIGURE 10.16
Belgian civilians ride a British Cromwell tank at the Liberation of Brussels, 4 September 1944. (Photograph by Sgt. A. N. Midgley, No. 5 Film and Photographic Unit, War Office, Second World War Official Collection, © IWM BU 509.)

FIGURE 10.17
Dress of parachute silk, Belgium, 1944. This was made after the Allies had landed.[11] (Modemuseum Hasselt no. 1994.0248.02. Photo by Frank Gielen © with many thanks.)

Conclusion

This comparative account of the fate of the couture and fashion textiles worlds in annexed, neutral and occupied European countries in World War Two testifies to the unceasing efforts made in Austria, Switzerland and Belgium to keep their own luxury fashion and textile businesses running. At the same time, Paris couture style retained its place as a key stylistic influence attesting to the strength of pre-war commercial and consumer adherences. In all three countries, however, whether as commercial concerns or as symbols of national cultural identity, everyone involved struggled, under circumstances well beyond their control, to keep businesses and trade alive. These survived most strongly in neutral Switzerland, where direct Nazi interference was at its weakest. In Occupied Belgium, the struggle was keen, though many of its couture businesses survived despite shortages and Aryanisation.

Fashion businesses in annexed Austria, under direct Nazi control, determined to retain their own national design identity but many foundered under Nazi anti-Semitic repression. Sultano writes that it took five years for the Nazis to destroy 'this significant element and tradition of Berlin. It took considerably less time to do the same in Vienna' (2007: 111).

References

Bernheim, N. (n.d.). 'Norine Couture, Brussels: The Embodiment of the Belgian Avant-Garde, 1915–1952', ongoing PhD at the Vrije Universiteit Brussel & Universiteit Antwerpen.

Bernheim, N. (2017). Personal e-mail to author, 1 January.

Elwyn Jones, F. (1938). *The Defence of Democracy*, London: Dutton.

Gedye, G.E.R. (1939). *Fallen Bastions, the Central European Tragedy*, London: Victor Gollancz.

Geller, J.H. (1999). 'Role of Military Administration in German-Occupied Belgium, 1940–1944', *The Journal of Military History, Society for Military History*, vol. 63, no. 1: 99–125. http://www.jstor.org/stable/120335 (accessed 28 August 2017).

Golson, E.B. (2011). *The Economics of Neutrality: Spain, Sweden and Switzerland in the Second World War.* London: London School of Economics and Political Science.

Guenther, I. (2004). *Nazi Chic? Fashioning Women in the Third Reich*, London: Berg.

Halbrook, S.P. (2003). *Target Switzerland: Swiss Armed Neutrality in World War II*. Cambridge: Da Capo Press.

Halbrook, S.P. (2006). *The Swiss and the Nazis. How the Alpine Republic Survived in the Shadow of the Third Reich*, Oxford: Casemate,.

Hayes, J.P. in Forward to Braunschweig, P. (2004). *The Secret Channel to Berlin, the Masson-Schellenbergconnection and Swiss Intelligence in Word War Two*, Havertown: Casemate.

Hervé Joly. (2005). 'Les Archives des entreprises sous l'Occupation'. Lille: IFRESI, 320. https://halshs.archives-ouvertes.fr/halshs-00536942/document (accessed 9 September 2017).

Holocaust Encyclopedia. (n.d.). ?The German Occupation of Belgium?. https://www.ushmm.org/wlc/en/article.php?ModuleId=10005432 (accessed 14 April 2019).

Independent Commission of Experts Switzerland – Second World War (ICE) (1999). *Switzerland and Refugees from the Nazi Era*. Bern: Author.

Institut national de la statistique et des études économiques. (1956). 'Etudes et conjoncture – l'industrie textile suisse', vol. 11: 934–945.

Karner, R. (2017). Personal e-mail to author, 12 June.

Kremer, R.S. (2007). *Broken Threads – the Destruction of the Jewish Fashion Industry in Germany and Austria*, London: Berg; see Loscek, I., 'Contributions of Jewish Fashion Designers in Berlin', 49–75 and Sultano, I., 'Ridding Vienna's Fashion and Textile Industry of Jews During the Nazi Period',110–124.

Mannes, M. (1944). 'In Lisbon – Dressed for Reaction', American *Vogue*, 1 Sept: 140–141, 198.

'Much Ado About Hats'. (1944). American *Vogue*, 15 May, no. 103: 103.

Pallmert, S. (2012). 'Artists, the textile industry and the Swiss Centre for Trade Promotion – an undertaking of a special kind', *Journal of Swiss Archaeology and Art History*, vol. 69, no. 2: 215– 225, http://doi.org/10.5169/seals-389710 (accessed 2 August 2017).

Petropoulos, J. (1997). 'Co-Opting Nazi Germany: Neutrality in Europe During World War II', *Dimensions*, 11.1 (Spring 1997), 15–21. Anti Defamation League, https://www.adl.org/news/op-ed/neutrality-in-europe-world-war-ii (accessed 5 September 2017).

Pouillard, V. (2000). *Hirsch & Cie, Bruxelles, 1869–1962*, Brussels: Editions de l'Université Libre de Bruxelles.

Pouillard, V. (2005). 'Les archives de la maison de couture, Hirsch & Cie. Perspectives pour l'histoire de la mode pendant la seconde guerre mondiale', in Joly, H. (ed.) *Les archives des entreprises sous l'Occupation*, Lille: Institut fédératif de recherche sur les économies et les sociétés industrielles, 167–187.

Pouillard, V. (2006). 'Aménager les échanges entre acheteurs belges et créateurs parisiens. La constitution d'une Chambre Syndicale de Haute Couture Belge pendant l'entre-deux-guerres', *Revue Belge d'Histoire Contemporaine*. no. 3–4, 410–447. http://docplayer.fr/13288251-Amenager-les-echanges-entre-acheteurs-belges-et-createurs-parisiens-1.html (accessed 10 June 2017).

Scaturro, S. (2007). 'Belgian Fashion Then and Now: An Interview with Nele Bernheim', www.fashionprojects.org/blog/194 (accessed 14 April 2019).

Settle, A. Archives, Design Archives, University of Brighton.

Shirer, W.L. (1941). *Berlin Diary, 1934–1941*, London: Hamish Hamilton.

Soie Pirate. (2011). *The History and Fabric Designs of Abraham Ltd*, Zurich: Swiss Marional Museum, with many thanks to Joya Indermule.

Sugarman, S. and McNeil, P. (2012). *Dressing Sydney, the Jewish Fashion Story*. Sydney: Sydney Jewish Museum.

Sultano, G. (1995). *Wie geistiges Kokain. Mode unterm Hakenkreuz, Viemnna Wien* (Like Mental cocaine . . . Fashion under the Swastika), Vienna: Verlag fur Gesellschaftskritik.

Veillon, D. (1990). *La mode sous l'occupation: débrouillardise et coquetterie dans la France en guerre (1939–1945)*, Paris: Payot.

De Waal, E. (2011). *The Hare with the Amber Eyes, a Hidden Inheritance*. London: Vintage.

Endnotes

1. United States Holocaust Museum,Washington, ?Austria', https://www.ushmm.org/wlc/en/article.php?ModuleId=10005447 (accessed 18 September 2017).
2. Ibid.
3. National Museum Zurich no. LM 118929, with thanks to Joya Indermuhle.
4. National Museum Zurich no. LM 118930.
5. Textile Designers for Album 2: Elsi Bosshard, Zurich; Serge Brignoni, Berne; Hans Fischer, Zurich; Cornelia Forster, Zurich; Elsi Giauque, Ligerz; Karl Hügin, Bassersdorf; E. Kappeier, Zürich; Walter Linsenmeier, Ebikon (Lucerne); Oscar Lüthy, Zurich; Marguerite Petermann, Agiez sur Orbe; Jonny Potthof, Zug; Noldi Soland, Zurich; Hans Wullschleger, Zurich.

    Manufacturing companies for Album 1: L Bally, shoe manufactuer, AG, Schönenwerd; Bischoff & Müller AG, embroidery, St. Gallen; F. Blumer & Cie. textile printing, Schwanden; M. Bruggisser & Co. AG, straw manufacture, Wohlen; C. Forster-Willi & Co, embroidery, St. Gallen; Aug. Giger & Co., Heer & Co. AG, Thalwil; Hufenus&Co, embroidery, St. Gallen; Heinr Otto Hürlimann, hand weaving, Arnegg; Schaffhausen & Derendingen, worsted spinning mills, Derendingen; Langenthai AG, Langenthai; Jacques Meyer & Co. AG, braid manufacture, Wohlen; A. Naef & Co., embroidery, Flawil; Edwin Naef AG, silk weaving, Zürich; J. G. Nef & Co., fabric manufacturer, Herisau; Reichenbach & Co., embroidery, St. Gallen; Ruepp & Cie, AG, knitwear, SarmenstSorf; Rüti AG, woolen mill, Rüti; Walter Schrank & Co., embroidery, St. Gallen; E. Schubiger & Cie, AG, silk weaving, Uznach; Stehli & Co, silk production, Zürich; Otto Steinmann & Co, AG, hat fabric manufacturer, Wohlen; Stoffel & Co., silk tissue, St. Gallen; Strub & Co., fabric innovations, Zürich; AG Stünzi Söhne, silk weaving, Horgen; Schweiz, Society for the Tulle Industry, AG, Münchwilen; Union AG.
6. Couturiers cited in Album 2: Elsa Barberis, Lugano; Bouchette, Zurich; Paul Daunay, Geneva; Grieder & Cie, Zurich; Sauvage Couture, Basel; R. Scheidegger-Mosimann, Berne; Andrée Wiegandt and Gaby Jouval.
7. Belgian Resistance, Revolvy, https://www.revolvy.com/page/Belgian-Resistance
8. Holocaust Encyclopedia. (n.d.). 'The German Occupation of Belgium'. https://www.ushmm.org/wlc/en/article.php?ModuleId=10005432 (accessed 14 April 2019).
9. Bakker, T. 'Hirsch & Cie en het Leidesplein', pp. 46-48, https://www.theobakker.net/pdf/hirsch.pdf (accessed 18 May 2019).
10. Bernheim, N. (n.d.). 'Norine Couture, Brussels: The Embodiment of the Belgian Avant-Garde, 1915–1952', ongoing PhD at the Vrije Universiteit Brussel & Universiteit Antwerpen.
11. With thanks to Karoline de Clippel, Dress, Curator, Fashion Museum, Hasselt.

Chapter 11
1944: London plans to become the 'meridian' of world fashion

Marie McLoughlin

In January 1944, Churchill's coalition government met to discuss the invasion of Europe. As it entered its fifth year of war, Britain was virtually bankrupt, but knew, now that Russia and America had entered the war on the Allied side, that it was only a matter of time before Nazi Germany was finally overthrown. Coalition politicians, from all sides of the political divide, were already preparing for the end of the war. The Labour MP, Ernest Bevin, trade unionist and Minister of Labour, was to be responsible for demobilising the forces and returning them to full employment. R.A.B. Butler, a Conservative MP and President of the Board of Education, was, in January 1944, introducing the Butler Education Act, which would provide free secondary and higher education. Meanwhile Lord Woolton, the British Minister of Reconstruction, at this time not affiliated to any party, asked how London could become 'the meridian of world fashion' once Europe was liberated (National Archive ED 46/892).

In fact, the end did not come as quickly as hoped. A week after the Allied landings in Europe, in June 1944, unmanned flying bombs – doodlebugs – bombarded Britain; Paris was not liberated until August 1944 and the war in Europe continued until May 1945. Back in January 1944, when plans for the invasion were being made, Woolton, who, before the war, had chaired a Committee on the Designer and the Dress Trade, hoped that the clothing industry would be an aid to British post-war economic recovery. Anticipating that the Paris dress trade would be in disarray, he asked the Board of Trade and the Board of Education to suggest ways in which London could take over as the world centre of fashion.

The Board of Education's perspicacious art inspector indicated that more than manufacturing capacity would be required: 'Before the war, the glamour of Paris as a centre of inspiration in women's dress transcended that of London or New York, and it is hard to tell how far shift of emphasis can be brought about deliberately' (Dickey 1944).

FIGURE 11.0
A scarf designed by Expressionist painter Felix Topolski entitled 'London 1944' depicting a group of British servicemen and women (Getty 106480761).

This chapter will examine the different responses of the two British government departments to this proposal, the Board of Trade and the Board of Education, responses that reflected British policies in manufacturing and design. What neither board seemed to realise was that Britain was already host to a substantial group of talented and successful textile manufactures who had fled Europe before the war, and to a group of Paris couturiers who had arrived in London after the Fall of France. The Board of Trade had dealings with both these groups yet seemed to overlook this resident expertise when approached by Woolton in 1944.

To examine these issues in the context of the links with Paris that existed in Britain during the war, this research uses material from the National Archives; contemporary reports in newspapers, magazines and Hansard; Howell and others on the Utility Scheme; Pouillard on post-war reconstruction in Europe; biographies and memoirs (two unpublished) and autobiographies from those directly involved.

The Board of Education

Dickey, quoted above, had worked with Woolton on the (unpublished) 1938 Dress Report.[1] He replied to Woolton immediately, repeating many of the recommendations of that report, notably that designers should be trained in the art schools, and accepted by the trade; whereas craftsmen and women should be trained in the technical schools. In his 1944 response, Dickey indicated his understanding of the difference between fashion and clothing production, emphasising fashion's need of a solid foundation in both education and marketing. He reported that the USA had already declared that it would spend millions of dollars on a new fashion centre (FIT, the Fashion Institute of Technology was consolidated in 1944); and the US spend on advertising was large. In New York, Mayor La Guardia had declared as early as 1940 that the city would become the international centre of the fashion industry.

Conscious of the competition that would be coming from New York, Dickey spoke of the need for a city of culture, a city with 'prestige'. Dickey identified the importance of design and propaganda to the fashion industry, the very tools used by the Paris couture as soon as Paris was liberated:

> If London is to become the centre of fashion, I think our publicity experts will have to get to work at top speed – but they must have some very good material to work with. I believe that if there were a few 'names' to whom great and glamorous publicity might be accorded, such as was given to Maggy Rouff and Schiaparelli, and that if the two Royal Princesses were to co-operate, London might go far towards capturing a world reputation for women's dress.
>
> (National Archive ED 46/892)

The Board of Trade

The Board of Trade was keenly aware of the need to move from the war-footing of industry controls and to seek ways of boosting the peace-time economy. A few days after Dickey's initial response, on 3 February 1944, Woolton wrote to the President of the Board of Trade, Old Etonian and socialist Hugh Dalton. Addressing him as 'Dear Hugh', Woolton explained the need to find new jobs as well as revive old ones – presumably in design as well as manufacture – and suggested revisiting his Designer and the Dress Trade report, continuing:

> Paris formerly attracted designers and acquired a considerable reputation in the dress trade, not only because of the couturier, but of the medium, [sic] class. After the last war Berlin tried to establish this trade, but were entirely unsuccessful: during the troubled inter-war years, largely due to the persecution of the Jews in Europe, New York has greatly developed it. If, after the fighting is over, Europe is slow in settling down, I believe there will be a great opportunity for making London into such a centre.

Woolton continued, referring to the need for the establishment of studios for the development of London fashion 'prestige', adding:

> By the way, my friend Sir Thomas Barlow [Director General of Civilian Clothing] . . . had the ridiculous idea that all – and only – French women were smart! I always insisted that if he had moved a quarter of a mile away from the Ritz . . . he would have found that this French 'chic' in clothes was not endemic and London girls were really quite smart! Ever yours Fred Woolton.
>
> (Handwritten letter to Hugh Dalton, 3 February 1944, National Archive BT 64/3579)

The Board of Trade, one of Britain's oldest government departments, did not reply to Woolton for several months, sending a note to the Board of Education in August 1944 to say it was 'waiting for Weir'.[2] In 1944, design education was the responsibility of the Board of Education; the Board of Trade had responsibility for all manufacturing and for exports. In that capacity, it oversaw the production of all civilian clothes during the war.

The Civilian Clothing Directorate

Sir Thomas Barlow, a Lancashire textile magnate, headed the department within the Board of Trade that had responsibility for civilian clothes. Clothes rationing was reluctantly introduced on 1 June 1941, quickly followed by a series of controls and restrictions on all aspects of clothing and textile production, which aimed to reduce the amount of labour and materials expended on clothing to an absolute minimum. These controls gave the British public not what they wanted, but what they needed. In effect, it changed the British economy from a demand economy, where supply is governed by demand – a central tenet of capitalist countries – to a command economy, where state-controlled production is limited to essential needs – a situation more commonly seen in Communist countries. The fact that this was not seen as unnecessarily oppressive, or Stalinist, is testament to the success of the 'fair shares for all' wartime propaganda.

More than six months after Woolton's enquiry, the first indication that the Board of Trade were beginning to grasp just how important the fashion industry might be after the war, was when *Women's Wear Daily* of 6 July 1944 reported that Schiaparelli had offered to design a frock for American production that would meet the requirements of the UK Utility Scheme. Asked if she could produce a dress for £6, she had said that it should not cost more than £2.10–£3.15. Clearly alarmed at the prospect of American-made, couturier-designed dresses competing financially with British-made womenswear, the Board of Trade made a note to contact the American Embassy for more details (Board of Trade 1944). With the pressures of overseeing clothing production, the Board of Trade failed to recognise that they already had direct contact with a core of specialists of international standing who could have provided the 'prestige' that Dickey called for.

Board of Trade quest for 'continental élan'

Northern textiles, Lancashire cotton and Yorkshire wool, were at the heart of the industrial revolution that made Britain the leading economic power of the nineteenth century. In the 1930s the North of England was hit hard by the economic depression; the Board of Trade issued a memo suggesting some 'continental élan' might be introduced to the textile trade by inviting European textile converters to set up businesses. West Cumbria, just to the north of Lancashire, suffered particularly badly. Fierce lobbying by local politician John Adams, later Lord Adams and Deputy Regional Controller of the Board of Trade, ensured that Cumbria was designated a 'special area'; consequently, several Jewish refugees from fascism set up businesses there.

Adams invited Miki Sekers, a Hungarian Jew who had trained in textile technology in Krefeld, Germany, to open a silk mill producing fashion fabrics. Cumbria already had Linton Tweed, set up by William Linton in 1912 to produce high-quality fashion tweeds. His close friend Captain Molyneux, the London-born, Paris-based couturier, introduced him to Coco Chanel in the 1920s and Linton has produced Chanel's iconic tweeds ever since. In the 1930s, Charles Creed, son of Henry Creed of the Paris couture house, studied for six months at Linton's, when Linton's key markets were Paris couture houses and the USA.[3]

West Cumberland Silk Mills

Sekers and his cousin, Tomi de Gara, arrived in England in 1937; both had trained in the textile industry in Hungary, France and Germany. They founded West Cumberland Silk Mills in 1938 in Hensingham, on the edge of the Lake District, with the intention of producing high-end fashion fabrics. However, the outbreak of war meant that the company was soon producing parachute silk, and experimenting with a new fibre, nylon. It produced two million yards of parachute nylon, a fibre Sekers saw could be developed for the home dressmaker and the ready-to-wear trade (Sekers Fabrics website).

Kangol

Jacques Spreiregen, of Russian/French Jewish descent, was another recipient of the Board of Trade Cumbrian development initiative. His aim was to set up a business, using the local wool, to produce berets. Spreiregen had been dividing his time between London and Paris as an exporter/importer, including exporting Basque berets from France to England. He was joined in Cumbia by his nephew, effectively his adopted son, Jo Meisner. Jacques set up a hatmaking business in an old linen factory in Cleator, Cumbria. The first berets came off the production line in 1938, cost 2s (10p), and were always made exclusively of wool, despite the name, Kangol, being an acronym of knitting, angora and wool.

The family had long been involved in the millinery industry and included a forebear who had been a Doucet model; continental élan had indeed come to Cumbria. Jo's daughter, born some years after the war, spoke of growing up in Cumbria: 'After Jacques Spreiregen's arrival, many other émigrés came, among them Miki Sekers (the Silk Mills). My childhood was, to some degree, spent as part of an enclave of Mittle Europeans with strong Hungarian-Austrian-whatever accents.' Jo, who was to become the managing director of the company after Jacques retired to Cannes, had arrived in Cumbria in 1934. He returned to France to do military service and was in Lyons, the French centre of textile production, when the Germans invaded. His daughter stated:

> He persuaded his commanding officer to demobilize him arguing that even Free France was very dangerous for a Jew and that he would be better occupied in England making berets for the British army. He managed to get a lift from Casablanca to Aberdeen on an American naval ship. On arrival he was arrested as an enemy alien, but this sounds to have been a formality, his arrival had been anticipated, and he was interrogated and debriefed for two or three weeks outside London before making his way to Cumbria and Kangol.[4]

Once there he did indeed make berets for the British Army, including Montgomery's iconic beret.

FIGURE 11.1 General Bernard Montgomery in England in 1943, wearing a Kangol beret © Imperial War Museum (TR 1036).

The Aschers

Zika and Lida Ascher arrived in the UK in 1939 following the German invasion of Czechoslovakia. Zika was interviewed by Deborah Barker in 1983 for an unpublished University of Brighton dissertation, *Artist Designed Textiles for Industry 1935–55*. His son Peter has been very helpful in providing additional information about his parents. As related to Barker, the Ascher family were textile retailers and Zika was sent to Lyon to study the silk industry. On his return to Prague he opened a shop retailing 'the best of French and British fabrics'. On arrival in the UK in 1939, he joined a firm importing silks from France. He told Barker that a commission to design and supply printed textiles for a Molyneux export collection of 1943 was a breakthrough in founding his own company. In fact, Zika had produced commercial printed fabrics from as early as April 1941, even before Ascher (London) Ltd. became an incorporated company in November 1941.

On the outbreak of war, Zika Ascher had enlisted in the Czechoslovak Army in Britain, so was unable to attend a meeting in 1942 with Molyneux to discuss printed textiles for a dress collection Molyneux was preparing for the American market, to earn dollars to pay for armaments. His son relates that his mother, Lida, together with her younger sister, went to meet Molyneux, taking some of Lida's tiny

FIGURE 11.2
Lida Ascher fabrics for a Molyneux collection for the USA. (*International Textiles* June 1943, no. 6: 21, © Peter Ascher.)

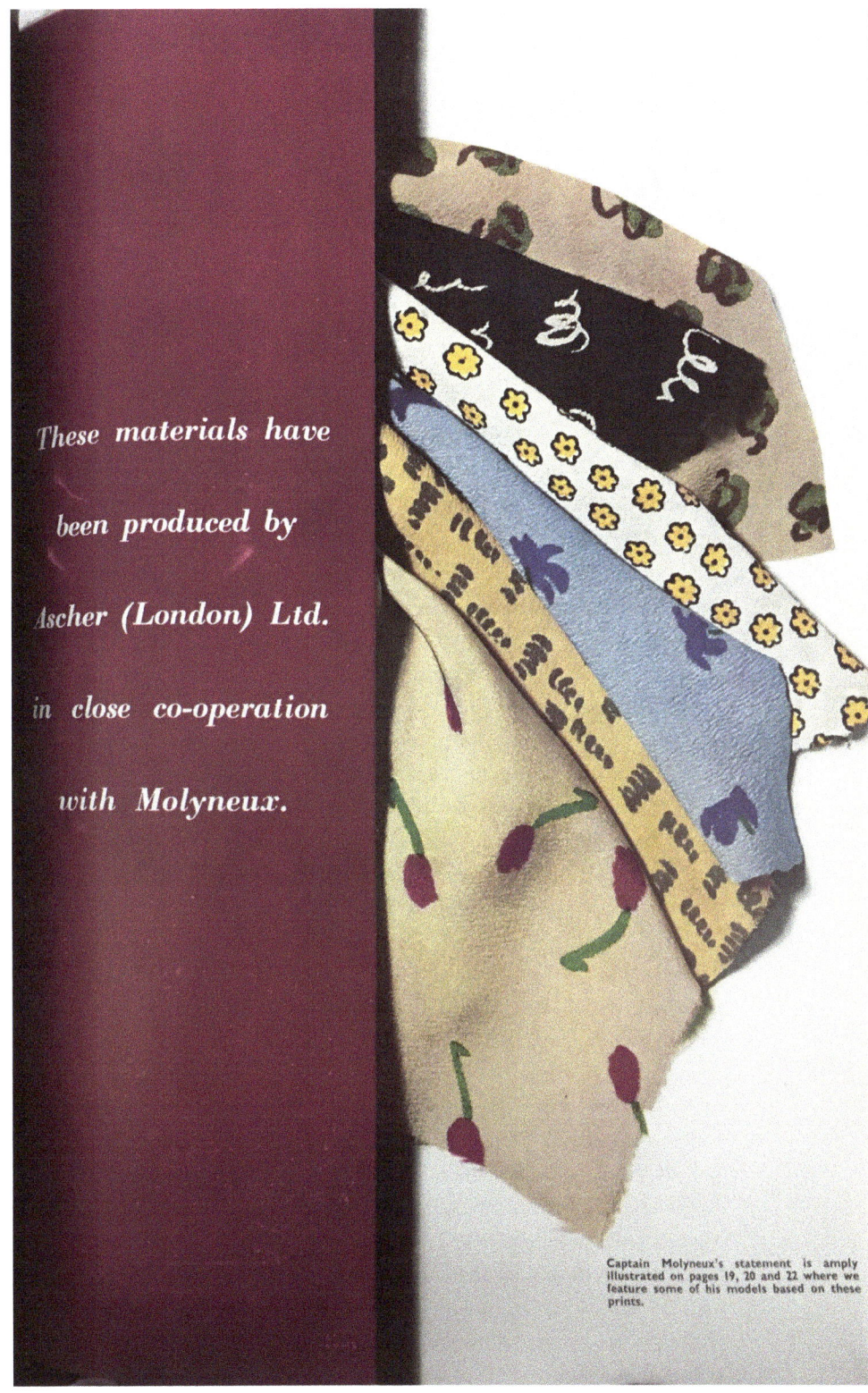

FIGURE 11.3
Molyneux drawings for Bergdorf Goodman, 1940, 1942 and 1944. (The Metropolitan Museum, Thomas Watson Library, Costume Institute, Bergdorf Goodman Sketches: Molyneux. Left: 1940: no. i207.9678_008; centre: 1942: no. 12079678_087; right: 1944: no. 12079678_116.)

sketches, the first designs she had ever done. He asked to see more. She promptly went out and bought a sketchbook and paints and spent the night creating more designs. Lida's naive spots and flowers were to become a trademark of the company, becoming popular with the French couture after the war. In 1943, Zika's recurring jaundice, although treated successfully at a US Army hospital in Salisbury, caused him to be discharged from the army on medical grounds. As related to Barker, he regarded the sale of Lida's designs, and Molyneux's use of them for the American market, as a breakthrough for the company. Swatches held in the Ascher Archive show alternative colourways and appear to be on a rayon crepe, a popular wartime alternative to silk.

Molyneux's work for the American market is described further in Chapter 12. *Vogue* indicates that he also designed in America, using largely British fabrics. The Thomas J. Watson Library has 165 Molyneux sketches done for Bergdorf Goodman.

Propaganda textiles and silk squares

Jack and Mary Lyons, who abbreviated their names to the more continental-sounding Jacqmar, had sold silk to the couture houses of London and Paris since 1932. Remnants were made into silk squares. As the headscarf became an essential wartime accessory for women of all classes, fabrics and squares were used to carry propaganda messages. Arnold Lever, of Jacqmar, even though he was serving in the RAF, designed a series of propaganda prints, with names like 'Fall in the Fire-bomb Fighters' (McDowell 1997: 106).

Ascher took this one step further, using artists to design silk squares bearing wartime slogans. Felix Topolski designed many propaganda scarves including 'London 1944', worn to show the image to greatest effect. Topolski had arrived in the UK from Poland in 1935 to draw the Silver Jubilee of King George V. Trained at

FIGURE 11.4
A scarf designed by Expressionist painter Felix Topolski entitled 'London 1944'. It depicts a group of British servicemen and women. (Getty 106480761.)

Warsaw Academy of Art and as an artillery officer, he would go on to be an official war artist, first for the Poles, then for Britain, witnessing many theatres of war. He was at Bergen-Belsen and the Nuremburg war trials.

Topolski was one of several official war artists whose work Ascher used, including Graham Sutherland and John Piper; British Pathé footage shows Ascher looking at Henry Moore's 'Shelter Drawings' at the National Gallery. In his interview with Barker, Ascher said he 'liked to look in their sketch book and from a silly little thing develop it', with the aim of maintaining morale whilst earning foreign currency abroad. Ascher had observed Josef Sochor's textile company successfully use Czech artists in this way in the 1920s and 1930s.[5] In December 1944, the New York fashion paper *Women's Wear Daily* enthused about the Ascher/British artists collaboration. In 1946 Ascher went to Paris and telephoned Picasso, Matisse and Derain – all designed textiles for him. Ascher's ease with the manners – and languages – of mainland Europe, a facility shared by other emigrés including Sekers, was something that the Board of Trade failed to recognise or capitalise upon when looking to rebuild the British textile industry after the war.

Hans and Elsbeth Juda

The Judas, editors of *Ambassador* magazine, are perhaps the most important emigrés of all. Stanley Marcus, of the American department store Neiman Marcus, doubted that 'the British Government ever realised what this remarkable magazine, and its publisher Hans Juda, contributed to its textile and garment industries' (Breward 2012: 37). The Judas had fled Berlin in 1933, arriving in London with only two suitcases and Hans' violin (Lipmann 2009). Hans immediately became the London editor of *International Textiles*, a trade magazine founded in 1933 in Holland and simultaneously produced in Amsterdam and London, in Dutch, English, German and French. The art editor in Amsterdam was the Hungarian Moholy-Nagy.[6] His typographic designs gave the magazine a modernist Bauhaus aesthetic that the Judas maintained until the magazine, called *Ambassador* after the war, closed in 1972. After the Nazi occupation of Holland in 1940, both magazines were produced under the title *International Textiles*, but all links were severed.

The British edition had an international circulation throughout the war. By 1945 it had overseas offices in forty-five countries. In January 1941, it had twenty-one overseas offices and agents including, as Japan and America were not yet at war, Kobe and Tokyo; New York and Los Angeles; Belgrade, not yet occupied by Germany; Helsinki, fighting a Russia which was not yet part of the Allied war against Nazi Germany; neutral capitals including Stockholm, Lisbon and Istanbul; Batavia, present day Jakarta, part of the Dutch East Indies, which supported the Free Dutch forces after the occupation of Holland; as well as cities that traditionally fell under British influence, like Sydney, Cairo and Haifa.

This not only gave *International Textiles* an extraordinary reach when promoting British fashions and textiles abroad, it also gave the journal unprecedented access to fashion reports from mainland Europe. On several occasions, it simply photographed and reprinted full-page spreads from French magazines, notably *l'Officiel* and *l'Art et la Mode*, alongside an interpretive narrative, at least once reprinting pages from the Austrian magazine *Juno*. In addition, it carried reports from travellers newly arrived from France. In January 1943, under the unlikely headline 'Seaweed and Cactus Tweeds – and Balenciaga's "Lovely Evening Dresses"', a British-born, French journalist, who had lived in France since the war began, told of innovative textiles being made in the South of France, using seaweed and cactus fibres, by a young soldier who had lost his machinery plant in Northern France following the Nazi invasion. All the French couture houses still in operation were listed.

In June 1943, under the title 'Paris Styles and Fabrics', the editor dissected a copy of *l'Officiel*, admitting it to be a few months old and emphasising that this reporting did not indicate sympathy for the Nazi regime. He reported that, whilst all the world class names had been preserved, many were often 'a mere façade . . . hiding second-class successors to first-class creators', as some of the eponymous couturiers had left Paris. But not all chic had disappeared he stressed, citing the hats, often made in fanciful materials. The editor, in discussing the French fashion trade, which it acknowledged was based on creating models for licensed copying, rather than mass production as in Britain, cautioned:

> To suppose that Paris has lost her skill and that her designers have remained at a standstill for the past three years is a gross mistake; yet there are many people who take the view that Paris is finished, and that the reputation that city held, as an illusion which has now been dispelled.
>
> (*International Textiles*, June 1943: 25)

L'Officiel's insistence on the need for skilled needlewomen, cutters and fitters was interpreted, not just as a means of keeping women out of the service of Germany, but 'clear proof that France has no intention of relinquishing her proud position as a fashion centre without a struggle'. The article, written over a year before the Liberation of Paris, observed that London may have made great strides in fashion exports whilst it had no competition during three years of war, but 'if London is to be a fashion centre . . . we must watch the activities of liberated Paris and not hypnotise ourselves in the belief that her fashion industry will have retrogressed in such a way it will have almost insurmountable difficulty to recover her export trade' (*International Textiles*, June 1943: 26).

This makes it clear that as early at 1943, some in the London trade press knew about both the styles of fashions coming out of Paris and the future challenges the British clothing industry faced. It is unclear why this level of strategic knowledge was not passed on to Woolton, especially as many of the designer names shown throughout *International Textiles*, now working in London, were from the Paris couture.

Paris couturiers in London

Several Paris couturiers had arrived in London following the Fall of France in June 1940. This was the second set of European exiles that were to cross the path of the Board of Trade. One such exile was Edward Molyneux. London born, he had trained with the London couturier Lucile before the First World War, in which he served with some distinction – his staff referred to him as 'the Captain'. He moved to Paris to create his own couture house in the 1920s, and ran two nightclubs with the American hostess Elsa Maxwell, who became a lasting friend. Loyally he dressed her ample figure, in every way the antithesis of his more usual clients Wallis Simpson and Princess Marina of Greece. In 1934, he made the wedding dress of the latter, at her wedding to Prince George, Duke of Kent, whose brothers were to become King Edward VIII (briefly) and King George VI.

Known for sophisticated, classic, pared-down designs in muted colours, Molyneux had branches in Monte Carlo, Biarritz, Cannes and London, this last

FIGURE 11.5
Wedding group of Prince George, Duke of Kent and Princess Marina of Greece and Denmark, with dresses by Molyneux, 1934. (Getty Universal History Archive 578343398.)

run by his sister Kathleen. Following the German invasion, he relocated briefly to Biarritz, where he opened his workroom facilities to other couturiers. Once Paris was occupied, he left for England, where he lived in Claridges for the duration.[7]

Another arrival from Paris was Charles Creed, the youngest son of Henry Creed, creator one of Paris' premier tailoring salons. Creed's origins reach as far back as 1710, as a tailor in St. James, London, before relocating to Paris in 1850; the house provided riding clothes for most of the crowned heads of Europe. Although based in Paris for generations, the family maintained their British links. Charles, educated at Stowe as a contemporary of David Niven, trained in Vienna and New York, then designed for his father's house in Paris in the late 1930s. Following the Occupation, Charles and his elder brother made different choices. Whilst Charles went to Britain, his brother returned to Paris to be with their father at the couture house (Creed 1961).

Also bringing Paris flair to the London couture were Bianca Mosca, who had arrived a little before the war, a cousin of Schiaparelli who had worked for Schiaparelli for fourteen years. Mosca, an Italian, was the house designer for Paquin, London. From 1939 she was also the dress designer for the previously mentioned textile company Jacqmar. Another Francophile was Elspeth Champcommunal, who had been the first editor of British *Vogue* from 1916–1922. A member of the Bloomsbury group, she spent most of the inter-war years

FIGURE 11.6
Suit from the House of Creed, February 1939. (Getty 55754899.)

living in France, where she ran an eponymous clothing label. In 1933 she became the designer for court dressmakers Reville-Terry, and when they bought Worth London in 1936, she became the head designer there. All these designers are discussed in more detail in Chapter 12.

The Incorporated Society of London Designers

These Paris refugees were to join up with the London couture, to form the Incorporated Society of London Designers, with Molyneux as chairman. Popularly known as IncSoc, they pooled their resources, both to promote elite fashion and to support the Board of Trade. They recruited the glamourous the Hon. Mrs. Reginald (Daisy) Fellowes to be their president.

Daisy Fellowes (1890–1962), born Marguerite Séverine Philippine Decazes de Glücksberg, had been the Paris editor of the American journal *Harper's Bazaar*, and heiress to the Singer sewing machine fortune. Her three daughters from her first marriage remained in France for the duration of the war. In 1919 Daisy married her second husband, Reginald Fellowes, a cousin of Churchill. Her favoured couturier was Schiaparelli, who named the colour Shocking Pink for her. Her 'shocking' set before the war (it was claimed that she lived off 'grouse, cocaine and other women's husbands'[8]) had included the Prince of Wales and Wallis Simpson. In short, she was rich, famous, knew about fashion and had friends, including Churchill, in high places; she was ideally placed to be the President of IncSoc.

FIGURE 11.7
The Hon. Mrs. Reginald (Daisy) Fellowes, President of the Incorporated Society of London Designers, wearing a Molyneux jacket with button trim, redolent of London's Pearly Kings and Queens, and Aage Thaarup's ostrich hat. Photographed by Cecil Beaton for *Vogue* in 1941. (Getty 507392200.)

Harry Yoxall, managing editor of British *Vogue*, writing in *A Fashion of Life* (Heinemann 1966), claims some credit for the founding of IncSoc, describing bringing together French and British couturiers and American buyers at a cocktail party at the Berkeley. His casual comment 'Meanwhile France fell, and suddenly Molyneux, Charles Creed, Madame Mosca and Angèle Delange found themselves refugees in London' ignores the fact that these designers, together with Champcommunal, the South African Victor Steibel and London couturiers Hardy Amies, Digby Morton, Peter Russell and royal couturier Norman Hartnell (not initially an IncSoc member), had already, before Yoxall's cocktail party, and before the formal foundation of IncSoc in 1942, come together to design a collection of model gowns for the Board of Trade to promote British textiles for export.

The South American collection: textiles, couture and propaganda

The South American market had been one of Britain's most successful trade destinations since the mid-nineteenth century, one strongly contested with the French (see Chapter 9). Determined not to lose this market during the war, a British export tour, under the aegis of the Board of Trade, was planned in the second half of 1940, to promote British textiles by showing them as couture garments worn by British debutants.

The London couture salons of Hartnell, Worth, Paquin, Molyneux, Digby Morton, Stiebel at Jacqmar, Creed at Fortnum & Mason, Worth and Peter Russell all took part, as British *Vogue* detailed in May 1941. It was a major undertaking, visiting Brazil (Rio de Janeiro and Sao Paulo), Argentina (Buenos Aires) and Uruguay.

FIGURE 11.8
Models leaving London for South America in March 1941, to publicise British fashion and textiles for the Board of Trade. Their gas masks, tied in silk scarves, would be left at the docks on departure. (Getty 138592010.)

(Montevideo) in spring 1941. The Export Councils for Cotton, Wool, Nylon, Lace, Silk Hosiery and Knitwear were all involved. Top fashion textile companies provided fabrics, including Tootal (cotton and rayon), John Heathcote (lace and voiles), Brocklehurst-Whiston and Hunt and Winterbotham (woollens) and Moygashel (linens). One gown was designed by Paquin in silk by A.C. Kay.[9] Even though hats, silk stockings, shoes, gloves and handbags were provided free by the manufacturers, the Board of Trade observed that the 'total [cost] was rather staggering' (National Archive BT 61/76/9). The largest expenses were for publicity, including a section in a special edition of *Harper's Bazaar* and a double-page spread in *Vogue*. There is no evidence that *International Textiles*, with offices in Chile, Peru, Argentina and Brazil, which did much to promote the collection, received any money.

A great effort was made, with much success, to seek publicity for the tour in the international press. Press reports and radio segments, some penned by Alison Settle, a former *Vogue* editor, were aired far and wide. A letter from Lord Derby, an elder statesman who had been Ambassador to France from 1918–1920, and was now Lord Lieutenant of Lancashire, Britain's textile heartland, was circulated to newspapers worldwide. His message was clear. Whilst the industry recognised the importance of London as a fashion centre, the collection was to sell textiles: 'Just as the famous dress houses in Paris were in fact "the shop windows" for the display of French silks, wools and laces, so will these displays of the latest London dress models serve the same purpose for our British textiles on the other side of the Atlantic' (National Archive file 61/78/4). The fact that textiles supplied by the export groups were to be shown to the lucrative South American market using eighteen live mannequins, one of whom was the niece of Lord Willingdon, leader of the trade mission and a former viceroy of India, caused questions to be asked in the British parliament in January 1941, months before the tour began. The girls were to wear seventy-seven models created by nine of the leading London couturiers; the Paris links of several of these designers was not mentioned.

The models travelled by sea to Halifax, then by train to New York, where their mission made for useful propaganda in a USA still reluctant to join the war. The day after the girls left London, on 16 March 1941, the *New York Times*, under the headline 'British, Nazis Battle for Latin Style Lead', had reported the joint collection by couturiers and textile manufacturers would be 'the opening gun in a "Battle of Fashion" between Britain and Nazi-dominated Paris in the luxury market of South America'. A report in the *London Gazette* of 16 February was quickly picked up and repeated throughout the Empire, from Montreal to Singapore. The *Examiner*, in Launceston, Tasmania, was particularly fascinated by the debutantes, models and actresses who were to 'sell' British fashions 'to help pay for guns, aeroplanes and tanks'. It revealed that the dresses, had been shown at a series of tea dances at Grosvenor House, but that British women could not buy them. The models were to be paid £3 a week plus hotel and travel expenses, far less than they would normally earn; Lord Willingdon's niece had given up her job as a nurse to join the group.

The *New York Times* of 2 April 1941, also made the girls the centre of the story, with a report headed 'British Girls Here Excited By Butter. Silk Is Also Thrilling'. They had travelled, at a time when many ships were lost to U-boats, on the Dutch ship *Bodegraven*,[10] first to Halifax, and then by train to New York. Whilst the article was dominated by the models' response to the availability of butter, 'a whole weeks ration in one serving', and their woollen stockings – silk stockings were not available in London – the newspaper did quote the Department of Trade officials accompanying the girls, who confidently stated that 'this is the first official trade mission to cross the ocean in an attempt to establish London as the heart of the fashion world and this showing is especially for South America'. The twenty-four cases of clothing that accompanied them would not be seen until they reached South America. The girls said patriotically that they wanted to see the sights rather than buy dresses, and, remembering the food shortages at home, said 'at this point . . . we'd prefer a string of onions to one of pearls' adding that they intended to return to war-torn Britain in June, as Parliament proposed to introduce conscription for all girls over eighteen.

The story of the tour reached the Far East and Australian press too. According to *The Singapore Free Press and Mercantile Advertiser* of 22 April, the shows were to open the next day, St. George's Day, simultaneously in Argentina and Brazil. There would be nine mannequins in each country (one for each designer) and all seventy-seven model garments had been produced in duplicate. After opening in Buenos Aires and Rio de Janeiro the fashion shows were to move on to Montevideo and Sao Paulo. An article on 3 May 1941, in the *Mail*, Adelaide, South Australia, headlined 'Britain's Hush Hush Fashions to Attack Foreign Markets', written by Margaret Gilruth in London, and sent by air mail, may have overstated the secrecy of the fashions sent overseas in wartime, but not the difficulties faced by the team putting the collection together, who were continually forced to move offices as they were bombed and lost bolts of precious cloth in the fire storms that were part of the London Blitz. Two *commères* accompanied the mannequins; Margaret Gilmore describes one of these, 'Mrs Tatton Brown, good looking, competent and charming, has been lent reluctantly by a Ministry for which she was doing hush-hush work, so that she can launch this fashion show in South America.' All her clothes had been designed especially for the occasion by Molyneux.

The collection was therefore an extraordinary collaborative effort to hold on to this luxury market, but sadly, after this 'opening gun', the battle was abandoned. It had been organised by a team from the British Colour Council, whose bills for the organisation of the project was the cause of much discussion in the Board of Trade papers. The marketing was undertaken by Crawford's Advertising Agency. Stefan Schwarzkopf suggests that Crawford's, influenced by the European emigrés arriving into Britain in the pre-war years, had established itself as having a modernist, highly visual style that placed Crawford's 'at the heart of the emergence of a cultural economy for which creative skills are a paramount source of value creation' (Schwarzkopf 2008 : 181). This key concept of commercial value lying in the creative industries, like fashion and design, rather than traditional manufacturing industries, like textile production, whilst understood by Dickey at the Board of Education, was never fully grasped by the Board of Trade, though their files reveal the marketing for this tour was both extensive and successful.

In May, British *Vogue* covered the South American collections using the *International Textiles* device of reproducing the American *Vogue* coverage as a photograph, displayed diagonally on the page, with an accompanying narrative. The various textile companies were listed and the couturiers were credited. The clothes had in fact, been photographed in the British *Vogue* studios before they left the UK. *Life* magazine of 16 June focused again on the glamourous society girls under the headline 'British Models Win Style Victory in South America'. Their upbeat prose was accompanied by photographs, not only of the fashions, but of the girls chatting to young men, one a British war hero, another a local playboy.

FIGURE 11.9
In Buenos Aires, to publicise British textiles, Paquin model Rosemary Chase, niece of Lord Willingdon, chats with socialite Tito Casares at party for models in an Argentine architect's house. (Getty 93704518.)

This extract gives some idea of how *Life* chose to report the visit to their American readers:

> Eighteen willowy English clotheshorse [sic] descended on South America last month to launch the first offensive in a campaign to win for England the rich South American fashion trade. Nine of the charmers disembarked at Rio de Janeiro. The other nine went on to Buenos Aires and to Montevideo. Reports indicate that this shapely battalion armed with subtle weapons of silk and spice and everything nice won a major British victory.

It added, perhaps as a sly reference to the *New York Times* headline about butter, that some of the models had 'put weight on in the wrong places' and that some hasty alterations were needed. The American reporting, as in the *Life* piece above, framed the venture in terms of war. The sacrifices and bravery of the 'shapely battalion' was constantly acknowledged. Irrespective of textile sales in South America, as far as the USA was concerned the expedition was a propaganda triumph. It was with some justification that the Board of Trade grumbled that much of the publicity costs should have been paid by the industrial publicity department of the Ministry of Information, but it was a triumph in publicity terms (National Archive BT 61/78/4).

British fashions and the United States of America

At the time of the South American collection Britain was still exporting fashions to the USA, and with increasing success. A report on London fashions in American *Vogue* in September 1940 pointed out that, by exporting, Britain could earn dollars to buy war supplies, adding 'Here is one way a [American] woman can help support democracy's fight. Buying a new British suit is as much a contribution to British defense [sic] as a sum of money' ('Fashion: London Collections . . . Undimmed' Sept. 1940: 73).

FIGURE 11.10
A group of models wearing new fashions for American women including sportswear and tailored suits at a preview in London, 18 August 1940. (Getty 3373912.)

On 15 April 1941, a month after the mannequins were photographed leaving for South America, under the headline 'More British fashions shown in New York', we learn that British fashions predominated at a show in aid of British war relief. The following month, *International Textiles* reported on a collection sent to New York by the London couture label Rahvis (*International Textiles* May 1941: 36). The December 1941 issue (p. 38) had photographs of the long evening dresses, modeled by Norma Shearer, who had bought them as her film wardrobe for the MGM Noel Coward film *When We Were Dancing*; that month the US joined the war with the Allies. The May 1941 edition had reported that 'Progressive London Hat Designers' had sent their collection to New York too, and there was an article on the newly formed Incorporated Society, with the news that models would be sold for copying, to increase the amount of fabric sold. Leading manufactures and couturiers were to accompany a collection to New York in the spring of 1942. Meanwhile, in September 1941 American *Vogue* had reported on 'a Molyneux Collection, designed in America' noting that in spring he had 'visited America, studied our markets, arranged to design clothes which could be made and sold in America. Half of them, at least, are to be of British fabrics, to stimulate trade, to amass British credit dollars here', adding that all his profits went to the Board of Trade.[11]

But this export trade was about to end, despite these upbeat editorials, and advertisements like that of a producer of millinery felts, of a double-page image of a British convoy with the headline, repeated in many languages, 'Britain delivers the goods – thanks to the British Navy'. In March 1941 America had introduced Lend-Lease, which provided material aid in the battle against Hitler, whilst the USA technically remained neutral. Throughout 1941 Britain fought on alone. Issue 9 of *International Textiles* (September 1941: 20–21) carried a dedication to the RAF boys who had fought in the Battle of Britain that summer; and Issue 10 (October 1941: 18–19) carried a similar dedication to the British Expeditionary Force, and the 'little ships' that helped their evacuation at Dunkirk the previous year. This last, Issue 10, ran a statement, in red ink, clearly prompted by government, explaining that Britain, as part of the Lend-Lease agreement, must not export goods that would be subject to restrictions in the USA. It was made clear that America would also be unhappy to see such goods advertised. The October editorial claimed that 'Wise Restraint' and 'On Merit Alone' were guiding principles for the trade, 'long before unfair and unfounded complaints reached these shores'. Manufacturers complained vociferously that America was being isolationist and there was no reason to curtail all British exports worldwide, as export markets once lost could not be restored.

A response from Prime Minister Churchill was printed in November 1941 (p. 29) in which, rather unconvincingly, he stressed that 'the reduction of exports is due to our increasing pre-occupation with warlike measures' rather than deference to the USA, and that the constraints of total war meant that 'a balance of merits' was needed. Whatever the arguments, and despite the success and 'staggering' costs of the South American campaign, government-supported British fashion exports effectively ceased from this point. However, some British companies continued to export to their regular markets. An article in *International Textiles* in December 1943 (p. 35) showed British woollens and worsteds, flown in from Savile Row to neutral Sweden, displayed in Stockholm shop windows. Another window, in the university town of Uppsala, was dominated by a large Union Jack leaving no doubt about the origin of the fabrics.

The Utility Scheme

The group of elite designers who had clustered around Molyneux in 1940 had proved the value of fashion as a propaganda tool with the South American shows. In 1942, IncSoc, was to help promote another Board of Trade initiative. Tom Heron, a member of the Civilian Clothing Directorate, recruited IncSoc to help launch the Utility Scheme. Rationing had led to increased prices and reduced quality; the Utility Scheme, of price and quality-controlled goods, would combat this, and eventually 85 per cent of all clothing sold was Utility. The scheme ensured the availability of warm serviceable clothing (and good basic furniture and household linens), at a time of great shortages, when many were losing all they had in the destruction of the Blitz. Sir Raymond Streat, of the Cotton Board, described it at the time as 'a floor for quality and a ceiling for prices'.

All non-Utility production of clothing, including garments made by London couturiers and costly because of high levels of purchase tax, was controlled by austerity regulations. This ensured that the rich, whilst only able to buy the same ration of clothing, could not demand fanciful or extravagant styles that might use

FIGURE 11.11
A tweed Utility ready-to-wear suit by Derèta, and a heavily taxed, much more expensive, emerald green frock, with matching jacket, by royal couturier Norman Hartnell, conforming to Austerity regulations, 1943. (Getty 154419538.)

FIGURE 11.12 September 1942, at a Board of Trade display in London, a couture suit on the left, part of the couturier prototype scheme to launch Utility, and a mass production copy. (Getty 100372763.)

scarce materials and labour. This ensured that a separate fashion silhouette did not emerge for the wealthier classes as it had in Paris. The Ministry of Information photograph of a tweed Utility suit by Deréta, a ready-to-wear company, and a green dress and jacket by royal couturier Hartnell, underlines the fact that the two clothing standards, Utility and Austerity, despite their very different price brackets, were not viewed as separate fashions.

In this context, Heron's idea of asking the IncSoc couturiers to each design a coat, suit, blouse and dress, anonymously, the patterns of which could be given to manufacturers for mass Utility production, was inspired. This famous experiment, covered by *Vogue* both in the UK and the USA, is still regarded as one of the triumphs of the British home front. In fact, few direct copy designs were put into production, but it did break style barriers between mass-produced and couture designed clothes and helped to maintain a homogenous wartime style across all classes. Molyneux, speaking to *Vogue* in October 1942 (pp. 23–31), described Utility as 'the democratic principle in action'.

Conclusion: 'creativity as capital'

To grasp why the Board of Trade did not turn again to this distinguished group of couturiers to help boost fashion at an international level when responding to Woolton in 1944, it is necessary to understand that at the end of the war the Board of Trade was concentrating on a Council for Art and Industry agenda, an agenda that focussed on manufacturing rather than design. Their aim was to restore the once-powerful British textile trade, in order to regain world export markets. The Board of Trade excuse of 'waiting for Weir', referred to the Weir Report on setting up the Council of Industrial Design and associated design centres. The Board of Trade felt that 'the next step for the clothing industry is to try to get them to subscribe for such a centre' (National Archive BT 64/3579). Their focus was on manufacturing, not the fashion leadership that Woolton had identified as a tool for post-war reconstruction.

Another Cecil Weir committee, the Heavy Clothing Working Party, set up in March 1946 (National Archive BT 64/2527), sheds further light on why a proposal to make London the 'meridian' of world fashion was unlikely to succeed. Weir's working party was one of many, set up to dismantle the wartime controls that had dominated clothing production, or, as it was put to the committee members, many of whom were manufacturers from the North of England, for 'industrial rehabilitation'. The minutes make it clear that the wartime restrictions of Utility, with its closing of small factories and the loss of a skilled workforce, contributed to the slow recovery of the industry. Clearly, the Board of Trade saw Northern manufacturing industrialists, rather than a handful of cosmopolitan fashion designers in London, as the key to the post-war reconstruction of the dress trade.

At no point therefore did the Board of Trade seek to capitalise on the wartime presence in London of well-established Paris couturiers, nor on successes of the South American export collection, or the Utility couture prototype scheme, by looking at the marketing and elite design skills that had made both such a success. The situation in Paris was the very opposite. Both Pouillard and Schwarzkopf cite creativity as a tool to rebuild capital, at a time when production is compromised. Paris used this tool to great effect with the *Thêatre de la Mode* in 1945.

The British Board of Trade, despite their earlier fashion experiences, and ignoring the Board of Education's exhortation for 'prestige', never took Woolton's call to make London the 'meridian' of the dress trade very seriously, but focussed on rebuilding heavy industry. The Board of Education however, with its post-war investment in free secondary and higher education for the most able, and the training of designers in an improved art school structure, did, eventually, make London a fashion centre to rival Paris. Ten years after the end of the war art school graduate Mary Quant opened Bazaar, a shop that was at the forefront of the 1960s Youthquake revolution; thirty years later Britain's art school system produced two more designers, John Galliano and Alexander McQueen, who even headed Paris couture houses.

References

Alison Settle Archive, Design Archives, University of Brighton, B0 405.19.
Barker, Deborah. *Artist Designed Textiles for Industry 1935–1955*. Unpublished BA dissertation, University of Brighton, 1983.
Board of Trade. Memo, July 1944. National Archive BT 64/3579.
Breward, Christopher. *Ambassador*. London: V&A Publications, 2012.

Blaszczyk, Regina Lee and Véronique Pouillard, eds. *European fashion: The creation of a global industry*. Manchester: Manchester University Press, 2018.

Creed, Charles. *Maid to Measure*. London: Jarrold Publishing, 1961.

Dickey, E.M. O'Rourke Board of Education, National Archive ED 46/892, January 1944.

'Fashion: London Collections . . . Undimmed'. *Vogue*, 15 September 1940, vol. 96, no. 6: 72–75, 128.

Howells, Geraldine. *From Haute Couture to Homemade, 1939–1945*. London: Bloomsbury, 2012.

International Textiles (1940-1945, all issues).

Lipmann, Maureen. *Elsbeth Juda: Portrait of a role model*. Jewish Chronicle, 23 April 2009.

McDowell, Colin. *Forties Fashion and the New Look*. London: Bloomsbury, 1997.

Pouillard, V. 'Haute couture goes global: networks, markets and challenges in the post-war era' presented at the V&A study day 'The Enterprise of Culture: The European Fashion System Around the World' (10 June 2016).

Schwarzkopf, Stefan. 'Creativity, capital and tacit knowledge: the Crawford Agency and British advertising in the interwar years'. *Journal of Cultural Economy*, 25 July 2008, vol. 1, issue 2: 181–197.

Sekers Fabrics website. http://www.sekersfabrics.co.uk/about-sekers/history/ (accessed 10 October 2017).

Endnotes

1. The University of Brighton Design Archive, which holds the archives of the Design Council and parent bodies like the Council for Art and Industry, has a rare copy of this report.
2. Cecil Weir, who wrote several reports, not all published, was an executive member of the Industrial and Export Council of the Board of Trade, on which he remained until 1946. In 1946 he became economic adviser, Allied Control Commission for Germany (*Oxford Dictionary of Biography*, accessed 5 July 2016).
3. The company's history is described both in Creed's autobiography and on the company website.
4. Email exchange between Jo's daughter and author, 2012.
5. Josef Sochor (1866–1931) was an industrialist whose core business was printed textiles and who achieved export success with artist designed textiles. This company became a public company in 1930 run by his three of his four sons. It was Aryanised in 1941 (Institute of Modern and Contemporary History, Austrian Biographical Dictionary).
6. Moholy-Nagy had resigned from the Bauhaus in the late 1920s and moved to Berlin, where he had a very successful studio practice. In 1933 he left Berlin, initially for Holland and then the UK. By 1937 he was in Chicago where he set up the New Bauhaus. He went on to be very influential in design education in Chicago and the USA.
7. Biographical details on Molyneux assembled from the *Oxford Dictionary of National Biography*, *Vogue* and *New York Times*, 9 Oct 1964.
8. Christopher Wilson, in a biographical essay, in the *Daily Mail*, 29 March 2014.
9. 'Export Drive: London Fashion for South America', p. 40–41; and pages reproduced from *Vogue*'s Special South American Edition, 1941, pp. 53–55, British *Vogue*, May 1941.
10. Although Germany occupied Holland in May 1940, the Royal Dutch Navy fought on the allied side throughout the war. The *Bodegraven*, a Dutch Merchant ship, was sunk by U-boat off the coast of Africa in 1944.
11. 'Fashion: Molyneux Designs for America', 1 Sept 1941, *Vogue*, vol. 98, no. 5: 72–75.

Chapter 12
Paris fashion: an international product for an international clientele

Marie McLoughlin, with postscript from Nancy Yeide

Paris fashion, as this book describes, was an international concept, one that went beyond couture clothes made in Paris, France. The phrase alone implied elegance, luxury and quality. Paris was the hub of a worldwide industry, one serving an international clientele of the richest and most discerning women in the world. It acted as a vortex, drawing in the world's most talented designers, the world's most sumptuous fabrics and the best craftspeople. For a designer to be considered 'world class', it was necessary to have a Paris address.

At the same time, this centrifugal force sent out evidence of its primacy in the form of exports and licensed copies sold throughout the world; international branches of its most famous couture houses and a never-ending stream of well-dressed women who moved through royal and wealthy circles, where they were photographed and admired in the latest Paris fashions. In the 1920s and 1930s the UK and Argentina were her main markets; the latter replaced by the USA until, following the Depression, the USA placed punishing taxes on imported French couture (Grumbach 2014: 40–45). This high cost seemed only to emphasise the exclusivity of Paris fashion abroad; its reputation continued to rise and anything that could advertise itself as 'Paris fashion' would attract a premium.

This chapter will examine two aspects of Paris couture fashion, its cosmopolitan workforce and its overseas marketing, to demonstrate that, by the time of the occupation of France, the Paris fashion industry the Nazis sought to regulate was no longer confined within the borders of France. It had long been an international industry whose creation and dissemination were not limited to clothes produced within the boundaries of Paris alone. Thus, it continued to manifest itself throughout the war through those branches of the industry already established overseas and through the work of its international designers. This assertion, which contradicts

FIGURE 12.0
Model, wearing a back-lacing corset by Detolle for Mainbocher, taken just before his relocation to New York, Horst, Paris, 1939. (Photo by Horst P. Horst/ Conde Nast. Getty 500685096.)

the popular belief that Paris fashion disappeared from world view between 1940 and 1944, will be proved by reviewing the pre-war diffusion of two of the grandest and oldest Paris couture houses, Worth and Paquin, and by examining the wartime careers of some of the top (non-French) Paris couturiers.

Molyneux, an Englishman, had no choice but to leave when the Nazis occupied Paris. Schiaparelli, Italian but holding a French passport, chose to leave Paris for the duration, whilst others, like Balenciaga and Piguet, stayed in Paris, but could cross French boundaries into their neutral home nations. This chapter will use magazine and newspaper reports from the period, biographies and autobiographies of leading designers and archival research, to build on the work of Dominique Veillon, Jean-Pierre Pastori, Meryl Secrest, Lesley Ellis Miller and Veronique Pouillard. It will show that Paris fashion of the late 1930s and early 1940s was international, both in conception and execution, as well as clientele.

Worth and the founding of the Paris couture

The founding father of Paris couture is generally agreed to be Charles Frederick Worth (1825–1895), an Englishman. He rose from working as a draper to dressing the crowned heads of Norway, Denmark, Belgium, Italy, Spain and Russia. Worth had had a branch in London from before World War One. Its clientele, as in France, were the upper classes and the rich. Work by E.-J. Scott (2015) has shown that Worth's reputation as an exclusive Paris couture house was contradicted by the large volume of its cheaper, simpler garments, which were not necessarily made in Paris.

Reville and Rossiter, later known as Reville-Terry, was the 'court dressmaker' who dressed Queen Mary, consort of King George V; in 1936 it bought the London branch of Worth and renamed it 'Worth London'. From this date, it was completely independent from the French branch, but the name, evoking the heyday of the birth of couture and the Second Empire, epitomised Paris fashion. It is doubtful that many customers realised that, when buying from Worth London, they were not buying a French product. Reville-Terry's head designer became the chief designer for Worth London. She had the pleasingly French sounding name of Elspeth Champcommunal (1888–1976). Indeed, she had run an eponymous label in France during the interwar years, but she was English and had been the first editor of English *Vogue* from 1916–1922. Born Elspeth Mary Hodgson, she had married a French artist, Joseph Champcommunal, who died in the first year of World War One (Squitieri 2014). She was a member of the Bloomsbury group, friend of Virginia Woolf and Roger Fry (Caws and Wright 2000) and long-time partner of Jane Heap, co-editor of the *Little Review*, where Joyce's *Ulysees* was first published. Champcommunal was a founder member of the Incorporated Society of London Designers, a group of couturiers which came together during the war, to both promote the couture and to support the Board of Trade in the war effort.

So here we have an English designer, located, through the Bloomsbury group, at the very heart of British modernist thinking, living an unconventional lifestyle with her partner Jane Heap, and wholeheartedly supporting the British war effort as a member of IncSoc. Her design for the Utility Couturier Prototype collection, a scheme covered in more detail in Chapter 11, shows a classic British tailor-made, offset with witty, slightly discordant, touches such as the rounded lapels, yellow blouse and slightly oversized yellow buttons (Figure 12.1). The outfit was completed by a yellow overcoat.[1] Although individual garments were anonymised at the time, the well-publicised fact that 'Worth' had supplied some of the designs imparted Paris kudos to a collection aimed primarily at the working classes.

The Victoria and Albert Museum (V&A) collection also has over a hundred sketches from the wartime Paris studios of Worth, drawn by Roger Worth, descendent of the founder. These 1943 designs show an exaggerated 'Occupation Style' silhouette, and occasional lavish embellishment quite at odds with the Champcommunal designs, despite the note of yellow (Figure 12.2). Even if few of the Paris Worth designs were put into production, the drawings give a clear indication of the tastes of the changed couture clients of occupied Paris, clients decribed by Taylor in Chapter 1. However, the Worth fashions that the outside world saw, in the pages of American *Vogue* and elsewhere in the 1940–1944 period, the one that still epitomised Paris chic, were the designs that were being created in London, not Paris.

Both the South American collection, sent by the British Board of Trade in Spring 1941, to publicise British textiles in Argentina, Brazil and Uruguay, and the Utility Couturier Prototype collection of 1942, were the subject of well-illustrated articles in both British and American *Vogue* and other magazines (Figure 12.3). Both cited clothes designed by 'Worth'. By 1944, fellow IncSoc designer Hardy Amies, formerly of Lachasse, was also designing for Worth. At this date, as Lt. Col. Hardy Amies, he was also head of the Belgian Section of Britain's Special Operations Executive (SOE). Following the Liberation of Brussels in September 1944 he entertained British *Vogue*'s war correspondent, Lee Miller, there. She photographed him and local resisters for British *Vogue* (copied to American *Vogue* in January 1945), which caused much agitation amongst Amies' seniors:

> What seems extraordinary to me is that a serving officer should lend himself and his Secret-service background in the interests of his private affairs, to wit, one of Englands [sic] chief dress designers employed by the House of Worth, to a gaudy publicity stunt together with posed photographs.
>
> (National Archive HS 9/29/2)

It is significant that this senior intelligence officer, in criticising Amies, cites the House of Worth as an embodiment of elite fashion.

FIGURE 12.1
Worth (Champcommunal) Utility suit in Scottish tweed, 1942 (V&A T.42&A&B-1942. © Victoria and Albert Museum, London.)

FIGURE 12.2
Fashion drawings, Roger Worth, Paris. Left: Winter 1943, no. E.18874-1957; centre: Winter/Summer 1943-44, no. E.18787-1957; right: Summer 1943 Winter 1943-44 E.18851-1957. Victoria and Albert Museum. (Copyright Ms. Nikita Mehta, Brand Development Manager, Akito Brands, SA Designer Parfums Ltd.)

FIGURE 12.3
Buenos Aires 1941. Peggy Meredith models a Worth dress and jacket as part of the Board of Trade South America tour. She is holding a show programme showing a British coat of arms and the heading 'Coleccion de Modes de Londres'. (1023007280 Getty/Life.)

Paquin

We have the evidence of the French Worth sketches in the V&A collection because, when the House of Worth finally closed in Paris in the 1950s, it was taken over by Paquin, which donated the albums of drawings to the V&A. Paquin, whose foundation dates from 1890, with a Maison de Couture situated next door to Worth in Rue de la Paix, can perhaps be seen as one of the first truly multi-national fashion houses. Jeanne Paquin (1869–1936) had trained at Rouff, a house which was to become one of the major Paris couture houses of World War Two. By 1896 Paquin had English backers and had opened a London branch. It needs to be stressed that Paris designs were produced in the London Paquin atelier. By the time of World War

One there were branches in New York, Buenos Aires and Madrid (Watson 2010: 326). The New York branch specialised in fur and by World War Two fur and fur trims were a signature of the house. Jeanne Paquin, who, at the time of World War One, became president of the *Chambre Syndicale de la Couture Parisienne*, was the first female head of a large couture house, which, at its height employed more than two thousand workers, more even than Worth (FIDM 2016).

Sirop writes that after her death in 1936 the house designer was the South American Ana de Pombo, whose wartime designs were regularly featured in *Modes et Travaux*, retaining the signature Paquin touches of filmy, layered chiffons and fur trimmings, but without the excesses seen in the Paris Worth drawings. Her assistant, the Spaniard Antonio del Castillo, succeeded her in 1941 after a spell at Piguet, where he had replaced Christian Dior (Figure 12.4).

Paquin closed in 1956 having bought the House of Worth, its neighbour and rival, in 1950. The two houses had always been close, on both sides of the Channel; when Paquin was bombed out in the London Blitz it moved into the same building as Worth, 50 Grosvenor Street ('British Vogue Weathers the Storm' 1940: 139).

In 1936 the London manifestation of Paquin took as its house designer Bianca Mosca. Italian, she was a cousin of Schiaparelli and had worked for her in Paris. In September 1940, just a few months after the Nazi occupation of Paris, American *Vogue* reported that Paquin London had become the company headquarters ('Fashion:

FIGURE 12.4
Antonio Del Castillo, designer for Paquin, France, 1944. (Getty 53375690.)

London Collections . . . Undimmed' 1940: 72–75, 128). Like Champcommunal at Worth, Mosca was to become a founder member of IncSoc and as such contributed to the Board of Trade's South American collection and to the Utility Couturier Prototype scheme as a representative of the House of Paquin. In 1939, in addition to her work for Paquin, Mosca had become the house designer for the British textile company Jacqmar, famous for its propaganda fabric and scarves. In August 1942 all the Utility prototypes were given to the V&A and placed for safe keeping in a Welsh slate mine.

Recent examination of a blouse designed as part of the Utility Prototype scheme shows that it bears a label in the side seam: 'BIANCA MOSCA at JACQMAR 16 Grosvenor St London' (Figure 12.5). A dress, without an attribution, also given as part of the Utility Prototype collection, has also been attributed to Mosca, as it bears the same curious notch in the rear collar. It is unclear if the links between Paquin and Jacqmar went beyond sharing Mosca as a designer, but what is clear is that the Board of Trade, and the Ministry of Information, chose to name the French house of Paquin as a contributor to the Utility Collection, rather than Mosca or Jacqmar.

FIGURE 12.5
Utility blouse given as part of the Couturier Prototype scheme. (V&A T.61-1942. © Victoria and Albert Museum, London.)

The IncSoc collection was promoted as a collection produced by leading couturiers, in *Vogue* and elsewhere. The designers, or the house to which they were attached, were named, but their individual garments were not identified.[2] The public were sceptical of government-controlled clothes, fearing a uniformity and lack of quality that would highlight the straightened circumstances in which many people found themselves. In this context, using IncSoc to demonstrate that the appearance of the clothes would be very similar to those clothes that were being designed for the middle and upper classes, was a great propaganda coup. As detailed in Chapter 11, few of the Utility Prototype clothes were put into mass production, but basic designs of simple, knee-length suits and dresses, using a minimal amount of fabric, became the abiding silhouette throughout Britain for the duration of the war.

Paris was never mentioned directly by the Board of Trade or the Ministry of Information, but, because of the way that the collection was promoted, stressing the design credentials of Molyneux, Creed, Worth and Paquin, it is clear that the intention was that the public should believe these clothes were imbued with all the attributes of 'Paris fashion'. What the British public did not see were the Paris Worth drawings or the embellished satin evening dresses being created by Paris Paquin (see Paquin dress in Figure Intro.2).

Creed

Henry Creed was a Paris couture house, famous for dressing both men and women in fine tailoring. Dating back to the time of Worth, it had its roots in Britain. Unlike Worth and Paquin, it did not have a London establishment, but during the war the name came in front of the British public as Charles Creed, the youngest, English-educated son of the Paris tailoring house. He came to Britain following the Nazi occupation of Paris, leaving his father and older brother running the Paris house. Although Charles did not open his own couture house until after the war, throughout the war, as a member of IncSoc, he was part of the various Board of Trade initiatives, working under the auspices of Fortnum & Mason.

This makes a Harrod's booklet from October 1940 particularly interesting. The full-colour illustrated booklet, sent to all account customers, was for a range of ready-to-wear tailored suits and coats made and sold at Harrods. Notification of an accompanying fashion show was struck through, no doubt cancelled as the London Blitz began in earnest. The oddity is that the clothes are advertised as being by Henri Creed. The name is unnecessarily 'Frenchified'. Despite trading out of Paris for a hundred years, the house was known as Henry Creed, and proud of its roots in British tailoring. The Paris origins of the Harrods clothes is stressed, but not explained:

> The couturier – whose name spells perfection in tailoring – designed the models specially for Harrods. We copied them diligently, line for line in the original superb British materials.

Millinery, sweaters, blouses and accessories of every kind have been dyed in tone with these CREED creations; exquisite warm-glowing shades including a brown we call 'Pottery Tan'.

The clothes, typical tweed tailored suits and coats, with some monochrome coats for city wear, came in three main colour palettes, moss green, airforce blue and snuff brown, in various tweeds, checks and tartans. The town clothes were available in black, violet and elephant. All came in a wide range of sizes.

It is likely that they were made in-house by Harrods in early autumn 1940, under licence (Figure 12.6). The name Henri may have been added for legal reasons, to distance Harrods from the Paris house, but it does emphasise the Paris connection, without any reference to the Nazi occupation. The clothes do have a continental air, with small, sophisticated details that are unlike those typically found on classic British suits, and the name of Creed was clearly well known to the British public. The Board of Trade made great play of the designs that Charles Creed did for IncSoc, never suggesting that his links with the parent company were severed for the duration.

FIGURE 12.6
Henri Creed, Harrods News, October 1940 fashion book. (Courtesy of Harrods Company Archive.)

Wartime Paris couture shown abroad before the Occupation

In the spring of 1940, two months before the German invasion of Paris and only a few weeks before the invasion of the Low Countries, *Match* reported on nine leading Paris-based couture houses taking a joint show to Amsterdam.[3] It was led by by M. Jean Howald of Maison Maggy Rouff, and held at the Hotel Carlton. The event was hosted by Hirsch et Cie and facilitated by the French Ambassador, Baron d'Arnault de Vitrolles, and the French Commercial Attaché, Paul Boncour, on condition that any proceeds be shared between French and Dutch war charities. The unequivocal message was that the Paris couture was still in business. The show was to have continued to New York, but this was almost certainly cancelled when the Low Countries were invaded in May 1940.

Reports in the Dutch press emphasise that the three fashion shows, held at the Carlton Hotel during dinner on 6–7 April 1940 and at Thé Dansant on Sunday 7 April, were highly unusual, as the couturiers did not normally show as a group (Figure 12.7).[4] The reports indicate they were well attended, quelling any rumours

FIGURE 12. 7
Paris couture show in Amsterdam. *Match*, 18 April 1940. (With thanks to the Dress History Teaching Collection, University of Brighton.)

that the Paris dress houses had closed or had been given over to making uniforms, as did the presence of many foreign buyers at the recent Paris spring shows, including forty from America. The show included a wide range of garments from sportswear, through tweed *tailleurs* and tartan day dresses, to sumptuous eveningwear and furs:

> How to describe to you, these clouds of georgette, lace, tulle and silk? Which refined simple white attire with their trimmings of bright green silk, gold ornaments, silver sequins, red-and-silver embroidery? That wide one, all little pink tulle and lace, topped with black? The stylish robes of black lace and silk? The evening capes and sheaths of marten and silver-fox and . . . and other fur? That incredibly witty evening sheath taffeta in colorful Scottish Tartans with enormous balloon sleeves?

The coverage went on to say:

> the models shown to us in this show were masterpieces. And even if we can never own these things, we can go to look at them, to enjoy as we enjoy a beautiful painting, a beautiful piece of music, a good book. . . . . . And if we also remember that these wonderfully beautiful things originated in a country which is at war, our admiration rises to deep respect. A. W.-V.
>
> (Utrechts volksblad: sociaal-democratisch dagblad, 11 April 1940)

The shows clearly showcased the best of Paris couture. The nine houses that participated in the Amsterdam show fall into three types. There were four old, established houses, where the creator had died or had handed over to someone else: Lanvin, Patou, Worth and Paquin. Paquin's South American designer Ana de Pombo sent fifteen of her latest designs, which subtly featured the *tricolore* of France, in linings, tartans and a floral-printed evening dress (Sirop 1989: 70).

There were three French designers: Alix, who as Mme Grès later created dresses in the red, white and blue of the French flag and whose house was closed by the Germans (Veillon 2002: 99); Lelong who, as chairman of the *Chambre Syndicale de la Couture Parisienne* was instrumental, by negotiating with the Nazis, in retaining the couture in Paris, and in doing so codified many of the strict rules of the *Chambre Syndicale* that we know today[5] (Grumbach 2014: 30); and Maggy Rouff, of Belgian heritage, whose parents had opened a branch of the Austrian fashion house Drécoll, and who, as Marguerite Besançon de Wagner, had familial links with the sponsor, Hirsch et Cie, a famous department store with branches in Amsterdam and Brussels.[6]

And finally, there were two designers who were not French, the British Molyneux and the Swiss Piguet. Both catered for similar clients: thin, rich, sophisticated women. Women whose social lives required elegant, but not overstated, clothes. The wartime careers of these two designers were to go in very different directions.

Molyneux

Captain Edward Molyneux was one of the big names of pre-war Paris couture, rivalling Chanel and Schiaparelli. He dressed many of the world's best dressed, including Wallis Simpson, the Duchess of Windsor. Born in Hampstead, he had trained with Lucile; by the time war broke out, in addition to his salon in Paris, he had branches in Monte Carlo, Biarritz, Cannes and London. An indication of his international stature is a *Vogue* article of 15 January 1939, 'Fashion: International Situation', which showed the same black moiré taffeta dress worn and accessorised by three different society women, French, English and American. The French styling was chic, with a black hat by Suzy; the English styling was classic, with black satin gloves and a red hat, both by Molyneux, and silver antique jewellery; whilst the American styling was more playful, with a pink Molyneux hat and pink gloves. This is evidence of a designer who understood the differing tastes of his international clientele, one who may have been based in Paris but whose business interests successfully extended far beyond France.

Following the shock of the German invasion of France in May 1940, many couturiers left Paris. Molyneux opened his Biarritz workrooms to Lelong and Schiaparelli, as reported by Schiaparelli to American *Vogue* in an interview. ('Needles and Guns' 1940: 57). As the Germans invaded Paris, Schiaparelli went on a planned lecture tour to the USA and Molyneux left for England. According to a piece written in American *Vogue* on his retirement in 1952, he travelled on a coal barge with his resourceful butler, Pawson, who served cocktails on deck. Alison Settle, in notes written in January 1941, described his London studio, a quarter the size of the one in Paris:

> work girls all in white gathered in the showing salon and told the importance of foreign exchange to the war effort and the need for secrecy . . . Staff canteen – 6d for a meal of meat and 2 veg . . . Capt Molyneux eats in it daily himself, instead of going back to Claridges [where he has a flat] for lunch. . . . the orders for export came in all the time – for Nassau, for San Francisco, for sports and summer clothes, for Australia an enormous order, New York wants glamour clothes while this country does not, so there have to be subtle changes with the same line and type.
>
> (University of Brighton Design Archive, ASTB4OS.19)

Only weeks after the occupation of Paris, in September 1940, American *Vogue* was reporting on the London Collections ('Fashion: London Collections . . . Undimmed' 1940: 72–75, 128) claiming, 'Tea now rationed, cocktails instead, but no shortage of material. Some houses showing as many as 70 models.' It went on:

Joining forces with the London designers are many of the Paris couturiers who fled from Paris. Captain Molyneux is now back in London, working on a Collection. Creed, another Englishman long resident in Paris and famous in the dressmaking world, has returned to his native land and is at work on an autumn showing. Paquin's London house is now headquarters for the firm . . . Worth, too, the house that was founded many years ago by an Englishman, has always maintained a large place in London and is carrying on in their Grosvenor Street house . . . High hopes for the future lies in this new combination of Paris houses and the young English houses . . . Out of this new concerted effort, this new union of talent, surely the designing ability that Europe contributed to the world will have a new lease on life.

It describes Molyneux as 'The greatest English designer of them all', adding 'No tailoring house in the world is more famous than Creed. No fame is more justly deserved.' Dark and petite, Mosca, who dressed the Queen of Spain, was described as the essence of French chic. A double page spread, from American *Vogue* 15 November 1940, announced 'Designed in London by Molyneux and Paquin' and depicted models posing on the steps of the American Embassy in Grosvenor Square close to Molyneux's London salon. The article added that the evening dresses were for export only – a small footnote suggests they were sold by Henri Bendell. We know that Molyneux also designed for Bergdorf Goodman, as seen in Chapter 11.[7]

In 1940 Molyneux told *The Bermudian*, whilst waiting for the Clipper to Lisbon, that he now exported more from his London house than he ever did from his Paris one (*The Bermudian* 1940). In addition to substantial sales to the USA, he made regular visits. In September 1941 under the headline 'Molyneux designs for America', *Vogue* stated that his designs were now coming from Grosvenor Square, London (Figure 12.10), rather than Rue Royale, Paris (Figure 12.8), and that soon, in addition to the imports, American women would be able to buy Molyneux clothes designed in America. 'This spring, he visited America, studied our markets, arranged to design clothes which could be made and sold in America. Half of them, at least, are to be of British fabrics, to stimulate trade, to help amass British credit dollars here.'

Throughout this time, he retained his premises in Rue Royale. Wartime fashion magazines show that unlike other Paris houses, it never adopted the extremes of the exaggerated 'Occupation Style' of huge sleeves, small waists and full skirts, perhaps in part because his signature style was a pared down, slim, modernist aesthetic. His London house, close to the American embassy, was bombed, yet continued to produce the restrained, demure clothes for which he was famous on both sides of the Channel.

FIGURE. 12.8
Molyneux's wartime premises in Rue Royale, run by his French team under the capable eyes of Georges. (Getty 107420771.)

FIGURE 12.9
Delivering perfumes in Occupied Paris without petrol. (Getty 50616899.)

FIGURE 12.10
(top) Molyneux's salon in Grosvenor Street, Mayfair, London, with an air raid shelter in the basement, 1941. (Getty 2674356.) (bottom) Two models wearing fashion by Molyneux stand in a London street with a bomb-site in the background. (Getty 3332663.)

FIGURE 12.11 (near right) Red spotted crepe dress, Molyneux, Paris, 1940. (With thanks to *Marie Claire* and the Dress History Teaching Collection, University of Brighton.)

FIGURE 12.12 (far right) Molyneux red crepe dress for Utility Couturier Prototype scheme, 1942. (V&A T 57.1942. © Victoria and Albert Museum, London.)

It is important to this account of Molyneux's Paris salon to note that his general manager in Paris, Yeo-Thomas, became the most decorated member of SOE, the Special Operations Executive of the British army, which worked behind enemy lines in occupied Europe (National Archive HS 9/1458). Molyneux's assistant, John Cavanagh, also left to join the British intelligence service. These facts were not known at the time. Molyneux was forced to defend his stance in a lengthy article in June 1943, in *International Textiles*, a British trade magazine (see Chapter 11), following reports of a New York interview that suggested he would return to Paris at the earliest opportunity. Despite the defensive tone of the article, it becomes clear that Molyneux saw Paris, and Paris alone, as the true home of the couture. After the war, he stated that he hoped to be able to export sportswear, based on British textiles, to both North and South America. Molyneux added:

> What I said I proposed to do (with the approval and sanction of the authorities here) would be to go immediately to America and also possibly to South America to meet American importers of Models from Europe all of whom I know and have known for at least twenty years – to ask them if they will include London on their first post-war buying trip so that the British designers in London should have a chance of obtaining a percentage of their purchases... At same time these buyers could place orders with British textile companies and be influenced by fabrics shown in collections.... and it would only be after I had done my utmost to establish this contact that I would return to my House of Couture in Paris where I would restart my model designing and creative activities, as I did before the war.
>
> (*International Textiles*, June 1943: 19)

In fact, following the Liberation, Molyneux did return to Paris, in October 1944, whether he had made these introductions first is not known, but he was back in his offices at Rue Royale seven months before the end of the war. The *Chambre Syndicale* gave a dinner to welcome him home.[8]

Throughout the war, and afterwards, he was lionised by American *Vogue*. On 1 February 1943, under the headline 'Fashion: Shoe-String Silhouette', very narrow Molyneux dresses were shown, available at Berdorf Goodman and Henri Bendel. *Vogue* observed that the slender dresses used even less fabric than permitted under the L-85 American restrictions, adding, 'The British, who have felt the pinch of fabric shortages longer than we, practically live in slim coat-dresses. They call them austerity fashions, but if this is austerity, let's have more of it.'

Molyneux was a regular visitor to the USA, it was an important part of his wartime output, even after the restrictions on British exports came into place following America's 'Lease-Lend' agreement in late 1941 (for more on this, see Chapter 11). His presence in Bermuda, a British colony and useful stopover for seaplanes making the Atlantic crossing, was not unusual. Schiaparelli is also recorded as making a stop there, as did the Duke and Duchess of Windsor, en route to take on the Governorship of the Bahamas. Like his close friend Noel Coward, Molyneux made a home in the West Indies. He was a complex, cosmopolitan figure who gave the proceeds of his London house to the Board of Trade, whilst his French house had SOE links not yet fully understood. An accomplished painter himself, he assembled a substantial collection of French paintings, which is now in the National Gallery of Art, Washington. This aspect of his life is discussed by Yeide in the postscript to this chapter.

Piguet

Like Molyneux, his fellow exhibitor in Amsterdam in April 1940, Robert Piguet's name appears in just about every issue of *Vogue*, American, British and French throughout the 1930s and 1940s. In December 1939, a few months after the start of the war, he is shown on the cover of *Marie Claire* with a Christmas-themed outfit and in American *Vogue* with an evening dress for Bergdorf Goodman. As Pastori writes, Piguet was the youngest of five brothers from a distinguished Swiss banking family and was a sickly child. Whilst his much older brothers pursued professional careers, Robert, declared unfit for military service, left for Paris in April 1918. At barely nineteen he had an exhibition of Batik textile designs in Lausanne followed by Geneva. A small shop in Avenue Montaigne, opened with his brother Edouard, did not prosper, and he returned to his home town of Yverdon-les-Bains, a Swiss spa town just over the border from France (Pastori 2015).

By 1922 he was working for an elderly Poiret, followed by a period as artistic director of the Paris-based, English tailoring house of Redfern. Whilst there, three of his brothers, including Edouard, died prematurely and his father suffered a fatal heart attack. Following the death of the owner of Redfern in 1931, the house temporarily closed in 1932. The following year, with the inheritance from his father and the support of two close friends from his Poiret days, Fanny and Alexander Clavel, he opened his own house. The Clavels, who were to remain his friends for more than thirty years, owned a Basle textile company, Clavel & Lindemeyer. Alexander Clavel became the house administrator at Piguet, other senior staff included members from Zurich and Geneva and Piguet's twenty-two-year-old nephew. Even when it relocated to large premises at the Rond Point, site of Poiret's greatest success, this Paris couture house was largely Swiss. According to Hubert de Givenchy, just one of a series of illustrious assistants which included Dior, Castillo and Bohan, the ambiance of the house was calm, reserved, elegant and very refined, it could be compared to a well administered Swiss Bank (Pastori 2015: Chapter 2 and Preface).

As detailed by Pastori, on opening his own house Piguet immediately courted an international clientele, inviting American buyers in 1934, the year of his first collection. The London society event that year was the marriage of the Duke and Duchess of Kent, the third son of King George V. Molyneux dressed the bride, but Piguet dressed some of the guests, resolving to have a London house, even though his clothes were already being sold in Harrods. He took 47 Grosvenor Street; his neighbours were Molyneux at 48 and Worth at 50 (Pastori 2015: 37). This places him firmly as a Paris couturier determined to operate on an international stage.

His first London collection was aimed at women invited to the coronation of George VI, held in May 1937. Dismissed by the British press as 'very young', Piguet expressed a liking for his British clients, who he saw as more daring than his French ones, who now included Greek and Egyptian princesses, high-class French women – he even had titled mannequins – and the Duchess of Westminster. However, the British business was not wholly successful, lasting less than two years and closing just two weeks before war was declared.

Piguet was a passionate supporter of Swiss textiles, designing the display for the Swiss Pavilion at the Paris World Fair of 1937, and again two years later in Zurich; he was often photographed with his arms draped with fabrics. His assistant, Christian Dior, who joined Piguet in July 1938 (Pastori 2015: 47), said he learned simplicity at Piguet. A later assistant, Marc Bohan, described Piguet's facility with fabrics, saying he could drape the cloth to achieve the effect he wanted without the help of his *premiers* (Pastori 2015: 54). His close relationship with fine Swiss fabrics, together with a home town, Yverdon-les-Bains, just over the French border, may have helped his wartime business. We know that during the war he was often seen, with his Hispano-Suiza and liveried chauffeur, in Yverdon-les-Bains.[9] Throughout the war, Piguet designs could be bought through the American stores, as is evident in American *Vogue*. His status as a Swiss national – Switzerland was neutral in the war – may have allowed him to continue to trade with the USA, perhaps from Switzerland. When asked about his designs for America, he is reported as saying

'Thank goodness for cable'. He is unusual as a designer who remained in his couture house in occupied Paris but whose designs continued to appear in America.

Schiaparelli

As the Nazis occupied France, Schiaparelli left for a pre-arranged lecture tour of America. There she remained, with occasional forays to Europe before America entered the war. With typical theatricality, Schiaparelli began her *Vogue* interview of September 1940 with these words:

> On my way to America, I left Lucien Lelong at the French frontier. "Please go for all of us" he said. "Try to do all that you can so that our name is not forgotten. We should like it to remain as it was. You must represent us over there. Assure everybody our work will start at the first opportunity . . ." So my duty is plain. War is behind me and I am given a definite assignment from the head of La Chambre Syndicale de la Couture.

Schiaparelli was uniquely qualified to do so. An Italian, before founding her couture business in Paris, she had lived for extended periods in both the UK and the USA. A large part of her pre-war clientele was American, wearing the simple black dresses and embroidered evening jackets that underscored her more outrageous fashions. Commercial licensing with American department stores meant that her customers did not need to belong to the elite set that travelled to Europe. A *Vogue* report headed 'Schiaparelli-via Clipper' (15 January 1940: 73), published before the occupation, appears to be aimed at this clientele, giving a detailed description, with photographs, of the wardrobe she had brought for a two-week flying visit to New York. Almost all black, it included two fur coats and eight hats, with touches of colour added by scarves and her trademark chiffon turbans. Emphasising her practicality, it added that she had worn the same costume for the thirty-hour trip. When Schiaparelli returned, in the early summer of 1940, she was welcomed, and her report of Paris and the occupation was published under the heading 'Needles and Guns'.

As German forces got nearer, at Molyneux's invitation, she moved part of her workforce to Biarritz to share his workrooms alongside Lelong. Lanvin already had workrooms in Biarritz. The plan was to jointly ship their collections to New York. She described a meeting, held in darkness, during a thunderstorm, with Mme Lanvin, Mme de Pombo (of Paquin), Molyneux, Piguet, Balenciaga, Heim, Patou and Lelong. In fact, Patou, champion of the sporty American figure, had died in 1936. His salon was run by his sister and her husband, but Schiaparelli, the consummate showman, was giving the American public what it wanted: the drama of the biggest Paris names, huddled together in the dark, with the stormy Atlantic lashing the windows. On reaching Lisbon, hearing of New York reports of forthcoming couture collections, she telegraphed Lelong in Paris. He replied that there would be no August collections, but it was too soon to make decisions.

Schiaparelli had instructed a handful of her staff to return to Paris and to sell what they could. Asked about a bird brooch she was wearing on arrival in New York in May 1940, she replied that it was a Phoenix, the bird that arises anew from the ashes, and that it represented France ('Needles and Guns' 1940: 57, 104–105). In her autobiography, Schiaparelli explained that she decided not to design whilst in America, as it would be disloyal to her Paris house, and instead devoted herself to charitable works and nursing. Like much of her auto-biography, the truth may be rather more nuanced. Her close friend and head of her press office was the American Bettina Jones, who married Gaston Bergery, a senior official in the Vichy government, later tried, and acquitted, as a collaborator (Secrest 2015: 286–287).[10] Perhaps because of this connection, Schiaparelli appears to have enjoyed easy passage between America and Europe through much of the war and wrote candidly of smuggling money in a hat (Schiaparelli 2007: 119). However, she was viewed with unease by both sides; the British even arrested her in Bermuda at one point when she was waiting for the Clipper to Lisbon (Schiaparelli 2007: 116–117), and America was initially reluctant to give her a visa to return to Paris when hostilities ended (Secrest 2015: 254–255). For more about Schiaparelli in America, see Chapter 6.

FIGURE 12.13 Wallis Simpson wearing Mainbocher for her 1937 marriage to the Duke of Windsor, formerly King Edward XVIII (Hulton Archive/Getty 2665979).

Mainbocher

This designer, the only American to create a successful pre-war Paris couture salon, returned to America just before the start of the war. His career has been reappraised in an exhibition in his city of birth, Chicago, called 'Making Mainbocher: The First American Couturier' (Chicago History Museum, 22 October 2016 to 20 August 2017). Following World War One he worked in Paris as an illustrator and as a fashion editor for both French and American *Vogue* before becoming editor-in-chief of French *Vogue* in 1922. In October 1926 he drew an archetypal 'little black dress' for American *Vogue*, immortalised as Chanel's 'Ford'. He set up his own couture house in 1929, shortening his name, Main Rousseau Bocher, to Mainbocher, usually Frenchified to be pronounced 'Mainboshay'. In 1937 he made the dress for the wedding between fellow

FIGURE 12.14
Model, wearing a back-lacing corset by Detolle for Mainbocher, taken just before his relocation to New York, Horst, Paris, 1939. (Photo by Horst P. Horst/ Conde Nast. Getty 500685096.)

American Wallis Simpson and the former King Edward VIII (Watson 2012: 300). It exemplified his pared down, elegant style.

Anticipating the German invasion, Mainbocher left Paris in 1939, successfully re-locating his salon on Fifth Avenue. From there, until 1971, he designed for many Hollywood stars and the American fashion editors Carmel Snow, Bettina Ballard and Diana Vreeland. (http://makingmainbocher.com). Whilst always retaining the cachet of the Paris couture, perhaps embracing the egalitarian attitudes of wartime, he worked with Warners, the makers of foundation garments (Figure 12.14). A 1939 Horst photograph of the back of a Mainbocher laced corset, made in pink satin by Detolle in Paris, is one of the most enduring images of the period immediately before the outbreak of the war and possibly hints at the corseted silhouette that was to emerge in 1947 with Dior's 'New Look'.

Balenciaga

This Spanish couturier is one of the few wartime couturiers whose star continued to rise post-war. He had founded his couture business, as Eisa Costura, in Spain in 1927, expanding to open establishments in Madrid in 1933 and Barcelona in 1935 (Watson 2012: 162). He fled to France in 1936, where he opened his eponymous French couture house to some acclaim, closing his Spanish premises for the duration of the Spanish civil war.[11] Originally a refugee from the Spanish Civil War, the close wartime relationship between Fascist Spain and Nazi Germany was to his advantage during the war years. As Miller writes, he could clearly move between occupied France and Spain freely, reopening his establishments in Madrid (1941) and Barcelona (1942) whilst still running a salon in Paris (Miller 2011: 18). In 1939 he reopened his Spanish operation, called Eisa after his mother, selling many of the same designs as his French house but rather more cheaply (Miller 2011: 84). His clothes were readily available in Lisbon, as discussed in Chapter 7.

Conclusion

This chapter has demonstrated that, like Molyneux, in terms of fashion supremacy, the Allied nations clearly believed in the pre-eminence of Paris, or at least of a Paris name, even when that city was behind enemy lines. When the British Board of Trade was promoting the couturier scheme in 1942, it publicised the names of Paquin and Worth, rather than Mosca and Champcommunal, because, it was understood, without needing to even mention Paris, that these names were premier labels in the world of Paris fashion – and Paris fashion was simply the best. Norman Hartnell complained in his 1955 biography 'Silver and Gold' that clients who liked his clothes would decide not to buy when they saw from the label that they were not made in Paris. (Hartnell 1955: 40). In the late 1920s, he twice showed collections in a hotel in Paris, and after 1930 took to having 'Paris-Londres' on his label.[12] In America, *Vogue* did not tire of applauding the Paris couturiers, notably Molyneux and Piguet, both of whose clothes were available in New York.

Even in her absence, the glamour of Paris fashion endured. Although Chanel had closed her couture house and was living in the Paris Ritz with her Nazi lover (see Chapter 1), Chanel perfumes were advertised in British *Vogue* in August 1943. It informed readers that whilst no perfume would be available for purchase until after the war, it would continue to produce lipstick, face powder and soap. Chanel perfumes was a separate company, one that Coco Chanel had tried, unsuccessfully, to have 'Aryanised' (see Conclusion), but few British readers would know this. The name still carried the cachet of a grand Paris couture house.

Vogue sent Cecil Beaton to Paris in the autumn of 1944 to photograph Paris fashions. He stayed with his old friend Lady Diana Manners, wife of Duff Cooper, the newly appointed British Ambassador to Liberated Paris. Beaton described the women who accompanied the stream of dignitaries who visited the Embassy:

> The women were a curiously dressed bunch in a fashion that struck the unaccustomed eye as strangely ugly – wide, baseball-players shoulders, Durer-esque headgear, suspiciously like domestic plumbing, made of felt and velvet, and heavy sandal-clogs which gave the wearers an added six inches in height but an ungainly plodding walk. Unlike their austerity-abiding counterparts in England these women moved in an aura of perfume.

Despite this coruscating appraisal, he praised the French fashions he was sent to photograph:

> after trying to install some sort of allure into my photographs of the 'stick in the mud' dowdiness of 'London's couturiers' these clothes give one wings. Balenciaga's line is very medieval and pregnant – nothing to do with the present day travelling in *métros* so over-crowded that one has to be pushed into the train by porters – but so rich and luxurious that it is stimulating to see.
>
> (Beaton 1972: 6)

He found the *Vogue* offices, which de Brunhoff and Lee Miller were re-establishing as described in Chapter 5, little changed, although the staff were clearly hungry and looked longingly at the vegetables he used as props. When he accompanied De Gaulle and Churchill to the front line – the war would continue for another six months – he bought a wheel of brie from a farmer and presented it to Mme Dilé, the studio manageress. He doubted giving any gift had given him more pleasure (Beaton 1972: 19). Despite his dislike of the clothes he saw on French women, adding that Clemmie Churchill found the high hats distasteful, he was clearly seduced by the couture, which was quickly embraced by the diplomatic corps.

Molyneux returned to Paris as quickly as he could and the *Chambre Syndicale* began work on the *Théâtre de la Mode*, which reasserted in March 1945, should

FIGURE 12.15
Lady Diana Cooper (née Manners) and Captain Molyneux at the gala opening of the Stage Door Canteen, Paris, March 1945. (Getty 50495942.)

292   Paris Fashion and World War Two: Global Diffusion and Nazi Control

there be any doubt, the primacy of the Paris couture (Figure 12.15). In March 1945 Molyneux was photographed with Lady Diana Cooper at the gala opening of the Paris Stage Door canteen, an entertainment centre for American servicemen and women, two months before Victory in Europe Day, and very quickly Paris resumed its place at the centre of the wheel of the international industry that was called 'Paris fashion'.

References

A. W.-V. (1940). Report in *Utrechts volksblad: sociaal-democratisch dagblad*, 11 April.
Beaton, C. (1972). *The Happy Years Diaries 1944-48*. London: Weidenfeld and Nicolson.
'British Vogue Weathers the Storm'. (1940). American *Vogue*, 1 December: 139.
Caws, M.A. and Wright, S.B. (2000) *Bloomsbury and France: Art and Friends*. Oxford: OUP
Chicago History Museum. Catalogue for the exhibition 'Making Mainbocher: The First American Couturier' (22 October 2016 to 20 August 2017).
'Fashion: International Situation'. (1939). *Vogue*, 15 January, vol. 93, no. 2: 46.
'Fashion: London Collections . . . Undimmed'. (1940). *Vogue*, 15 September, vol. 96, no. 6: 72–75, 128.
'Fashion: Shoe-String Silhouette'. (1943). *Vogue*, 1 February, vol. 101, no. 3: 58–58).
FIDM (Fashion Institute of Design and Merchandising) Museum. (2016). http://blog.fidmmuseum.org/museum/2016/03/jeanne-paquin.html (accessed 7 November 2017).
Grumbach, D. (2014). *History of International Fashion*. Northampton, MA: Interlink Books.
Hartnell, N. (1955). *Silver and Gold*. London: Evans Bros. Ltd.
Miller, L.E. (2011). *Balenciaga*. London: V&A, Reprint. First edition 2007.
'Needles and Guns'. (1940). American *Vogue*, 1 September: 57, 104–105.
Penrose, A. (1985). *The Lives of Lee Miller*. London: Thames & Hudson.
Pastori, J.P. (2015). *Robert Piguet. Un prince de la mode*. Lausanne: La Bibliothèque des Arts.
Pouillard, V. (2000). *Hirsch & Cie, Bruxelles: 1869–1962*. Bruxelles: Editions de l'Université libre de Bruxelles.
Scheips, C. (2014). *Elsie de Wolfe's Paris: Frivolity Before the Storm*. New York: Abrams.
Schiaparelli, E. (2007). *Shocking Life: The Autobiography of Elsa Schiaparelli*. London: Victoria & Albert Museum. First published 1954.
Scott, E.-J. (2015). Unpublished MA. University of Brighton.
Secrest, M. (2015). *Elsa Schiaparelli: A Biography*. London: Penguin Books.
Sirop, D. (1989). Catalogue of exhibition 'Paquin, Une Retrospective de 60 Ans de Haute Couture', Paris. Adam Biro.
Squitieri, K. (2014). *A Tale of Two Elspeths: Forgotten Couturières and Their Impact on Modern Fashion*. Paper given at FIT conference 'Modes of Modernity: The Ephemeral and the Eternal in Twentieth Century Fashion', 10 May 2014.
The Bermudian. (1940). Volume 11, Issue 7; Volume 12, Issue 12: n.p.
Veillon, D. (2002). *Fashion Under the Occupation*. London: Berg.
Watson, L. (2010). *Vogue Fashion*. London: Carlton.

Archives

Harrods Company Archive.
National Archive, Kew. Various papers, especially those generated by the Board of Trade (BT) and the Board of Education (ED).
University of Brighton Design Archive. The Alison Settle Archive.

Endnotes

1. According to Schiaparelli, writing in American *Vogue* on 1 September 1940 ('Needles and Guns': 57, 104–105), yellow dye, alongside metal and leather, became unavailable in Paris once war broke out.
2. They were Molyneux, Creed, Amies, Morton, Russel, Stiebel, Worth and Paquin. *Vogue* called them the 'Eight Pillars of Wisdom'. Royal couturier Norman Hartnell felt it would be inappropriate to contribute but was later persuaded, in part by Queen Elizabeth herself, to do some Utility designs for Berkertex.
3. Alix, Jeanne Lanvin, Lucien Lelong, Maggy Rouff, Molyneux, Paquin, Jean Patou, Robert Piguet and Worth. Paris *Match*, 18 April 1940, '*Robes de Luxe Pour Pays en Paix*', 24–25.
4. Many thanks to Ben Wubs, Associate Professor, Erasmus University Rotterdam, for help in finding contemporary Dutch press reports, via the Dutch language digital newspaper archive *Delpher*.
5. According to Grumbach, the couture was formalised in 1943, following an argument about which couturiers could belong and therefore gain authorisation for access to raw materials. Therefore, in 1942, Lelong sent out a questionnaire to members of the Chambre that gave the information on the number of staff and outfits that was to govern couture for decades (Grumbach 2014: 32).
6. For more on the history of this Brussels department store, which had a German Jewish founder and branches in Germany, see Veronique Pouillard, *Hirsch et Cie, Bruxelles, 1869-1962*, Editions de l'Université de Bruxelles, 2000.
7. The Costume Institute of the Metropolitan Museum, New York, has 167 drawings by Molyneux for Bergdorf Goodman, done between 1940–1949.
8. Article on Molyneux's retirement, 15 August 1952, Talmey, Allene. *Vogue*, 120, 132–133, 178–181.
9. With many thanks to Anna Corda, Directrice, Musée Suisse de la Mode and Piguet archive, Yverdon-des-Bains. Her many conversations with the Piguet family, still resident in Yverdon-des-Bains, enabled her to confirm Piguet's wartime visits.
10. Gaston Bergery was involved in the creation of the Vichy government in 1940 and wrote some of Pètain's speeches before being posted to Russia as Ambassador for Vichy. Secrest 2015: 244–245, 286–287.
11. For first-hand accounts from Balenciaga's French staff, see Oskar Teledor's 2009 film *Balenciaga: Endurance in an Ephemeral World.*
12. Such was the success of his white wardrobe for the newly bereaved Queen Elizabeth when she accompanied her husband, King George VI, on a state visit to France in 1938, that Hartnell seriously considered opening a Paris branch, but the international situation intervened (*Les Annees Trentes*).

Postscript:
Captain Edward Molyneux: Art collector*

Nancy H. Yeide

'My clothes are the frame to help the picture, and it is important that the picture should have a good and suitable frame', said Edward Molyneux.[1] The metaphor is apt, since Molyneux was an avid collector of paintings who had planned a career in the fine arts. Most of his art collection has been in the possession of the National Gallery of Art in Washington since 1970. However, its relationship to Molyneux is overshadowed by its strong association with Ailsa Mellon Bruce, daughter of Andrew W. Mellon, founder of the National Gallery of Art, who bequeathed 183 paintings to the institution upon her death. A selection of these accessible and popular paintings, mostly of the French Impressionist school, were subsequently featured in special exhibitions highlighting the Mellon Bruce gift, and a portion remained permanently on view for decades.[2] In fact, Mrs. Bruce acquired almost a third of her paintings from Molyneux, who had assembled a very personal collection of art to adorn his apartments in Paris and London.

Molyneux worked for Lucile, Lady Duff Gordon until the onset of World War One. Wounded twice, Molyneux was awarded the British Military Cross in 1917. His second injury, which occurred in April of 1917, resulted in severely limited use of his right index finger. Molyneux wrote to the Secretary of the War Office to argue for a war gratuity greater than the 250 pounds which he had received, on account of his being 'an artist by profession'. Discharged in April of 1919, he was subsequently always referred to as Captain Molyneux.[3]

Molyneux clearly began collecting as soon as his means permitted. The sources of his art acquisitions are not well documented as his own records have not been discovered, although he certainly must have begun to purchase paintings in Paris as he gained success. His first interest was in eighteenth-century French art, including

---

*All works mentioned are now in the collection of the National Gallery of Art, unless otherwise noted.

two drawings by Fragonard also now in the collection of the National Gallery of Art.[4] By the mid-1930s, however, he had changed interests. In 1938 he wrote to the dealer Jacques Seligmann, whose agents had been courting him,

> It is quite true I have started collecting French nineteenth century pictures, and if you ever hear of anything that might be interesting, I wish you would let me know. I only want pictures of very tip-top quality; I do not like big ones, but only the smaller ones. I believe the Seligmanns are sending me a Degas to see. I am looking forward to that when I get back to Paris.[5]

Despite its small size, Molyneux doesn't appear to have liked the Degas that Seligmann sent, which was being sold from the collection of the Museum of Modern Art in New York. Molyneux did eventually find a Degas he liked, also a race horse scene, which Ailsa Mellon Bruce acquired and gave to her brother, racing and Degas enthusiast Paul Mellon.[6]

Little is known about this initial, more conservative collecting interest of Molyneux, which parallels the habits of fellow couturier-collector Jacques Doucet. Doucet shocked the art world in 1912 by selling his collection of eighteenth-century French art and subsequently devoting his attention to more modern art. He continued to improve his assembly of impressionist, post-impressionist, cubist and fauve art, which eventually included Picasso's landmark 1907 *Les Demoiselles d'Avignon*.[7] Like Doucet, Molyneux discarded his early interest in conservative collecting in favor of more modern art.

In interviews and letters, Molyneux noted that he often bought directly from artists or their families in France, but this only partially true, and a somewhat misleading statement. Most of the artists he sought were long dead by the time he began to collect – for example Boudin (d. 1898), Corot (d. 1875), Manet (d. 1883), Morisot (d. 1895) and Seurat (d.1891) – their works having gone into the art trade, often changing hands several times before Molyneux. Dealers he frequented to obtain these works included Seligmann, Paul Rosenberg, and Bernheim-Jeune in Paris and, in London, Alex Reid & Lefevre, and Arthur Tooth & Sons.

For some artists, however, the second-generation family was the only realistic source, as the artists had been so successful that the only works potentially available for purchase would be those descended in the family. Claude Monet died in 1926 after a prosperous commercial career and left his entire estate to his sole surviving child, Michel. For the next thirty or so years, Michel sold off his father's paintings when he needed money. Molyneux purchased Renoir's *Madame Monet and Her Son* from Michel (Michel's brother Jean, who had died in 1914, is pictured), apocryphally because the latter needed money to buy camels for a safari.[8] *Bazille and Camille (Study for Déjeuner sur l'Herbe)* also came from Michel, as did *The Red Kerchief: Portrait of Mrs. Monet*.[9]

FIG 12.16
Renoir, *Madame Monet and Her Son*. (Courtesy of the National Gallery of Washington, 1970.17.60.)

Berthe Morisot's *The Artist's Sister at a Window* came from the artist's son-in-law, Ernest Rouart, who had inherited it from his cousin, the daughter of the sitter. Rouart was a collector in his own right, as well, and inherited the collection of his father, Henri, an artist and friend of the Impressionists. Likewise, Morisot's *Harbor at Lorient*, a gift from her to her brother-in-law Edouard Manet, also moved about through the family and was ultimately with a cousin of the artist, from whom Molyneux doubtless obtained it.

Molyneux relocated to London during World War Two, and brought along his art collection to brighten his hotel suite at Claridge's.[10] While there, he made the rounds of dealers and continued to acquire paintings that suited his taste. He seems to have a developed a regular relationship with Arthur Tooth & Sons, who sold him several paintings, including works by Boudin, Sisley, Monet and Pissarro. In addition, Tooth provided Molyneux with insurance, cleaning, restoration and framing for his collection.

The Molyneux pictures at the National Gallery of Art vary widely in quality, but include undisputed masterpieces such as Claude Monet's glorious *Bazille and Camille (Study for Déjeuner sur l'Herbe)*, Berthe Morisot's thoughtful view of her sister reclining near a window, a study for *La Grande Jatte* by Georges Seurat and Henri de Toulouse-Lautrec's *Carmen Gaudin*. Auguste Renoir, clearly a favorite of Molyneux, is represented by no less than seventeen pictures.

At first, Molyneux based his selections on personal taste. A representative of the Seligmann firm visited Molyneux in the fall of 1938, and lamented that the collection betrayed no personality or taste. Seligmann had the feeling, however, that Molyneux was

FIGURE 12.17
Morisot, *The Artist's Sister at a Window*. (Courtesy of the National Gallery of Washington, 1970.17.47.)

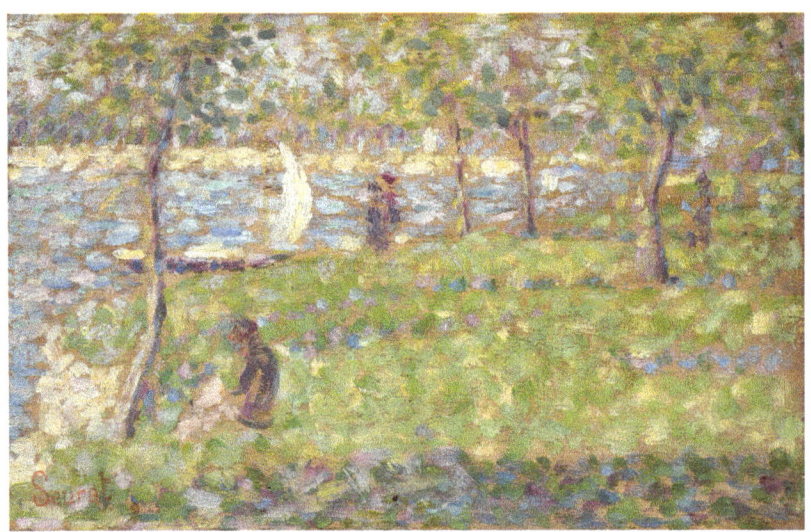

FIGURE 12.18
Seurat, *Study for 'La Grande Jatte'*. (Courtesy of the National Gallery of Washington, 1970.17.81.)

open to professional advice.[11] At that time Molyneux was anxious to acquire a van Gogh or a Cezanne, both of which he did eventually obtain, although not through Seligmann.

Working with dealers in Paris and London, the quality of the collection increased significantly from the impoverished state in which Seligmann's agent found it in 1938. Through Wildenstein in Paris, Molyneux obtained Sisley's *Boulevard Héloïse, Argenteuil* and Seurat's *Study for 'La Grande Jatte'*. Bernheim-Jeune procured for him one of the two van Goghs that Molyneux eventually acquired, as well as several Bonnards.[12] The legendary Parisian dealer Ambroise Vollard was the source of at least half of the Renoirs in the collection.

FIGURE 12.19
Sisley, *Boulevard Heloise, Argenteuil*. (Courtesy of the National Gallery of Washington, 1970.17.82.)

One might think Molyneux would be drawn to the images of fashionable women so popular in the late nineteenth century, but this doesn't appear to be the case. With two noteworthy exceptions, Monet's *Bazille and Camille (Study for Déjeuner sur l'Herbe)* and Morisot's *The Artist's Sister at a Window*, detailed attention to costume is lacking in Molyneux' collection.

Molyneux himself painted throughout his life. His own work was small format, intimate pictures obviously influenced by impressionism, with its soft focus and open brushwork. His subjects were primarily nature – small landscape and narrowly focused floral still lives – but rarely figural. Exhibitions of Molyneux's work were held at the Galerie André Weil in Paris (1953) and at the Hammer Galleries in New York (1967). Molyneux' former business partner Elsa Maxwell bought his *Pont de l'Alma* from the exhibition at the Galerie André Weil.[13] Four of Molyneux's own paintings were included in the Ailsa Mellon Bruce gift to the National Gallery of Art.

Molyneux retired from fashion design in 1950. One of his first projects was arranging the US exhibition of his collection. He had rarely lent previously, although in 1939 he did send two paintings to the French Pavilion of the New York World's Fair.[14] In the fall of 1950, Molyneux was visited by David Finley, Director of the National Gallery of Art, and Chief Curator John Walker. A few months later, through the intermediary of David Bruce, US Ambassador to France and former husband of Ailsa Mellon Bruce, Molyneux offered the National Gallery of Art the long-term loan of his collection. Arrangements for transporting the collection from Paris to Washington were complicated, however, due to French export permits, and it was not until March of 1952 that the Molyneux exhibition opened at the National Gallery of Art. Molyneux himself did not attend the opening but made a brief stop in Washington to witness the installation. The exhibition went on to the Museum of Modern Art in New York. John Walker characterized the collection:

> Captain Molyneux has been especially attracted to paintings which convey with romantic intensity the deliciousness of life before World War I. This exhibition is in a way, therefore, a nostalgic tribute to a vanished world, a world nowhere more vividly recorded than in the canvases of the Impressionist and Post-Impressionist painters.[15]

Encouraged by David Finley, in 1955 Ailsa Mellon Bruce purchased the entire Molyneux collection with the exception of Paul Cézanne's *Le Pont de Mennecy*, which was acquired by the Louvre rather than allow its export from France; it is now at the Musée d'Orsay in Paris.[16] 'I want you to know how happy I am that you will be enjoying all these pictures in the near future. They all have such a very personal appeal', wrote Molyneux to Mrs. Bruce in the spring of 1955.[17] As he had done before her, Mrs. Bruce displayed the Molyneux paintings in her homes. She disposed of only about fifteen of the Molyneux paintings, by sale, gift or in trade.

Somewhat surprisingly, Molyneux continued to purchase pictures between the US exhibition planning and the 1955 sale of his collection, perhaps with an eye to enhancing its legacy. The London dealer Reid & Lefevre acquired for him *Ships Riding on the Seine at Rouen* by Monet and *Pont de la Tournelle, Paris* by Lepine at the estate auction of the collection of Gabriel Cognacq (1880–1951), heir to the Paris Samaritaine department store fortune. Likewise in 1951 Reid & Lefevre sold him a Boudin that had recently appeared at auction in Paris, following its return to the owner from whom it had been confiscated during the war.[18] Molyneux also obtained two Vuillards from the collection of Prince Antoine Bibesco,

A chevalier of the Legion d'Honneur, Molyneux died in Monte Carlo in March of 1974 and is buried in the French town of Biot, where he had a home. His highly personal and beloved collection remains a popular favourite at the National Gallery of Art.

Endnotes

1. *Current Biography*, New York, 1942: 601.
2. Temporary exhibitions featuring the Bruce gift included 'French Paintings from the Collection of Mr. and Mrs. Paul Mellon and Mrs. Mellon Bruce', 1966 and 'Small

French Paintings from the Bequest of Ailsa Mellon Bruce', 1978. 'Small French Paintings' became a permanent installation for decades, featuring works by Pierre Bonnard, Paul Cézanne, Edgar Degas, Henri Matisse and Camille Pissarro from Mrs. Bruce and other donors in galleries designed specifically for their display.

3. Molyneux's official military record is housed at the Public Record Office in Kew, England, WO339/24364.
4. *The Reading*, 1765/1775, 1991.217.16, and *Visit to the Nurse*, 1780/1790, 1991.217.19.
5. Letter dated 17 February 1938 from Molyneux to Hans Wegen of the Seligmann firm, Box 69, Jacques Seligmann & Co. Records, Archives of American Art, Smithsonian Institution.
6. This painting has not been identified, although it was lent by Molyneux to the National Gallery of Art and recorded in Ailsa Mellon Bruce's notebook without further description or image.
7. The Picasso is now in the collection of the Museum of Modern Art, New York. On Doucet's collection, see A. Joubin, 'Jacques Doucet', *Gazette des Beaux-Arts*, 1930, 6th period, no. 3: 69; and J.-F. Revel, 'Jacques Doucet, couturier et collectionneur', *L'Oeil*, December 1961, no. 64: 44–51.
8. Allene Talmey, 'Captain Molyneux', *Vogue*, 15 August 1952: 132.
9. *The Red Kerchief* was sold by Molyneux in the late 1940s and is now in the collection of the Cleveland Museum of Art.
10. 'Molyneux Designs for America', *Vogue*, September 1941: 73.
11. 'l'emsemble est très froid, and ne prouve auxune personnalité, ni surtout aucune culture de la part de Molyneux. Il a été extrèmement gentile, et j'ai l'impression que nous nous sommes très bien ententudus.' Letter from German Seligmann to Hans Waegen dated 18 October 1938, Box 404, Jacques Seligmann & Co. records, Archives of American Art, Smithsonian Institution.
12. *Farmhouse in Provence* was acquired from Gaston Bernheim de Villers; *Vineyard au Auvers*, now at the Saint Louis Art Museum, was purchased from the Paul Rosenberg Gallery in Paris.
13. *Look*, 23 March 1954, 18, no. : 117.
14. The exhibition at the French Pavilion was entitled 'Five Centuries of History Mirrored in Five Centuries of French Art'. Molyneux sent Monet's *The Red Kerchief*, now at the Cleveland Museum of Art, and Cezanne's *Viaduct at l'Estaque*, now Allen Memorial Art Museum, Oberlin.
15. National Gallery of Art press release, 24 February 1952, extensively quoted in press reviews of the exhibition. Limited records concerning the exhibition can be found in RG7, Central Files, Reel 13 and RG 24, Registrar, Boxes 3–4, Gallery Archives, National Gallery of Art.
16. Charles Sterling, 'Le pont de Mennecy par Cézanne', *La Revue des Arts* 5 (December 1955): 195–198.
17. Letter from Molyneux to Ailsa Mellon Bruce, RG39, Box 1, Gallery Archives, National Gallery of Art.
18. In 1940, Boudin's *On the Jetty* was confiscated from the Levy de Benzion collection in Paris, and subsequently selected by Hermann Goering for his own collection. The painting was recovered in the spring of 1945 with Goering's collection in Berchtesgaden and restituted to France. It was returned to the Levy de Benzion family on 10 May 1946.

Chapter 13
The liberation of Paris and the state of the haute couture industry: late August 1944–1946

*Lou Taylor with Marie McLoughlin**

First of all, Paris had to be liberated . . .

The Battle for Paris and the aftermath of Liberation

The Battle of Paris lasted from 18 August to 25 August 1944. It was won by the FFI (Forces Françaises de l'Intérieur), the Resistance forces, *'les fifi'*, commanded by Col. Rol Tanguy, fighting alongside the Forces Françaises Libres, the Free French Forces of de Gaulle's regular army led by the Second Armoured Division of General Philippe Leclerc, and General Bradley's American forces (Dansette 1946: 397). As troops neared the city, having fought their way from the Normandy beaches, Paris Resistance leaders called for an uprising. Intense fighting across the city went on for five days. On 18 August 2,000 Paris police occupied their prefecture. By 20 August the collaborationist press was shut down, the Resistance took over the presses and started to publish its own newspapers and finally the French tricolour flag and not the swastika flew over the Hotel de Ville. By 21 August, Paris Radio was reclaimed and 600 FFI barricades had gone up all over the city.

Whilst the American forces moved inland, de Gaulle had travelled from North Africa to Normandy and met with Eisenhower, the Supreme Allied Commander. General Montgomery and British forces moved along the French coastline to free Belgium. By agreement, Leclerc's Second Armoured Division was to be the first

FIGURE 13.0
Young woman combatant for Forces Françaises de l'Intérieur during the Battle of Paris, August 1944 (Getty 104410856).

---

*Translations from French by Lou Taylor.

FIGURE 13.1
Young woman combatant for Forces Françaises de l'Intérieur during the Battle of Paris, August 1944 (Getty 104410856).

of the liberating troops to enter Paris. On 25 August as Gen. Choltiz, the Nazi Commander of Paris surrendered to Gen. Leclerc and Col. Rol Tanguy, de Gaulle reached the city and by 12:30 on 25 August the tricolour flew once again over the Eiffel Tower (Levisse-Touzé and Trouplin 2010). On Saturday, 26 August, as de Gaulle led the victors in a triumphant parade down the Champs Elysées, snipers were still firing from inside Notre Dame and from the Paris rooftops. Documentary photographs show British and Canadian troops amongst the throng. Dansette wrote in 1946 that 'Paris had liberated herself but at the cost of 1,100 civil and military deaths with 700 people injured' (Dansette 1946: 401, 422).

Democracy, social division and *épuration*

Peace did not come to France however until 7 May 1945. The country was by then in a state of economic collapse and extreme upheaval as millions returned from forced labour, from concentration and prisoner-of-war camps and from abroad. France set about re-establishing democracy and directing its economy away from Third Reich policies and back to its own interests. A provisional government was set up by autumn 1944 led by de Gaulle. *Épuration* (Purge) committees were formed to pass judgement on collaborators and elections were organised with French women granted the vote for the first time. A socialist-led Fourth Republic was declared on 26 January 1946. Laborie described the strangeness of this Liberation moment as a time of 'concealment, of masks, pretence and ... codes of connivance' (Laborie 2011: 30).

Mouré has commented that economic choices during the Occupation had 'displayed considerable variety ... the struggle to survive skewed individual behaviours, encouraging the pursuit of self interest' (Mouré 2007: 125). This now had to be set right. Dansette stressed that alongside the joy of the Liberation, there was an atmosphere of hatred and an explosion of long-controlled, vindictive violence

FIGURE 13.2
Alison Settle in her war correspondent uniform, 1944, the Alison Settle Archive, University of Brighton Design Archives, no. AS97 (with thanks).

with summary executions (1946: 386–387). Bertin[1] believed that disproportionate levels of scapegoat blame and humiliation were thrown at ordinary women who had slept with Germans and collaborators (1993: 352).

Alison Settle, a British journalist who knew the Paris haute couture world intimately, went to Paris in August 1944 and 1946 as a war correspondent. She was shocked by the profound social contrasts she found. Reporting on the first post-war election in 1946 – the first in French history that gave women the vote – she interviewed some of the women election candidates, some still using their Resistance code names.

She commented on the contrast between their clothes and extravagance of the Paris couture Occupation style still to be seen in Paris. They 'dressed as our own women MPs, quietly, with the greatest reserve'. She noted that Mme. LeFaucedy, from l'Organisation Civile et Miltaire, wife of the new administrator of the now-nationalised Renault car company, who had rescued her husband from a Weimar prison, was 'elegant and feminine in her 1939 black cloth suit with a tawny orange scarf folded at the throat'. Settle, whose own son nearly died at the crossing of the Rhine in March 1945, reflected that 'everywhere the women to whom I talked stressed the terrible dangers of having on the one side even a small class of women who have spent money and effort to secure for themselves comfort and an unruffled life under the German Occupation, as against the vast bulk of the women of the nation who have endured and suffered and lost everything, home, possessions and money' (Settle 1945, *Tricolore*, ATS.B.45.1).

The row over Occupation style, late August 1945 to 1946: 'subtle sabotage'?

Paris couture found itself drawn into these controversies and obliged to respond to sharp questioning about the extravagance of Occupation style. This issue became an international scandal, as British and US reporters and photographers, totally unused to these styles, published deep criticisms of Occupation fashion. This scandal threatened the unity of the Allies now that France was back fighting in the war again. The very future of Paris haute couture was at stake as Allied troops continued fighting for the freedom of France until May 1945. During the Battle of the Bulge in the Ardennes in the fearful winter of December 1944 to January 1945 (Figure 6.8), American troops suffered approximately 81,000 casualties.[2]

Lee Miller, then a war correspondent for British *Vogue*, arrived in Paris on the day of Liberation. She wrote that

> Everywhere in the streets were dazzling girls, cycling – crawling up tank turrets – their silhouette was very queer and fascinating to me after utility and austerity in England – full floating skirts-tiny waist lines.... The G.I.s gasped *en masse* at a town full of flying pin-up houris – and thought that tales of wild women in Paris had come true.
>
> (British *Vogue* October 1944: 62)

FIGURE 13.3 The Liberation of Paris, August 1944. Parisiennes throw flowers to US soldiers in a jeep. (Getty 526785428.)

Miller had worked in pre-war Paris couture circles and became quickly aware of the commercial dangers that news of the extravagant styles posed to the future of the couture trade and immediately wrote a defence of Occupation style, declaring that US troops

> settled for the evidence that, good and bad . . . all had deliberately organised this style of dressing and living as a taunt to the huns, whose women were clumsy and serious women dressed in grey uniforms. . . . If three meters of material were specified, they found fifteen for a skirt alone - saving material and labour meant help to the Germans – and it was their duty to waste instead of to save.
>
> (British *Vogue* October 1944: 62)

Many however were not convinced by this explanation. Sarcastic headlines hit the international press. Unaware that the stylish shoes were mostly made with wooden soles, the *New York Times* of 1 September 1944 headlined:

> What is this happy, prosperous place whose beautifully shod women our own style-conscious women can only envy without apparently hoping to rival? It is Paris . . . It now seems that the Scepter [of Fashion] never actually departed from the banks of the Seine. Apparently it needs a much larger German occupation than four years to undermine the prestige of centuries.

FIGURE 13.4
Paris pre-Liberation styles. Left to right: Alix Marcelle Tizeau, Nina Ricci, Anny Blatt, Jacques Fath, *Modes et Travaux*, June–July 1944, no. 538 (with thanks to the Dress History Teaching Collection, University of Brighton).

All of this added fuel to the fire of US hostility towards Vichyism in France (Chapters 5 and 6). The English left-wing journal *Picture Post* also carried a damning editorial in the same vein: 'Cities may fall, governments may crumble and nations may perish, but the modistes carry on their work. . . . French dress designers . . . knew that though Frenchmen might die in the Maquis, the future of French fashion was secure.' The headline read: 'The Fashion Trade is ready for peace'. The conclusion read: 'Perhaps it is truer to say that the French fashion designers have always been ready for peace since they never knew war. There were always buyers for their models' (*Picture Post* 7 October 1944: 19). It needs to be emphasised that most of the women joyously greeting the French and Allied troops in Paris on 25–26 August did not wear these styles. Street photographs show older and middle-aged women in shabby summer clothes. Figure 13.1 has already shown street fighting clothes worn by a young FFI woman.

Soon after the Liberation, Alison Settle, Britain's most respected fashion journalist, to her astonishment, received Foreign Office instructions to help resolve this rift between France and the Allies as soon as possible. Settle 'was far up the Dutch fighting area' with British forces in late August 1944 when she was ordered to Paris. There she met Lelong, head of the *Chambre Syndicale de la Couture Parisienne*, whom she had known before the war. As Settle remembered later:

> He wanted to explain to the English-speaking world that he and the couture generally had not been co-operating with the Germans, as many believed, but was fighting a rear-guard battle to retain the Paris couture and its skilled workers and designers, in Paris and not have them transported to Berlin as the Germans planned.
>
> In notes for an unpublished autobiography, Settle remembered that in Brussels, as noted in Chapter 10, she had already 'been staggered by the French women whom I saw in huge over decorated hats, . . . and wide skirts with padded hips . . . "to keep up the spirits" they said' (ATS.B40s.6).

James Laver, the English fashion historian, was unforgiving. He declared that the fashions 'represented the desires and hopes of the collaborators and the Germans themselves' (English *Vogue* 1944: 31). Edna Woolman Chase, international editor of *Vogue*, remembered the scandal and the

> outspoken shock and displeasure of the Press and the American buyers when they saw the fussiness, the extraordinary luxury of French couture and thought of the American boys who had died on the Normandy beach heads and were continuing to do so across France. It was all very well to say that the luxury was a challenge to the Nazi invaders – the rationed Americal retail houses and manufacturers accepted that. What they could not do was to reconcile

the French amplitude with the continuous pleas to send American clothing to France because the need was so great. With enough material in every Paris frock to make two dresses, people kept asking me why. Explanations were difficult.

(Woolman Chase 1954: 315–316)

Woolman Chase, as international editor of *Vogue*, became involved with diffusing these tensions. In autumn 1944, in a trans-Atlantic radio broadcast to an American radio audience, she spoke to Michel de Brunhoff (by then once again editor of French *Vogue*), Lucien Lelong and the designer Mad Carpentier. Their words were published in British *Vogue* in December 1944 under the banner 'ICI PARIS+ICI PARIS'. De Brunhoff explained he had personally been able to work in independent Monte Carlo, 'without selling out to the Germans', as Kurkdjian has discussed in Chapter 5. He claimed too that the 'most extravagantly wasteful [designs] which could be imagined' were created 'to tease the enemy and flaunt the regulations', but that 'now we are sober and responsible'.

Lelong stressed his struggle against Nazi plans to move the couture to Germany and how 'at the end of the four years, we had actually saved 97% of the couture work force'. By staying open, '12000 workers had been saved from unemployment and consequent labour in German war industries'. He made no reference to style. Mad Carpentier however described the Occupation styles as a defence against the 'Boche' who 'liked to think themselves as our conquerors'. In flaunting such designs, she declared, 'I believe we won a moral victory' ('Ici Paris' 1944: 45, 82).

Whilst, thanks to Lelong, the '*petits mains*' had remained, several of the key arbiters of good taste – both clients and designers – were absent. These included, as this text has shown, Molyneux, Schiaparelli and Chanel, albeit that their absences were for profoundly different reasons. Noone mentioned in this December 1944 interview that some salons had done well through the Occupation. Guillaume writes that Fath's staff numbers had grown along with his success, from 76 in 1942 to 240 by 1944 (Guillaume 1993: 29). New salons had opened including Charles Montaigne, Jaques Griffe, Marcelle Dormoy and one run by Marcelle Chaumont, Vionnet's daughter (Chapsal 1989: 114).

Grumbach confirms that throughout the Occupation 'protected from any kind of competition in France, the price of haute couture and its revenues soared' (1993: 56). He details that in the month of February 1942, the house of Lelong used 1,053 metres of woollens and 4,002 metres of silk, Lanvin used 718 metres of woollens and 3,200 of silks, Piguet 514 metres of woollens and 1,771 of silks, whilst the salon using least was Molyneux, with 743 metres of woollens and 544 metres of silks (1993: 265, Annexe 1), perhaps reflecting that the master was living in London. Sales made in the hundred or so salons that stayed open (ATS.B405.5.8) 'multiplied by five-fold between 1941 and 1943' (Grumbach 1993: 265, Annexe 1). The salons, as this text has detailed, had determined to keep both their designs and export sales alive and did so with success, albeit with far less overseas income than in pre-war years. Once Paris was liberated, they energetically set about re-energising their businesses.

The first post-Liberation collections and the continuing scandal

The war in Europe ended on 7 May 1945. Economic recovery in devastated France was, however, slow, as severe shortages of basic necessities from food to coal and petrol remained in place as France suffered fearful winters in 1945 and 1946. The need for international credit, especially with America, became an absolute economic priority. The French government recognized that French luxury trades were of immediate value in this respect. As American *Vogue* clarified on 16 October 1946, 'France has to export for the dollar credits needed to rebuild her industries. Luxury trades bring her the quickest profits and also the luxury trades were the least touched by the Germans'. The immediate post-war years were, however, despite this government support, marked by painfully slow recovery rather than instant success for the Paris haute couture trade. As the war ended, from September 1944 shortages of every kind reached crisis point and the collapse of Nazi regulatory control systems, though hated, caused confusion. The trade faced new challenges, especially the independent strength of fashion design that had blossomed in America through the war (see Chapter 6). The need to re-establish French control of all aspects of the haute couture industry and to build up and extend pre-war levels of business was paramount.

No seasonal fashion showings had been cancelled throughout the entire war and the first post-Liberation couture collections were duly held in early October 1944, a few weeks after the Liberation of Paris. Ten days of shows were presented, each with forty models. No buyers from Allied countries were as yet present. Lelong told American *Vogue* in November 1944 of the difficult shortage conditions under which these collections were put together. In a statement that mirrors exactly the findings in the chapters of this book, with many of the Occupation-period clients fled, dead or in hiding, target clients from neutral countries who had been clients throughout the Occupation remained the same. Lelong stated, 'We could not resist showing several [grand evening] dresses to prove [we] haven't lost our touch. . . . These dresses can still be sold to wives of Spanish, Portuguese, Swiss or Swedish diplomats. . . . We didn't count on selling Allies these models' (15 November 1944: 74).

Molyneux, who returned to Paris at the first opportunity, to the evident joy of the *Chambre Syndicale*, as well as Lelong, were both particularly aware of the damaging international trade ramifications of the Occupation style scandal. Thus they declared a new mode of simplicity, slimness and restraint 'in keeping with France's new role of fighting alongside the Allies' (British *Vogue* December 1944: 53). Gertrude Bailey, writing for *Tricolore*, described this design transition as 'sudden', noting however that not all the Paris houses were as quick as Lelong to establish a sudden note of restraint appropriate for a country again at war. Maggy Rouff, whose show opened the October 1944 collections, insisted her designs were 'comparatively restrained' but one US WACS Army nurse in the audience said: 'It seems terrible to see huge velvet skirts and sequins when the world is at war.'

Bailey noted that 'everything about the silhouette had been inflated. Yardage . . . was inflated. They lavished fabric into parachute sleeves, elaborately draped bodices, . . . and outsize hats that were over trimmed. . . . Some of the couture were frankly embarrassed by it.' Accepting Miller's Liberation day rationale for the styles, Bailey added: 'The hangover of this defiance [of Nazi rules] was evident' (Bailey 1944: 102).

The Nazi authorities had indeed imposed yardage restrictions on the couture salons on 11 February 1941. Veillon gives the example of the woollen yardage, which was reduced down to 60 per cent of that used in 1938. She adds that the restrictions system did nevertheless provide one hundred tonnes of textile raw material through the war years – just enough to keep 97 per cent of workers employed (1990: 160–161). Defiance of the rules was punished. In January 1944, for example, the Germans ordered the closure of Mme. Grès salon because her complex draped designs broke yardage regulations. She adapted them somewhat and reopened in March of that year (Veillon 1990: 176).

A reporter for the influential US magazine *Time*, on 16 October 1944, however did not blame the extravagance in the autumn couture collections on any kind of defiance of the German occupiers:

Dunkirk not yet liberated. The Gaullist government has not yet been recognised. . . . The spectators were almost as arresting as the mannequins. . . . in towering electric blue or mustard yellow hats at Maggy Rouffs [sic] . . . Designers used materials lavishly, too lavishly for US and British women limited by regulations and rationing.

In September 1944, Bob Landry, a well-established *Time* war photographer, and seemingly sharing the view of the Women's Army Corps nurse, took a series of photos of extravagantly styled couture models standing outside leading haute couture salons, posing incongruously against an American tank and jeeps.

Thus, styles did not suddenly become simpler and so this serious Allied scandal continued to threaten the future success of the Paris couture trade. Cecil Beaton noted on 29 October 1944 that Paris hats looked 'suspiciously like domestic plumbing, made of felt and velvet' (Beaton 1972: 19). (See also Chapter 12.) Bettina Ballard, a leading American fashion journalist but then serving in Paris in the US Red Cross, described Balenciaga's silhouette in December 1944, with its snug suit jackets with long stiffened 'peplums that rolled out away from the hips. . . . They were shown

FIGURE 13.5
Unpublished photograph of Paris haute couture model next to American tank, September 1944. (Photo by Bob Landry. Getty 50493367.)

with enormous incongruous hats of tulle and lace, with roses' (Ballard 1960: 197). The very taste values of the couturiers were therefore still under question months after the Liberation of Paris.

Efforts to resolve the style scandal and overcome accusations of loss of taste

Lelong and Molyneux continued to offer their simpler designs, with British *Vogue* reporting by April 1945 that in Paris hat design 'exaggeration has departed, height is deflated' (British *Vogue* April 1945: 38). The Maggy Rouff design on the front cover of *Modes et Travaux* for March 1945, however, belies this suggestion.

Interestingly in May 1945, London, too, favoured 'high hats for high summer' (British *Vogue* May 1945: 44–45). The London *Evening News* of 7 March 1945 published a cartoon by the popular English cartoonist Joseph Lee showing a uniformed ATS (Auxiliary Territorial Army) woman returning home by train with the British Liberation Army wearing a towering, fanciful Paris hat instead of her uniform cap. The caption read, 'It's a little Paris creation. I couldn't bear it to get crushed.' In truth, most Paris couturiers continued with their extravagant styles throughout 1945 and well into 1946 despite the shortages, and high styles were still being copied across Europe, as seen in the Belgian magazine *Femmes d'Aujourdhui* in January 1946, and the row rumbled on.

FIGURE 13.6 Maggy Rouff, pastel tartan dress, *Modes et Travaux*, March 1945 (with thanks to the Dress History Teaching Collection, University of Brighton).

FIGURE 13.7 Cartoon by Joseph Lee, *Evening News*, 7 March 1945 (Cartoon Centre, University of Canterbury, with permission from *Evening News*/Associated Newspapers Ltd.).

FIGURE 13.8
High turban on cover of *Femmes d'Aujourdhui*, Belgium, 19 January 1946 (with thanks to the Dress History Teaching Collection, University of Brighton).

As a solution to the criticisms, the morally cleansing viewpoint expressed by Lee Miller on Liberation day – that it had been an anti-Nazi duty for the salons 'to waste instead of to save' (Miller 1944: 51) – gathered increasing force. New face-saving terms like 'High Hat Resistance' and 'subtle sabotage' became phrases that were accepted in the international press and thereafter have been forever used by those eager to fight off, or deny, critical comments. The term 'High Hat Resistance' (see also Chapter 2) proposed, as had Mad Carpentier, that the flaunting of fancy hats was a form of serious resistance. Carmel Benito believed these hats to be a slap in the face to the Boche. 'Women have shown that they don't need a gun to fight', she wrote (Benito 1944), despite the fact that thousands of French women, as this book has shown, had in truth taken up guns to fight, to resist and many had died.

The French wife of Air Vice-Marshal Addison (Air Officer Commanding 100 Bomber Support Group) kept a remarkable press cutting from the *Daily Mail* that was published in London the day after the German surrender in Paris. This newspaper coined its own phrase, 'subtle sabotage', stating boldly that 'Paris Tricks the Germans'. Whilst critical of the styles, this view exonerated the makers from accusations of loss of taste and commercial collaboration. British readers needed plausible reasons why their beloved Paris fashion now appeared vulgar.

> French fashion houses have played tricks on Frau Boche. Wealthy German women have been beguiled into wearing ludicrous hats and dresses. Buxom

women bought – and innocently wore – elaborate and costly creations that could only be carried off by the really smart Parisienne. This subtle sabotage is revealed in copies of *l'Art et la Mode* and *l'Officiel* published a few days before Liberation and just received in London.

German officers and rich business men have also made stupid purchases believing them to be the latest French models, to send home to their wives and sweethearts. . . . A member of the British Colour Council stated 'Is it possible that the French couturier is designing with his tongue in his cheek, knowing that the German women, who will have been the main clients, could not carry off these fashions.'

The caption attached to photos of three bizarre Paris high hat designs read: 'Foolish fashions for Frau – No Parisienne would be seen dead in a "creation" such as this. Paris designers persuaded German women it was "the latest" and then sat back to smile' (*Daily Mail* August 26 1944).[3]

This was, as the chapters in this book have shown, very far from the truth. As *Picture Post* had already publicised in an angry article 'Clothes for Wealthy Collaborators', the 2,000 'wealthy collaborators whose names are on the approved list for *cartes d'acheteurs*, were in fact French' (1 May 1943: 10–11) with 'only 200 German women clients' (Veillon 1990: 204–205). From the end of August 1945 and well into 1946 as the high hair styles, high hats and full skirts continued to be designed in many salons, the scandal continued. It was by then nearly two years since the Nazis had been vanquished in Paris, so stories of 'High Hat Resistance' began to ring hollowly. Mrs. Robert Henrey, on her first visit to Paris from London to see her mother after a six-year parting, found herself deeply out of fashion. Wishing for her own 'high coiffure', she went to a smart hairdresser near the Rue Royale and was astonished to hear of the use of postiches to build up height and marvelled at 'the tremendous speed' with which her sixteen year old hairdresser 'built up the edifice' (Henrey 1954: 285). In 1946, Settle commented that Occupation styles were still evolving and the shoulder line had even extended again, with 'very, very wide shoulders' (ATS. B405.26.1).

Many young women in their Occupation styles would have styled their own 'high coiffures' and made their own dresses that summer out of any fabrics they could find, following paper patterns and fashion drawings in popular magazines such as *Modes et Travaux*. As in pre-war days, if Paris couturiers proposed that these styles were fashionable, then they had to be followed, and so the style lasted and spread long after the departure of the Nazis from Paris. In 1947, Queen Elizabeth, consort of King George VI of England, was photographed informally wearing a high, draped turban when sailing to South Africa on a state tour.

FIGURE 13.9
Queen Elizabeth in a high turban en route to South Africa, 1947. (Still from film *Royal Family in South Africa*, with thanks to British Pathé Ltd.)

The controversial and shocking issue of loss of taste remained unresolved. In 1946, Settle had been pleased to see 'a swing away from the vulgar and ostentatious hats' (ATS.B405.23). She wrote later that she had been 'horrified at the lack of proportion of the clothes then worn... The critical faculty had temporarily vanished' (ATS.B405.34.1). As Veillon has explained in this book (Chapter 3), the justification that the couturiers and milliners gave for their extravagant styles was that they were determined to maintain age-old, sophisticated, hand techniques in garment sewing and in the creation of complex embroidery, and other trades, despite the fearful shortages. Hence, for example, the painstaking, hand-crafted manufacture of high, wide, fancy hats designed to fill the working hours of their staff and save them from forced labour in Germany.

Hardy Amies, the London couturier, defended the Occupation style in British *Vogue*: 'These are not the wish fulfilments of the collaborationists; they are the serious creations of the backroom boys and girls who cannot stop making clothes. I believe in these new clothes. I feel them in my bones' (British *Vogue* September 1944: 86). He was one of the very few who did. Even Schiaparelli returned to her own salon from New York in 1945 determined 'to sweep away the ugliness of the clothes and the incredible horror of the hats' (Schiaparelli 2007: 156). It was not, however, until 1947 that Occupation style and all talk about loss of taste was swept away.

References

Bailey, G. (1944), 'Report on October Collections', *Tricolore*, November, vol. 11, no. 8: 102.
Ballard. B. (1960), *In My Fashion*, London: Secker and Warburg.
Beaton, C. (1972), *Beaton Diaries. The Happy Years. 1944–1948*, London: Weidenfeld and Nicolson.
Benito, C. (1944), *High Hat Resistance*. American *Vogue*, 1 November, vol. 104, no. 8: 124, 125.

Bertin C. (1993), *Femmes sous l'Occupation*, Paris: Stock.
Chapsal, M. (1989), *La Chair de la Robe*, Paris: Fayard.
Dansette, A. (1946), *Histoire de La Liberation de Paris*, Paris: Arthème Fayard.
Grumach, D. (1993), *Histoires de la Mode*, Paris: Seuil.
Henrey, Mrs. R. (1954), *Madelaine, Young Wife*, London: Dent.
'Ici Paris'. (1944), British *Vogue*, December, vol. 100, no. 12: 45, 82.
Laborie, P. (2011), *Le Chagrin et le Venin. Occupation, Résistance, Idees reçues*, Paris: Gallimard.
Laver, J. (1945), 'French Fashions in London', *Art and Industry*, January, vol. 40, no. 235: 1–19.
Levisse-Touzé, C. and Trouplin, V. 'La libération de l'Ile-de-France', Musée de la Resistance 1940–1945, en ligne. http://www.museedelaresistanceenligne.org/expo.php?expo=84 (accessed 3 September 2017).
Mouré, K. (2007), 'Economic Choice in Dark Times – the Vichy Economy', *French Politics, Culture & Society*, Spring vol. 25, no. 1: 108–130.
Picture Post. (1943), 'Clothes for the 2000 Wealthy Collaborators', 1 May: 10–11.
Settle, A. (1945). In *Tricolore - News of France at War*, journal of the Free French Forces in London, published by the Service d'Information de la France Libre (later Service des Publications de la France Combattante), London. University of Brighton Design Archives, Alison Settle Archive, no. ATS.B.45.1.
Settle, A. University of Brighton Design Archives, Alison Settle Archives, no. ATS.B40s.6.
Veillon, D. (1990), *La Mode Sous l'Occupation*, Paris: Payot.
Woolman Chase, E. and I., (1954), *Always in Vogue*, London: Gollancz.

Endnotes

1. See Chapter 1, footnote 19.
2. Holocaust Encyclopedia. (n.d.), 'Battle of the Bulge', https://encyclopedia.ushmm.org/content/en/article/battle-of-the-bulge (accessed 18 June 2018).
3. With many thanks to Chris Boydell, Maryse Addison, Beezy Marsh and staff of the *Daily Mail* who confirmed the date of this press cutting.

Chapter 14
The end of the war in Europe to 1947: rejuvenating the international business of haute couture

Lou Taylor with Marie McLoughlin

FIGURE 14.0
Drawing of Dior design 'Ketey' on official Lucien Lelong notepaper, probably late 1946 (with thanks to Archives Dior, Paris).

The war in Europe finally ended on 7 May 1945, but whilst the celebrations were unbounded, this brought no immediate relief to the Paris fashion industry. Firstly, the Occupation style row continued to fester long after the Liberation of Paris, and secondly, the business of haute couture had to function within the collapsed state of the French economy whilst urgently trying to build up dollar credits in order to rejuvenate their export markets, especially to the USA. A third urgent problem was the need to stave off any global fashion leadership takeover attempts, especially from the USA and the UK (as discussed in Chapters 6, 11 and 12), whilst fourthly dealing with extremes of shortages of fabric, heating and so on.

This situation impacted fundamentally on the Paris haute couture trade. Many were aware that 'luxury trades bring [France] the quickest profits and . . . the luxury trades were the least touched by the Germans' (American *Vogue* 16 October 1946: 106). Nonetheless, Pouillard writes of the immediate post-war need to rebuild basic infrastructure 'including new hotel and improved transport facilities' to encourage private couture clients and professional corporate buyers back to Paris. Raymond Barbas of the *Chambre Syndicale* noted that travel from New York to Paris by air now took only 'fourteen hours for $160' and that this opened up 'a huge stratum of American clientele. It is our national duty to attract them to Paris, because the clients will spend much more money here than if we export to America' (Pouillard 2013: 819).

Settle, too, well understood that 'France was putting all her encouragement and all possible knowledge to rehabilitate her country's exports.... Luxury creation was to be encouraged' (ATS.B405.6). She noted however that because of the desperate state of the French textile industry, as detailed in Chapter 2, 'there was still a 7 to 8 months delay in making suitable export textiles' (ATS B405.24). From late 1944 and into 1947, with serious disruptions in communications and transport, there were also extreme shortages of coal, oil and heating, which the citizens of France both at home and at work had to endure through two fearfully cold winters. When Célia Bertin had returned to Paris in late 1944, she found 'nothing at all', only 'a dead landscape where everything was broken and everything was lacking' (Bertin 1990: 365).

Thèâtre de la Mode

Unable to offer garments for international sale, the Chambre Sydicale astutely organised its *Thèâtre de la Mode* over the summer of 1945, an event that has been discussed throughout this book. It was the most vital tool in the couture's post-war international, commercial publicity tactics. It was a profoundly Parisienne creative tool featuring twelve little sets of Paris life with quarter life-size model figures displaying styles for the autumn 1945 season (see Chapter 9). Albeit that these were, one year after the Liberation of Paris, still in the controversial Occupation style, the high hats, full sleeves, wide skirts and heavy, wedge-heeled shoes were somehow charmingly inoffensive when modelled by the sophisticated miniature dolls.

In his August 1945 introduction to the catalogue of the London showing, Lelong stressed with no lack of *sans froid* the Thèâtre's charitable, rather than commercial, role. He stated that its aim was to confirm that Paris couture was functioning and that the salons had 'sought to safeguard their independence and their workers [throughout the Occupation]'. The Thèâtre, he declared, had already raised 52 million francs for Entraide Française. 'Since the Liberation, the dressmakers have intensified their efforts in this cause. In all workrooms, dresses have been made for the bombed out and the sufferers from the war, while each month considerable sums of money have been handed over to *l'Entraide Française*.' Lelong concluded defensively, that 'it is not intended to represent luxury or lavish use of materials; it is instead a proof of ingenuity and good taste' (Thèâtre de la Mode 1945).

Style criticisms, however, continued. James Laver, whilst saluting 'the consummate artistry' of the sets and dolls, commented that 'one cannot help wondering whether these delightful figures . . . do not in fact rather look back to the last days of the Occupation . . . hats and coiffures tower upwards' (Laver 1946: 15). The *Thèâtre de la Mode* was nonetheless a huge marketing success and was received by enthusiastic crowds wherever it was shown, as detailed in chapters in this book already. Refitted in 1946, it ended triumphantly in San Francisco.

1946 style

Laver's assessment of Paris styles in 1946 was accurate. Whilst Lelong and Molyneux continued with their more pared down styles, the *Album de la Mode du Figaro*, no. 8 of autumn 1946, by then published in Paris, also shows little basic change in the couturiers' silhouettes. Some of the wide shoulders, by Balenciaga for example, seemed a little softer at the crown of the shoulder, large patch pockets filled out the hips and hem lies were becoming somewhat longer – both hints at future changes. Amongst the usual heavy wartime platform shoe styles, new designs developed by eleven prestigious Paris *haute-botterie* creators in February 1946 witnessed their efforts to re-introduce far more delicate high heels.

Couture hats became dramatically smaller and neater – a swift reaction, doubtless, to the avalanche of international criticism of Occupation millinery. Another hint of change lies in a hairstyle photographed for the Paris salon of *Guillaume*, titled '*Retour au Naturel*', a simple, shoulder-length cut with the hair brushed naturally over the crown. This was a very far cry from Mrs. Henrey's 1946 Paris 'haute coiffure' discussed earlier.

FIGURE 14.1
Molyneux suit, Paris, April 1946, cover of *La Femme*[1] (with thanks to Sue Breakell).

FIGURE 14.2
'*Les Beaux Souliers de Paris*', *La Femme*, no. 36, 20 February 1946 (with thanks to the Dress History Teaching Collection, University of Brighton).

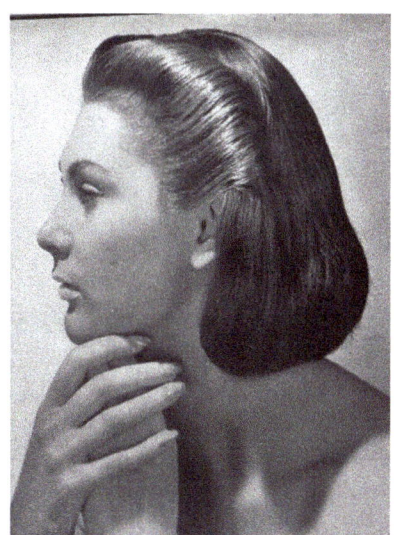

FIGURE 14.3
Hairstyle by Guillaume, Paris, autumn 1946, *Album de la Mode du Figaro*, no. 8, autumn 1946: 80 (with thanks to the Dress History Teaching Collection, University of Brighton).

Neutralising the scandal: the value of luxury couture exports

Deeply aware of the personal and commercial consequences of the criticisms, Lelong had already asked that a '*commission d'épuration de la couture*' be established. Between October 1944 and January 1945, fifty-five cases were examined – none directly related to couture. None of the salons were charged on any count, giving them public exoneration from accusations of economic collaboration (Veillon 1990: 247). Veillon explains that prosecutions against big business and famous companies, with strong export and foreign currency potential, were seen as counter-productive at a time when such exports were vital to the reconstruction of the destroyed French economy (1990: 249). Settle recognised this too in 1946: 'The whole strength of the French Government and the tremendous French textile trade [was] put behind the rehabilitation of couture as the world's showcase of fashion' (Settle 1946, B405.24 and 26).

Despite this, Palmer explains that in the immediate post-war years 'it was not legal [for the couture salons] to export any clothing' but garments could be sold directly to private international clients who were able to get to Paris (Palmer 2001: 22*)*. Thus direct selling became crucial to the rejuvenation of the trade. Lelong had already made an official business visit to New York in mid-May 1945, just ten days after the ending of the war in Europe (see Chapter 6).

Late 1945–1947: international private clientele begin to return

Wealthy, international private clients with good diplomatic or military connections were able to reach Paris by autumn 1945. *La Femme* magazine reported on 20 February 1946 that Princess Faiza, the sister of King Farouk of Egypt, had returned to Paris to order her new dresses. So too had Mme. Germaine Brusse-Urtebise, a pre-war couture client from Belgium[2] who bought her new post-Liberation hats in Paris from the Legroux Soeurs, including one featured on the cover of *Claudine* of October 1945. In dark green felt with a small brim, and bearing in mind the autumnal season (see also Figure 3.1) it had an entire pheasant, including its long tail, wrapped around the crown. Now in the Rijksmuseum, it is similar to a hat by Maud et Nano drawn in the autumn 1946 *Album de la Mode du Figaro*.[3]

Madelief Hohé, curator at the Gemeentemuseum in the Hague, notes that Dutch women were amongst the first to return to Paris for their haute couture clothes.[4] Amongst them was Elsa Rijkens, a famous Dutch classical singer, whose wardrobe is in the Gemeentemuseum. In Paris in autumn 1946, she ordered the most spectacularly beautiful evening ensemble – a gown of black silk crêpe-satin, with a short jacket and charming little pagoda-styled hat, both in cream-coloured satin from Balenciaga. Titled 'La Perse', the jacket and hat are covered with rich

FIGURE 14.4
Hat by Maude et Nano, Paris, autumn 1946, *Album de la Mode du Figaro* (with thanks to the Dress History Collection, University of Brighton).

oriental-style embroidery in gold thread, glass beads and chenille, perhaps by Maison Lesage.[5]

As to clients from North and South America, Kauffman writes that the Brazilian beauty Aimée de Heeran, then married to the son of the owner of the Wanamaker department store (see Chapter 6) and whose name is threaded through this book, on her return to Paris, bought herself a bright red silk, long-sleeved dress with a skilfully draped and knotted front bodice, dropped waist and very full, short skirt from Piguet's second post-liberation collection for spring 1945. It is now in the collection of the Fashion Institute of Technology, New York. The startling, immediate post-war feature of this rare dress is that its back is entirely plain, without any draping or even full gathering to the skirt, evidently due to fabric shortages (Kauffman 2012: 6).

FIGURE 14. 5
Evening ensemble, 'La Perse', Balenciaga, Paris, autumn 1946 (Gemeentemuseum Den Haag, no. 1030958, with many thanks).

FIGURE 14.6
Front and back of Piguet, red silk dress, spring collection, Paris, 1945, worn by Aimée de Heeran. (The Museum at FIT, no. 70.57.61. Gift of Mr. Rodman A. Heeren, with thanks to FIT and Valerie Steele.)

Palmer notes that, also in 1945, the Canadian Mrs. Berschinger purchased a knee-length, apricot-coloured lace and silk chiffon dress directly from Jean Dessès in Paris.[6] Wilcox confirms that the Duchess of Windsor, an American, who had returned with the Duke to their Paris residence on 23 September 1945,[7] bought two Schiaparelli pieces from the salon's first post-war collection in December 1945: a green taffeta gown and a tailored black moiré suit (Wilcox 2007: 166).[8] A year later, in 1946, Stella Carcano, daughter of the post-war Argentine Ambassador in Paris, married Viscount Edman, the 4th Earl of Dudley. For her wedding in Paris, she wore a dress designed by Balmain. The Victoria and Albert Museum (V&A) owns the quilted and beaded white satin jacket and little matching pill box hat which went with her dress. She also ordered in the same year a spectacular, slim, full-length black evening dress in black velvet and tulle from Lelong, which is also in the V&A collection.[9] Her mother, Mme. Miguel Angel Carcano, bought haute couture too in 1946: a beaded white, satin jacket by Balenciaga, now in the V&A collection.[10]

British women had far more of a struggle to obtain Paris haute couture. Even when they were legally allowed to buy it, they were hampered by severe currency restrictions and very heavy import duty charges imposed by the new socialist government, which made such purchases prohibitive. Nancy Mitford described one way around this problem – a debutante dress, 'chosen in Paris . . . and bought over in the bag of some South American diplomat to save duty' (Mitford 1949: 89). British *Vogue* had various suggestions for obtaining French styles without the necessary currency: from the ready-to-wear boutiques of the big houses and licensed copies made in the UK by stores like Liberty, and through the use of Vogue Couturier Patterns, often made up and modelled in the magazine. The Paris couture often used British woollens, so there was little difficulty in obtaining the same fabrics from which to make copies, but the craftsmanship could not be replicated.

A very few English women in diplomatic circles did manage to obtain Paris couture in the years of 1945–1947, when others were simply not able to do so, though the styles caused genuine shock. The first to do so seems to have been Lady Diana Cooper, wife of Duff Cooper, then the British Ambassador in Paris when she returned briefly to London in February 1945 wearing Paris couture clothes. Emily Russell wrote in her diary on 21 February that Diana 'seemed glamorous to me in her French clothes, elegant hat, veil, earrings and faint smell of good scent. . . . Diana's appearance – as it were from another world and another kind of life – unsettled . . . me' (Russell 2017: 275). Lady Alexandra, daughter of Earl Haig and the wife of Cpt. Howard-Johnson, the Naval Attaché at the British Embassy in Paris in 1947, had the rare good fortune to be given a Jacques Fath couture dress even before she moved to Paris. In 1946 she was gifted a slim, black, crepe cocktail dress with a low dropped waist and elegant horizontal drapery bought back to London for her and now in the V&A collection.[11] In 1946, she also wore a summer hat by one of the leading Paris milliners, Mme. Suzy – a small boater covered in white silk and encircled with huge white organza flowers with large yellow stamens.[12]

For British women living in Paris itself and frequenting diplomatic circles, purchase was possible if they had the money. The writer Nancy Mitford, daughter of Lord Redesdale, one of the famous Mitford sisters, visiting Paris from London, went to Lelong's salon on 25 September 1946. Her lover Gaston Palewski, then back in Paris, had been de Gaulle's Director of Political Affairs for the Free French movement in London. Mitford was shocked by the prices but loved the styles: 'Why is it that the clothes in these places always dangle well out of one's reach', she wrote afterwards to her sister, Diana.[13] (Mosley 1993: 183). However, once she had moved to live in Paris in the early summer of 1947, she began to visit couture salons regularly, attending shows at Piguet (1993: 252) and many at Dior.

As for Lady Alexandra, her couture good fortune continued in 1948 because she became a *mannequin mondaine* at the House of Jacques Fath and then at Lanvin, wearing their supremely elegant clothes, for free, at smart social occasions in France, Britain and indeed around the world (Lynn 2008: 172). The accessory trades were rejuvenated too, though still with a shortage of exotic plumes. On 10 March 1948, Nancy Mitford wrote to her sister, 'I've two new hats of a beauty indescribable – one is a cloud of roses and pink tulle, the other a seagull with a bunch of violets in its mouth' (Mosley 1993: 252).

New style and new business approach: Dior and the Corolle line collection of 1947

The post-war economic policies of the French government, its support for the couture trade and the energetic activities of the haute couture salons slowly became successful. International journalists returned to Paris in 1947 to pick up the seasonal style threads again and to place their orders. Fascinatingly few undated Dior designs survive in the Archive Dior, Paris, drawn seemingly for buyers on official Lucien Lelong, Avenue Matignon, Paris notepaper, complete with collection numbers. One is of particular interest with its ankle-length, amazingly full pleated skirt, a tiny waist, natural shoulder line and wide-brimmed, low-crowned hat. Its date remains uncertain but this may well be one of the first images of Dior's 'Corolle' (New Look) designs. It is titled 'Ketey', *Marque Deposé, Reproduction Interdite*, with the words 'Kindly return the sketches you have not chosen as soon as possible.' It is stamped no. 7297. This was almost certainly created whilst Dior was still in his last few months of employment at Lelong's salon in late 1946.

This idea is not confirmed but seems probable because Dior, whilst still at Lelong's, was already organising the opening of his own new salon, Christian Dior. Palmer writes that this was legally established on 8 October 1946, opening for business at Ave. Matignon with Lelong's blessing, with the first collection on 13 February 1947 (Palmer 2008: 25).[14] This was the moment when Dior's 'Corolle' line created such a sensation.

Just six days later, on 19 February, Nancy Mitford ordered a Dior suit from this opening collection. Despite the currency restrictions, which meant that she was short of money, she spent £120 on the suit. She wrote that 'Evening dresses start at £342. Impossible to get inside the building. I had to use my INFLUENCE to be allowed inside' (Acton 2001: 76).[15] Harold Acton believed that Nancy Mitford was the first English woman to appreciate Dior's 'New Look' (2001: 76). She explained to her sister, Diana, that 'the skirt has sort of stays at which one tugs until giddiness intervenes – the basque of the coat stuck out with whale bone . . . terribly pretty' (Mosley 1993: 224). She wrote on 17 May 1950 that her private dressmaker in Paris declared that for a full-skirted evening dress, '30–40 yards is the minimum [yardage] if it is not to look skimpy' (Mosley 2008: 289).

Price comparisons with London couture are startling. Hattrick details that a formal strapless evening dress dating from about 1950–1952 from the Norman Hartnell salon in still-rationed London, with a full skirt decorated with a deep embroidered band and using just twelve yards of fabric, cost £140 and thirteen coupons (Hattrick 2011: 177).[16] The lowest price evening dress at Dior in 1947 was thus almost three times more costly and came without the beading. These prices were so high that, as Nancy Mitford wrote to her sister Diana on 4 April 1948, many French couture *habituées* could not afford Dior's evening clothes (Mosley 2008: 261).

The commercial success of the new Dior fashion house was, nonetheless, unrivalled. It was built on Dior's unquestioned talent both as a designer and as a businessman with a very different approach to his products. He soon created his own lines of branded luxury accessories such as stockings, produced at affordable – albeit still high – prices for an entirely new and less exclusive clientele. Pouillard writes

> Dior adopted two intertwined strategies to a level unprecedented for a Haute Couture house: the worldwide expansion of his company and the licensing of several lines of clothing and accessories under Dior's name. In October 1946, he opened a 'boutique' on the side of his Paris Haute Couture, bespoke business. The boutique sold presents, scarves, gloves, perfumes, beachwear and holiday clothes.
>
> (Pouillard 2013: 825)

Palmer notes that in September 1947, Dior was invited to receive the annual US Fashion Oscar awarded by the Neiman Marcus department store in Dallas

FIGURE 14.7
Drawing of Dior design 'Ketey' on official Lucien Lelong notepaper, probably late 1946 (with thanks to Archives Dior, Paris).

(Palmer 2009: 77–78). Pouillard confirms too that in 1948, Boussac and Dior 'founded Christian Dior New York, Inc. and Christian Dior Perfumes-New York, Inc.' Significantly, too, Christian Dior-New York opened in October 1948 as a 'wholesale salon' (Pouillard 2013: Part 1V). By the late 1940s and early 1950s, leading international couture salons, high-end department stores and ready-to-wear companies around the world were able to purchase the right to make legal copies of Paris haute couture garments in a far more commercialised and greater scale than in pre-war days. These included, to give just one example, the salon of the Amsterdam couturiere Catharina Kruysveldt-De-Mare, who took over the salon of Mme. Borgeaud in 1948. Mme. Brusse-Urtebise, cited above, was a regular client, purchasing licensed copies of designs by Dior, Fath and Balenciaga in the post-war period.[17]

As for Dior, his business success was built on the wealth of his financial backer, Boussac, a French textile millionaire and famous race horse owner, who had profited considerably through his economic collaboration with the German Occupiers. Bertram defines economic collaborators as those who 'sought financial gain, adventure or revenge against personal enemies' and/or as 'French business interests which saw enlarged opportunities in German dominated Europe' (Bertram 1980: 18). In Boussac's case, his support of Nazism had been evident. Broche and Muracciole have described him as financing 'Parisienne ultracollaboration', giving money to support Luchaire's pro-Nazi newspaper *Le Nouveau Temps* and encouraging all forms of economic collaboration by others (Broche and Muracciole 2017: 220). Boussac had made a fortune supplying canvas for French airplanes in World War One and made another in World War Two. His close relationships with leading Nazi commanding officers and Jean Bichelonne, the Vichy Minister of Industrial Production, enabled him to keep his textiles factories open.

After the war he was not investigated by *épuration* committees as a consequence of the public thanks offered him by his employees returning from deportation in Germany. They found that Boussac had continued conscientiously to pay their salaries to their families in their absence (Cousin 2009). Boussac's vital support for the couture industry and its consequent export profits would also have been noted. Dior, with his successful 'Corolle' line, led the way to international style leadership recovery for Paris haute couture, not only through his joyous, bold, feminine lines but also through the initiatives of his new lucrative business developments (Palmer 2018). After the four grim Occupation years and the three-year post-Liberation struggle against chaos, criticisms, recriminations, export restrictions and fearful shortages, this was good news indeed.

References

Acton, H. (reprint 2001), *Nancy Mitford*, London: Gibson Square Books.
Bertin, C. (1993), *Femmes sous l'Occupation*, Paris: Stock.

Bertram, M. Gordon. (1980), *Collaboration in France During World War 2*, London: Cornell University Press.

Broche, F. and Muracciole, J-F. (2017), *Histoire de la Collaboration, 1940–45*, Paris: Tallandier.

Chapsal, M. (1989), *La Chair de la Robe*, Paris: Fayard.

Cousin, R. (2009, Nov. 20), 'Memoires de Guerre, Marcel Boussac', http://la-loupe.over-blog.net/article-boussac-marcel-39741704.html (accessed 1 October 2017).

Hattrick, J. (2011), 'A life in the archive: the dress, design and identity of the London couturier Norman Hartnell, 1921–1979', doctoral thesis, University of Brighton.

Kauffman, M. (2012), *The Couture Client as Patron of the Art of Fashion*, https://process.arts.ac.uk/sites/default/files/michelle-kauffman-the-couture-client.pdf (accessed 2 September 2016).

La Femme, 20 February 1946.

Laver, J. (1946), 'French Fashions in London', *Art and Industry*, January, vol. 40, no. 235: 1–19.

Levisse-Touzé, C. and Trouplin, V. 'La libération de l'Ile-de-France', Musée de la Resistance 1940–45, http://www.museedelaresistanceenligne.org/expo.php?expo=84 (accessed 3 September 2017).

Lynn, E. (2007), 'Lady Alexandra', in Wilcox, C. (ed.) *The Golden Age of Couture – Paris-London 1947–57*, London: V&A.

Mosley, C. (1993), *Love from Nancy – The Letters of Nancy Mitford*, London: Sceptre-Hodder and Staughton.

Mosley. C. (2008), *The Mitfords: Letters Between 6 Sisters*, London: Harper Press.

Mitford, N. (1949), *Love in a Cold Climate*, London: Hamish Hamilton.

Mouré, K. (2007), 'Economic Choice in Dark Times – the Vichy Economy', *French Politics, Culture & Society*, spring vol. 25, no. 1: 108–130.

Picture Post. (1943), 'Clothes for the 2000 Wealthy Collaborators', 1 May: 10–11.

Palmer, A. (2001), *Couture and Commerce – the Transatlantic Fashion Trade in the 1950s*, Toronto: ROM.

Palmer, A. (2009), *Dior, A New Look, a New Enterprise*, London: Victoria and Albert Museum.

Palmer, A. (2018), *Christian Dior, History and Modernity, 1947–57*, Chicago: Chicago University Press.

Pouillard, V. (2013), 'Keeping designs and brands authentic', *European Review of History*, 24 October: 815–835, http://dx.doi.org/10.1080/13507486.2013.833720.

Russell E. (ed.). 2017. *A Constant Heart. The War Diaries of Maud Russell. 1938–1945*. Wimborne Minster: Dovecote Press.

Théâtre de la Mode. (1945), 'London catalogue', Paris: Aljanvic Publicité.

Time. (16 October 1944), 'Black Lace and Woolen Undies: Paris Fashion 1944', http://style.time.com/2012/09/24/paris-fashion-1944-by-bob-landry-tk-tk (accessed February 2016).

Veillon, D. (1990), *La Mode Sous l'Occupation*, Paris: Payot.

Wilcox, C. (ed.). (2007), *The Golden Age of Couture – Paris-London 1947–57*, London: V&A.

Woolman Chase, E. and I. (1954), *Always in Vogue*, London: Gollancz.

Endnotes

1 This journal was published bi-monthly in Paris, see Bibliotheque National Paris website (gallica.bnf.fr). (La Femme Paris 1945). The first edition was printed on 15 March 1945, seven months after the Liberation of Paris and two months before the final end of World War Two in Europe. Published for two years only, 1945–1946, in sixty editions, it was attached to the Movement de Liberation National (MLR), one of whose

founders was the Resistance heroine Lucie Aubrac, who was the director of this journal throughout its two years of functioning.
2. 'The Wardrobe of Madame Brusse', exhibition at the Rijksmuseum, Amsterdam, 30 January–7 June 2015; https://www.rijksmuseum.nl/nl/de-garderobe-van-mevrouw-brusse (accessed 6 August 2018), with many thanks to Madelief Hohé for this reference.
3. Ibid.
4. E-mail to the author, 18 January 2018.
5. With many thanks for help and advice to Madelief Hohé, who notes that an exactly similar ensemble is to be found in the collection of the Balenciaga Museum in Gataria, Spain.
6. This dress is in the collection of the Seneca Fashion Resource Centre, Seneca College of Applied Art and Technology, no. 1-9945-14-00300 (Palmer 2001: 22).
7. *The Advertiser*, Adelaide SA, Monday, 24 September 1945, 'The Duke of Windsor in Paris', National Library of Australia, https://trove.nla.gov.au/newspaper/article/4866905 (accessed 10 July 2018).
8. Wilcox, C. (ed.). (2007), *The Golden Age of Couture – Paris-London 1947–57*, London: V&A, quoting *Time* magazine, 24 December 1945.
9. Vickers, H. (2007), 'Cecil Beaton and his Anthology of Fashion', in Wilcox, C. (ed.), *The Golden Age of Couture – Paris-London 1947–57*, London: V&A. Jacket and pill box hat, 1946, Balmain, Paris, V&A, and black evening dress, Lelong, Paris, 1946, V&A.
10. Mme. Miguel's white Balenciaga jacket, V&A, 1974.
11. Cocktail dress, black crepe, Fath, Paris, 1946, V&A, no. T 304.1977. In 1947 Lady Alexandra, later Lady Dacre, became a *mannequin mondaine* for the House of Jacques Fath. She bequeathed many clothes from the salons of Fath and Lanvin from late 1940s and the 1950s to the V&A. Brighton Museum also has a small collection.
12. Hat, Madame Suzy, Paris, 1946, V&A, no. T.269.1961, given by Lady Alexandra Dacre.
13. Diana Mosley, the wife of Oswald Mosely, Founder of the British Fascist Party.
14. Palmer, A. (2009: 25), *Dior. A New Look, a New Enterprise*, London: Victoria and Albert Museum; and La Maison Dior, 'The Story of Dior', https://www.dior.com/couture/en_gb/the-house-of-dior/the-story-of-dior/30-avenue-montaigne (accessed 14 April 2019).
15. Acton quoting a letter from Nancy Mitford to Haywood Hill. (This starting price for the evening dress indicates a plain dress without beading and with little trimming.)
16. See Norman Hartnell sales sketch and price docket, no. 31 and 33 for the white satin evening dress with a band of emerald green with an embroidered band priced at £140 and a matching emerald green, heavily beaded, satin evening coat for £157. In Hattrick, J. (2011), 'A life in the archive: the dress, design and identity of the London couturier Norman Hartnell, 1921–1979', doctoral thesis, University of Brighton, 177 Figure 4.4, Hartnell-Mitchison Archive, Box 5/File 9.
17. 'The Wardrobe of Madame Brusse', exhibition at the Rijksmuseum, Amsterdam, 30 January–7 June 2015; https://www.rijksmuseum.nl/nl/de-garderobe-van-mevrouw-brusse (accessed 6 August 2018), with many thanks to Madelief Hohé for this reference.

— VERA BORÉA —
Jaquette classique en toile exotique. Les longs revers fermés très bas sont nouveaux

ROBERT PIGUET — Jaquette en tweed. Les découpes sont ornées par des abeilles... les carrées

Conclusion

Lou Taylor and Marie McLoughlin

Paris couture style diffusion throughout the Occupation

Many chapters in this book have detailed the continuation of the international business of Paris couture all through the war. This of course varied, as this text has shown, dependent upon each country's relationship with Nazi Germany and on the initiatives of the local fashion press, the Paris couturiers themselves, their international business partners and their clients. The American *Vogue* correspondent Marya Mannes wrote waspishly at the moment of the Liberation that 'France – war torn France – has never stopped being the fashion centre of Europe . . . Paris couture has been doing very nicely under the Germans' (American *Vogue* 1 September 1944). The trade had indeed 'multiplied by five-fold between 1941 and 1943' (Grumbach 1993: 56)

To summarise the findings of this book, Axis countries aside, it was neutral countries that received the most regular news. The fashion presses in Sweden, Portugal and Switzerland, for example, offered regular fashion descriptions and images from Paris. Couture goods were received around the world. Luxury silks from Abraham, Zurich, went by air to Stockholm and in that city, Paris couture gowns arrived via Spain or Italy (see Chapter 4 and Figure 4.6). In Lisbon, buyer trips to Paris were possible, as was the regular availability of original couture and hats, which were also sold in Switzerland. Paris copy styles were made in all these countries and sold alongside their own designs (see Figure 7.7A–D). Amongst the Occupied countries, Denmark received less and less Paris news and no Paris garments as the war continued, though some news filtered in from Stockholm (Chapter 8). In Belgium, fashion buyers could sometimes get German passes to travel from Brussels to Paris and Lyon. Pouillard can even track what Paris couture garments were bought and copied and for which wartime Brussels clients (Chapter 10). In Allied countries, seasonal style reports as well as couture clothes and hats were available in America for sale and copy in top stores across the country until the USA joined the war at the end of 1941. After that some snippets of news arrived through 1942–1944.

Brazil, even though the country sent troops to fight on the Allied side, received regular information and even, by one route or another, garments all through the war

FIGURE CONCL.0 Red tweed jacket with small hat, Paris, drawn by Gruau, *Marie Claire*, 12 April 1940 (copyright SIC/Marie Claire France, 163, with kind permission).

(Chapter 9). In London, the trade magazine *International Textiles* reported on Paris occupation styles in 1943 when it obtained a copy of *l'Officiel*. Whatever British manufacturers thought of the styles, they knew that wartime restrictions ensured they could not be reproduced in Britain (Chapters 11 and 12). However, Britain did enjoy a welcome injection of Paris style as some top Paris couturiers relocated to London following the Fall of France (Chapter 12). Several Paris couture houses had had overseas branches for many years before the war and these continued to trade, keeping the Paris names in the public eye even when trading links with the parent house were severed. Thus, the allure of Paris couture remained alive in the hearts of even the most patriotic of Allied fashion minds.

The chapters in this book have shown too that travelling Paris couture shows became a key element in maintaining contacts abroad, arranged to prove the salons were still functioning – until Nazi control stopped them. Amsterdam hosted one in mid-April 1940, two months before the German invasion of Paris (Chapter 12) and couture shows were held in New York in 1939 and 1941 (Chapter 6). Lelong secured a major coup when given Nazi permission for the March 1942 couture fashion show in Lyon (see Chapter 2, and Figure 2.9). This was for an audience including over 300 trade professionals from neutral countries – Swiss, Spanish, Portuguese, Turkish and North African (Veillon 1993: 166).

After the Liberation, official Chambre fashion shows abroad were even more vital as proof that Paris haute couture had never gone away. Major shows were consequently held in Rio de Janeiro and São Paolo in September 1945 (Chapter 9) and in Copenhagen on 9 November 1945 (Chapter 7). Paris haute couture had received the help of loyal supporters all over the world through the war years and many international commercial contacts had been kept alive, as this book has shown. The 'ownership' of Parisian salons, through the nationality of head designers, had never only been in French national hands, from Charles Worth onwards. Thus, as our chapters have noted, Molyneux designs were available in Paris, London and across the USA. Piguet designs could be bought in Paris, New York, Stockholm, and Zurich and Balenciaga in Paris, Madrid, Barcelona, Lisbon, Stockholm – and as Kauffman writes, in 1946, in Rio (Kauffman 2012: 3).

Chapters in this book have for the first time in one publication also offered witness to the vastly differing wartime experiences of the fashion trades in Occupied, neutral and Allied countries and their differing access and responses to Paris Occupation style. It has detailed, too, the full range of personal responses made by the haute couturiers and their clients to the Occupation's restrictive trade regulations, including (as noted in Chapter 10) that Chanel tried and failed to use Nazi legislation for her own ends. The entire Chanel company, both fragrances and fashion, is now owned by the grandsons of the Wertheimer brothers, from whom Chanel had tried unsuccessfully to wrest control of the fragrance company using Nazi anti-Semitic Aryanisation regulations. (Vaughan 2011). Images have also detailed here the complex

FIGURE CONCL.1
(above left) Summer hat, Agnes, *Modes et Travaux*, June 1943 (University of Brighton Teaching Collection). (above right) Design in gouache on paper for 'Captive Bird' brooch, Cartier, Paris, 1942 (Archives Cartier, Paris, © Cartier Collection, with many thanks).

creative reactions of the luxury accessory companies at this time of extreme shortage (see Veillon, Chapter 3). The astonishing Agnès Occupation-style hat festooned with roses,[1] and the Gaullist Resistant Cartier '*Oiseau en cage*' brooch of 1942 were made by companies committed to profoundly contrasting political stances. They were, nonetheless, united in their work through the struggle to overcome shortages of every kind and the need to keep their businesses alive and their staff in work.

This text has detailed the international row over the extravagance of styles, triggered once the Allies reached Paris. It has shown how the designers and their supporters struggled to overcome criticisms of Occupation style extravagance, finally doing so with the new post-war 'Corolle'/New Look style of Dior and the new mood in the designs of his colleagues from 1947. As Veronique Pouillard has detailed (Pouillard 2013), international contacts were thereafter assiduously expanded. Many of the Paris salons named in this book – Dior, Balmain and Balenciaga to name just three – flourish still today in new global branded forms as a consequence of collective policies that were put into play in Paris in the 1940–1947 period.

This text has at same time assessed the impact of Nazi barbarism, racism and belligerency on France and on Europe as a whole from 1939–1945 and the consequent upheaval wreaked on its fashion world. Hitler's anti-Semitic legislation caused many anti-Nazi and Jewish fashion professionals from Paris, Berlin, Vienna,

Budapest, Prague and Brussels to flee from persecution, carrying their deep commitments to supporting Paris couture to their new homelands and so spreading old allegiances right around the world, from London (Chapter 11) to Sydney, Australia (Sydney Jewish Museum 2012). We have respectfully acknowledged the loss of many, many thousands of Jewish women and men who had been working at all levels of the fashion trade from textile manufacture to ready-to-wear and couture, in Germany and France as elsewhere. The contributions they could have given to post-war European fashion re-construction will never be known.[2] Goldstein has written that 'after the war it was extremely difficult for the textile centres in Berlin and Vienna to regain the reputation they had previously enjoyed due in part to the Jewish textile industry' (Goldstein 2005: 117).

Fanny Berger, the young, couture milliner from Paris, who was murdered at Auschwitz-Birkenhau at the age of twenty-eight, was one whose future contributions were lost forever, though just a few of her elegant little hats dating from 1940–1941 survive. (See Chapter 3 and Figures 3.3A and B.) The Jewish Museum Milwaukee rescued memories of the work of another murdered Jewish fashion designer from the ashes of the concentration camps in their exhibition 'Stitching History from the Holocaust' of 2015. Hedwig Strnad was a talented Jewish dressmaker and designer from Prague with relatives in Milwaukee, Wisconsin, USA. In 1939 they were struggling to arrange a US entry Affidavit of Necessity for Hedwig and her husband, Paul. Eight sophisticated fashion drawings were sent with the affidavit request to impress the US immigration authorities as to her high standard of professional skills, but to no avail. The couple did not survive. Hedwig and her husband, Paul, were rounded up by the Nazi authorities in Bohemia. She was sent first to Theresen Stadt, in April 1942, then to Treblinka and died in Poland in 1943.

Based on one surviving letter, a photograph and the eight fashion drawings, all that was left of Paul and Hedwig, the museum created a remarkable and touching exhibition. At the centre were Hedwig's fashionable 1942 drawings painted in Prague, showing early Paris Occupation couture style, complete with small hats tilted over the forehead. In 2015, the museum had these garment designs made up for the very first time by Jessica Jaeger, a costumier for the Milwaukee Repertory Theatre, and displayed in Hedwig Strnad's memory over seventy years after she was murdered.[3]

Airey Neave's view, discussed in Chapter 1, was clear. Nazis were 'ordinary people . . . invested by Hitler with unbridled power. . . . As their power increased they learned to wield it without restraint. Manipulation, perversion and corruption of the law, allied to absolute rule unchecked by legal or democratic sanction, turned many of them into beasts' (Neave 1978 : 27, 25–26). Above all, when examining human and business reactions to the relentless grip the Nazi Occupiers held on Paris haute couture, as we have done throughout this book, and quoting Célia Bertin again, 'When we think about these years, we must never forget the great weight of moral as well as material misery in which we lived' (Bertin 1993: 133).[4]

FIGURE CONCL.2
Hedwig Strnad, fashion drawings on paper, Prague 1942. (near right) Floral printed day dress with flared skirt and short puffed sleeves. (far right) Flared blue coat worn over a floral printed pleated summer suit. The Jewish Museum, Milwaukee, with thanks.

Postscript

The image in Figure Concl.3 shows an undated letter with a drawing of a bird's nest, sent to Lou Taylor when she was four years old, in spring 1946, from bomb-blasted Nuremberg by her father, F. Elwyn Jones, MP, a member of the British Prosecuting Team at the International Military Tribunal. He was Labour MP for West Ham South from 1945–1974 and Lord Chancellor 1974–1979. His wife, the artist and writer, Pearl Binder, was Jewish. The letter was written on British War Crimes Executive notepaper as he was immersed in the trials of Nazi leaders responsible for horrors of the Nazi slaughter across Europe. He prosecuted, for one, SS Standartfuehrer Wolfram Sievers, Reich Manager of the Ahnenerbe (Ancestral Heritage Society) for Sievers's personal involvement in the creation of the 'Jewish Skeleton Collection', including the heads and bodies of eighty-six specifically murdered Jews from the Auschwitz concentration camp. At the 'Doctors' Trial' in 1946, Sievers was found guilty, convicted and sentenced to death.[5]

The letter reads:

Dearest Lou,

Daddy saw another bird's nest in the garden this morning with two little birds in it, like this.

A big kiss from Daddy. X.

Nearly forty years later Elwyn Jones wrote:

Of the twenty-one who were charged [at Nuremberg] on what was believed to be reliable evidence, three were acquitted when that evidence was put to the judicial test. The death sentence on the ten condemned men were carried out on 10 October 1946. Their bodies and that of Goering, were cremated in Munich and their ashes thrown into the river Isar and borne by the Danube to the Black Sea. Nothing of them was left to become a shrine and focus for any possible Nazi revival.

(Lord Elwyn-Jones, *In My Time – an Autobiography*, Weidenfeld and Nicolson, 1983: 124)

FIGURE CONCL.3
Undated letter from Nuremberg, spring 1946. (With thanks to Lou Taylor.)

BRITISH WAR CRIMES EXECUTIVE [E.S.]

Dearest Love,

Daddy saw another bird's nest in the garden this morning with two little birds in it. Like this

A big kiss from Daddy. X

References

Bertin. C. (1993). *Femmes sous l'Occupation*, Stock : Paris

Goldstein, G.M. (2005). *The Perfect Fit, The Garment Industry and American Jewry, 1860–1960*, New York: Yeshiva University Press.

Grumach, D. (1993). *Histoires de la Mode*, Paris: Seuil.

Kauffman, M. (2012). *The Couture Client as Patron of the Art of Fashion*, https://process.arts.ac.uk/sites/default/files/michelle-kauffman-the-couture-client.pdf (accessed 2 September 2016).

Neave, A. (1978). *Nuremberg, a Personal Record of the Trials of the Major Nazi War Criminals in 1945-6*, London: Hodder and Stoughton.

Pouillard, V. (2013), 'Keeping designs and brands authentic', *European Review of History*, 24 October: 815–835, http://dx.doi.org/10.1080/13507486.2013.833720 (accessed April 2016).

Sydney Jewish Museum. (2012), *Dressing Sydney, the Jewish Fashion Story*, Sydney: Sydney Jewish Museum.

Vaughan, H. (2011). *Sleeping with the Enemy. Coco Chanel Nazi Agent*, London: Chatto and Windus.

Veillon, D. (1990). *La Mode Sous l'Occupation*, Paris: Payot.

Endnotes

1. Veillon has noted that Mme Agnès, a leading couture milliner, along with Jeanne Lanvin, Marcelle Dormoy, Paquin, Marcel Rochas, Jean Dessès and Jacques Fath, attended a cocktail party on 11 February 1941 to celebrate the hundredth edition of Jean Luchaire's notorious collaborationist newspaper *Les Nouveaux Temps* (Veillon. 1990.191).

2. *Remembrance, Reflection, Responsibility,* vol 2. 'Fashion and Persecution – the Fate of Jewish clothiers in the Nazi Dictatorship on the Premises of Today's Justice Ministry,' (2016). Berlin: German Ministry of Justice and Consumer Protection, *www.bmjv.de/SharedDocs/.../DE/Konfektion_und_Repression.*

3. Milwaukee Jewish Museum *Stitching History from the Holocaust. 2015:* Milwaukee. *stitchinghistory.org/* accessed Sept, 23, 2017.

4. See Footnote 19, Chapter 1.

5. Wolfram Sievers was Reich manager of the *Ahnenerbe* (Ancestral Heritage Society.) This organisation put together the 'Jewish Skeleton Collection' of the heads and bodies of Jews from Auschwitz Concentration Camp for August Hirt, Director of the Anatomical Institute at the Reich University of Strasbourg for 'anthropological purposes.' Schmidt, U. (2004.123) *Leo Alexander and the Nazi Doctors Trial:* London, Palgrave Macmillan. See also the prosecuting role of F. Elwyn Jones in: *'Nuremberg trial cross-examination of Wolfram Sievers 8/8/1946,'* https://www.youtube.com/watch?v=tGSUGXimqMk.

List of Illustrations

Cover Image

Adapted from Göta Trägårdh's fashion drawing *Hats in Red*. Copies of Paris couture millinery designed and made by Stockholm milliners, *Bonniers månadstidning*, 7 November 1942.

Introduction

Intro.0 Summer hat, straw with silk flowers and veiling, by Agnès, Paris, *Modes et Travaux*, June 1943, Dress History Teaching Collection, University of Brighton.

Intro.1 French fashion magazines, 1942–1943 (University of Brighton, Dress History Teaching Collection).

Intro.2 Paquin, green chiffon evening dress with gold sequins for winter 1939 (Kerry Taylor Auction House, Lot 60, June 2010).

Intro.3 Cover of *Modes et Travaux*, June–July 1944 (University of Brighton, Dress History Teaching Collection.

Intro.4 Summer straw hat with silk flowers and veiling by Agnès, Paris, *Modes et Travaux*, June 1943 no 528, University of Brighton, Dress History Teaching Collection.

Intro.5 Jeanne Lanvin, Paris, evening dress in beaded, ivory rayon satin, 1944 (Kerry Taylor Auction House, Lot 94, 23 June 2015,with thanks).

Chapter 1

1.0 1941–42, German Reich, Nazi Occupied, neutral, and Allied territories across Europe. (Map adapted from Wikimedia Commons, licence CC-BY-SA-3.0).

1.1A Emmy and Herman Goering with Magda and Joseph Goebbels, Reich Minister for Propaganda, attending a press ball in Berlin, 3 February 1935 (Getty 541086559).

1.1B Hans Frank, Governor General of Occupied Poland's General Government, with his wife, Brigitte, and Goebbels at a soirée in Krakow on 1 September 1940, marking the first anniversary of the outbreak of war (with thanks to the National Digital Photographic Archive, Warsaw, no: SM02-3385. Photograph by Paul Brander).

1.1C Arthur and Maria Greiser at the Hunters Ball, 5 November 1937. (Copyright Bundesarchiv 183-C15532.)

1.2A Anneliese Ribbentrop, Inge Ley and Mme. Alfieri, the wife of Dino Alfieri, the Italian Ambassador and leading Italian Fascist, at a reception on 22 May 1939 (Getty 545920705).

1.2B College blazer badge for the Augusta-Victoria College, Bexhill-on-Sea, Sussex, attended by one of Ribbentrop's daughters, in about 1937 (Bexhill Museum, no. BEXHM: 2018.41.1, with thanks to Julian Porter, curator).

1.2C Left: Summer evening dress in purple silk crepe georgette and gelatin sequins, salon of Stanowksi, Dussledorf, 1936–1938 (No.T-A79/252). Right: White evening dress in rayon tulle, 1938, worn by the actress Gundel Thormann (No. T-80/654). Both garments from the Münchner Stadtmuseum, with thanks to Isabella Belting.

1.3 Robert and Inge Ley in a motorcade, 6 June 1930, with Max Amman (photograph by Hugo Jaeger, Timepix/The LIFE Picture Collection/Getty Images, 50714939, 1939).

1.4A and B Fashionable linen suit and dirndl, both from *Der Goldene Schnitt*, Hamburg, 1938 (with thanks to the Dress History Teaching Collection, University of Brighton).

1.5 Frau Mia Renner and children in dirndl styled dresses, Karlsruhe, summer, 1937. (Photographer Dr. A.E. Haffner, with thanks to Janet Hammond.)

1.6 Map of divided France, June 1940 (Map adapted from Wikimedia Commons, licence CC-BY-SA-3.0).

1.7 Chambre des Deputés in Paris, 1941, with German V for victory sign and banner: 'Germany Triumphs On All Fronts' (Getty 3313255).

1.8A Evening dress in cream-coloured lawn with red, white and blue floral embroidery and lace ruffles, 1939–1940, Chanel, Paris. (Museum of the City of New York, no. 45.111.3A and B. Gift of Mrs. Harrison Williams, 1945. © The Metropolitan Museum of Art Photograph Studio.)

1.8B General Schellenberg, head of the SS Intelligence Service in Berlin, September 1943. (Copyright Bundesarchiv 101III-Alber-178-04A. Photographer Kurt Alber.)

1.9 Carven, Paris, summer suit with hunting print, 1945 (Kerry Taylor Auction House, LOT 73, 23 June 2013, with thanks).

1.10 Violette Szabo in floral print dress, probably 1942–1944, from a Lambeth newspaper published in 1946 (by kind permission of London Borough of Lambeth, Archives Department, lambethlandmark.com).

Chapter 2

2.0 Jacket and pleated skirt in red, white and blue, Lanvin, *Modes et Travaux*, May 1943, no. 527, with thanks to Dress History Collection, University of Brighton.

2.1 Checking papers at a French police station at the Demarcation Line between the Vichyist Zone Libre and the Nazi-Occupied zone, at Moulin, Auvergne, 1940. (Roger Viollet. Getty 92424721).

2.2 Pétain propaganda poster featuring wild field flowers, 1940. (Alamy CW8ME9.)

2.3 Hans Kehrl, in his uniform as the Head of the Planning Office, Ministry of Armaments and War Production, Germany, 1942. (Bundesarchive, 183-1998-0525-500/CC-BY-SA 3.0. Bundesarchiv 101III-Alber-178-04A. Photographer: Kurt Alber.)

2.4 Montage of fifteen Coudurier-Fructus-Descher silk and rayon designs (Musée des Tissus, Lyon, 1941–1942 with one of 1942, no 21397 from Collection Départementale des Musées de l'Ain/ Fonds des Soieries Bonnet, with thanks). Top Row, Left to right: MT 39848.6.6; CDF 1942, vol. 82, no. 25521; CDF 1941, vol. 101, no. 53978; MT 39847.8verso.43137. Second Row, Left to right: MT 39848.19.2.47154; MT 39847.6.1; MT 39847.14 verso; MT 39847.7 verso.43126. Third Row, Left to right: MT 39843.7recto.43125; CDF 1943, Vol. 111, no. 46072; CDF 1942, Vol. 113, no. 25544; Soieries Bonnet.1942, no. 21397 from Collection Départementale des Musées de l'Ain/ Fonds des Soieries Bonnet. Bottom Row, Left to right: CDF 1942, vol. 97. 37; MT 39843.10recto.43144; MT 39848.9.8. 47121; MT 39843.5verso.43109.

2.5 Photograph of the giant paper mise-en-carte jacquard weaving plan of 1941 for the silk portrait of Pétain published in *l'Illustration* (5 July 1941:306; with thanks to Lou Taylor Collection). Small silk copies (45 cm x 35 cm) were sold to raise funds for the Secour Nationale. One example remains in the Musée des Tissus today.

2.6A Abstract, warp-printed and woven sample, with a red, white and blue moiré effect, 1941. (Coudurier-Fructus-Descher, vol. 111. no 53978. Musée des Tissus, Lyon with thanks.)

2.6B Jacket and pleated skirt in red, white and blue, Lanvin, *Modes et Travaux*, May, 1943, no. 527 with thanks to the Dress History Collection, University of Brighton.

2.7 Lelong, 1943, summer dress with pleated tartan skirt, *Modes et Travaux*, July 1943. (No. 52 with thanks to the Dress History Collection, University of Brighton.)

2.8A Sheep, rabbits and geese, reversible weave, Coudurier-Fructus-Descher, 194 (CDF 1942, Vol. 113, no. 25544). (Musée des Tissus, with thanks.)

2.8B Daisies with red, white and blue centres, Coudurier-Fructus-Descher 1940, MT 39847.7 verso.43126. (Musée de Tissus, with thanks.)

2.9 Paris haute couture fashion show in Lyon, March 1942. (Getty 558642441, photo by Keystone-France/Gamma-Rapho.)

2.10 The Liberation of Lyon, 3 September 1944. French parachutists of the Forces Françaises Libres and Allied troops meet up with French Forces of the Interior soldiers of the French Resistance at Lyon Town Hall. (Bibliothèque Municipale de Lyon no.P0706 001 00004, photo by Pik, with thanks.)

2.11A Floral print summer dress, *Modes et Travaux*, July 1943, no. 529. (With thanks to the Dress History Collection, University of Brighton.)

2.11B Design for Resistance fabric print '*canard*' by Colcombet, Lyon, 1940–1944, The Studio, December 1945, vol. CXXX, no. 633, 175–176. (With thanks to St. Peters House Library, University of Brighton.)

Chapter 3

3.0 Turban in beige jersey with brown bow, c. 1943 (Kerry Taylor Auction House, Lot 307, 12 February 2013, with thanks).

3.1 Hat and muff by Agnès, *Marie Claire*, January 20th, 1943 (copyright SIC/Marie Claire France, 269, with kind permission).

3.2 'A Sheep in your Cupboard', advertisement for Pingouin Wools, urging the re-knitting of old jerseys. *Marie Claire*, back page, 20 January 1943 (copyright SIC/Marie Claire France, 269, with kind permission).

3.3 (top) Two hats by Fanny Berger, in white and pink felt, 1940–1941 (Musée de la mode de la Ville de Paris Palais Galliera, GAL.1959.43.3 and 4, © Topfoto and Roger-Viollet) and (bottom) a hat in fine black straw with feather trimming, 1940–1941 (Caroline Last Collection with thanks).

3.4 Handbag by Duvelleroy made from a Kashmir Shawl of the 1850–1870 period, Paris, 1943. (Palais Galliera, Musée de la mode de la Ville de Paris GAL.1998.83.1, 1942. © Topfoto and Roger-Viollet.)

3.5 Winter shoes with wedge heels of cork covered in brown leather and with knitted brown gaiters attached, c. 1943–1944. (Fonds Chauvin, with kind permission of the Musée des Métiers de la Chaussure, Saint-André-de-la-Marche. Photo copyright Olivier Rahard.)

3.6 Forces Navales Françaises Libres Officer's badge in enamel and brass, probably designed by George Charity in the Cartier Studio, London and made in London, c. 1941–1943 (with thanks to Jane Hattrick).

3.7 Left: 'Freed Bird' brooch, Paris, 1944, in gold, diamonds and lapis-lazuli (photo by Vincent Wulveryck, Archives Cartier, Paris, © Cartier Collection, Paris, with thanks to Anne Lamarque and Violette Petit). Right: Design in gouache on paper for 'Captive Bird' brooch, Cartier, Paris, 1942 (Archives Cartier, Paris, © Cartier Collection, with many thanks).

3.8 'Pagode' shoes with rigid wooden soles and red leather uppers recycled from stitched-together belts or handbag handles, made by the 'Imperial' brand at Aixe-sur-Vienne (with kind permission of the Neuville collection, Musée des Métiers de la Chaussure, Saint-André-de-la-Marche; photo copyright: Olivier Rahard).

3.9A Two models wearing scarves made into fashionable turbans, Paris, 1944. (Getty 2696639. Photo by Fred Ramage.)

3.9B Turban in beige jersey with brown bow, c. 1943 (Kerry Taylor Auction House, Lot 307, 12 February 2013, with thanks).

3.10A Straw boater piled with wide coloured ribbons, cover, *Marie Claire*, 12 April 1940 (copyright SIC/ Marie Claire France, 163, with kind permission).

3.10B Felt hat with 'knife' feather, shown at the haute couture fashion show in Lyon 8–10 March 1942 (Getty 558642453).

3.11A High red felt hat with black-and-white striped silk trimming, 1943–1944 (Musée de la Mode de la Ville de Paris, Palais Galliera, no GAL. 1959. 43.3 and 4, © Topfoto and Roger-Viollet).

3.11B High green felt hat with feather trimmings by Gabrielle, dress by Jacques Heim, *Modes et Travaux*, December 1943 (with thanks to the University of Brighton Dress History Teaching Collection).

3.12 Red, white and blue prototype, wedge-heeled shoe, designed to celebrate the Liberation of France, Manoukian, Paris (Musée Carnavalet, 1944 OM 4248. © Topfoto and Roger-Viollet).

Chapter 4

4.0 Göta Trägårdh fashion drawing '*Hattar i rött*' (Hats in Red), *Bonniers månadstidning*, November 1942 (with many thanks to Li Thies-Largergren).

4.1 French censorship stamp in 'Från modefronten mycket nytt', *Bonniers månadstidning*, January 1940 (with thanks to the National Library Stockholm).

4.2 A typical French fashion image by the Parisian photographer Laure Albin Guillot. Couturier unknown. *Bonniers månadstidning*, March 1944 (with thanks to the National Library Stockholm).

4.3 Fashion drawings by the French illustrator Pierre Pagès. Report by Jean de France titled 'Modebrev från Paris', *Bonniers månadstidning*, September 1942 (with thanks to the National Library Stockholm).

4.4 Piguet design in *Bonniers månadstidning*, January 1940 (with thanks to the National Library Stockholm).

4.5 Paris haute couture fashion spread, 1943, including designs by Lanvin, Jacques Fath, M. Dormoy, Bruyère, Maggy Rouff and Hermès. In 'Paris just nu', *Bonniers månadstidning*, July–August 1943 (with thanks to the National Library Stockholm).

4.6 Göta Trägårdh's illustrations of Paris couture garments sold in Stockholm, *Bonniers månadstidning*, April 1944 (with thanks to the National Library Stockholm).

4.7 Göta Trägårdh fashion drawing, '*Hattar i rött*' (Hats in Red), *Bonniers månadstidning*, November 1942 (with many thanks to Li Thies-Largergren).

Chapter 5

5.0 'Velasquez', Piguet evening dress, *l'Album de la Mode du Figaro*, 1943 (from De Holden Stone, 'French Fashion Survives the Nazis', *Art and Industry*, July 1945, vol. 39, no. 229: 3, London, with thanks to St. Peter's House Library, University of Brighton).

5.1 German censorship of the French Press May 1944. (Getty 46390343.)

5.2 Michel de Brunhoff and the staff of French Vogue before the war, in 1937. (Getty 110260487.)

5.3 (left) Cover of *Vu*, no. 436, 22 July 1936 (with thanks to the Dress History Teaching Collection, University of Brighton). (above) Vogel's name on cover as Director of *Vu*, no. 436, 22 July 1936 (with thanks to the Dress History Teaching Collection, University of Brighton).

5.4 Photo of Lucien Vogel and his daughter, 1931. (Getty 541041423.)

5.5 'Velasquez' Piguet evening dress, *l'Album de la Mode du Figaro*, 1943 (from De Holden Stone, 'French Fashion Survives the Nazis', *Art and Industry*, July 1945, vol .39, no. 229.3, London, with thanks to St. Peter's House Library, University of Brighton).

5.6 Evening jacket, House of Schiaparelli, Paris, *Modes et Travaux*, December 1941 (with thanks to the Dress History Teaching Collection, University of Brighton).

5.7 Cover of *Glamour* USA, Christmas 1943. (Getty 531289852.)

5.8 Paris *Vogue* staff, Brunhoff, Woolman-Chase and four others, 1950. (Getty 533413038.)

Chapter 6

6.0 Blue day dress, Schiaparelli, Spring-Summer 1940 (the Metropolitan Museum Digital collections, the Thomas Watson Library, the Costume Institute, Bergdorf Goodman Sketches Collection no. i2079650_364).

6.1 Poster for New York World Fair, Hall of Fashion, c. 1939. (Miller Art Co., Museum of the City of New York, no. X2011.34.4319.)

6.2A French hat, Elsa Schiaparelli, straw, cotton and silk, summer 1940. Brooklyn Museum Costume Collection at the Metropolitan Museum of Art, New York. Gift of Millicent Huttleston Rogers, No. 2009. 300. 1837. (Image copyright the Metropolitan Museum of Art/Art Resource/Scala, Florence.)

6.2B French dinner dress, Elsa Schiaparelli, silk, ceramic, plastic, summer 1940. Brooklyn Museum Costume Collection at the Metropolitan Museum of Art, New York. Gift of Arturo and Paul Peralta-Ramos, no. 009.300.1210. (Image copyright the Metropolitan Museum of Art/Art Resource/Scala, Florence.)

6.3 Left, blue dress, Schiaparelli design for Bergdorf. Right, evening dress, Paquin for Bergdorf, 1940. Both sketches from the The Metropolitan Museum Digital collections, the Thomas Watson Library, the Costume Institute, Bergdorf Goodman Sketches Collection. Left: Blue dress, Spring-Summer, 1930, no. i2079650_364. Right: Evening dress, 1940, i2070653_002.

6.4 US Navy WAVES uniform, yeoman third class, 1942, designed by Mainbocher, worsted serge, rayon and cotton. (Museum of the City of New York, 46.293.a-d.)

6.5 Evening dress, Madeleine Vionnet, cotton, metallic, Paris, 1939, and shown the following year at the Wanamakers charity fashion show, 1940. (New York, Metropolitan Museum of Art. Gift of Mrs Harrison Williams, C.I.52.24.2a, b. Copyright the Metropolitan Museum of Art/Art Resource/Scala, Florence.)

6.6 US service women window shopping at Saks Fifth Avenue, New York, 1944. (United States Office of War Information. Museum of the City of New York, no. 90.28.22.)

6.7 (left) Peggy Morris of Bergdorf Goodman, New York, draping French satin, August, 1940. (Getty 72399398.) (right) Emmet Joyce of Saks examining his design of Paris silk for an American clientele, August, 1940. (Getty 72399402.)

6.8 US tank at the Battle of the Bulge, France, December 1944. (Getty 72432865.)

6.9 Dinner dress, Mainbocher, silk, c. 1945, designed and made in America, worn by Millicent Rogers. (Brooklyn Museum Costume Collection at the Metropolitan Museum of Art, New York. Gift of Arturo and Paul Peralta-Ramos, no. 1945. 2009. 300.172. Image copyright the Metropolitan Museum of Art/Art Resource/Scala, Florence.)

6.10 Roger Worth, Paris, fashion drawing for dress (Eglantine) for the first *Thèâtre de la Mode*, Paris, late 1944 to early 1945. (Ms. Nikita Mehta, Brand Development Manager, Akita Brands, SA Designer Parfums Ltd. and Victoria and Albert Museum, E.22247-1957, with thanks.)

6.11 Day dress, Claire McCardell, New York, 1948. (With thanks to the Ohio State University, College of Education/Human Ecology Historic Costume and Textiles Collection, no. 1988.318.73.)

Chapter 7

7.0 Models by Amelia de Morais, Lisbon, *Eva*, New Year, 1944 (with thanks to the Hemeroteca Municipal de Lisboa).

7.1 Pan-American Clipper, moored on the Tagus River, Lisbon, unloading passengers, 1940. (Getty 50612043.)

7.2 Women at a beach bar in Estoril, 1936. (Photo by Eric Borchert/ullstein, Getty 548787407.)

7.3 Refugee passengers still on the *SS Quanza* at the dockside in Norfolk, Virginia, 11 September 1940 (photograph by Charles Borjes, the *Virginian Pilot* Photograph Collection, Sargeant Memorial Collection, Norfolk Public Library).

7.4 'Lisbon the capital of fashion': An elegant Lisbon woman as graceful as a Parisian woman dressed in Rue de la Paix. (Mundo Gráfico, no. 1, 15 October 1940: 7, with thanks to the Hemeroteca Municipal de Lisboa.)

7.5 Left: 'Morning walk on Avenida da Liberdade'. Centre: 'The Portuguese have become accustomed to walking without a hat'. Right: 'A French refugee in her white dress with geometric lines and no hat'. (*Mundo Gráfico*, no. 1, 15 October 1940: 7, with thanks to the Hemeroteca Municipal de Lisboa.)

7.6 Top: Silk day dress with small, navy blue, floral print on white ground, Gomez, Porto, 35603/1. Bottom: Silk day dress, with larger floral print, white on a mid-blue ground, Gomez, Porto, no. 5602/1. (Both from the Museu Nacional do Traje, with thanks to the Directorate-General of Cultural Heritage/Documentation Archive, Lisbon. Photographer, Luisa Oliveira.)

7.7A Designs by Paquin, Lecomte and Lanvin available in Lisbon; drawings by Janine, *Eva*, October 1944 (with thanks to the Hemeroteca Municipal de Lisboa).

7.7B Obtainable from Mme. Valle in Lisbon, left to right: Legroux hat, Jane Laforie draped silk dress and Lecomte dress with large *broderie anglaise* collar trim (with thanks to the Hemeroteca Municipal de Lisboa).

7.8 (above) Evening dress, in pink, about 1940, Albertina Naar, Avenidia de Liberdade, Lisbon, no. 35036. (top right) Close up of its gold, floral, appliqué neck trimming, no. 35036. (bottom right) Black jersey jacket, Beatriz Gomez, 1940–1945, no. 35610. (From the Museu Nacional do Traje, Lisbon with thanks to the Directorate-General of Cultural Heritage/Documentation Archive. Photographer, Luisa Oliveira, 2017.)

7.9 (top) Evening wear by Bobone, Mme Valle and Amélia de Morais and (bottom) models by Amelia de

Morais, Lisbon, both images from *Eva*, New Year, 1944 (with thanks to the Hemeroteca Municipal de Lisboa).

7.10 Four Lisbon hats. (top left) Hat, black felt, 1939, no. 7821, Museu Nacional do Traje, Lisbon. (With thanks to the Directorate-General of Cultural Heritage/Documentation Archive, Lisbon. Photographer Luisa Oliveira, 2017.) (top right) Hat by Bobone, *Eva*, May 1944. (bottom left) Hat, with violets, cover, *Eva*, January 1945. (bottom right) Hat by Amelia de Morais, *Eva*, New Year, 1944: 24. (With thanks to the Hemeroteca Municipal de Lisboa.)

7.11 Fur fashions from Paris, October 1946, *Eva*, drawn by Janine (with thanks to the Hemeroteca Municipal de Lisboa).

Chapter 8

8.0 Marie Gudme Leth, 1943, 'Friendship', a print in five colours on twill woven cellulose fibre fabric. (Designmuseum Danmark, no. 198, 1999. Photo by Pernille Klemp.)

8.1 Exhibition of synthetic fabrics arranged by the National League of Danish Manufacture, 1942 (with thanks to the *Magasin du Nord* Archive).

8.2 Six bridesmaids wearing dresses, in printed fabric, 1943, by Marie Gudme Leth, titled 'Birds'. (*Tiden Kvinder*, 1943, 22: 15, photo by Pernille Klemp.)

8.3 Tailored *culotte* suit for cycling in Copenhagen during World War Two (with thanks to the *Magasin du Nord* Archive).

8.4 Dress and jacket in Allied colours, from the Fonnesbech department store, Copenhagen. (Designmuseum Danmark, no. 179 a-b/1987. Photographs by Pernille Klemp.)

8.5 Marie Gudme Leth, 1943, 'Friendship', a print in five colours on twill woven cellulose fibre fabric. (Designmuseum Danmark, no. 198, 1999. Photo by Pernille Klemp.)

8.6 General Montgomery and British forces welcomed in Copenhagen's Straget Street on 12 May 1945. (Getty 514704308.)

8.7 Liberation flag dress, 1945. (Designmuseum Danmark, no. 228/2013. Photo by Pernille Klemp.)

8.8 Front cover of *La Femme*, no. 36, 20 February 1946 (with thanks to the Dress History Teaching Collection, University of Brighton).

8.9 Chicken wire figure made in Copenhagen by Jean Saint-Martin to promote the showing of the *Thèâtre de La Mode*, *La Femme*, 20 February 1946 (with thanks to the Dress History Teaching Collection, University of Brighton).

Chapter 9

9.0 (opposite) Fashion drawing from the collection 'Brazilian Beige' by Worth and Hermès, *Sombra*, May 1941 (with thanks to the Biblioteca Nacional, Rio de Janeiro).

9.1 (right) Walking on the famous mosaic pavement at Copacabana Beach, Rio de Janeiro, 1941. (Getty 50453673.)

9.2 The Brazilian Expeditionary Forces marching past Castel Nuovo, Naples, 1944. (Getty 82031815.)

9.3 London fashion models leaving for South America on 15 March 1941 to exhibit British fashions, posing with British sailors at the railway station en route the docks to catch their ship. (PastPix/TopFoto.)

9.4 London model at the Copacabana Palace Hotel dressed in a design by Worth, London, in striped Moygashel from the British collection. *Correio da Manhã*, 7 July 1941 (with thanks to the Biblioteca Nacional, Rio de Janeiro).

9.5 'Brazilian Beige' collection, fashion drawings of designs by Worth and Hermès, *Sombra*, no. 4, May 1941 (with thanks to the Biblioteca Nacional, Rio de Janeiro).

9.6 Brazilian socialite Sylvia Regis de Oliveira in dress by Maggy Rouff, *Sombra*, no. 2, February–March 1942 (with thanks to the Biblioteca Nacional, Rio de Janeiro).

9.7 From right to left: Sras. José Lima Guimarães, Silvio Matos, Mario Ipanema Moreira and Abel Ribeiro attending a cocktail party in Rio de Janeiro, *Sombra*, no. 2, May 1943 (with thanks to the Biblioteca Nacional, Rio de Janeiro).

9.8 Sra. Aimée Rodman de Heeren at the French Embassy ball in Rio, *Sombra*, August 1945 (with thanks to the Biblioteca Nacional, Rio de Janeiro).

9.9A French models arriving in Rio de Janeiro from Paris, 22 August 1945, *Correio Carioca*, ano XVIII, no. 5271, August 1945 (with thanks to the Biblioteca Nacional, Rio de Janeiro).

9.9B Paris couture dress with frilled peplum shown at the fashion show during the Great Exhibition of French Art in Rio de Janeiro, *Sombra*, August 1945 (with thanks to the Biblioteca Nacional, Rio de Janeiro).

9.9C Dress with fashionable full-frilled peplum, from the 'Port of Nowhere' scene by Georges Wakhévitch, from the *Thèâtre de la Mode* catalogue for London, printed in Paris, autumn 1944 (with thanks to the Dress History Collection, University of Brighton).

9.10 Figures from the *Thèâtre de la Mode* shown in Brazil from late August into September 1945, *Revista Rio*, no. 75, September 1945: 88 (with thanks to the Biblioteca Nacional, Rio de Janeiro).

9.11A Four *Thèâtre de la Mode* figures in the '*Rue de la Paix*' scene by Touchagues, shown in Rio and São Paulo, late August–September 1945, *Revista Rio*, no. 75, September 1945: 89.

9.11B Four *Thèâtre de la Mode* figures in the '*Rue de la Paix*' scene by Touchagues from a photograph in the London catalogue of the exhibition, printed in Paris in August 1944 (with thanks to the Dress History Teaching Collection, University of Brighton).

Chapter 10

10.0 Swiss design, Paris style: 'New designs for spring suits', *l'Illustré*, Swiss French edition, Lausanne, 5 March 1942. (Dress History Teaching Collection, University of Brighton with kind permission from *l'Illustré*.)

10.1 *Hitlerjugend* forcing Jewish women and men to scrub a street, Vienna, Austria, 1938. (Getty Images 566465051. Photo from Universal History Archive/UIG.)

10.2 (left) Silver fox fur coat by Schuler Wien (Getty 548144067). (right) Elégance Wien showed a slim evening dress with jewelled belt and flowing cape displayed at a fashion show at the Palais Lobkowitz in 1943, Vienna (Getty 548791963).

10.3 Day dress in rayon crepe de chine, Austria, 1940–1944, which is very similar to Molyneux's day dress photographed in *Marie Claire* shown in Figure 12.11. (© Salzburg Museum, no. 22539.)

10.4 Machine embroidery by Els Bossard for C. Forster-Willi, St. Gallen, 1943 (Schweizerisches Nationalmuseum, Landesmuseum Zürich, no. LM 118929).

10.5 Lyon *haute nouveauté* silk exhibition, Palais de Congrès, Zurich, April 1942. (*La Semaine de la Femme*, Issue 2, 9 January 1943, with thanks to Musée Suisse de la Mode, Yverdon-les-Bains.)

10.6 Album *ETUDE I/ETE 1943*. Left: watercolour design on paper by Cornelia Forster. Right: the same design, printed linen by Langenthai AG. (Schweizerisches Nationalmuseum, no. LM 118929.)

10.7 Summer dress by Scheidegger-Mosimann in Strub fabric, *Annabelle*, August 1943, Swiss French edition, Lausanne (Dress History Teaching Collection, University of Brighton, with kind permission from *Annabelle*).

10.8 Hat with lace veil, Gaby Jouval, cover of *l'Illustré*, French edition, 5 March 1942, published in Lausanne (Dress History Teaching Collection, University of Brighton, with kind permission from *l'Illustré*).

10.9. Swiss winter fashions for sportswear, *Marie Claire*, 11 October 1941. (Photograph by Werner Bischof, with the kind permission of the Bischof Estate, Lausanne and the Dress History Teaching Collection, University of Brighton.)

10.10A (above left) Fashion show of Swiss lace, Swiss Fashion Week, spring 1942, *l'Illustré*, 5 March 1942, no. 21 (Dress History Teaching Collection, University of Brighton, with the kind permission of *l'Illustré*).

10.10B (above right) Gaby Jouval's collection made in Swiss 'Ticinella' fabric by Strub and Co, *l'Illustré*, 5 March 1942, no. 21 (Dress History Teaching Collection, University of Brighton, with the kind permission of *l'Illustré*).

10.11A (near right) Swiss design, Paris style: Swiss lace skirt and bolero over black dress. *Annabelle*, August 1943. (Dress History Teaching Collection, University of Brighton, with thanks to *Annabelle*.)

10.11B (far right) Fashion drawing, 'Les Parisiennes Sont Toujours Élégantes', *l'Illustré*, 13 January 1944 (with thanks to the Musée Suisse de la Mode, Yverdon-les-Bains and with kind permission from *l'Illustré*.)

10.12 Lucile Manguin summer coat, *Semaine de la Femme*, 15 May 1943 (with thanks to Musée Suisse de la Mode, Yverdon-les-Bains.)

10.13 Swiss design, Paris style: 'New designs for spring suits', *l'Illustré*, 5 March 1942 (Dress History Teaching Collection, University of Brighton, with kind permission of *l'Illustré*.)

10.14 Dress with frilled cape, in floral print, Belgium, late 1930s (Hasselt Fashion Museum, no. 2011.0027.01, photo by Frank Gielen © Modemuseum Hasselt/Frank Gielen.)

10.15 German soldier reads *West-Front*, a German propaganda newspaper in a café in Brussels, 1940. (Getty Images 542367797.)

10.16 Belgian civilians ride a British Cromwell tank at the Liberation of Brussels, 4 September 1944. (Photograph by Sgt. A. N. Midgley, No. 5 Film and Photographic Unit, War Office, Second World War Official Collection, © IWM BU 509.)

10.17 Dress of parachute silk, Belgium, 1944. This was made after the Allies had landed. (Modemuseum Hasselt no. 1994.0248.02. Photo by Frank Gielen © with many thanks.)

Chapter 11

11.0 A scarf designed by Expressionist painter Felix Topolski entitled 'London 1944' depicting a group of British servicemen and women (Getty 106480761).

11.1 General Bernard Montgomery in England in 1943, wearing a Kangol beret © Imperial War Museum (TR 1036).

11.2 Lida Ascher fabrics for a Molyneux collection for the USA. (*International Textiles* June 1943, no. 6: 21, © Peter Ascher.)

11.3 Molyneux drawings for Bergdorf Goodman, 1940, 1942 and 1944. (The Metropolitan Museum, Thomas Watson Library, Costume Institute, Bergdorf Goodman Sketches: Molyneux. Left: 1940: no. i207.9678_008; centre: 1942: no. 12079678_087; right: 1944: no. 12079678_116.)

11.4 A scarf designed by Expressionist painter Felix Topolski entitled 'London 1944'. It depicts a group of British servicemen and women. (Getty 106480761.)

11.5 Wedding group of Prince George, Duke of Kent and Princess Marina of Greece and Denmark, with dresses by Molyneux, 1934. (Getty Universal History Archive 578343398.)

11.6 Suit from the House of Creed, February 1939. (Getty 55754899.)

11.7 The Hon. Mrs. Reginald (Daisy) Fellowes, President of the Incorporated Society of London Designers, wearing a Molyneux jacket with button trim, redolent of London's Pearly Kings and Queens, and Aage Thaarup's ostrich hat. Photographed by Cecil Beaton for *Vogue* in 1941. (Getty 507392200.)

11.8 Models leaving London for South America in March 1941, to publicise British fashion and textiles for the Board of Trade. Their gas masks, tied in silk scarves, would be left at the docks on departure. (Getty 138592010.)

11.9 In Buenos Aires, to publicise British textiles, Paquin model Rosemary Chase, niece of Lord Willingdon, chats with socialite Tito Casares at party for models in an Argentine architect's house. (Getty 93704518.)

11.10 A group of models wearing new fashions for American women including sportswear and tailored suits at a preview in London, 18 August 1940. (Getty 3373912.)

11.11 A tweed Utility ready-to-wear suit by Derèta, and a heavily taxed, much more expensive, emerald green frock, with matching jacket, by royal couturier Norman Hartnell, conforming to Austerity regulations, 1943. (Getty 154419538.)

11.12 September 1942, at a Board of Trade display in London, a couture suit on the left, part of the couturier prototype scheme to launch Utility, and a mass production copy. (Getty 100372763.)

Chapter 12

12.0 Model, wearing a back-lacing corset by Detolle for Mainbocher, taken just before his relocation to New York, Horst, Paris, 1939. (Photo by Horst P. Horst/Conde Nast. Getty 500685096.)

12.1 Worth (Champcommunal) Utility suit in Scottish tweed, 1942. (V&A T.42&A&B-1942. © Victoria and Albert Museum, London.)

12.2 Fashion drawings, Roger Worth, Paris. Left: Winter 1943, no. E.18874-1957; centre: Winter/Summer 1943-44, no. E.18787-1957; right: Summer 1943 Winter 1943-44 E.18851-1957. Victoria and Albert Museum. (Copyright Ms. Nikita Mehta, Brand Development Manager, Akito Brands, SA Designer Parfums Ltd.)

12.3 Buenos Aires 1941. Peggy Meredith models a Worth dress and jacket as part of the Board of Trade South America tour. She is holding a show programme showing a British coat of arms and the heading 'Coleccion de Modes de Londres'. (1023007280 Getty/Life.)

12.4 Antonio Del Castillo, designer for Paquin, France, 1944. (Getty 53375690.)

12.5 Utility blouse given as part of the Couturier Prototype scheme. (V&A T.61-1942. © Victoria and Albert Museum, London.)

12.6 Henri Creed, Harrods News, October 1940 fashion book. (Courtesy of Harrods Company Archive.)

12.7 Paris couture show in Amsterdam. *Match*, 18 April 1940. (With thanks to the Dress History Teaching Collection, University of Brighton.)

12.8 Molyneux's wartime premises in Rue Royale, run by his French team under the capable eyes of Georges. (Getty 107420771.)

12.9 Delivering perfumes in Occupied Paris without petrol. (Getty 50616899.)

12.10 (top) Molyneux's salon in Grosvenor Street, Mayfair, London, with an air raid shelter in the basement, 1941. (Getty 2674356.) (bottom) Two models wearing fashion by Molyneux stand in a London street with a bomb-site in the background. (Getty 3332663.)

12.11 (near right) Red spotted crepe dress, Molyneux, Paris, 1940. (With thanks to *Marie Claire* and the Dress History Teaching Collection, University of Brighton.)

12.12 (far right) Molyneux red crepe dress for Utility Couturier Prototype scheme, 1942. (V&A T 57.1942. © Victoria and Albert Museum, London.)

12.13 Wallis Simpson wearing Mainbocher for her 1937 marriage to the Duke of Windsor, formerly King Edward XVIII (Hulton Archive/Getty 2665979).

12.14 Model, wearing a back-lacing corset by Detolle for Mainbocher, taken just before his relocation to New York, Horst, Paris, 1939. (Photo by Horst P. Horst/Conde Nast. Getty 500685096.)

12.15 Lady Diana Cooper (née Manners) and Captain Molyneux at the gala opening of the Stage Door Canteen, Paris, March 1945. (Getty 50495942.)

12.16 Renoir, *Madame Monet and Her Son*. (Courtesy of the National Gallery of Washington, 1970.17.60.)

12.17 Morisot, *The Artist's Sister at a Window*. (Courtesy of the National Gallery of Washington, 1970.17.47.)

12.18 Seurat, *Study for 'La Grande Jatte'*. (Courtesy of the National Gallery of Washington, 1970.17.81.)

12.19 Sisley, *Boulevard Heloise, Argenteuil*. (Courtesy of the National Gallery of Washington, 1970.17.82.)

Chapter 13

13.0 and 13.1 Young woman combatant for Forces Françaises de l'Intérieur during the Battle of Paris, August 1944 (Getty 104410856).

13.2 Alison Settle in her war correspondent uniform, 1944, the Alison Settle Archive, University of Brighton Design Archives, no. AS97 (with thanks).

13.3 The Liberation of Paris, August 1944. Parisiennes throw flowers to US soldiers in a jeep. (Getty 526785428.)

13.4 Paris pre-Liberation styles. Left to right: Alix Marcelle Tizeau, Nina Ricci, Anny Blatt, Jacques Fath, *Modes et Travaux*, June–July 1944, no. 538 (with thanks to the Dress History Teaching Collection, University of Brighton).

13.5 Unpublished photograph of Paris haute couture model next to American tank, September 1944. (Photo by Bob Landry. Getty 50493367.)

13.6 Maggy Rouff, pastel tartan dress, *Modes et Travaux*, March 1945 (with thanks to the Dress History Teaching Collection, University of Brighton).

13.7 Cartoon by Joseph Lee, *Evening News*, 7 March 1945 (Cartoon Centre, University of Canterbury, with permission from *Evening News/Associated Newspapers Ltd.*).

13.8 High turban on cover of *Femmes d'Aujourdhui*, Belgium, 19 January 1946 (with thanks to the Dress History Teaching Collection, University of Brighton).

13.9 Queen Elizabeth in a high turban en route to South Africa, 1947. (Still from film *Royal Family in South Africa*, with thanks to British Pathé Ltd.)

Chapter 14

14.0 Drawing of Dior design 'Ketey' on official Lucien Lelong notepaper, probably late 1946 (with thanks to Archives Dior, Paris).

14.1 Molyneux suit, Paris, April 1946, cover of *La Femme* (with thanks to Sue Breakell).

14.2 'Les Beaux Souliers de Paris', *La Femme*, no. 36, 20 February 1946 (with thanks to the Dress History Teaching Collection, University of Brighton).

14.3 Hairstyle by Guillaume, Paris, autumn 1946, *Album de la Mode du Figaro*, no. 8, autumn 1946: 80 (with thanks to the Dress History Teaching Collection, University of Brighton).

14.4 Hat by Maude et Nano, Paris, autumn 1946, *Album de la Mode du Figaro* (with thanks to the Dress History Collection, University of Brighton).

14.5 Evening ensemble, 'La Perse', Balenciaga, Paris, autumn 1946 (Gemeentemuseum Den Haag, no. 1030958, with many thanks).

14.6 Front and back of Piguet, red silk dress, spring collection, Paris, 1945, worn by Aimée de Heeran. (The Museum at FIT, no. 70.57.61. Gift of Mr. Rodman A. Heeren, with thanks to FIT and Valerie Steele.)

14.7 Drawing of Dior design 'Ketey' on official Lucien Lelong notepaper, probably late 1946 (with thanks to Archives Dior, Paris).

Conclusion

Concl.0 Red tweed jacket with small hat, Paris, drawn by Gruau, *Marie Claire*, 12 April 1940 (copyright SIC/Marie Claire France, 163, with kind permission).

Concl.1 (above left) Summer hat, Agnes, *Modes et Travaux*, June 1943 (University of Brighton Teaching Collection). (above right) Design in gouache on paper for 'Captive Bird' brooch, Cartier, Paris, 1942 (Archives Cartier, Paris, © Cartier Collection, with many thanks).

Concl.2 Hedwig Strnad, fashion drawings on paper, Prague 1942. (near right) Floral printed day dress with flared skirt and short puffed sleeves. (far right) Flared blue coat worn over a floral printed pleated summer suit. The Jewish Museum, Milwaukee, with thanks.

Concl.3 Undated letter from Nuremberg, spring 1946. (With thanks to Lou Taylor.)

End Papers

Five-colour print design, 'Friendship', by Marie Gudme Leth, on twill-woven cellulose fibre fabric, 1943 (Designmuseum Danmark, no 198_1999 photo by Pernille Kemp).

Index

Abetz, Otto, 37–8, 39, 43, 49n15, 50n16–17
Abraham and Co, 231, 333
Abraham, Ludwig, 231
Accessories, 5
   belts, 82–3
   gloves, 85
   handbags, 83–4
   hats, 12, 20, 78, 80, 81, 90, 92, 93, 176, 237, 256, 311, 312-14, 316, 320, 322
   head scarves, 88, 91
   jewelry, 86–7
   shoes, 79 80, 85, 88–90, 94, 187, 320, 321
   stockings, 85–6
   turbans, 76, 90, 91, 108, 314, 316
   wartime functions of, 82–93
Acton, Harold, 328
Adams, John, 250
Agius, Christine, 98
Agnes-Drécoll, 196
Agnès, Madame, 20, 78, 92, 335, 340n1
Albrecht, Donald, 142
Albouy, 92, 176
Album de la Mode du Figaro, 94, 115, 126, 127, 134, 311, 321, 322, 323
Alexandrine (Queen), 196
Alfieri, Dino, 29
Alfieri, Mme., 29
Alix – Madame Grès, 100, 109 118, 168, 196, 205, 236, 281, 307
Almanak Silvá, 177–8
Amark, Klas, 98
American Quakers, 148
American *Vogue. See Vogue* (magazine)
Amies, Hardy, 242, 260, 273, 316

Amman, Max, 31, 49n11
Annabelle (Swiss French edition magazine), 234, 237
Anne-Marie (magazine), 242
Antelme, Sandy, 89
Archives Cartier, 87, 87n6-8, 88
Archive Dior, 318, 319 327, 328
Archive: National Digital Photographic, Warsaw, 27
Armistice agreement, 80
Aryanisation, 32, 37, 61, 80, 227, 240, 334
Ascher, Zika and Lida, 252, 253, 254, 255
Aubrac, Lucie, 331n1
Augusta-Victoria College, 28–9
Auschwitz, 28, 34, 80, 87, 133, 336, 338, 340n5
Austria, 225–9
   Anchluss, 226
   fashion industry 227,
   House of Fashion, *Haus der Mode*, 19, 201n8, 227, 229
   Nazi anti-Semitic legislation and repression, 226, 227, 243

Bailey, Gertrude, 310–11
Bailly, Reine, 90
Baker, Josephine, 44, 51n28
Balenciaga, 20, 41–2, 44, 55, 109, 118, 134, 146, 171, 177, 196, 213, 214, 216, 236, 256, 288, 290–1, 322, 324, 326, 334, 335
Ballard, Bettina, 43, 290, 311
Balmain, Pierre, 42, 43, 134, 192, 335
Barbas, Raymond, 319
Barbie, Klaus, 45
Barioz, Jean, 57
Barker, Deborah, 252
Barlow, Sir Thomas, 249
Battle of Paris, 302, 303–4, 307
Battle of Sedan, 119
Battle of the Bulge, 153, 159n3, 306, 317n2

Bérard, Christian, 134
Beaton, Cecil, 104, 162, 163, 168, 177, 179, 291, 292, 311
Beatrix Gomes, 173, 174
Beaumont, Germaine, 94, 126
Becker, Jacques, 39
Becker, Max, 30
Belgium
   Belgian couture, 240–1
   Buyers' visits to Lyon, 241
   couture salons of Hirsch and Norine, 240–2
   dress of parachute silk, 243
   Nazi Occupation of, 239
   Paris couture in, 238, 240
   wartime couture in Brussels, 238–40
Belting, Isabelle, 18, 29, 30
Bendel, Henri, 144, 156, 283, 286
Benito, Carmel, 314
Bérard, Christian, 134
Bergdorf Goodman, 139, 141, 142, 144, 145, 152, 156, 159n2, 214, 254, 283, 286
Bergery, Gaston, 289, 294n10
Berliner Modelle Gesellschaft (BMG), 185, 191, 200n3, 201n8, 229
Bernheim, Nele, 225, 238, 241, 242
Bernstein, [Berger] Odette Fanny, 39, 80, 95n1, 336
Bertin, Celia, 36, 50n23, 72, 320, 336
Bestegui, Charles de, 43
Beurre-Oeufs-Fromages (Butter-Eggs-Cheese) women, 43–4, 100
Belting, Elizabeth, 34
Bevin, Ernest, 247
Bichelonne, Jean, 58, 329
Birck, Preben, 186
Bizot, Edmond, 57
Blatt, Anny, 67, 307
Blom, Holger, 186
Blossac, Bernard, 126
Board of Education, UK, 248

Index   349

Board of Trade, UK, 209, 211, 248, 249, 255, 260, 264, 265, 266–7
Bobone, 174, 175, 176, 177
Bobowski, Andrzej, 41
Bodegraven (ship), 262
BOF (Boeuf, Oeufs et Fromages) women, 43–4, 100
Bohan, Marc, 287
Boinet, Max, 86
Bonabel, Elaine, 197
Bonali, Giulia, 181n1
Boncour, Paul, 280
Bonfils, Robert, 65
Bonnet, Mme. Henri, 155
Bonniers manadstidning (periodical), 97–8, 100, 101–4, 105–11
Borea, Vera, 178
Boussac, Marcel, 329,
Bradley.O.M. General, 303
Brazil, 203–6, 220
    business, 204–5
    Expeditionary Forces, 204,
    fashion, 1943, 212
    fashion press and social reportage during World War Two, 206, 208–13
    French culture in, 205
    impressions of fashion show in, 213–19
    Mena Fiala as sales director of Casa Canadá, 207–8
    newspapers and magazines, 206, 222
    politics in WW2, 203
    Portuguese royal family, 222n1
Brazilian Beige, 202, 210, 211
Breker, Arno, 37
Bricianer, Henry Moise, 45
British Colour Council, 262, 315
British Vogue. See *Vogue* (magazine)
Brochier, Joseph, 59, 232
Brouckère, Suzanne de, 37, 42
Bruce, Ailsa Mellon, 295–6, 299, 300

Bruce, David, 300
Brunhoff, Michel de, 19, 115, 116, 117–19, 121, 125–8, 133–4, 135, 292, 309
Brunhoff, Pascal de, 121
Brunius, Célie, 105
Brussels, 239, 241, 242
    Liberation of, 242
Bruyère, 107, 171, 236
Brydegaard, Uffe, 186
Bueno, Maria Lúcia, 208
Bulletin des Soies, 68
Bürckel, Josef, 227
Bureau Otto, 42
Butler, R. A. B., 247
Butler Education Act, 247

Callot Soeurs, 171
Cameron, Roderick, 163–4
Campos, Hortensia Redig de, 212
Cannell, Kathleen, 145, 146
Capanema, Gustavo, 212
Carcano, Stella, 326
Cardin, Jo, 83, 95n4
Carmona, Oscar, 161
Carnegie, Hattie, 14, 144, 214
Carnton, Eleanor, 152
Carpentier, Madeleine, 196, 309, 314
Carter, Ernestine, 107
Carte-d'acheteur, 34
Cartier et Cie, 45, 87–8, 87n7–9, 335
    Captive bird brooch, 88, 335
    'Freed Bird' brooch, 88
Carven, Marie Louise, 45, 46, 171
Casablanca (film), 181n6
Casa Bobone, 173, 175, 176, 177, 178
Casa Canadá, 203, 210, 213, 214, 220. See also Brazil fashion house in Rio de Janeiro, 206–8
    Mena Fiala as sales director of, 207–8
Castillo, Antonio Del, 44, 276 (also image)
Cavanagh, John, 285

Censorship, Nazi regulations for French *Vogue* and *Jardin des Modes*, 122–4
    of Swedish fashion press, 102–3
Cézanne, Paul, 300
Chagas, Beatriz, 174
Chambre des Deputés in Paris, 36
Chambre Syndicale de la Couture Parisienne, 15, 16, 38, 39, 56, 99, 117–18, 124, 140, 143–44, 146, 154, 196, 197, 216, 218, 276, 281, 292, 308, 319
Chambre Syndicale des Fabricants, 16
Chambrun, René, 41, 50n22
Champcommunal, Elspeth, 258, 260, 272, 274, 291
Chanel, 33, 40, 41, 45, 50n21, 54, 218, 250, 291, 309, 334
Charity, George, 87
Charles, Robert, 62, 65
Chase, Rosemary, 263
Chatillon-Mouly-Roussel, 65
Chaumont, Marcelle, 41, 309
Churchill, Clemmie, 292
Churchill, Winston, 247, 265, 292
Claudine (magazine), 322
Clavel, Alexander and Fanny, 287
Cognacq, Gabriel, 300
Colcombet, Hilaire, 75n21
Collections de Costumes Suisse Originaux (Meyer), 32
Colette, 83,
Colombier, Janet, 176–7
Communist party, 120, 136n4
Condé Nast Publications, 115, 117, 122, 131, 133
Connor, Marcia, 143
Cooper, Duff, 326
Cooper, Lady Diana, 292, 293, 326
Copeland, Joe, 152
Copenhagen, 21
    Liberation, 1945, 192
    Shortages, 187, 189
Corolle line collection (1947), 327–9, 335

Correio Carioca (newspaper), 206, 216, 217
Correio da Manha (newspaper), 206, 209
Costa, Lúcio, 216
Costebelle, Georges, 56
Costes, Mme. Dieudonné, 151
Cotte, Albert, 59
Coudurier-Fructus-Descher, Silk manufacturers, 54, 62, 63, 64–6, 68
Couture industry
  Belgian couture, 240
  Danish couture, 186–7
  enforcement of Nazi policies, 21–2
  German couture, 29–30, 99
  millinery from Paris to Lisbon, 176–7
  Paris couture in Lisbon, 171, 173
  Paris couture in Switzerland, 236–7
  style diffusion throughout occupation, 333–6
  wartime Paris couture abroad before Occupation, 280–1
  Worth and founding of Paris couture, 272–3, 274
Coward, Noel, 265, 286
Creative imagination, shoes and hats and, 88–90
Creed, 20, 210, 213, 214, 278–9
Creed, Charles, 214, 250, 258, 260, 278–9
Creed, Henry, 250, 258, 277, 278–9
Crome & Goldschmidt, 186, 187, 194
Crosses of Lorraine, 86
Curie, Eve, 164
Curie, Marie, 165
Curtiz, Michael, 181n6

Daily Mail (newspaper), 314
Dali, Gala, 165
Dali, Salvador, 165
Dalio, Marcel, 166, 181n6

Dalton, Hugh, 249
Daunay, Paul, 235
Daves, Jessica, 154, 155
d'Ayen, Solange, 126, 130
de Brouckère, Suzanne, 37
'Decadent' art, 37
de Gaulle, Charles, General, 34, 45, 73, 75n23, 86–7, 88, 95n9, 119, 133, 165, 215, 292, 303, 304, 327
Descat, Rose, 45
De Holden Stone, James, 126–8
Delange, Angè, 260
Deligny, Jacques, 110
Demarcation Line, France, 55, 56, 126, 133,
Democracy, 304–6
Demornex, Jacqueline, 105
Denmark, 183–4, 198–9, 133
  home diligence in, 187–9
  influence of Paris on, 184–6
  invaded by Germany, 183
  liberation flag dress, 195
  liberation of, 183, 184, 190, 192–7, 198
  momentum for Danish couture, 186–7
  occupation by Germany, 183
  shortages, 182, 183, 187, 189
  silent resistance, 189–90
  using alternative materials during shortage, 187–9
Der Goldene Schnitt (magazine), 32
Descat, Rose, 45
Designmuseum Danmark, 182, 183–4, 190, 191, 194, 196
Dessès, Jean, 43, 196, 326, 340n1
Deutche Zellwolle-und Kuntseide-Ring, 66
Deutsches Mode-Institut (DMI), 30, 201n8, 227
d'Houville, Gérard, 90
de Vinci, Leonardo, 28
De Waal, E, 227
Diário Carioca (newspaper), 206, 220
Diário de Noticias (magazine), 177

Dickey, E. M. O'Rourke, 247–50, 263
Die Mode (magazine), 33
Dincklage, Baron von, 33, 40
Dior, Christian, 42, 43, 192, 276, 287, 319, 327, 329
  Corolle line collection (1947), 327–9, 335
  design 'Ketey', 318, 328
Dormoy, Marcelle, 43, 118, 236, 309, 340n1
Doucet, Jacques, 296
Duff Cooper, Diana, (Manners) 291, 292, 293, 326, 327
Dufy, Raoul, 65
Duhamel, Georges, 126
Duvelleroy, handbag by, 84

Edman & Anderson, 109
Edward VIII (King), 290
Eisenhower, D. Supreme Allied Commander, 303
Elégance Wien, 227, 228
Elizabeth (Queen), 315, 316
Elizabeth Arden studio, 86
ELLE (magazine), 134
Elwyn-Jones, F. 26, 26n2, 49.2, 229, 338, 339
Englebert, Ejnar, 196
Épuration (purge), 304–6, 322, 329
Ernst, Max, 166
Eisenhower, Dwight, General, the Supreme Allied Commander, 303
Estoril Casino, 164
Etude 1and 2, Textiles Suisses pour la Mode/ÉTÉ 1943 and 1944 (albums) 232–4
Eude-Altman, Micheline, 83
Eva (magazine), 161, 165, 171, 172, 177, 178–9
Evening News (newspaper), 312, 313
Exhibitions
  Barcelona International Fair, Lyon textiles, and Paris haute couture, 1942, 69

Exhibitions, *continued*
  Copenhagen, *La Mode Française*, 1946, 184
  Lyon, Foire de Lyon, Textiles, 1941, 61, 67
  Lyon, International Lyon Textile Fair, 1941, 62
  London: Brazilian Art, 1943, 211
  New York, World Fair, 1939–40, Paris couture presence, 142
  New York, Auditorium of Wanamaker's, Paris haute couture, 1940, 148
  Paris, the Orangerie, Arno Breker, 1942, 37
  Paris, Palais de Tokyo, Lyon Textiles, 1942, 67
  Paris, Palais de Tokyo, *Soieries Lyonnaise*, 1943, 67
  Paris, Petit Palais, *Exposition de la France Européene*, 1941, 37
  Paris, Port de Versailles, New Shoe Exhibition, 1942, 89
  Rio de Janeiro, Great Exhibition of French Art, September 1945, 156, 217, 220
  Rio de Janeiro, *Thèâtre de la Mode*, Aug-Sept. 1945, 154 (see *Thèâtre de la Mode*) Zurich, Palais de Congrès, Lyon Textiles 1942, 69, 231, 232
  Zurich, Palais de Congrès, Swiss Textiles 1943, 232

Fabius, Odette, 39, 44
  Fabricants, 54, 58
Falbalas (film), 39, 44, 50n20
Falluel, Fabienne, 2, 13–15
Fashion industry
  Paris, under occupation, 99–101
  political and economic dimension of, 124–5

Fashion shows
  Amsterdam, Paris haute couture, April, 1940, 280, 281
  Copenhagen, Hotel d'Angleterre, German/Austrian fashions, 1943, 190, 229
  Copenhagen, Town Hall, Paris haute couture, 1945, 196
  Lyon, Paris haute couture, 1942, 67, 92
  Madrid, Paris Haute couture at the Barcelona International Exhibition, 1942, 69
  New York, World's Fair, Paris haute couture, August 1940, 146
  Rio de Janeiro and Buenos Aries, London couture Export Collection, 1941, 209–10, 260–4, 275
  Rio de Janeiro, Paris haute couture, Copacabana Palace Hotel, August 1945, 216
  Sao Pāulo, Casa Canada, April/May 1945 Paris haute couture, 213–14
  Sao Pāulo, Paris haute couture, Nov. 1945, 219
  Zurich and Geneva, first Swiss Fashion Week Feb–March 1942, 235
Fashion textile industry in France
  design and manufacture under Nazi control (1940–1944), 57–9
  designing Lyon fabrics, 61–2
  import and export markets, 68
  in Lyon, 53–4
  replacement textiles, 59–61
  in Spain, 69
  in Switzerland, 69–70, 231–2
  Vichyist designs, 62–6

Fath, Jacques, 39, 100, 107, 171, 178, 196, 205, 220, 236, 240, 307, 309, 326, 331n11, 340n1
Fellowes, Daisy, (The Hon. Mrs. Reginald Fellowes), 259
Femina (journal), 101, 117, 123
Ferier, Bianchini, 66
Fernande Desgranges, 84
Ferrand, Louis, 126
Fiala, Mena, 206, 207–8, 220
Filho, Abel Ribeiro, 212
Filpas leg dye, 86
Finley, David, 300
Fischer, Leon, 235
Flöge, Emilie, 225
Forces Françaises de l'Intérieur (FFI resistance) 303, 304
Forces Françaises Libre (FFL - De Gaulle's forces), 34, 87, 88, 95n9, 133, 165, 303
Forces Navales Françaises Libres, 87
France
  censored fashion information, 101–4
  couture trade in 1940, 34, 36
  Demarcation Line in, 55
  map of divided, 35
  Nazi anti-Semitic legislation in France, 39
  Nazi control over French culture, 37
  Otto Abetz and 'cultural cooperation', 37–8
  Paris couture trade after Occupation (June 1940), 38–9
  resistants in the world of French couture, 44–5, 47
  wartime Paris couture abroad before Occupation, 280–1
Frank, Brigitte, 27, 28
Frank, Hans, 25, 27, 28, 49n6
Frederik (Crown Prince), 196
Free Dutch Forces, 256

Free France, 86, 128, 251
Free World (magazine), 133
Free Zone, (Zone Libre) 34, 55, 56, 67, 69, 79, 80, 122, 126, 151
French press, German censorship, 116
French 'Romantic Realist' art, 37
French *Vogue*. *See Vogue* (magazine)
Fructus, M., 62
Fry, Roger, 272

Gabrielle, 93
Galliano, John, 268
Ganterie (journal), 82
Gara, Tomi de, 251
George V (King), 206, 254, 272, 287
George VI (King), 257, 287, 294n12, 315
Gedye, G.E.R, 226–7
Gerda Janson & Co., 109
Germain, Viola, 109
German couturiers, 29, 30
German Foreign Intelligence Agency, 40
German Military Administration Zone, 79
German National Fashion Institute, 30
German National Socialist art, 37
German Textiles and Leather Distributor, 68
Germany, First Ladies of Fashion in, 33–4
Gerson, Hermann, 30
Gervais, Louis, 215
Gilmore, Margaret, 262
Gilruth, Margaret, 262
Ginsburg, Madeline, 140, 141
Givenchy, Hubert de, 42, 205, 287
Gladstone, Josephine, 50n22
Glamour (magazine), 131, 132, 133

Gluzman, Cândida, 208, 220
Goebbels, Joseph, Reich Minister for Propaganda 27, 29, 31, 37, 38, 39, 41,122
Goebbels, Magda, 27, 29
Goering, Emmy, 27, 33, 42, 70
Goering, Herman, Reichsmarschall, 25, 26–7, 33, 41, 49n4, 56, 70, 122, 338
Goetz, Richard, 30
Gomez, Beatriz,169, 170, 173, 174
Goodman, Andrew, 141
Gordon, Lady Duff, 295
Gorin, Daniel, 61, 117–18
Göta Trägårdh
 couture garments, 108
 fashion drawing, 185, 201n5
 hats, 96, 109, 110
Great Depression, 140, 141, 142, 271
Greiser, Arthur Karl, 28, 49n7
Greiser, Maria, 28
Gresy, 89
Griffe, Jaques, 309
Grumbach, Didier, 15, 38, 54, 309
Grumberg, Dr., 80
Guenther, Irene, 29–34, 225, 227, 229
Guggenheim, Peggy, 166
Guillaume, 321
Guillot, Laure Albin, 103
Gutton, Marie-Laure, 14

Haffner, Dr. A. E., 32, 33
Hammond, Janet, 32, 33, 49n12
Handbags, 83–4
Hansson, Per-Albin, 98
Harper's Bazaar (magazine), 140, 141, 261
Harrods, 278–9, 287
Hartman, M., 57–8
Hartnell, Norman, 260, 266, 267, 291, 328, 331n16

Hats, 90, 92–3
 Agnès, 78
 American salons, 214
 couture millinery from Paris to Lisbon, 176–7
 Fanny Berger, 81
 felt, with knife feather, 92
 Göta Trägårdh fashion, 96
 high green felt, 93
 high red felt, 93
 straw boater with wide colored ribbons, 92
 style (1946), 321
Hattrick, Jane, 87, 328, 331n16
Haus der Mode, 185, 200n3, 227, 229
Haute couture, 13–16
 Paris fashion spread, 107
 wartime clientele, 40–3
Haute nouveauté textiles, 54, 61, 70, 237,
Havas agency, 209, 222n3
Hawes, Elizabeth, 140
Head, Edith, 194, 201n12
Heap, Jane, 272, 273
Heavy Clothing Working Party, 268
Heeren, Aimée, Rodman de, 42, 148, 205, 215, 323, 325
Heim, Jacques, 39, 55, 89, 100, 101, 288
Heise, Annemarie, 30
Henri à la Pensée, 85
Hermès, 67, 84, 210, 240,
Hibbelen, Gerhard, 124
Hirsch Department Store, Brussels, 68, 240, 241, 281
Hirsch, Amsterdam, 280, 281
Hirsch, Jean-Paul, 240
Hirsch, Robert, 240
Hitler, Adolf, 25, 26, 31, 37, 68, 226, 239, 335
Hochsmann, Gertrude, 225
Hodgson, Elspeth Mary, 272
Hohé, Madelief, 322, 331n2, 331n5
Holmes, William C., 144

Horst, 270, 290
House of Worth, 83, 85, 273, 275, 276. *See also* Worth, Charles Frederick
Hoyas, Erica, 168

Illum department store, 186, 187
Images de France (magazine), 82
Imperial War Museum, 18, 252
Incorporated Society of London Designers, 20, 258, 260, 273, 277
Informations (bulletin), 69
International Military Tribunal, Nuremberg, 25, 27, 49n9, 74n3, 338
International Textiles (magazine), 38, 256, 257, 261, 265–6, 285, 334
Ipanema, Otavio Moreira de, 212

Jac Olsen department store, 185, 186
Jacqmar, 254, 258, 260, 277
Janin, Suzanne, 62
Janine, 172, 177–8
Jardin des Modes (magazine), 115, 117–19, 122–4, 134
Jewish communities
　Australia, 336
　Austria, 225–7
　Belgium, 240
　Denmark, 26
　France, 36, 38
Jewish textile designers in Paris, fate, 61–2, 62n4
Jewish fashion professionals 335–6
Jewish Refugees
　in Switzerland, 229–30
　in Portugal, 163, 166–7, 167n5
　to the USA, 167
Jewellery, 86–7
Jewish Museum Milwaukee, 336, 337
Johansson, Alf W., 98
Join-Diéterle, Catherine, 14

Jonas, Jacqueline, 236
Jones, Bettina, 289
Jornal de Noticias (magazine), 177
Jornal do Brazil (journal), 206
Jornal Feminino da Mulher para a Mulher (magazine), 161, 177
Joséphine (Empress), 37
Journal de la Chaussure Française (journal), 79, 89
Jouval, Gaby, 111, 234, 235
Joyce, Emmet, 152
Juda, Elsbeth and Hans, 256

Kangol, 251
Karner, Regina, 227, 229
Kerl, Hans, 26, 58, 57–8, 60, 66, 74n3
Kehrl Plan, 58, 60, 74n3, 125
Kernan, Thomas, 123–4
King, Elizabeth, 139
Kruysveldt-De-Mare, Catharina, 329
Kuhnen, Paul, 30

Lachasse, 273
Lady with an Ermine (de Vinci), 28
Lafaurie, Jeanne, 172, 185
La Femme (magazine), 196, 197, 201n17, 321
La Gazette du Bon Ton (magazine), 115
La Guardia, Fiorello H., 143, 248
Lambauer, Barbara, 38
La Mode sous l'Occupation (Veillon), 14, 53
Landry, Bob, 311, 312
Landscape With the Good Samaritan (Rembrandt), 28
Lanvin, Jeanne, 22, 41, 42, 43, 45, 51n29, 52, 64, 100, 107, 109, 118, 143, 196, 281, 288, 340n1
Lasseux, Marcel, 82

Last, Caroline, 81
Laval, Josée, 41–2
Laval, Pierre, Head of *Milice* 1943, 41, 42
Laver, James, 308, 320, 321
Laverniere, Guy de Voisins de, 43
La Vigiere, François D'Austier de, 214, 215, 222n5
Lazareff, Hélène, 134
Lebeau, Madelaine, 166, 181n6
Leclerc de Hauteclocque, General, P. F.M. 303
Lecomte, Germaine, 118, 172, 177, 185
Leduc, Violette, 90
Lee, Joseph, 312, 313
Le Figaro (magazine), 126
Legroux Soeurs, 172, 176, 322
Lelong, Lucien, 38, 39, 41, 42, 55, 56, 65, 84, 99–100, 111, 124, 126, 134, 143–4, 146, 152–55, 178, 192, 196, 214, 216, 236, 281, 288, 308, 309, 310, 311, 318, 319–21, 327, 328
Lend-Lease, 265
Le Petit Echo de la Mode (journal), 83
Le Petit Journal (journal), 119
Les Nouveaux Temps (journal), 82, 86, 92, 340n1
Leth, Marie Gudme, 2, 182, 187, 188, 189, 190, 192, 194, 201n7, 201n20
Lever, Arnold, 254
Levisse-Touzé, Christine, 14
Lewis, Mary, 146
Le Wita, Beatrix, 13
Ley, Inge, 29, 31, 42, 49n10
Ley, Robert, 31, 49n9
Liberation of Paris, 93
　aftermath of, 303–4
　post-Liberation collections, 310–12
Life (magazine), 151, 263–4
L'Illustré (magazine), 234, 235, 236, 237

Lima, Isaura José Guimarães, 212
Linder, Jan, 98, 101
Linton, Tweeds, 250
Lisbon. *See also* Portugal
   couture millinery from Paris to, 176–7, 333
   dresses, 169, 170
   fashion leaders in, 168
   Paris couture in, 171, 173
   Porto couture in wartime, 173–4
Lister, Adele, 225
London, 247–8
   the Aschers, 252–4
   Board of Education, 248
   Board of Trade, 249, 267
   Board of Trade quest for 'continental élan', 250
   British fashions and the USA, 264–6
   Civilian Clothing Directorate, 249–50, 266
   creativity as capital, 267–8
   Hans and Elsbeth Juda, 256–7
   Incorporated Society of London designers, 259–60
   Kangol, 251
   Paris couturiers in, 257–9
   propaganda textiles and silk squares, 254–5
   scarf by Felix Topolski, 246, 255
   South American collection, 260–4
   West Cumberland Silk Mills, 251
London Gazette (journal), 261
L'Oréal, cosmetic company, 125
Luchaire, Corinne, 43, 44, 50n25
Luchaire, Jean, 37, 42, 329, 340n1
Lyon, 241
   Designers of *haute nouveauté* fabrics, 53, 61–2, 66–7
   eighteenth century context of, 54–5
   at end of World War Two, 70–3
   exhibitions abroad, 68
   fashion textile manufacturing, 53–4
   import and export markets, 68
   Liberation of Lyon, 70
   Paris haute couture fashion show in, 67
   at start of World War Two, 55–6
   Vichyist designs, 62–6
Lyons, Jack, 254
Lyons, Mary, 254

McCardell, Claire, 157
McQueen, Alexander, 268
Magasin du Nord, Copenhagen, 186, 189, 196
Mahrenholzp, Harald, 30
Mainbocher, 20, 54, 146, 147, 154, 289–90
Malraux, Andre, 47
Manet, Edouard, 297
Manguin, Lucile, 236, 237
Mannes, Marya, 162, 168, 169, 171, 173, 174, 176, 177, 231, 333
Map of divided France (1940), 35
Maravilhas, Ana, 173
Marcelle Chaumont, 41
Marcus, Stanley, 151
Marianne (journal), 119
Marie Claire (magazine), 78, 79, 83, 92, 101, 124, 234, 235, 286, 332
Markström, Ingeborg, 103–4
Marly, Diana de, 100
Mass, Walter, 131
Matos, Silvio de, 212
Maude et Nano, 322–3
Maxwell, Elsa, 257, 299
Meisner, Jo, 251
Mellon, Andrew W., 295
Mellon, Paul, 296

Meredith, Peggy, Worth dress, 275
Messidor (newspaper), 119
Metropolitan Museum, Digital Library, 214
Milice, 42
Miller, Lee, 199, 201n19, 273, 292, 306, 307, 313
Miller, Lesley Ellis, 272, 291
Millinery. *See* Hats
Mitford, Nancy, 326–8, 331n15
Modas & Bordados (magazine), 161, 177
Mode du Jour (journal), 83, 101
Modes et Travaux (magazine), 19, 20, 93, 129, 307, 312, 313, 315
Molyneux, Edward, 20, 45, 47, 54, 55, 100, 118, 146, 165, 178, 196, 205, 209, 210, 213, 214, 216, 228, 250, 252, 253, 254, 257, 258, 260, 265, 267, 278, 281, 282–6, 288, 291, 321, 295–300, 309, 310, 311, 334
Mogens Wieth, 196
Monet, Claude, 296, 297, 299
Montaigne, Charles, 178, 185, 309
Montgomery, Bernard, L. Field, 1st Viscount Montgomery of Alamein, 194, 251, 252, 303
Monuments, Fine Art and Archives (MFAA), 49n4
Morais, Amélia de, 173, 174, 175, 176
Morais, Judith de, 173
Morel, Henry, 55
Morisot, Berthe, 297, 298, 299
Morris, Peggy, 152
Morton, Digby, 260
Mosca, Bianca, 258, 260, 276–7, 291

Moulin, Jean, 45
Mourgue, Pierre, 126
Mundo Gráfico (magazine), 161, 169, 171, 177
Munn, Mrs. Ector, 148
Murrow, Edward, 165

Naar, Albertina, 173, 174
Napoleão, 173
Nast, Condé, 115, 121, 133, *See also* Condé Nast Publications
National Gallery of Art, Washington, 295–7, 299–300
Nazi control
  censorship of French *Vogue* and *Jardin des Modes* under, 122–4
  couture industry and, 21–2, 310
  cultural 37, 38
  economic 34, 36
  Lyon silk and synthetic textiles, 58–9
  occupation of Paris, 77, 94, 118, 146
  reactions of couturiers to anti-Semitic legislation, 39–40
  Swedish relationship with Nazism, 98
Nazi Germany, 18, 25–6
  high society, 26–8
  luxury goods and couture fashion in, 28–34
Nazi National Socialist policies, 32, 34
Neave, Airey, 25, 25n1, 48n1, 49n6, 336
Nettleback, Colin, 34
Neutrality
  Lisbon of neutral Portugal, 161–3
  Swedish policy of, 98–9
  Switzerland, 229–30
New York and Paris fashions after Liberation, 152–6

  before World War Two, 139–42
  defending Parisian fashion in, 128–31
  industry without Paris, 146–51
  war beginning in Europe (1939), 117, 142–6
New York Times (newspaper), 33, 70, 142, 145, 146, 154, 261, 262, 264, 307
New York World Fair, 1938–39, 142
Niemeyer, Oscar, 216
Nostalgia, 65
Noth, Louis, 69
Notre Coeur (magazine), 124
Nouveaux Temps (newspaper), 43

Occupied France, 97
  couture trade in, 36
  map of, 35
  subtle sabotage of style, 306–10
Occupied Zone, 34, 37, 55, 79, 83, 122–3, 126
Ohio State University, 157
O Imparcial (newspaper), 209
Oliveira, Sylvia Regis de, 211
Oliveira Salazar, Antonio de, 161
O Século (magazine), 177
Ottolini, Guida, 177
Pagès, Pierre, 103, 104, 126
Palais de Tokyo Salon des Artistes Décorateurs, 67
Palmer, Alexandra, 100, 322, 326, 327
Pan-American Clipper, 162, 165
Paquin, Jeanne, 43, 100, 109, 145, 171, 178, 196, 205, 216, 210, 213, 260, 261, 263, 275–8, 281, 282, 291, 340n1
  dresses by, 171, 172
  evening dress, 145
  green chiffon evening dress, 19

Paris. *See also* Accessories; Fashion textile industry; Lyon; New York and Paris fashions
  accessories and wartime functions, 82–93
  Battle for, 303–4
  changes in fashion style, 107–8
  couture scandal, 312–16, 322
  couture style, 333–6
  couture trade after Occupation (1940), 38–9
  defending Parisian fashion in New York, 128–31
  Dior and Corolle line collection of 1947, 327–9
  economic and political contexts, 77, 79–80, 82
  fashion industry under occupation, 99–101
  fashion upheaval by war, 77
  influence on Denmark, 184–6
  international private clientele returning (1945–1947), 322–3, 326–7
  Liberation of, 21, 43, 302–5
  Nazi Occupation of, 77, 79–80
  Occupation couture style, 108–11, 256–7, 306–10
  post-Liberation collections, 310–12
  resolving style scandal, 312–16
  styles of 1946, 321
  Tout Paris social circles, 37, 41, 42
  wartime couture clientele, 40–3
Paris fashion, 271–2, 291–3
  salons and First Ladies of Fashion in Germany, 33–4

356 Paris Fashion and World War Two: Global Diffusion and Nazi Control

wartime Paris couture abroad before Occupation, 280–1
Worth and founding of Paris couture, 272–3, 274
Paris Office of Art and Creation (OFAC), 155
Park, Nona, 144
Pastori, Jean-Pierre, 272
Patcévitch, Iva, 122, 133
Patou, Jean, 55, 100, 118, 177, 196, 214, 281, 288
Patriotism, 31, 150
Paulette, 172
Pelicks, Jacob, 206, 208, 209, 220
Penrose, Elizabeth, 131
Penteado, Honório, 214
Penteado, Olívia Guedes, 214
Penteado, Yolanda, 214
Perugia, 88, 89
Pétain, Maréchal, 34, 55, 56, 57, 58, 59, 62, 64, 65, 66, 67, 69, 72, 75n23, 79, 88, 119, 128, 231, 232
Phoney War, 115, 117–19
Picken, Mary Brooks, 143
Picot, Gérard, 84
Picot, Geneviève, 84
Picture Post (journal), 308, 315
Piguet, Robert, 20, 67, 100, 105, 106, 127, 171, 214, 236, 276, 281, 286–8, 291, 309, 323, 325, 334
Pingouin Wools, 'A Sheep in your Cupboard' advertisement, 79
Pinto, Clara Vaz, 181n2
Piper, John, 255
Politiken (newspaper), 196
Pollak, Rosy, 174
Pombo, Ana de, 59, 276, 281, 288
Pope, Virginia, 142, 145, 146, 152, 153
Porter, Julian, 26
Portugal. *See also* Lisbon
arrival borders of, during the war, 163–5
couture millinery from Paris to Lisbon, 176–7

Estado Novo totalitarian regime, 162
fashion in World War Two, 168–9
fashion magazines of, 177–8
Liberation of Paris nearing, 178–9
Lisbon and Porto couture in wartime, 173–4
neutrality of, 161–3
Paris couture in Lisbon, 171, 173
refugees and travelers leaving, 165–7
Portuguese Illustration (magazine), 177
Pouillard, Veronique, 21, 68, 155, 225, 238, 240, 272, 329, 238, 319, 329, 333, 335
Pourcher, Yves, 41
Pour Elle (magazine), 90, 124
Presle, Micheline, 39, 44
Prince George, Duke of Kent. Wedding of, 258
Propaganda Abteilung (Propaganda Ministry), 37, 38, 122, 124, 360
Propaganda poster, Pétain, 57
Proust, Marcel, 200n2
Puhl, Emil, 26
Quant, Mary, 268

Rahvis, 265
Ravensbrück, 39, 44, 47, 133
Rauch, Madeleine de, 118, 171, 178
Reboux, Caroline, 41
Refugees, leaving Portugal, 165–7
Reich Fashion, 31
Remédios, Mário, 173
Renner, Mia, 32, 33
Renner, Wilhelm, 32
Renoir, Auguste, 296, 297
Resistance Information Service, 44
'Retour à la Terre' textiles, 71–2, 232

Reville-Terry, 259, 272
Reville and Rossiter, 272
Revista Rio (magazine), 206, 218, 219
Revolution Nationale, Travail, Famille and *Patrie* (Pétain), 56, 62
Reynaud, Paul, 117, 119
Rhonheimer, Hans George, 231
Ribbentrop, Anneliese, 28, 29
Ribbentrop, Joachim Von, 49n8
Ricci, Nina, 85, 171, 177, 178, 196, 307
Rijkens, Elsa, 42, 322
Rio De Janeiro, 21, 204, 205, 209
Copacabana Beach, 202
Casa Canada, 203, 206–8, 210, 220
Hotel Copacabana Palace, 208, 209, 210
Reboux, Caroline, 41
Rochas, Marcel, 39, 42, 43, 205, 340n1
Roche, Daniel, 13–15
Roche, Madelaine de, 171
Romatzki, Hilda, 29
Roosevelt, Eleanor, 167
Rose, Kirsten, 190
Rothschild, Elisabeth, 38
Rothschild, Baron Philippe de, 39
Rothschild, Baron Louis, 227
Rouff, Maggy, 29, 39, 42, 45, 85, 100, 107, 171, 178, 196, 211, 236, 248, 280, 281, 311, 312, 313
Rouleau, Raymond, 39
Rourke, Jenny, 87, 95n7
Russell, Peter, 260
Rydeberg, Marga, 97, 109

Saint-Martin, Jean, 197, 198
Saks Fifth Avenue, 145–6, 150, 152
Salva, Ricardo Espirito Santo, 165
Sampaio, Sérgio, 173
Sandler, Richard, 98
Sass, Ignazy, 226
Sass, Stephanie, 226

Sasse, Antoine, 45
Schellenberg, Walter, General, 40, 49n2, 50n21
Schiaparelli, Elsa, 20, 34, 39, 42, 55, 66, 83, 92, 100, 109, 118, 129, 130, 138, 143–5, 146, 148, 155, 164, 165, 168, 171, 196, 205, 209, 248, 250, 258, 282, 288–9, 309, 316
Schmidtke, Heinz, 122
Schueller, Eugène, 125
Schultz, Clara, 30
Schwarzkopf, Stefan, 262
Scott, E.-J., 272
Secrest, Meryl, 272
Seixas, Cristina, 203, 207
Sekers, Miki, 250, 251
Seligmann, Jacques, 296, 297
Selmer, Ketty, 185, 201n4
Semaine de la Femme (journal), 231–2, 234, 236
Sereville, Monique de, 126
Settle, Alison, 100, 242, 261, 305, 308, 315, 316, 320, 322
Seurat, Georges, 297, 298
Shearer, Norma, 265
Shirer, William, 165–7, 179, 225, 226, 227
Shonnard, Sophie, 144
Sievers, Wolfram, 338, 340n5
Silk and synthetic textile design, Nazi control in Lyon, 58–9
Simplicity Patterns, 128
Simpson, Wallis, 257, 259, 282, 289, 290
Singapore Free Press and Mercantile Advertiser (newspaper), 262
Sleeping with the Enemy (Vaughan), 40, 50n21
Smelflex, 89
Snow, Carmel, 141, 144, 147, 290

Sobrinho, Francisco Matarazzo, 214
Sochor, Josef, 255, 269n5
Social Democratic Party, 98
Social division, 304–6
Soie Informations (journal), 54
Sombra (magazine), 206, 210, 212–13, 215–18
Sonnemann, Emma, 70
South American collection, textiles, couture and propaganda, 260–4
Spain, 69
Spanish Civil War, 117, 120, 290
Speer, Albert, 25–6
Spreiregen, Jacques, 251
SS Excambion, 166, 179, 181n4
SS Quanza, 16
SS Serpa Pinto, 216
St. Martin, Jean, 198
Stadt, Theresen, 336
Steibel, Victor, 260
Stohrer, Baroness, von, 33, 34, 42
Stone and Blythe, 226, 227, 229
Streat, Sir Raymond, 266
Strnad, Hedwig, 336, 337
Strnad, Paul, 336
Suggia, Guilhermina, 164
Sultano, Gloria, 225
Sutherland, Graham, 255
Suzy, 177, 282, 326
Sweden, 68, 97
 fashion journalism, 97–8
 fashion studios, 106
 Paris couture in, 236
 Paris Occupation couture style development in, 108–11
 policy of neutrality, 98–9
 relationship with Nazism, 98
 source of Paris fashion information, 185
Swedish *Statens Informationsstyrlrelse* (SIS), 101

Switzerland, 69–70, 229–30, 237, 238
 album: *Etude 1, and 2, Textiles Suisses pour la Mode/ETE 1943 and 1944*, 232–4
 fashion textile exports, 230–1
 Nazi activities in, 229
 Paris couture in, 236–7
 policy of armed neutrality, 229–30
 Textile designers and companies, 245n5
 wartime fashion textiles, 231–2
 world of couture in wartime, 234–5
Symington, Judith, 168
Szabo, Tania, 45
Szabo, Violette, 45, 47
Szkonikoff, Elfrieda, 43
Szkonikoff, Michel, 42

Tanguy. Col. Rol, 303
Tartan, 47, 65, 83, 90, 279, 281, 313
Taylor, Kerry, 33, 49n13, 76
Teixeira, Maria Luisa Silva, 173
Textile. *See* Fashion textile industry
Textiles, synthetic, 37, 58, 59, 60, 61, 189, 235
Théâtre de la Mode, 21, 134, 154, 156, 184, 198, 215, 217, 218–19, 223n8, 220, 268, 292, 320
Third Reich, 25, 34
Thormann, Gundel, 30
Tidens Kvinder (magazine), 184–92, 198–9, 200n1
Tildi, Madame, 198
Time (magazine), 311
The Times (newspaper), 146, 151, 152, 153, 156, 226
Tizeau, Alix Marcelle, 307
Tobé, 140, 150

Topolski, Felix, 247, 254, 255
Toussaint, Jeanne, 95n8
Toute La Vie (journal), 84
Tout Paris social circles, 18, 37, 41, 42, 44, 205
Trachtenkleidunge' style dirndl dress, 31–2, 33
Trägårdh, Göta, 2, 97, 108–110, 185, 201n5
Train, Susan, 217
Treanor, Tim, 163, 165
Treaty of Friendship and Commerce, Brazil and France, 204, 222n2

United States of America, British fashions and, 264–6
  Fashion industry in, 139–43
  War Production Board and L85 restrictions on styling, 150
  New York, as 'world fashion centre' in, 151
University of Brighton-Dress History Teaching Collection , 16, 19, 20, 64, 65, 71, 252, 307, 323
US Navy WAVES uniform, 147
Utility Couturier Prototype, 273
Utility Prototype scheme, 250, 266–8, 277, 278

Vaillant-Couturier, Marie-Claude, 133, 136n6
Vaillant-Couturier, Paul, 120
Valéry, Paul, 126
Valle, Madame, 171, 172, 175, 177
Valois, Rose, 92
Van Hecke, Paul-Gustave, 241
Vargas, President, Brazil, 204, 205, 212
Vaughan, Hal, 40

Veillon, Dominique, 12, 13–15, 17–18, 34, 38, 39, 53, 57, 58, 59, 99, 100, 109, 111, 199, 272, 316, 317, 322
Vestir (journal), 168–9, 174
Vichy, 34, 55, 72, 122, 130, 149, 308
  Culture, 56, 65
  Ideology, 56, 62, 66, 71, 72, 73, 82, 232
Vienna, 124, 225
  day dress, 228
  fashion and couture, 99, 227–9
Vionnet, Madeleine, 45, 149, 205, 309
Vogel, Cosette, wife of Lucien Vogel, 119, 125, 128
Vogel, Lucien, 19, 115, 117–19, 119–22, 128, 133–4
Vogel, Marie-Claude, daughter of Lucien Vogel, 114, 120, 121, 131, 133
Vogel, Pascal, son of Lucien Vogel, 121, 134
Vogue (magazine), 101, 154, 286
  American *Vogue*, 122, 130–1, 161, 162, 165, 230–1, 237, 265, 267, 282–3, 286, 289, 310, 333
  British *Vogue*, 118, 169, 258, 260, 263, 267, 273, 291, 307, 312, 316
  French *Vogue*, 115, 117–19, 122–4, 125n19, 134, 135–37, 289
Vollard, Ambroise, 299
Volpi, Maria Cristina, 203, 207, 208
Von Dincklage, Baron Hans Günther, 33, 40
Votre Beauté (magazine), 125
Votre Bonheur (magazine), 123
Vourlat Pienoz, studios of, 62
Vreeland, Diana, 290

Wakhévitch, Georges, 217, 218
Walker, John, 104, 300
Wallerstein, Monique Saint de, 215–16
Wanamaker department store, 148, 149, 157
Wanamaker, Fernando, 148
War, Kostio de, 130
War Production Board (WPB, USA), 149–50
Wartime propaganda campaigns, 21
Weigandt, Andre, 235
Weir, Cecil, 268, 269n2
Wertheimer brothers, 334
Westerby department store, 184, 186, 194
West-Front (newspaper), 239
When We Were Dancing (film), 265
White, Nancy, 141
Wieth, Mogens, 196
Williams, Mrs. Harrison, 148
Winckler, Paul, 124
Windsor, Duke and Duchess of, 33, 165, 282, 286, 289, 290, 326
Wittelsbach, Maria Isabel de, 215
Women's Wear Daily (magazine), 250, 255
Woolf, Virginia, 272
Woolman Chase, Edna, 55, 121, 130–1, 135, 308–9
Woolton, Lord, 247–50, 257, 267–8
World's Fair of 1939, 142
World War One, 9, 55, 118, 133, 139–40, 241, 272, 295, 329
World War Two, 9, 13, 16
  Brazil during, 203–6
  fashion industry before, 139–42
  fashion in Portugal, 168–9

Index 359

World War Two, *continued*
   fashion press and social reportage in Brazil, 208–13
   Lyon at end of, 70–3
   Swedish press during, 111–12
Worth, Charles Frederick, 50n23, 171, 196, 210, 260, 334
   Paris couture founding, 272–3
Worth, London, 210, 258, 260, 272–7, 281, 291
Worth, Paris, 83, 171, 196, 275
Worth and Hermès, 202, 203, 211
Worth, Roger, 154, 273, 275

Yad Vashem World Holocaust Remembrance Center, 45, 51n30
Yeo-Thomas, Forest, Wing Commander, 45, 285
Yoxall, Harry, 121, 122, 260

www.ingramcontent.com/pod-product-compliance
Ingram Content Group UK Ltd.
Pitfield, Milton Keynes, MK11 3LW, UK
UKHW050052040326
468610UK00002B/793